coories

Health Economics

Introduction to the Pharmacy Business Administration series

Books in the Pharmacy Business Administration series have been prepared for use in university-level graduate and professional-level courses, as well as for continuing education and self-study uses. The series includes books covering the major subject areas taught in Social and Administrative Pharmacy, Pharmacy Administration, and Pharmacy MBA programs.

World-class authors with well-regarded expertise in the various respective areas have been selected and the book outlines, as well as the books themselves, have been reviewed by a number of other experts in the field. The result of this effort is a new integrated and coordinated series of books that is up to date in methodology, research findings, terminology, and contemporary trends and practices.

This is one book in that series of about 12 subjects in total. It is intended that each of the books will be revised at least every 5 years. While the books were intended for the North American market, they are just as relevant in other areas.

Titles in the series currently include:

Health Economics
Health Policy and Ethics
Pharmaceutical Market Research
Principles of Good Clinical Practice
Research Methods for Pharmaceutical Practice and Policy
Pharmaceutical Marketing: A Practical Guide
Pharmaceutical Marketing Research: Principles and Practice
Financial Analysis in Pharmacy Practice

The series editor-in-chief is Professor Albert Wertheimer PhD MBA of Temple University School of Pharmacy, Philadelphia.

Suggestions and comments from readers are most welcome and should be sent to Commissioning Editor, Pharmaceutical Press, 1 Lambeth High Street, London SE1 7JN, UK.

Health Economics

FIRST EDITION

Jordan Braverman MPH MSFS

London • Chicago **PhP Pharmaceutical Press**

Published by the Pharmaceutical Press
An imprint of RPS Publishing

1 Lambeth High Street, London SE1 7JN, UK
100 South Atkinson Road, Suite 200, Grayslake, IL 60030-7820, USA

© Pharmaceutical Press 2010

(**PP**) is a trade mark of RPS Publishing

RPS Publishing is the publishing organisation of the Royal Pharmaceutical Society of
Great Britain

First published 2010

Typeset by Thomson Digital, Noida, India
Printed in Great Britain by TJ International, Padstow, Cornwall, UK

ISBN 978 0 85369 867 8

A catalogue record for this book is available from the British Library.

Dedication

To my parents, Morris and Molly Braverman, who both lived well into their mid-90s and taught my brother, Irwin, and myself good health practices so as to maintain our health in as best a state as possible.

Contents

Preface

American health care is in crisis; the system is broken and must be fixed – words that are spoken so often that they have become part of the American lexicon. Every day Americans hear about the high costs of prescription drugs; that millions of Americans are uninsured; that without health insurance coverage a stay in hospital can bankrupt the patient in a matter of days; that health care costs are out of control; that the poor and disadvantaged have trouble finding access into the health care system to receive care – the list of problems appears endless.

Another word that has become part of the American language when speaking about the American health care system is 'reform.' We will cover the uninsured through state or national health insurance programs; we will include more preventive care in insurance benefits to keep Americans healthy in order to ward off more serious and costly illnesses at a later date; we will make drugs affordable for the elderly by including such a benefit under Medicare; we must control the cost of technology and not use it unnecessarily – the list of reforms goes on.

It sounds so simple to describe the US health care problems and solutions. Yet the complexity and causes of the US crisis today, especially in terms of costs, may not be completely understood by the many who work outside the health care system or even by those within it who are making these pronouncements. That is the purpose of this book. This book is an introductory discourse of health care in the USA today, especially its economics. This book is not a discussion of health care economics in the theoretical sense but a practical analysis of how our economic problems developed historically, the magnitude of the economic problems, why they developed, and how health care economics impacts the various segments which constitute the health care field, like physicians, pharmacists, nursing homes, hospitals, prescription drugs, health maintenance organizations, public programs like Medicare, and other elements within the health care field, as well as the whole of American society itself.

To understand health care economics it is necessary to understand each of the fields themselves and the complexity of the financial mechanisms which are unique to each field. The financial mechanisms that affect physicians are not necessarily the same mechanisms which affect hospitals or prescription drugs. So this book serves a dual purpose. It presents an introductory discussion of health care itself and of each relevant field, and then the economics of that field in particular detail with all the socioeconomic and political ramifications both within and outside the health care system.

Health care financing and economics is not a monolith of a single financial mechanism where a person buys private health insurance, or joins a health maintenance organization, or signs up for Medicare or Medicaid; visits a health care provider like a physician for a particular problem; the third-party payer like the insurance company pays the provider's bill, wholly or in part; and the health care transaction between patient, provider of care, and third-party payer is finished. That is all that most people know when viewing their experiences within the health care system.

While these actions are true on the surface, they do not represent the complexity and reality of the health care system as it actually functions. That is why this book was written. It is the purpose of the book to explain to the reader and give the reader an understanding in practical terms of the economic complexity of each of the fields that constitute the US health care system along with the major problems or issues with which each of these fields must contend. While each field is part of the overall health care system, in reality each of these fields occupies its own particular universe in and of itself, apart from the rest of the health care system with its own particular economics. There is an old saying that 'if you are not part of the solution, then you are part of the problem.' To be part of the solution in resolving the US health care crisis requires some fundamental knowledge of this field. Any proposed solutions will necessitate the input of many people both within and outside the health care field. But no one can help resolve the US health care problem if they do not basically understand the nature of the field itself. This book will present readers with such a basic knowledge and understanding so that they can contribute their own inputs, so that every American today and those who are yet to be born can and will be able to live in as healthful a state as possible and receive health services, when needed, at prices that are reasonable for all Americans to afford.

Jordan Braverman
October, 2009

Acknowledgments

I want to thank Dr. Albert Wertheimer, Professor of Pharmacy Adminis-tration, and Director, Center for Pharmaceutical Health Services Research, Temple University, for his continuous support and interest. Discussions with Dr. Wertheimer about the necessity for this kind of book led to its writing.

I also want to thank Christina De Bono, Commissioning Editor, the Pharmaceutical Press of the Royal Pharmaceutical Society of Great Britain, for accepting the manuscript for publication. I express my appreciation to Louise McIndoe for her valuable advice regarding manuscript submission. In addition I am grateful for the valuable assistance given by Rebecca Perry, Editorial Assistant, Linda Paulus, Production Editor, Tamsin Cousins, Production Manager, Marion Edsall, Proofreader, and Celina Edwards, Marketing Executive, for bringing the manuscript into production and to the attention of readers throughout the world.

I want to express my appreciation to Jeff Gold for drawing to my atten-tion some of his own readings concerning American health care. I also want to thank The Commonwealth Fund, New York City, and the Committee of Economic Development, New York City, for granting me permission to reproduce some of their charts and figures.

About the author

Jordan Braverman is an author of many books, newspaper columns, and magazine/journal articles for the lay public and health care groups/professionals on health care policy and economics. He has served as Director of Legislative and Health Policy Analysis at Georgetown University's Health Policy Center. He has also directed health policy activities at the American Pharmaceutical Association, the Pharmaceutical Manufacturers Association, Blue Cross Association, US Department of Health, Education, and Welfare, as well as being a consultant to private and public organizations, and was managing editor of *Topics in Health Care Financing*. Jordan is a graduate of Harvard, Yale, and Georgetown Universities. He lives in Washington, DC.

Introduction

As the USA enters the 21st century, it confronts socioeconomic and political challenges which it has never yet had to face since declaring independence as a nation on July 4, 1776. Energy-challenged, it must now compete for the same natural energy resources with countries such as India and China, whose own growing economic powers are only at their initial stages. American businesses are no longer insular to the USA but have become global entities. Jobs are being transferred out of the USA to countries where the wages are lower so that corporate profits can be higher. The USA finds itself for the first time an aging society. As the baby boomers of the 1940s and beyond reach retirement age, more and more must be supported by a smaller American workforce under 65, whose taxable incomes must support an increasing number of beneficiaries in public programs such as social security and Medicare, and whose life expectancies are expanding, with more chronic illnesses and the increasing costs attendant in treating those illnesses. While the USA spends $2 trillion a year on health care services, with no end in sight to its spending appetite, countries like Japan spend much less and their populations live much longer and enjoy better health. At a time when modern media like the internet, television, radio, newspapers, magazines, and other sources have provided Americans with access to more information about health care than ever before, Americans still find themselves uninformed about nutrition, the value of exercise, and health programs that have been in existence for decades that can help them maintain their personal health in as healthful a state as possible.

How does a nation reach a point where more and more of its monies constitute a greater percentage of its gross domestic product with no end in sight, crowding out expenditures that are also required for other societal needs? How does a nation that is constantly told about the value of exercise and good nutrition face an epidemic of obesity not only among its adult population but among its children as well? How does a nation find itself in a situation where millions of people cannot afford to buy health insurance to pay for the health services they need to maintain their own healthful status? How is a nation in the forefront of technological progress unable to devise systems to prevent unscrupulous people from defrauding the American public of billions of dollars from their public medical programs? These are some of the issues that confront the USA in both the health and nonhealth fields in the 21st century.

This book is about the economics of the health care field, not from a theoretical perspective, but in the sense of economic problems that readers confront on a practical everyday basis. Health care is one of the top problems with which American society is concerned in the 21st century. A problem cannot be solved unless it is understood. The purpose of the book is to acquaint the reader with many of the economic issues within health care today. Issues discussed embrace costs and affordability, how they developed historically, the magnitude of the economic crisis, factors contributing to the cost crisis such as medical technology, drugs, hospital care, and inefficient planning, and the mechanisms that are available today in the USA to help consumers combat, afford, and pay for the high costs of health care, in addition to their successes, failures, and the reasons why. Each of the separate health care payment systems has its own unique financial mechanisms and these concepts will be explained.

Although health care is discussed as a monolithic entity – the health care industry – readers must understand that it is not just a single monolithic industry. It is many industries placed under the caption of the health care in-dustry, and the financial worth of each of these industries is measured in many billions of dollars. There is the drug industry, hospital industry, nursing home industry, home health care industry, private health insurance industry, man-aged care industry, and many professional groups like physicians, dentists, pharmacists, podiatrists, physical therapists, and many others. Each has its own payment mechanisms, problems, and particular issues, which makes it difficult to grapple with these cost issues on a universal basis. Many books propose solutions and explain health care problems in terms of strictly eco-nomic theories and discussion, such as inelastic and elastic demand, micro-economics, and macroeconomics. While economic terminology will be used in this book, wherever relevant, this is not a book on theoretical economics, nor an advice book on how to find, judge, and pay for health care services as economically as possible, nor a book based solely on academic studies trying to explain our current health care economic problems. Rather it is a plain explanation of the economics of the health care industry so that readers will understand why we have a cost crisis; how it came about; some of the con-tributing reasons; the success or failure of today's cost control mechanisms; and what the future might hold. Hopefully, readers will have a more complete understanding of the health care field and be able to make a contribution to the national debate as the USA tries to bring about equitable solutions to its various health system problems, not only for individual consumers who use its services, but also for those who provide the services.

1

History of health care financing in the USA

Introduction

During the US presidential election of 2008, US Senator Hillary Rodham Clinton proposed the enactment of a universal mandated health insurance plan as part of her campaign platform when contesting for the presidential nomination of the Democratic Party. Her advocacy of such a position is not new in American history. In fact, the very principle of compulsory participation can be traced as far back as 1798, when the US government established a marine service hospital (forerunner of the US Public Health Service), and required owners of merchant ships to contribute 20 cents a month into a sickness fund for each seaman in their employ. In fact, the basic principle of individuals pooling their resources in order to spread their economic risks can be traced as far back as the so-called funeral societies of ancient Greece. Originally established to pay members' funeral costs, the societies ultimately came to have a variety of social and relief functions. Similarly, medieval craft guilds, forerunners of modern labor unions, often established welfare funds to assist sick and/or needy members. As the industrial revolution gathered momentum in the 19th century, a number of labor unions and individual employees required that workers join relief funds, many of which eventually came under government regulation.

In addition to the previous principle of pooling resources to spread economic risks, the idea that government should share some of the responsibility for health care can be traced as far back as Greece and its city states where citizens enjoyed the services of tax-supported public physicians. Centuries later, the first broad-gauged compulsory health insurance law was enacted by the state of Prussia in 1854, 29 years before Germany was united under Chancellor Otto von Bismarck. The Chancellor was thus able to draw upon this precedent in 1883 when he persuaded the German Reichstag to extend compulsory health insurance to workers throughout the German nation. When Bismarck's program proved highly successful, it soon spread to other European countries, notably the UK, and eventually expanded into the comprehensive system of worker protection that is known today as 'social insurance.'[1] In 1911 David Lloyd George, UK Chancellor of the Exchequer, convinced parliament to pass the National Health Insurance Act, which provided a cash payment in the event of maternity or disability and medical services if a worker became ill. Other countries, including Austria, Hungary, Norway, Russia, and the Netherlands, also took the same steps through 1912. In addition, other European countries, including Sweden in 1891, Denmark in 1892, France in 1910, and Switzerland in 1912, subsidized mutual benefit societies that workers had established among themselves. Meanwhile, during this same period of time the USA did not take any action to subsidize voluntary funds or make sickness insurance mandatory, because the federal government thought this responsibility belonged to the states. The states, in turn, thought this function was the responsibility of private and voluntary programs. Thus, the national debate in the USA as to how best to protect American citizens against the costs of ill health has never concluded – a debate that has now extended into the 21st century.

Today, all kinds of proposals are being offered to help Americans pay for their health care services. Nationally, it is proposals for a national health insurance program. Some want it to be mandated, others do not. In the private sector, there are all kinds of plans like health savings accounts, managed care, private health insurance policies, and other private programs for those who are working. For senior citizens, whether they are still working or not, there is not only Medicare and Medicare supplementary health insurance (known as Medigap), but also managed care plans under Medicare as well as Medicare's new prescription drug program that began in 2006 for those who find drug costs a financial burden. So, how did America reach this point in its history where so many different proposals, both public and private, are being implemented or proposed to resolve its health care cost crisis? It is the intent of this chapter to present a brief historical overview of how America reached the situation today where the receipt and purchase of health care services have become more of a burden rather than a relief for America's citizenry, regardless of their socioeconomic and demographic status.

The 19th century

Private health insurance originated in the USA in the middle of the 19th century when a few insurance companies responded to the public's demand for coverage against rail and steamboat accidents. Then, during the latter half of the 20th century, the concept of the mutual aid society which had originated in Europe, notably in Germany, was adopted in the USA. As already noted, small contributions were collected from each member in return for the promise to pay a cash benefit in the event of disability through accident or sickness. Early providers of health insurance, therefore, included fraternal benefit societies. Also, a number of mutual benefit associations, called 'establishment funds,' began to be formed in 1875 within the USA. Comprising the workers of a single organization, these funds, sometimes partially financed by employers, provided small payments for death and disability. Toward the end of the 19th century, with the entry of accident insurance companies into the field, health insurance began to demonstrate substantial growth. At about the same time, life insurance companies made accident and health insurance available. Thus, between two eras – the mid 19th and the mid 20th century – the private health insurance industry dramatically evolved.

The Progressive Era

As the 19th century melded into the 20th century, the Progressive Era emerged in the USA. Reformers sought to improve the social conditions of the working class. In the early 1900s, patients either lived or died. Care was largely confined to preventing disease, by keeping clean, recommending good diets, providing good nursing, performing basic surgery, and praying for rapid recovery. Unlike in Europe, there was no strong support emanating from the working class for social insurance, which is an insurance program carried out or mandated by a government. Social insurance protects against various economic risks such as loss of income due to sickness, old age, or unemployment, and is considered one kind of social security, though both terms are used interchangeably. In addition, labor and socialist parties were not united in their support for health insurance or sickness funds and benefits, as they had been in Europe. Even though President Theodore Roosevelt supported health insurance and the Progressive Party, for which he was the presidential nominee and candidate, in 1912 included in its party platform a national health insurance proposal for the USA, the federal government did not act. However, there was support for such a program outside government. One such progressive group was the American Association of Labor Legislation (AALL). It was co-founded in 1905 by John R. Commons, an economist at the University of Wisconsin, to lobby for health reform, and disbanded in 1943. The AALL sought to reform capitalism rather than abolish it, and campaigned for health insurance in 1906. In 1915 it drafted a model bill that limited coverage to the working class and all others who earned less than $1200 a year, including dependants. The bill included the services of physicians, nurses, and hospitals as well as sick pay, maternity benefits, and a death benefit of $50 to pay for funeral expenses. The model was a blend of health insurance and disability. It would have covered both health care costs and sick pay for 26 weeks. Costs were to be shared between workers, employers, and the state.

Even the American Medical Association (AMA) at that time was in favor of a compulsory health insurance plan and by 1916 was working with the AALL on such a proposal. In 1917 the AMA's House of Delegates favored compulsory health insurance, which the AALL had proposed. However, many state medical societies were not in favor of such a program and because the manner in which physicians were to be paid could not be agreed upon, the AMA leadership soon disavowed that it had ever favored such a proposal.

In the meantime, the president of the American Federation of Labor (AFL) denounced compulsory health insurance as an unnecessary paternalistic reform. (This is in contrast to its advocacy as the American Federation of Labor–Congress of Industrial Organizations (AFL–CIO) (now renamed) in 1955.) The reasons for the denunciation were that now the state would have created a system to supervise people's health and, by taking over the union's role in providing social benefits, the government would weaken the union's strength. Remember, at this time labor unions did not have the legal right to engage in collective bargaining. Another group opposed to compulsory health insurance at the time was the commercial insurance industry. The reformers' health insurance plan contained benefits that paid for funeral expenses, which was in direct conflict with the insurance industry that also sold policies to working-class families which paid for death benefits and covered funeral expenses. Thus, life insurance companies saw a compulsory health insurance plan as a threat to their income. Then, in 1917, the USA entered World War I and bad feelings against the Germans increased. The government even commissioned articles that denounced 'German socialist insurance' and the opponents of health insurance called it a 'Prussian menace' that was not in line with American values. Also, in 1917 the War Risk Insurance Act was passed and extended medical and hospital care to veterans, amending the War Risk Insurance Act of 1914 that insured American shipping and cargo.

The 1920s

During the early 1920s the USA went through a period called the Red Scare, when the nation sought to eliminate the remnants of radicalism from its midst. Opponents of compulsory health insurance associated this idea with the bolshevism of the Soviet Union and buried the concept under a torrent of anticommunist rhetoric. This ended the debate over enacting a compulsory health insurance plan in the USA until the 1930s.

Meanwhile, the costs of health care, especially those of hospitals, began to rise slowly. From 1918 to 1929 hospital costs increased from 7.6% of total family medical bills to 13%.[2] According to the *Historical Statistics of the United States*,[3] average annual earnings in all industries and occupations in 1926, when farm labor was excluded, were $1473.[4] Surveys of medical expenditures from 1928 show that US urban families, with above-average annual incomes of $2000–3000, and that had no expenses for hospitalization, spent an average of $67 a year (2–3% of their income) on medical care. With hospitalization, the average was $261 or 8–13% of annual income.[4] In spite of price increases, most people still paid for medical care out of their own pockets. Estimated health expenditures in 1929 were $3649 million. Of that amount consumers paid $2937 million, public sources paid $495 million, and philanthropy paid $217 million.[4] However, the year 1929 was also the beginning of another great event in American history: the Great Depression, that extended itself throughout the 1930s. As the Depression became worse and unemployment rose, the public became increasingly aware that new methods were required to help pay the costs of medical care. These conditions led a number of teachers and the Baylor Hospital in Dallas, Texas, to develop an arrangement whereby the teachers would receive 21 days of hospitalization care on a prepayment basis for $6.00 per year.[4] This development had a significant effect on the insurance industry, foreshadowing the arrival of reimbursement policies for hospitals and surgical care. At the same time, another form of prepayment services was beginning in Los Angeles, California, where a group of health care providers assumed the responsibility for organizing and integrating medical services on a prepaid basis, that is, combining group practice with prepayment. This physician-sponsored organization, known as the Ross–Loos Medical Group, named after its founders Donald Ross and H. Clifford Loos, contracted with the Los Angeles Department of Water and Power to provide prepaid comprehensive health care to its employees and their dependants. This group was the predecessor of programs such as the Kaiser Foundation Health Plan of California and served as the prototype of today's emerging medical care foundations and health maintenance organizations (HMOs).

The 1930s

Beginning in 1927 and ending in 1932, a committee appointed by President Calvin Coolidge and composed of 50 economists, physicians, public health specialists, and major interest groups, met as a group called the Committee on the Costs of Medical Care (CCMC). Privately funded by philanthropic organizations such as the Rockefeller, Milbank, and Rosenwald Foundations and established because of concerns over the costs of and distribution of medical care, they published their findings over a period of 5 years in 26 research volumes and 15 smaller reports. The CCMC documented the severe and widespread problems Americans faced in obtaining and paying for medical care and recommended that more national resources ought to be directed to medical care. The CCMC saw voluntary, not compulsory, health insurance as a means to cover these costs and the care, which is provided through groups, would be paid for by taxation or insurance. The AMA considered the report as a radical document promoting socialized medicine.

Meanwhile, hospitals that were hit hard by the Great Depression wanted to make sure they were paid and rushed to embrace plans for prepaid health care. Bank failures began to mount and Americans were not going on spending sprees. By 1931, private hospitals had their occupancies reduced to 62%, while public hospitals that accepted charity care filled 89% of their beds.[5] Whether their income was declining or not, and whether patients were using the facilities or not, hospitals still had to support their physical plant and pay their staff. Hospitals knew that prepaid health plans could help them greatly by providing them with a steady source of income. Therefore, the American Hospital Association began to market prepaid hospitalization plans as something that could be financially beneficial to hospitals and patients alike and relieve patients, especially those on low income, of a financial burden when they became sick. Since hospitals operated their own prepaid plans, they began to compete with each other. To diminish this competition, community hospitals began to organize with each other to offer network hospital coverage. These plans eventually came together under the auspices of the American Hospital Association, which, in 1939, adopted the Blue Cross name and logo as the national symbol of plans that met the American Hospital Association's requirements. Member hospitals began offering discounts to Blue Cross plans in the 1930s. State legislatures were more than agreeable to permit the American Hospital Association to establish the terms under which hospital health insurance would operate. States did not consider Blue Cross plans as insurance because hospitals owned the plans. Thus, states exempted the Blue Cross plans from normal insurance company requirements. The Blue Cross plans were permitted to operate as nonprofit corporations and did not have to pay the taxes of 2–3% of premiums that most states levied upon and received from private insurance companies. States also exempted the Blue Cross plans from reserve requirements that were designed to make sure that regular insurance companies were solvent. Since Blue Cross brought hospitals together into a network that impeded competition from stand-alone institutions, its structure made it very difficult for any kind of insurer to offer benefits that were very different from the Blue Cross standard. When the Blues began, in their early years, they used a method of establishing health insurance premiums called *community rating* in which everyone, regardless of age, sex, or preexisting condition, paid the same premiums. And when private insurance companies entered the market they used a methodology to establish premiums called *experience rating* which calculated relative risk and avoided the riskiest potential customers altogether. Experience rating is computed on the basis of past losses and expenses which are incurred by the insurance company in the settlement of claims and other expenses involving a particular group of risks. To survive as business entities, the Blues eventually adopted this method of establishing premiums, and for the most part, have lost their tax advantages and are basically like other health insurers.

Meanwhile, as hospitals began operating their own prepaid health plans, the idea of enacting a US national health insurance plan had not yet died. The first attempt was made in 1935 when the social security legislation came up for a vote in the US Congress. With millions of people out of work, unemployment insurance became an administration priority, followed by old age benefits. President Roosevelt's Committee on Economic Security, which the president established in 1934, was afraid that if national health insurance, which the AMA opposed, was included in the social security bill, it would threaten the passage of the entire social security legislation. Therefore, national health insurance was omitted from the social security bill, which did become law. The Social Security Act of 1935 (PL 74-241) established a categorical assistance system in which the federal government shared with the states the cost for providing maintenance to the aged who were needy, the blind, families with dependent children, and, subsequently, the permanently and totally disabled. The Social Security Act did not make any special provisions for medical assistance, but it included the cost of medical care in the individual's monthly assistance payment, for which federal participation was available. Without any restrictions on how to spend their payments, many welfare recipients neglected their personal medical care – often because states set the overall payments so low that it was not enough to pay even for basic food and shelter. However, the Roosevelt administration made one more attempt in the 1930s to enact national health insurance through the Wagner National Health Insurance Act of 1939. While not totally supported by President Roosevelt, the proposal emanated from the president's Tactical Committee on Medical Care, established in 1937. The national health plan was to be supported by federal grants to states and administered by states and localities. The essential elements of the technical committee's reports were included in the Wagner bill. However, the bill was never enacted into law because of the declining fortunes of the New Deal as the 1930s neared its end and World War II began.

While the debates over national health insurance continued at the national level, and as hospitals during the Depression established their own prepaid plans to buttress their own financial viability, physicians began to be concerned that hospitals would expand the prepaid concept to embrace physician services as well. In 1934 the AMA adopted 10 principles that were directed at answering proponents of national health insurance and hindering hospitals from underwriting physician services. Legislation exempting prepaid physician service plans from insurance regulations and establishing their nonprofit status was passed, along with requirements that made sure that there was physician representation on plans that provided prepaid physician services. In 1939, the first prepaid physician services began operations in California. The

AMA encouraged state and local medical societies around the country to establish similar plans, and in 1946 they affiliated and became known as Blue Shield. By the end of the 20th century, the individual entities, the Blue Cross Association and the Blue Shield Association, had merged under the single banner of the Blue Cross and Blue Shield Association, representing the political and economic interests of its members on a national level.

The 1940s

In 1939, private health insurance covered only 6% of the American population for hospitalization. By 1941, the number had risen to 12.4%. Fifty-one percent of those covered had a Blue Cross–Blue Shield policy, 33% had group or individual polices from insurance companies, and almost 14% received insurance coverage from community groups, individual practice plans, unions, private group clinics, or similar arrangements.[4] Then, on December 7, 1941, the Japanese attacked Pearl Harbor, Hawaii, and the USA entered World War II. During this time a major change took place in the health insurance field. The 1942 Stabilization Act imposed price controls on employers by limiting employee wage increases. However, since price controls also have problems, at the request of employers the Act included a loophole permitting employers to compete for scarce workers by offering health insurance to employees as a pre-tax fringe benefit. Fringe benefits then became a significant part of collective bargaining, eventually including group health insurance.

In the postwar years, three powerful forces came together to provide modern health insurance with its strongest impetus to growth. First, in 1948 a decision by the US Supreme Court held that fringe benefits, including health insurance, were a legitimate part of the collective bargaining process; the second was the sharply increasing costs of medical care; and third was the capability of the private health insurance industry to introduce new kinds of coverage and broaden existing benefits. An important spur in the growth of group health insurance, for example, was the favorable treatment that group coverage received.

However, despite the development of Blue Cross and Blue Shield plans at this time and the expansion of commercial health insurance, interest in passing a national health insurance plan for the entire country had not waned. The Wagner bill of 1939 (Senator Robert Wagner, Democrat – New York (D-NY)) had changed from a proposal for federal grants-in-aid to a proposal for national health insurance. First introduced in 1943, it became known as the Wagner–Murray–Dingell bills for its sponsors in both the US Senate and US House of Representatives and, subsequently, reintroduced into Congress in 1945, 1947, and 1949, all to no avail in terms of its passage. The bill called for compulsory national health insurance and a payroll tax. Opposition to the bill was immense. Although there was a great deal of debate, with very great opposition to the bill, the US Congress never passed it, despite its constant reintroductions. Had the bill passed, the law would have established a national health insurance program, funded by payroll taxes.

After Harry S. Truman had succeeded Franklin D. Roosevelt as US president upon the latter's death on April 12, 1945, the president thoroughly supported the enactment of a national health insurance program. However, after the end of World War II the US Cold War with the former Soviet Union ensued and the opponents of national health insurance began equating it with 'socialized medicine' which, in turn, became a symbolic issue in the enlarging crusade against communism in the USA. Unlike President Roosevelt's national health insurance plan of 1938, which was a separate proposal for the medical care of the needy, President Truman's plan was a single universal comprehensive health insurance plan for all Americans, regardless of class, rather than just for the working class. And the president even eliminated the funeral benefit that contributed to the defeat of national health insurance during the Progressive Era. But opposition to the plan was intense and included opponents such as the American Hospital Association, American Bar Association, and the AMA. When the Republican party took control of the Congress in the 1946 elections, it had no interest in the concept and viewed national health insurance as one part of a large socialist scheme. When President Truman was reelected in 1948, again national health insurance was linked with socialism and, as anticommunist feelings rose in the USA, the Korean war began in 1950. Truman's proposal died in Congressional Committee – even compromises could not save it – and proponents of national health insurance began to direct their attention to a more modest goal: hospital insurance for the elderly and the beginnings of Medicare. Rather than have a single system of national health insurance for the entire population, the USA would have a system of private health insurance for those who could afford to purchase it and public welfare services for the poor.[6]

The 1950s

As already noted, the Social Security Act of 1935 allowed the cost of medical care to be included in the monthly assistance payments, but the rate for such payments was so low recipients could barely afford food and shelter and, therefore, neglected their personal medical care. Beginning in 1950, Congress passed a series of amendments to the Social Security Act that expanded the public definition of public assistance to include money for 'vendor payments' – that is, direct payments by the state to physicians, nurses, and health care institutions, rather than to welfare recipients. This change created an administrative framework for a welfare medical program. By

1958 the federal government was sharing not only in cash payments but also in a separate category of medical payments to those who met the state's definition of being 'needy.' As of 1960, most of the states made vendor payments in federally aided categorical assistance programs and many states, in calculating their cash payments to welfare recipients, also allowed for the purchase of some items of medical care.[7]

Meanwhile, by 1952 the Truman administration had turned away from trying to enact a national health insurance program and in 1952 began advocating for a medical care for the aged program – what would become Medicare in the 1960s. The AMA opposed it. In 1957 the debate over Medicare reached new heights of discussion when Congressman Aime Forand (D-RI) introduced a bill in the House Ways and Committee to cover hospital costs for the aged on social security and, again, the AMA and other opponents were able to prevent it from being reported out of the Committee for a Congressional vote. The AMA portrayed a government insurance plan as a threat to the patient–doctor relationship but the tenor of the debate had shifted. Rather than seeking to cover the entire American population with a national health insurance plan, its proponents were now seeking to cover only the elderly. At this time organized labor united for the first time behind the idea for Medicare. For nearly a decade with the AMA and its allies on one side and some politicians and elements of the public on the other side, the debate over Medicare resulted in a Congressional standoff with no Congressional action. Finally, a compromise proposed by Senator Robert Kerr (D-OK) and Representative Wilbur Mills (D-AR) sought to substitute, in place of a federal Medicare program covering aged social security beneficiaries, a state-based welfare program covering only the medically indigent, persons who did not qualify for welfare but were still too poor to purchase medical care (the 'medically needy'), and the aged state welfare rolls. This program was enacted into law in September 1960. Kerr–Mills differed from Medicare in three ways: (1) it was a welfare benefit in its scope for those able to demonstrate a lack of financial means; (2) it was state-based rather than federal; and (3) the program was entirely an option of the state. If a state chose not to contract a health care program (Kerr–Mills), it did not have to do so. Initially even this program was opposed by the AMA, but finally, giving in to political reality, the AMA dropped its opposition to Kerr–Mills. By November 1964, 39 states and the District of Columbia had established programs providing medical assistance for the aged. All covered hospital services, 30 covered nursing home care, 34 covered physician visits, and 25 covered prescription drugs.

While these activities were being pursued on a national level in the public sector, in the private sector health insurance continued to be innovative in terms of new products and expand in terms of beneficiaries who were covered. In the early 1950s insuring organizations introduced the most comprehensive insurance coverage yet developed – major medical expense coverage. This

policy had been defined as insurance especially created to offset heavy medical expenses resulting from catastrophic or prolonged illness or injury. From its beginning, major medical has grown rapidly as families responded to the need to protect themselves against quickly rising hospital, medical, and surgical costs. Benefit levels under comprehensive major medical expense policies increased from a range of $50 000 to that of several million dollars. The rapidly developing economy in the years following World War II also led to the emergence of protection in the form of long-term disability benefits, stressing once again the idea of income replacement during times of disability and other financial emergencies.[4,8] In addition, the insurance industry began selling other forms of insurance. Vision insurance was introduced in 1957 and in 1959 extended-care facility benefits as well as insurance for dental care became available to the public.

The 1960s

As the 1960s began, Kerr–Mills was the law of the land, but the debate was still not over in terms of federal financing of medical costs. Those who were still proposing a Medicare program for the elderly had not given up on trying to enact such a program. After the Forand bill was defeated and John F. Kennedy was elected president in November 1960, Medicare's proponents introduced a new version of the legislation, called the King–Anderson bill, named after its sponsors Congressman Cecil King (D-CA) and Senator Clifford Anderson (D-NM). The King–Anderson bill was the predecessor of the Medicare program and would have paid for the hospitalization of the elderly through the social security system, and covered 14 million recipients of social security over the age of 65. The King–Anderson program was only half of the Medicare program which itself came into existence in 1965, but it did have President Kennedy's support. It proposed to cover the costs of hospital and nursing home care, as already noted, but not surgical costs and not outpatient physician services. It was scaled back from the Forand bill, which, in addition, offered coverage for surgical expenses. Between 1960 and 1965, the King–Anderson bill never received Congressional approval. After the assassination of President Kennedy on November 22, 1963, his successor, President Lyndon B. Johnson, took up the cause to enact a Medicare program and failed in his attempt to pass his hospitalization bill in 1964.

After the 1964 presidential election, when the Democrats took control of the US Congress, the climate that eventually allowed for the passage of Medicare and Medicaid had changed. However, before that had happened, the AMA developed an alternative to the Medicare proposals which they called Eldercare, an expansion of the Kerr–Mills program. It promised much more generous benefits than Medicare but again was limited to the welfare population rather than to all aged social security beneficiaries. The program, a voluntary insurance plan with broader benefits and physician services, was to be operated by insurance carriers and states, with premiums for the low-income elderly subsidized out of federal–state revenues. In response, the government expanded its proposed legislation to cover physician services and what came of it were Medicare and Medicaid. Finally, with debates over Medicare still proceeding in July 1965, Wilbur Mills, Chairman of the House and Ways Committee, substituted his own bill and King–Anderson was eventually voted out of Committee, the Senate approved the bill, and Medicare became law on July 30, 1965 (the Social Security Amendments of 1965, PL 89-97).

The Act was developed in closed sessions of the Ways and Means Committee without any public hearings that would have stimulated public debate. During the closed sessions the necessary political compromises and private concessions were made to the doctors (reimbursements for customary, reasonable, and prevailing fees), to the hospitals (cost plus reimbursement), and to the Republicans was granted a three-part plan. This plan included the Democratic proposal for comprehensive health insurance (Part A), the revised Republican program of government-subsidized voluntary physician services (Part B), and Medicaid, a federal means-tested program for the poor in which federal and state governments shared the costs, half and half, and offered a minimum set of benefits to those who were eligible, with other benefits being made optional, allowing states to devise their own programs. Because the federal government paid half of all charges it encouraged states to replace the state programs that previously helped the poor and the ill and essentially removed all financial responsibilities from consumers. Medicare at the time was expected to help relatively few people aged 65 years and older since men born in 1950 had a life expectancy of 66 years and women, 71.7 years.[9]

The 1970s

As the 1960s turned into the 1970s, rising health expenditure continued to be a problem and a new administration was now in Washington, that of President Richard M Nixon. From 1950 through 1965, when Medicare became law, national health expenditures (NHE) rose from $12.7 billion to $41.8 billion or an increase of about $29 billion in 15 years. From 1965, after Medicare was enacted into law to 1970, NHE increased from $41.8 billion to $73.1 billion or about $32 billion in just 5 years.[8] In other words, the amount of NHE expended in just 5 years (from 1965 to 1970) was equivalent to the amount spent in the 15 years before the enactment of Medicare and Medicaid. Consequently, when health care costs began to rise dramatically in the period following the implementation of Medicare and Medicaid, a reexamination of the health system seemed urgent. The Nixon administration undertook such a study. In the course of analyzing the system, the administration considered health maintenance as one means of containing the runaway costs of health care. After a thorough study of the concept, the government decided to promote health maintenance organizations (HMOs) as a major federal initiative.[10] Former President Nixon announced this undertaking in his 1971 message to Congress. The administration noted in a White Paper on health care that HMOs emphasize prevention and early care; provide incentives for holding down costs and for increasing the productivity of resources; offer opportunities for improving the quality and distribution of care; and by mobilizing private capital and managerial talent, HMOs reduce the need for federal funds and direct control.[11]

But despite this prognosis, there were still various reasons why prepaid group practice required federal assistance at this point in history. First, the movement was growing at a very slow rate. While older plans such as the Kaiser Foundation Health Plan and the Health Insurance Plan of Greater New York were well established, there was not enough pressure or incentives for their expansion or for the development of new plans in other locations. Second, health care providers were not really convinced that HMOs should grow in great number. Hospitals had little to gain from a system which stressed outpatient care; and many medical professionals viewed any form of organization, even if privately controlled, as a step toward socialized medicine. Furthermore, the AMA, in strong opposition, had raised serious questions about the ability of HMOs to deliver high-quality care. Even without opposition from the health care establishment, HMOs' growth faced an uphill battle. Financial requirements for organizing even a modest HMO system and covering its operational deficits were prohibitive to all but the wealthiest of potential sponsors. Consumers were expected to support the HMO movement once they understood its long-range promise of financial savings and better care, but consumer education is an expensive effort. Finally, the laws in many states were unfavorable to the operation and formation of HMOs. The existence of these impediments made it clear that the federal government had to give some kind of assistance if a substantial number of HMOs were to develop.[12] Consequently, a series of bills were introduced by the Nixon administration, another by Senator Edward M. Kennedy (D-MA) and still another by Congressman William R. Roy (D-KS). Public hearings were held on the bills and discussions took place with representatives of various elements of the health care industry. Legislative language was revised, compromises achieved, and, finally, in the late fall of 1973, Congress passed the Health Maintenance Organization Act of 1973 (PL 93-222) and President Richard M. Nixon signed it into law in December of that year.

But the federal government was not the only resource developing HMOs in this period. The private sector also began to examine these prototype organizations as another way of lowering the costs of delivering health care. Physician and consumer groups, Blue Cross–Blue Shield, and commercial insurance carriers, to name but a few sponsors, began to establish HMOs. From February 1971 to December 1975 the number of HMO-like delivery systems had increased from 33 to 178 organizations, serving almost 6 million persons compared to 3.6 million in 1971.[13] In fact, by the mid-1970s 30 Blue Cross plans were involved in 98 HMO-like organizations. During 1975 enrollment in Blue Cross-affiliated HMOs increased by 14% to 1 168 900 people compared with estimated 8% nationally for all HMOs. Blue Cross estimated at the time in the 1970s that by 1980 it would have invested $57 million in an effort to offer subscribers HMO programs as an alternative to traditional health coverage.[14] Thus, in the 1970s when the Blue Cross efforts were coupled with that of other insurance carriers and groups, the HMO movement looked promising in terms of future growth. To spur their growth even further, in 1976 Congress passed the Health Maintenance Organization Amendments, which relaxed requirements for HMOs to qualify for federal assistance. Like the Blues, initially, HMOs were mainly nonprofit entities, but once business saw an opportunity to make a profit, these profit-making HMOs' share of the market increased to about two-thirds by 1997. Oriented to the bottom line, for-profit HMOs became more aggressive about denying treatments. While HMOs were able to contain cost increases for a while during the 1990s, they could not contain them forever and eventually costs began rising again slowly, contributing to the current US crisis and the renewed call for a national health insurance plan in the Democratic presidential campaigns of 2008.

But HMOs were not the only federal efforts being undertaken in terms of health care financing during this decade. In 1972 Congress passed the Social Security Amendments (PL 92-603), which expanded Medicare by extending health insurance benefits to the disabled and to end-stage renal disease patients, These 1972 amendments also established professional standard review organizations (PSROs) whose purpose was to monitor the quality of health care by determining, for example, whether the hospitalization of Medicare, Medicaid, and Maternal and Child Health program recipients is necessary, of appropriate duration, and met professional recognized standards of quality, in part to control costs. In October 1977 the Medicare and Medicaid Anti-Fraud and Abuse Amendments (PL 95-142) broadened the mandate of the PSROs to undertake ambulatory care review within 2 years of becoming designated as a PSRO. These PRSOs eventually evolved into the professional review organizations (PROs) of the 1980s, which, in turn, evolved into the quality improvement organizations (QIOs) of the early 21st century.

Then, in 1974, private health insurance received another form of expansion when Congress passed the Employee Retirement Income Security Act (PL 93-222), also known by its acronym ERISA. As a result of this law, which encouraged the growth of self-insurance and because of rising health care costs, various companies rapidly began to develop self-insurance plans in which the companies themselves pay their employees' doctor and hospital bills, providing the company with significant cost advantages. The original purpose of the law was to protect workers' fringe benefits. Although the law was primarily directed at pensions, the courts over the years have interpreted ERISA as overriding state regulation of employee health insurance plans in instances where the employer insures itself. In the 1970s before ERISA became law such corporate self-insurance was rare. Today, as a result of ERISA more than one-half of all US workers are employed by companies that self-insure, compared to only 5% in the 1970s, because self-insurance is less expensive than purchasing health insurance from a third party. The reason for this is that self-insurance allows companies to cover only those ailments which they choose and to exclude a wide variety of coverage that the state laws require of conventional insurance. In addition, to lower their medical bills further some large corporations have begun to combine their self-insurance system with the provision of general medical services by in-house medical clinics, staffed by their own doctors, or provided by contract medical firms. Besides saving on drugs and tests, companies can save money by avoiding unnecessary hospitalizations through careful case monitoring and negotiating lower fees with hospitals – a possibility when a firm can guarantee a hospital a lot of patients.

And once again, despite all these other financial developments in the health care field during the 1970s, the issue of enacting national health insurance as in previous decades was never far from a president's agenda, whether it be a Republican like Richard M. Nixon or a Democrat like Jimmy Carter. A few days after what would turn out to be his final State of the Union address on February 6, 1974, President Nixon introduced his Comprehensive Health Insurance Act and called for universal access to health insurance. He told the American public that his program with vastly improved protection against catastrophic illnesses would assure comprehensive health insurance protection to millions of Americans who, at the time, could not receive or afford it. President Nixon stated that his plan would build on existing employer-sponsored insurance plans and would provide government subsidies to the self-employed and small businesses to ensure universal access to health insurance without creating a new federal bureaucracy. His plan also did not require all Americans to purchase health insurance. President Nixon's interest in national health insurance in 1974 was not new. In fact, as a conservative Congressman in 1947 from California, he first proposed the enactment of national health insurance because, after losing two brothers to tuberculosis and then seeing the disease cured, the necessity for such a private–public partnership was very personal to him. Despite his problems with the widening Watergate break-in and cover-up scandal that eventually led to his resignation, his proposal was wending its way through Congress but then, according to a political almanac published by the *Congressional Quarterly*,[15] a national leader in political journalism since 1945, the AFL-CIO and United Automobile Workers Union lobbied successfully against its passage, hoping to get a better deal after the 1976 presidential elections. In his 1992 book, *Seize the Moment*,[16] President Nixon wrote, 'we need to work out a system that includes a greater emphasis on preventive care, sufficient public funding for health insurance for those who cannot afford it in the private sector, competitions among health care providers and health insurance to keep down the costs of both, and decoupling the costs of health care from the cost of adding workers to the payroll.'[17]

Four days after President Nixon resigned on August 8, 1974, his successor President Gerald Ford addressed Congress and asked for a bipartisan effort to pass national health insurance. But the economy was deteriorating and President Ford wanted to contain government spending and national health insurance did not move out of Congress. However, the Ford administration did create one program that impacts on the purchasing of prescription medicines by public programs. In August 1976, a new program called maximum allowable cost (MAC) went into effect. The program places a price ceiling on prescription drugs whose patents have expired, which are produced by more than one company, and which are covered by Medicare, Medicaid, and Maternal and Child Health Programs. At that time, Part D of Medicare (Medicare's new prescription drug benefit program) was still almost 30 years away from becoming federal law. In 1975, the AMA, the Pharmaceutical Manufacturers Association, and five physicians filed a suit against the US Department of Health, Education, and Welfare (HEW), which developed the MAC program, in the Chicago District Court. The AMA argued that the MAC program would interfere with the traditional prerogatives of the physician. The Pharmaceutical Manufacturers Association argued that the program would intrude on the professional prerogatives of the doctor and the pharmacist, would disrupt pharmaceutical distribution patterns, and possibly result in inferior drugs for Medicare and Medicaid patients. In March 1977, the Chicago Federal District Court dismissed the suit against HEW with a 74-page opinion which concluded that all of the objections to the MAC program were without merit. In establishing the MAC program, HEW announced that it would send lists of drug price comparisons to physicians and pharmacists alike to encourage them to reduce patient costs. HEW considered the MAC program as essential and one of the building blocks to control health care costs in the event any national health insurance program would be enacted.

While the Watergate scandal ruined the presidency of President Nixon, it did help propel a Democrat named Jimmy Carter into the presidency in the 1976 elections. With his election the debate about national health insurance continued. The Carter administration in 1979 put forth a plan – Health

Security – that combined requirements for employers to offer health insurance to their employees with tax credits for small business, together with an expansion of the Medicare and Medicaid programs. Health costs were to be controlled by employing high patient out-of-pocket spending requirements. Senator Edward M. Kennedy (D-MA) and Representative Henry Waxman (D-CA) also promoted their own bill – Healthcare for All Americans Act – that combined a national health budget with insurance plans offered to all employers and individuals through a consortium of companies. With a non-unified Democratic party and the continued opposition, as in the past, of organized medicine, business, the insurance industry, and conservative Republicans, the possibility of legislative action was nonexistent. In the aftermath of this failure, Medicaid was modestly expanded to include coverage for pregnant women and children, and in 1983 new reimbursement methods under Medicare for hospitals were introduced in an effort to contain their costs. The political atmosphere at the time of the Nixon and Carter administrations helped contribute to the defeat of national health insurance proposals. One was the threat that any reform would certainly increase pressure on the federal budget. Another was that the public seemed to prefer a smaller government. The third was the inability to agree on just one single proposal.

The 1980s

In the administrations of Ronald W. Reagan as well as of George H.W. Bush (1981–1993), the focus of health policy was principally on cost containment rather than expanding coverage through programs such as national health insurance. However, the private health insurance industry was not quiescent during the 1980s in seeking to control health care costs and introduced new insurance products. Managed care was beginning to attract more and more subscribers such as businesses, for example, which sought to contain their own health costs, but also the insurance industry began to introduce new forms of health delivery systems. One such popular system by the mid-1980s was called preferred provider organizations (PPOs). PPOs are a combination of traditional fee-for-service and HMOs. When patients use doctors and hospitals that are part of a PPO – these providers are called 'preferred' and at other times, 'network' providers – patients can have a larger part of their medical bill covered. Patients can use other doctors who are out-of-network providers, but at a higher personal cost. Basically, a PPO is a group of doctors and/or hospitals that negotiate a contract with a company, union, or insurance firm to provide medical services for reduced fees. In return, that provider (doctor or hospital) is promised increased patient volume and prompt payments. Evolving from the concept of PPOs and HMOs, other kinds of health delivery plan developed, such as point of service (POS) plans and exclusive provider organizations (EPOs). The POS plan contains the features of both

PPOs and HMOs, sometimes called HMO–PPO hybrids or open-ended HMOs. The health plans allow the covered person a choice to receive care from a participating or nonparticipating provider, with a different set of benefits associated with the use of participating providers. It is an HMO option that permits the beneficiary to use doctors and hospitals outside the plan for additional cost. On the other hand, an EPO is an organization that allows provider coverage for services only from network providers.[18] In this arrangement health care providers deal directly with buyers of health care services rather than deal with middlemen like insurers or HMOs, according to a negotiated discount or fee schedule.

Meanwhile, while private health insurers were introducing new products into the marketplace, the US Congress was passing new laws that altered the health care delivery system while trying to control its costs. In 1982, Congress passed the Tax Equity and Fiscal Responsibility Act (TEFRA), which made Medicare the secondary payer, brought federal employees under Medicare, and made changes in hospital reimbursement under Medicare. In 1983, in response to TEFRA, Congress enacted a payment system for hospital care for Medicare enrollees. The payment system is called a prospective payment system (PPS) and is a method for reimbursement in which Medicare payment is made, based upon a predetermined fixed amount. In other words, the Centers for Medicare and Medicaid Services (CMS), then called the Health Care Financing Administration, switched from a retrospective fee-for-service system to PPS, under which hospitals receive a fixed amount for treating inpatients diagnosed with a given illness, regardless of the length of stay or type of care received. The payment amount for particular services is derived based upon a classification system of that service (for example, diagnosis-related groups for inpatient hospital services). CMS today uses separate PPS for reimbursement for inpatient hospitals, home health agencies, hospice, hospital outpatients, inpatient psychiatric services facilities, inpatient rehabilitation facilities, long-term care hospitals, and skilled nursing facilities.

The Omnibus Deficit Reduction Act (PL 98-369) in 1984 extended Medicare as a secondary payer for elderly spouses of workers under 65. Then, on July 1, 1986 Congress passed the Consolidated Omnibus Budget Reconciliation Act (PL 99-272), also known by the acronym COBRA, which required that employer group health plans offer continued coverage to workers and their dependants upon termination of employment and to workers' spouses and dependants who would lose such coverage because of the death of the worker, divorce, or Medicare eligibility. The Act made the coverage of private employers' health care plans primary to Medicare coverage that was now secondary for active workers and their spouses who also have Medicare coverage, required that third-party payers reimburse for certain care rendered in government-operated veterans and military hospitals, and established a task force to study long-term care insurance policies.

Also, in 1986 Congress passed the Tax Reform Act (PL 99-514), which, in part, removed the federal tax exemption for Blue Cross–Blue Shield organizations providing commercial-type insurance. Then, in 1988, Congress passed the Medicare Catastrophic Coverage Act (PL 100-360), which represented the largest expansion of the Medicare program since its establishment in 1965. Benefit changes included the elimination of all cost sharing for inpatient hospital care after meeting the hospital deductible, a cap of $1370 on out-of-pocket expenses for physicians' services, and minor changes in skilled nursing home, home health, and respite care benefits. A phased-in outpatient drug benefit was to be added to Medicare in 1991. But the financing of the program by the elderly caused so much controversy that Congress eventually repealed the law in 1989. The Medicare beneficiaries were to pay for the added benefits through premium increases and an income surtax.

Thus, throughout the 1980s active debate over national insurance coverage lay rather dormant with both the private insurance industry and the Congress concentrating on new insurance products, new reimbursement systems, altering the relationship between private and public insurance coverage when a beneficiary has both kinds of coverage, protecting workers for a period of time from losing health insurance coverage when they leave one job for another, as well as other proposals for containing health care costs.

The 1990s

Then, in 1990, as part of the Omnibus Budget Reconciliation Act, Congress passed reforms (Medigap Insurance Reforms) to help states regulate Medicare supplementary insurance. Two of the most significant provisions were designating only 10 Medicare supplementary packages as marketable and requiring that all policies be guaranteed renewable.[8]

In February 1992, President George H.W. Bush announced a health insurance proposal which included vouchers for the poor to purchase private health insurance and tax credits or deductions for families with incomes up to $80 000, as well as the creation of small business pools and health insurance networks. In November 1992, William J. Clinton was elected president and national health insurance continued to be at the fore of national debate. After his election the president designated the First Lady, Hillary Rodham Clinton, to lead administration efforts to design and pass a national health insurance bill. On September 22, 1998, Clinton addressed a joint session of Congress to describe the plan, historically titled 'Health Security.' The Clinton plan took elements of previous plans with complex and new ideas for cost containment and a management of insurance companies. The principal concept of the Clinton plan would have mandated employer-purchased coverage through 'accountable' provider plans contracting with state-regulated consumer alliances. Employers were required to pay 80% of the premium (up to a maximum of 7.9% of payroll), with the family share of premiums not to exceed 3.9% of income. Low-wage employees, self-employed, and the near poor would be subsidized by public funds. The alliance would manage competition to make sure there was access to health care services and risk pooling. The plan was to be financed by substantial Medicare and Medicaid savings, an increase in the tobacco tax, and cross-subsidies among employers within risk pools. But the plan's complexity, the administration's poor management of the political process, and strong opposition by insurance company health plans and organized medicine combined to defeat the Clinton plan. The after-effects of the health care reform debacle helped elect the conservative Republican Congress in 1994 and, once again through 2008, national health insurance in terms of any kind of enactment went into Congressional hibernation.

While the attempt to establish a national health insurance plan was one of the highlights and failures of the Clinton administration to reform the health care delivery system, much smaller legislative steps were enacted by Congress in the following years. In 1996, Congress passed the Health Insurance Portability and Accountability Act of 1996 (also known as the Kennedy (D-MA) and Kassebaum (R-KA) bill) and whose acronym is HIPAA. The Act's principal focus is to make health insurance coverage portable and continuous for workers. Employees who change or lose jobs and meet eligibility conditions must either be accepted into a group plan or offered an individual policy. Also, under HIPAA Congress established as a test medical savings accounts (MSAs) as a way to pay medical bills: policyholders and employers were not taxed on their contributions. From 1997 through the year 2000 insurance companies could sell up to 750 000 high-deductible policies for large medical expenses. Deductibles were established between $1600 and $2400 for individuals and between $3200 and $4800 for families. Money in the account can be withdrawn tax-free to pay for medical care expenses, including premiums. After age 65 the money can be withdrawn for any reason, but under age 65 any withdrawals, unless for medical expenses, are subject to income tax, plus a 15% penalty. MSAs have now been supplanted by health savings accounts (established by the enactment of the Medicare Prescription Drug, Improvement, and Modernization Act of 2003), into which they can be rolled over. While existing MSAs can continue, new ones cannot be created.

In that same year of 1996, Congress also passed the Mental Health Parity Act, which requires a group health insurance plan, if they choose to offer mental health benefits, to provide the same level of coverage for such benefits as they provide for medical and surgical benefits, including the same aggregate lifetime limits and the same annual limits, if any. The Act does not apply to groups of fewer than 50 persons, substance abuse or chemical dependency treatment, or to groups whose health plan costs would increase at least 1% because of such an offering. This Act was amended on October 3,

2008 when Congress passed the Paul Wellstone and Peter Domenici (US Senators) Mental Health Parity and Addiction Equity Act of 2008 which closed loopholes that existed in the 1996 Mental Health Parity law. The law does not require that health insurers cover mental health. However, if insurers do offer this benefit, they must provide coverage and treat psychological and addictive disorders just like any other physical medical condition. Thus, they cannot limit the number of outpatient visits or allowable days in hospital or charge higher deductibles or copayments. Mental health care must be equal to the benefits an insured individual receives for any other disease, also including day limits, dollar amounts, coinsurance, and out-of-pocket maximums. As in the case of the 1996 Mental Health Parity Law, the 2008 law applies to health plans covering more than 50 employees, preserves state mental health parity laws which typically do not govern large corporate health plans as covered by federal law and consumer protection laws, and extends protection of mental health services to 82 million Americans not protected by state laws. The law ensures coverage for both in-network and out-of network services. According to the National Institutes of Mental Health, more than 57 million Americans suffer from a mental health disorder. The nonprofit Mental Health Association estimates that 67% of adults and 80% of children requiring mental health services do not receive assistance, in large part because of discriminatory insurance practices.[19–21]

Then, in 1997, Congress enacted the Balanced Budget Act, which introduced several legislative initiatives that affected the health insurance industry, from both a public and private perspective. The Act:

- expanded private plan alternatives to the original fee-for-service program (Part B) of the Medicare program through Medicare + Choice (Part C: managed care, now renamed Medicare Advantage)
- created a new state health insurance program for children: the Children's Health Insurance Program
- clarified the tax provisions contained in the HIPAA 1996 for long-term care insurance.

Thus, the US Congress continued to deal with the problems of health insurance coverage in a partial rather than comprehensive fashion.

The 21st century

In 2000, Congress passed the Long-Term Care Security Act, which provided for the establishment of a program under which long-term care insurance would be available to federal employees, members of the uniformed armed services, and civilian and military retirees. Thus, after being defeated in its enormous effort to redesign the US health care delivery system, the Clinton administration and Congress chose smaller steps to expand, protect, and offer new choices for health insurance coverage for the elderly, children, and the working population. As already noted, trying to resolve the problems of containing health care costs was still being dealt with in piecemeal fashion after efforts to control health care costs and improve its quality through a wholly revamped systematic approach were defeated.

When President George W. Bush came into office, the concept of enacting a national health insurance plan was not on the agenda of the Republican Congress. Rather, Congress's emphasis on controlling health care costs was through consumer-driven plans in which consumers became responsible for their own health expenses as well as protecting the elderly from the rising costs of prescription drugs.

As the 21st century began, other new programs began emerging in the private sector. In these programs providers like physicians are being reimbursed on the basis of their performance because in providing services they attain goals of quality of care. This is in contrast to the system that reimburses doctors, hospitals, or other providers regardless of whether they provide good services or whether patients are satisfied with their care. In requiring high quality, the programs are trying to eliminate from the health system expensive mistakes as well as inefficiencies relating to various kinds of medical treatments and the management of patient care. As a result, doctors are reimbursed at higher fees, those in the middle are reimbursed with standard payments, and the worst providers receive a reduction in fees. As pay-for-performance develops over time, the next logical step would be to supply consumers with a shopping guide that gives them information about their provider's cost and quality of care. As new challenges arise, the health insurance field continues to demonstrate its innovation and flexibility to meet them.

Another major development occurred in 2003 when Congress enacted the Medicare Prescription Drug, Improvement, and Modernization Act of 2003 (PL 108-173). Aside from covering the elderly for the costs of prescription drugs under Medicare, this law created a new kind of mechanism for consumers to pay for their health care costs. It is called a health savings account. Basically, the health savings account is a combination of a type of individual retirement account (IRA) with insurance policy directed at only medical expenses. The health savings account can be used to pay for routine medical bills and the insurance policy for larger medical expenses. Participants can choose among an array of investment options within the IRA-like account – that is, the money can be invested in a mutual fund, brokerage, bank account, or the like. Each year consumers or their employers can fund the health savings account with an amount equal to the deductible, subject to a limit, and the amount issued to pay for health expenses or to be invested. The money going in would be pretax dollars and withdrawals for medical expenses would be tax-free. If consumers use the money for nonmedical expenses before age 65, they pay a penalty in addition to income tax. After age 65, consumers do not incur a penalty if they use the money for nonmedical expenses, but would still have to pay income tax on the money. As long as the high deductible health plan meets the requirements of this federal program, it can be an HMO, PPO, or an indemnity plan. This arrangement, sometimes called a 'consumer-driven plan,' is intended to encourage workers to look for inexpensive treatment and to avoid unnecessary spending.

As noted, the creation of health savings accounts was just one program in a law that essentially broadened the scope of Medicare itself by creating a new prescription drug benefit known as Part D – the fourth element of Medicare after the hospitalization insurance (Part A), voluntary medical services insurance (Part B), and managed care plans or Medicare Advantage (Part C). This is a voluntary insurance program that everyone can join if they are enrolled in the original Medicare program (with either Part A or Part B coverage, no matter what their income may be), or in a Medicare Cost plan, or in a Medicare Fee-for-Service plan that does not cover prescription drugs. Consumers do not have to take any physical examination for this coverage nor can the program turn consumers down for health reasons. In addition, consumers do not have to sign up and enroll in this prescription drug program if they do not wish to do so. For purpose of definition a consumer cost plan is a kind of HMO. In a Medicare Cost plan, if a patient receives services outside the plan's network without a referral, the patient's Medicare-covered services will be paid under the original Parts A and B of Medicare, except the cost plan does pay for emergency services or urgently needed services outside the service area. A private fee-for-service plan is a kind of Medicare Advantage plan (Part C) in which a patient may go to any Medicare-approved physician or hospital that accepts the plan's payment. The insurance plan, rather than Medicare, decides how much it will pay and what consumers will pay for the services they receive. Consumers pay more or less for Medicare-covered benefits and may have extra benefits which Medicare does not cover. Despite the establishment of Medicare Part D, Medicare Part B will continue to cover drugs such as those administered in a hospital or a doctor's office as it has in the past.

As a final example, when the US Congress enacted the Deficit Reduction Act of 2005 (PL 109-171) it also established elements of consumer-driven plans called health opportunity accounts for Medicaid patients to use in these state programs.

The year 2012

The year 2012 marks the 100th anniversary since Teddy Roosevelt ran as a candidate of the Progressive Party for the presidency of the USA with the enactment of national health insurance as a plank in his political party's platform. Since that time, almost every administration since President Roosevelt has proposed the enactment of such a program for the USA, yet all have failed. Meanwhile, running almost in parallel with the health activities of the federal government, as in the enactment of Medicare and Medicaid, HMOs, HIPAA, COBRA, prescription drug coverage, PROs, ERISA, and TEFRA, and other programs which were enacted into law, the private sector in the form of the insurance industry has developed all kind of programs to protect consumers from the costs of ill health and to ensure they receive quality care. These include programs such as major medical insurance, disability income insurance, dental insurance, vision insurance, HMOs, PPOs, POS, long-term care insurance, and other programs to insure against the costs of medical care. Yet, nothing has stemmed the tide of rising costs. Today, employers are placing more and more of the burden of paying for their own health care services on employees by reducing or simply eliminating health care benefit coverage; hospitals are merging and becoming less friendly to low-income patients; and more and more of the population cannot afford to buy health insurance at all and, thus, remain uninsured as the portion who can afford it continues to decline in direct proportion to the increase in the number of uninsured. In 1950 the USA spent $12.1 billion on health care and in 2007 an estimated $2.2 trillion, and the costs keep rising. No one knows what new proposals the next few years until 2012 and beyond will bring to resolve America's health care crises, not only for those who have insurance and find they must pay more and more of the costs out of their own pocket, but also for the 47 million Americans who cannot afford insurance at all. The only reality that the country knows is that by October 2009, with just a few years remaining until the arrival of the hundredth anniversary of the first national health insurance proposal in this country, none had become law; public and private programs have not worked to stem the tide of the rising costs of health care as well as solve problems of access to quality health care; shortages of health professionals in various parts of the country, rural and urban, have not been eliminated; the US population is aging, living longer and with longer lives come more illnesses that may be very costly to treat, yet the costs of programs such as Medicare to pay for such illnesses are dependent upon the payroll deduction contributions of a smaller workforce than in the past as the baby boomers of the 1940s begin to join the ranks of senior citizens.

If the past is any prologue, the national debate over the enactment of a national health insurance plan is not yet over and the private sector will continue to develop programs as yet unknown to try and stem the tide of rising health care expenses and improve the quality of care. Thus far, be they public or private, programs in existence today have not enjoyed a permanent success for the nation as a whole as more of the nation's medical expenditure becomes a larger part of gross national domestic product (the total market value of all the goods and services produced in the USA), although, on an individual personal budget level for many, but not all, persons, the opposite may be true. Somewhere in the future there is the answer, as yet to be discovered, that is appropriate to the USA to resolve its health care crisis.

References

1. Braverman J. National compulsory health insurance: yesterday's theory – tomorrow's reality. *J Am Pharm Assoc* 1970; 10: 266–267.
2. Ross J H. The committee on the cost of medical care and the history of health insurance in the United States. *Einstein Q* 2002; 19: 130.
3. US Department of Commerce. *Historical Statistics of the United States*. Washington, DC: Bureau of the Census, 1949.
4. Gorman L. *The History of Health Care Costs and Health Insurance*, vol. 19, no. 10. Hartland, WI: Wisconsin Policy Research Institute, 2006: 4, 6–8, 10.
5. Davis M M, Rorem C R. *The Crisis in Hospital Finance and Other Studies in Health Economics*. Chicago, IL: University of Chicago Press, 1932.
6. Palmer K S. *A Brief History: Universal Health Care Efforts in the US*. Chicago, IL: Physicians for a National Health Program, 1999.
7. *A Commission Report: Intergovernmental Problems in Medicaid*. Washington, DC: Advisory Commission on Intergovernmental Relations, 1968: 3–4.
8. *Source Book of Health Insurance Data, 2002*. Washington, DC: Health Insurance Association of America, 2002: 100 (Table 5.3), 179, 181–183.
9. Kinsella K G. Changes in life expectancy 1900–1990. *Am J Clin Nutr* 2002; 55 1197s.
10. Seubold F H. HMOs – the view from the program. *Public Health Rep* 1975: 100.
11. *Toward a Comprehensive Health Policy for the 1970s: A White Paper*. Washington, DC: US Department of Health, Education, and Welfare, 1971: 31.
12. Rosoff A J. Phase two of the HMO development program: new directions after a shaky start. *Am J Law Med* 1975: 211–212.
13. *HMO Reports*. Washington, DC: US Department of Health, Education, and Welfare, December 19, 1975 (press release).
14. Blue Cross plans increase HMO efforts. *Blue Cross Consumer Rep* 1976; January.
15. CQ Almanac, 93rd Congress, 2nd session. *Congressional Q* 1974; XXX: 386–394.
16. Nixon R M. *Seize the Moment: America's Challenge in a One Super Power World*. New York: Simon & Schuster, 1992.
17. Hall K G. Democrats' health plans echo Nixon's failed GOP proposal. *McClatchy Newspaper* November 26, 2007, available online at: http://www.mcclatchydc.com/226/story/22163.html); accessed on May 21, 2008.
18. Braverman J. *Your Money and Your Health: How to Find Affordable High Quality Healthcare*. Amherst, NY: Prometheus Books, 2006: 225, 587, 595.
19. Americans one step away from receiving mental health coverage. *MarketWatch* October 3, 2008, available online at: http://www.marketwatch.com/news/story/Americans-one-step-away-receiving/story.aspx?g. . .; accessed on October 4, 2008.
20. Roberson J. Provision in bailout bill seeks mental health parity from employers. *Dallas Morning News* 2008; October 2.
21. Bender B. Mental-health parity law a big win for Kennedys. *Boston.com*, October 4, 2008 (Boston Globe) available online at: http://www.boston.com/news/nation/articles/2008/10/04/mental_health_parity_law_a_big...; accessed October 4, 2008.

2

The costs of American health care

Introduction

Millions, billions, trillions – words beyond comprehension that describe the costs of American health care today. The term encompassing those who pay on behalf of others, such as insurers, produce the goods, such as manufacturers, and deliver the services, such as physicians and pharmacists, is called the health care industry. Yet, this term is a misnomer. There is no single health care industry in the USA but a number of distinct industries and fields, each of whose individual revenues add up to many millions and billions of dollars which are, in turn, summed into the trillions of dollars of US health expenditure today. There is the hospital industry, the pharmaceutical industry, the nursing home industry, the home care industry, the hospice care industry, the private health insurance industry, the managed care industry, public programs like Medicare, Medicaid, the Veterans Administration health care system, the military health care system, and myriad professional groups like physicians, dentists, podiatrists, chiropractors, nurses, physical therapists, occupational therapists, and speech therapists. Each of these singular groups or industries can be further delineated into even more distinct subgroups which comprise the specific industry. For example, the pharmaceutical field is composed of brand-name pharmaceutical manufacturers and generic pharmaceutical manufacturers or a combination of both, chain drug stores, independent retail pharmacies, apothecaries, drug wholesalers, community-based pharmacists, pharmacy benefit managers, hospital-based pharmacists, nursing home-based pharmacists, consulting pharmacists, and other classifications. When all the revenues of each of these classifications are aggregated for the total revenue amount of that one industry and subsequently added to each of the totals of the other individual health care industries, in addition to the costs of public and private health programs, then the amount of monies which the USA spends on health care services today is staggering.

Some economic definitions

One tool that is in the forefront of trying to resolve America's health care problems is the discipline of economics. Economics is the social science that studies human welfare: the production, distribution, and consumption of resources which may be scarce or bountiful; how individuals, firms, governments, and other organizations make choices; and how these selections determine the manner in which wealth is produced and distributed. Scarcity means that not enough resources are available to meet everyone's wants and needs, such as a shortage of physicians in rural and inner-city areas that makes it difficult for patients to obtain needed medical care.

The meaning of economics may be found in the Greek language: *oikos* (house) and *nomos* (custom or law), therefore 'rules of the house(hold).' By extension, economics also studies national economies. An economy is the system of human activities relating to the production, distribution, exchange, and consumption of goods and services of a nation or area. Economies, in turn, can be further delineated, for example, by their ideological structure, such as capitalist or socialist, and by their range, such as global or transitional. In addition, economies can be described in terms of regulation, such as market, mixed, or planned.

However, regardless of the kind of economy that is being discussed, economies can also be divided into two broad classifications, macro and micro, within which there are many subdisciplines, such as energy, labor, and health, to name but a few. In terms of definition, *microeconomics* is a branch of economics that studies how individuals, families, and firms may decide how to allocate resources, typically in markets where goods and services are bought and sold. Resources are the factors of production and represent land, labor, and capital. Land is the natural resources that people use like forests, water, and other elements. Labor is a person's ability to produce goods or services such as his/her skills, physical labor, and other qualities. Capital is the goods people employ to produce goods and services, such as equipment, factories, and other factors.

In economics, a market exists when a buyer wishing to exchange money for a good or a service is in contact with a seller wishing to exchange a good or a service for money. Thus, a market is defined in terms of the fundamental forces of supply and demand, and is not necessarily confined to any particular geographical area. The law of demand states that when the price of an item declines, the demand for the item increases, since people who could not afford to purchase the item or were not willing previously to buy the item can or will now purchase it. The law of supply states that when the sales price of an item rises, more people will make the item. Since the higher price means more profit for the producer of the item as the price rises, more people will be willing to produce the item when they realize they can make money.

The price of an item is said to be in equilibrium when there is a buyer for each individual product that is produced. If the price of a product is set too high, then more goods will be produced than sold and surplus will result. If the price of the item is set too low, there will be a demand for a higher quantity of the item than is being produced and a shortage will take place. If a change in price does not affect the demand for the product, the demand is said to be *inelastic*. For example, if people need a particular medication to survive and there is no substitute for the medicine, the change in the price of the medication will not affect demand for the medicine; people will still need the medication just as much, not less, even though the price has increased. If price changes do affect the demand for an item, that is called *elastic* demand because a cheaper substitute is available that a person can use. Rather than drive an automobile more at high gasoline prices, people can use public transportation, bicycles, and other transport means which are less expensive.

The concept of the market is basic to most contemporary economics since in a free-market economy this is the mechanism by which resources are allocated. A free-market economy is an economy in which the allocation of resources is determined only by the supply and the demand for them. This is mainly a theoretical concept as every country, even capitalist ones, places some restrictions on the ownership and exchange of commodities. Microeconomics examines how these decisions and behaviors affect the supply and demand for goods and services, which, in turn, determines prices, and how prices, in turn, affect the supply of goods and services. On the other hand, *macroeconomics* looks at the performance of the economy as a whole and is concerned with aggregates such as national income, consumption, and investment. Macroeconomics examines subjects such as economic growth, inflation, changes in employment and unemployment, international trade with other countries (i.e., a nation's balance of payments) and the relative success or failure of government policies. Economics also uses various kinds of methodologies or tools in studying a particular subject. For example, one such tool is econometrics, which is the application of mathematical and statistical techniques to analyze data related to economic models that result in making quantitative generalizations such as testing or refining a theory, describing the relation of past variables, and forecasting future variables.

As already noted, the subject of this book is health economics. In order to understand the concepts of this relatively new field, it should be noted, as the discussions in the ensuing chapters demonstrate, that there are four factors important to the field of health economics: *government intervention, uncertainty, asymmetric knowledge,* and *externalities.* The health care industry is heavily regulated by government such as the Food and Drug Administration's oversight of the pharmaceutical industry while government programs such as Medicare and Medicaid not only tend to be the largest payers within the market but also establish regulations for the providers who participate in these federal–state programs. Uncertainty is intrinsic to health, in terms of both patient treatment outcomes and the financial concerns of the consumer. The knowledge gap that exists between a health provider such as a physician and a patient, for example, gives the physician a distinct advantage relative to the patient, and this knowledge gap is called asymmetric knowledge. Finally, within health care there are many effects that occur between two parties that do not involve monetary compensation, called externalities, such as catching someone's illness and entering the health care system to become well. The impact of all these factors can be found in the trillions of dollars the USA spends on health care services today and within a system which many authorities describe as 'broken.'

What US health care spending has not solved

Health care spending in the USA is consuming an increasing share of the gross domestic product (GDP) over time (Figure 2.1). For example, in 1970 total health care spending was only $75 billion, or only $356 per person. In less than 40 years these costs had grown to $2 trillion, or $6687 per person As a result, the share of economic activity devoted to health care had risen from 7.2% in 1970 to 16.0% in 2005.

By the year 2015 the Centers for Medicare and Medicaid Services (CMS) projects that health care spending will be nearly one-fifth of GDP (19.6%). Between 1970 and 2005, the average growth in health spending had exceeded the growth of the US economy as a whole by between 1.3% and 3.1%.

For example, in more specific terms, in 2005, of total national health expenditures (NHE) of $1.987.7 trillion, the USA spent $611.6 billion in

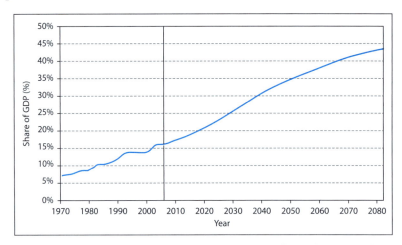

Figure 2.1   National health expenditures as a percentage share of gross domestic product (GDP) 1970–2082. Note: historical data are used before 2007 and projections from 2007 forward. Source: Centers for Medicare and Medicaid Services, Office of the Actuary, and as cited in Caldis TG (2008) *The Long-term Projection Assumptions for Medicare and Aggregate National Health Expenditures.* Baltimore, MD: Centers for Medicare and Medicaid Services, p. 15.

hospital care (30.8%), $121.9 billion in nursing home care (6.1%), $421.2 billion in physician services (21.2%), $200.7 billion in prescription drugs (10.1%, but contributing to the 14% growth in spending), as well as additional monies of other industries and professional groups. Health spending was fairly evenly divided between the private and public sectors in 2005, with private health spending accounting for about 55% of the total and public spending the rest. Private spending includes private health insurance (64%), out-of-pocket payments by individuals (23%), and the remainder (13%) was expenditures by other private sources like philanthropy. CMS has projected that by 2016 the private share of national health spending will decline to 51%. The growth in public spending (to 49%) is taking place primarily because of the growth of Medicare's share of health spending (to 21% in 2016). One important contributor to the growth in Medicare's share of the spending was implementation of the Medicare prescription drug benefit on January 1, 2006, which reduced private out-of-pocket spending and increased public spending for prescription drugs.[1-3]

In terms of economics, by 2006 health expenditure again continued its rise and exceeded $2.106 trillion a year (Figures 2.2 and 2.3).

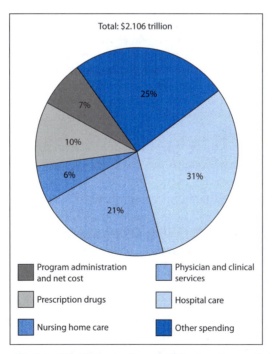

Figure 2.2   The nation's health dollar, calendar year 2006: where it went. Note: other spending includes dentist services, other professional services, home health, durable medical products, over-the-counter medicines and sundries, public health, other personal health care, research and structures and equipment. Source: Centers for Medicare and Medicaid Services, Office of the Actuary, National Health Statistics Group.

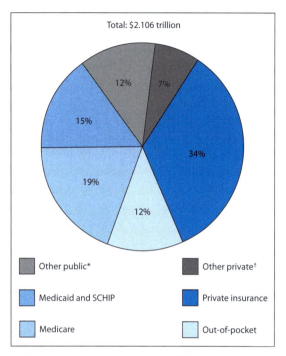

Figure 2.3 The nation's health dollar, calendar year 2006: where it came from. *Other public includes programs such as workers' compensation, public health activity, Department of Defense, Department of Veterans Affairs, Indian Health Service, state and local hospital subsidies and school health. †Other private includes industrial in-plant, privately funded construction, and nonpatient revenues, including philanthropy. Note: numbers may not add up to 100% because of rounding. Source: Centers for Medicare and Medicaid Services, Office of the Actuary, National Health Statistics Group.

Yet, despite expenditures of $2.1 trillion, today in America about 18 000 people die prematurely because they lack health insurance. People file for bankruptcy at a rate of one every 30 seconds because of medical bills. The average employer-based family premium rose 87% from 2000 to 2006, to $11 500. Fewer than 60% of people under age 65 have employer coverage, a decrease from 70% in 1987. In 2006 CMS projected that health care expenditures are expected to rise to over $4 trillion by 2015. In 2006, per-person health spending in the USA was $7110 and is projected to increase to $12 320 by 2015. CMS estimates that health spending between 2006 and 2015 will increase at an annual average growth rate of almost 7.2% (2.3 percentage points faster than the average annual GDP), with total aggregated health spending in the 2006–2015 period of about $30.3 trillion. As one example of increasing costs, in 2008 New York State records showed that in New York City between 2002 and 2008, the city health maintenance organizations (HMOs) had raised their rates by double digits 49 times. All nine HMOs serving New York City had raised their rates during the past year, two-thirds of them by at least 19%. For those buying their own insurance some premiums had soared to $5000 a month. Data have also shown that 36 401 city residents purchased their own coverage in 2005 and, by the end of 2007, that figure decreased to 24 000 or by more than one-third, according to state records. 'We're beyond crisis,' said Troy Oechsner, the state deputy superintendent for health insurance, 'We're in what economists call an adverse selection death spiral. Only the sick people stay on because they need the coverage, while healthy people flee because it's too expensive, which just drives the prices up and up and up,' he added. The HMO industry blames the rapidly rising costs of premiums on a state law that establishes benefits and copayments for those buying coverage individually – a law that has not changed since 1996. But Oechsner argues that giving HMOs more flexibility on the benefits they provide and copayments they charge will only place more of the costs on patients.[4–6]

In a study supported by the US-based Commonwealth Fund, comparing preventable deaths in 19 industrialized countries, researchers at the London School of Hygiene and Tropical Medicine found that the USA ranked last in terms of preventive care. While other countries improved dramatically between the two study periods, 1997–1998 and 2002–2003, the USA improved only slightly on the measure of international rates of 'amenable mortality' – that is, deaths before age 75 from certain causes that are potentially preventable with timely and effective health care. Diseases such as diabetes, treatable cancers, and cardiovascular diseases are conditions considered amenable to health care treatment. According to the study's authors, if the USA had been able to reduce amenable mortality to the average rate achieved by the three top performing countries, there would have been 75 000–101 000 fewer deaths annually by the end of the study period. Between 1997–1998 and 2002–2003, amenable mortality declined by an average of 16% in all countries except the USA, where the decline was only 4%. By 2002–2003, the USA dropped to last place, with rates of death of 109.7 per 100 000 people compared to the mortality rates per 100 000 recorded in the three leading countries – 64.8 in France, 71.2 in Japan, and 71.3 in Australia. In 1997–1998, the USA on this measure ranked 15th out of 19 countries with a rate of death of 114.7 per 100 000 people – ahead of only Finland, Portugal, the UK, and Ireland. The study's authors concluded that the US health system underperforms in several key indicators compared with other industrialized countries.[7]

In addition, a new Commonwealth Fund survey in 2007 of 12 000 adults in seven countries – Australia, Canada, Germany, the Netherlands, New Zealand, the UK, and the USA – found that among adults in these seven countries, US adults reported the highest overall error rates, including laboratory and medication errors. Well above the rates of the other six countries, 37% of all US adults surveyed (42% with chronic conditions) skipped

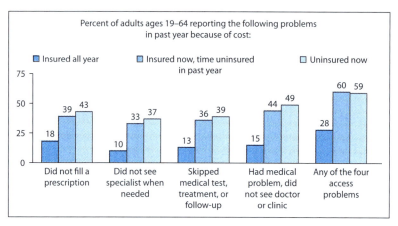

Figure 2.4 Lacking health insurance for any period threatens access to care. Source: Cozens SR, David K, Doly MM *et al.* (2006) *Gaps in Health Insurance: An All-American Problem.* New York: The Commonwealth Fund. Reprinted with permission of The Commonwealth Fund, New York, NY, and cited at: http://www.commonwealthfund.org/chartcartcharts/chartcartcharts_show.htm? doc_id=526.

medications, did not see a doctor when sick, or did not obtain recommended care in the past year because of cost (Figure 2.4).

With the USA the only country of the seven without universal health insurance, half or more adults in Germany, the Netherlands, and New Zealand reported having rapid access to physicians, while in the USA only 30% of adults said that could get same-day appointments with their doctors when sick. Nearly one-fifth (19%) of US adults have a serious problem paying medical bills, more than double the rate in the next highest country, while nearly one-third (30%) of US survey respondents spent more than $1000 in the past year (2006–2007) in out-of-pocket medical expenses compared to only 19% in Australia and 12% in Canada, and the rates were even lower in the other four countries.[8] Yet, according to the Commonwealth Fund, all these problems were occurring despite the fact that the USA spends twice what other countries spend on average. Per-capita spending in the USA in 2004 was $6102, two to three times that of Germany's $3005, Canada's $3165, New Zealand's $2083, Australia's $2876, and the UK's $2546 per person.[9] While health care spending reached 16% of GDP in 2005 in the USA or 4.3 times the amount spent on US national defense, the International Organization for Economic Cooperation and Development reported that health care spending accounted for only 10.9% of GDP in Switzerland, 10.7% in Germany, 9.7% in Canada, and 9.5% in France (Figure 2.5).[10]

In terms of societal demographics, the gap between medical care for blacks and whites may be becoming smaller. Since the 1980s, many studies have documented racial gaps in health care standards, blaming

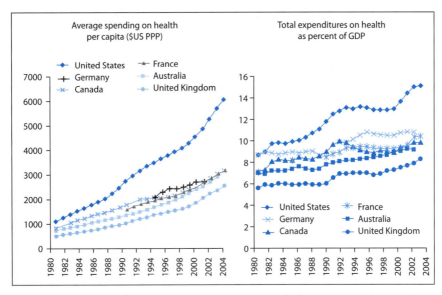

Figure 2.5 Health care costs in USA markedly exceed those of other countries, and are increasing more rapidly. Data from OECD Health Data 2005 and 2006. Source: Commonwealth Fund National Scorecard on US Health System Performance, 2006. Reprinted with permission of the Commonwealth Fund, New York, NY, and cited at: http://www.commonwealthfund.org/chartcartcharts/chartcartcharts_show.htm?doc_id=472.

economic, cultural, and even biological differences between the races. Black Americans have a much lower life expectancy and worse health outcome than white Americans. Blacks have less access to better doctors, hospitals, and health plans and the medical system treats whites and blacks differently. In a study of the Medicare program for the elderly, published in the *New England Journal of Medicine* in August 2005,[11] evidence appeared that racial disparities in US health care have become smaller, at least for some patients and treatments, but have not totally disappeared. Researchers looked at nine procedures, categorized according to the coding of the *International Classification of Diseases, Ninth Revision* (ICD-9) with exclusions and restrictions to certain coded diagnoses: abdominal aneurysm repair, back surgery, coronary artery bypass grafting (CABG), percutaneous transluminal coronary angioplasty, cardiac valve replacement, carotid endarterectomy, total hip replacement, total knee replacement, and appendectomy. The researchers found that racial differences in the rates of use of the nine procedures among black and white persons enrolled in Medicare between 1992 and 2001 did not narrow meaningfully during this decade. The rates of procedures performed were greater among whites than among blacks for every procedure examined. Racial differences in these rates widened for five procedures, narrowed for one (surgical repair of the abdominal aortic aneurysm, and that rate was due to the disproportionate receipt among whites of a procedure involving new endovascular techniques instead of the traditional surgery for repair of an abdominal aortic aneurysm), and the rates remained statistically unchanged for three. There were no hospital referral regions by 2001 (79 for black men and white men and 79 for black women and white women, or a total of 158 regions) where racial differences in care were completely eliminated, especially in regard to hip replacement, CABG, and carotid endarterectomy. (The rates for these three procedures changed significantly in 22 hospital referral regions, widened significantly in 42, and were not significantly changed in the remaining hospital referral regions.) Numerous other studies have shown that gaps in care represent, in part, both underuse among black persons and overuse by white persons. Researchers concluded that new efforts toward a better understanding of and closing of these gaps in care between black persons and white persons are needed.[11]

However, disparities in health care are relevant not only to blacks and whites but among all ethnicities and racial groups in the USA. In March 2008, a publication of the Commonwealth Fund, New York, listed a whole series of disparities among racial and ethnic groups (blacks, whites, Asian, Hispanics, and Native Americans/Alaska Natives), a few of which are listed as follows:

- Black men and women are more likely to die from heart disease than all other racial/ethnic groups.
- Almost 2.5 times as many Hispanics as whites report having no doctor.
- American Indians/Alaska Natives are more likely to have diabetes than other groups.
- Hispanics are most likely to lack health insurance coverage, with more than one-third uninsured. Even at high income levels Hispanics are more likely to be uninsured. Also, Hispanics are least likely of all racial ethnic groups to use a private doctor and most likely to use a federally qualified health center, an outgrowth of the community health center established in the 1970s, as their usual place of care.
- Life expectancy at birth is 5 years lower for blacks compared with whites. Infant mortality rates are still twice as high for blacks than for whites, despite a slight decline for all groups since about the year 2000.
- Asians/Pacific Islanders and Hispanics are more likely to die from complications in hospital care than whites and blacks.
- Blacks are more likely than whites or Hispanics to visit the emergency department for conditions that could have been treated by a primary care provider; blacks are more likely than whites to leave the emergency

department without being seen. Also, blacks are two to four times more likely than whites and Hispanics to be hospitalized for potentially preventable conditions.

- Asians and Hispanics are more likely than whites and blacks to go without needed care.
- Blacks are more likely to forgo dental care and prescription drugs than whites; American Indians/Alaska Natives are most likely to go without prescription drugs.
- Disparities in blood pressure control are smaller at Veterans Administration hospitals compared with other hospitals.
- Minorities with depression are less likely than whites to receive treatment for their condition.

In view of the fact that minorities constituted one-third of the US population during the first decade of the 21st century, with Hispanics composing the largest minority, followed by blacks, the impact of the $2 trillion being spent on health care services in the USA appears to be bypassing to some degree a large segment of the US population in terms of improving their health care status relative to other groups such as whites. By 2050 minority groups will compose almost half of the US population; the biggest increase will occur within the Hispanic population, which is younger on average than other demographic groups in the USA.[12]

In terms of demographics, a nationwide survey conducted by Erickson Health in 2007 showed that retirees are feeling especially vulnerable about health care costs affecting their financial stability. Almost one-half of retirees (49%) were concerned most about health care costs, followed by loss of their independence (41%), future changes in Medicare (38%), and their wellness (36%).[13] According to the US Centers for Disease Control and Prevention (CDC), most health care dollars are spent on adults aged 65 years or older. And, out of every Medicare dollar spent in 2005, 96 cents went toward the treatment of chronic disease, like heart disease and arthritis. Approximately 80% of older adults have at least one chronic disease and 50% have at least two. To pay for these various illnesses, government programs pay for about 45% of health care costs. Unfortunately, Medicare is spending more money than it receives, according to the Urban Institute. Most of Medicare's money (revenues) comes from the payroll tax, which has remained at the same rate of 2.9% since 1986. More than half the payment of health care costs come from private funds – the largest portion from private health insurance. In the case of Medicare, private health insurance policies like Medigap supplement the benefits and costs which Medicare does not cover. And these health insurance premiums are rising faster than inflation. In addition to the previous payments, out-of-pocket health care expenditures by Medicare beneficiaries are high and are expected to keep rising. Older Americans spend two-thirds of their cash incomes on health care – including 44.5% of their social security incomes – according to a 2007 report by the National Center for Policy Analysis.[13]

The previous examples are cited to illustrate the fact that, although the USA now spends slightly more than $2 trillion a year on health care, these huge expenditures have not resolved many of the problems that beset the American health system, whether they be in terms of economics, differences in the receipt of care by different ethnic groups within American society, or in the provision of services that could prevent more serious illnesses at a later stage in a person's life. According to Helen Darling, president of the National Business Group on Health, which represents large employers in the USA, 'We get so little for what we put in, compared to well-off European countries [that] deliver quality health care for half what we pay.'[14] In 2007 Darling stated that large companies say that the price of providing health care – an average of $8400 for each employee – makes them less competitive abroad. But there is also a cost for not providing health care coverage. When uninsured people receive care in an emergency room – the most expensive kind of care – and can't pay the hospital bills, these bills are often paid by tax-funded state programs. But in many cases, according to Paul Fronstin of the Employee Benefit Research Institute in Washington, 'the hospital raises its rates for people with insurance coverage in order to recoup the costs.'[14] So, in many ways, Darling says, 'everybody is negatively affected by rising costs.'[14] This is true whether the consumer does not have the ability to pay for health care or whether the consumer can do so at higher personal costs, whether it be out-of-pocket or through health insurance coverage with higher and higher premiums.

Background of rising costs

The problem of rising health costs has reemerged as a national issue as some candidates in the US presidential campaign of 2008 called for universal health insurance as a panacea for resolving America's health care systematic problems. Unfortunately, by 2008, as the costs were rising, the American economy headed into a recession, the nation's budget showed a deficit rather than a surplus, and the nation was focused on the worldwide war against terrorism. Rather than allocating the monies to resolve the problems confronting the US health care system, education, transportation, and other aspects of its societal infrastructure, these funds were instead being diverted into national security and defense.

Since the enactment of Medicare and Medicaid in the mid-1950s, no approach that the USA has attempted to control rising health care costs has worked out, nor has had a lasting impact – perhaps they may have in the short term, but certainly not over the long term. When Medicare and Medicaid became law, the new public programs relieved the private sector of some of the burden of health spending, but only temporarily. By the late 1960s the rate of increase in private health spending began to rise. In the early 1970s wage and price controls during the Nixon administration had a dampening effect on health care costs. But again, the impact did not last a long time and the rate of increase in private health spending again rose dramatically after a few years. When President Jimmy Carter threatened stringent cost containment regulations in the 1970s, the health care industry organized what it called the 'Voluntary Effort.' The rate of increase in per-capita private-sector health spending decreased rapidly but then bounced back within a few years. Managed care and the threat of the Clinton health reform plan appeared to have had a dramatic effect on the rate of increase in private health spending in the mid-1990s, but by the late 1990s it was increasing again, reaching double-digit rates of increase by 2001. In summary, regulation, voluntary action by the health care industry, and managed care and market competition have not had a lasting impact on our nation's rising health care costs.[15]

Some believe that the rationing of medical care is the possible solution for controlling health care costs. Others state that the obvious failure to control health care costs is really a reflection of the American people who want to have the very best and latest innovations in health care treatment, but try small corrections at the edges of the system, complain about rising costs, and ultimately will do nothing but pay the bill, perhaps feeling helpless in not knowing what they can do as lay consumers to control these spiraling expenses. Some believe that the federal government is the answer to resolving our health cost problems through universal health insurance. Others believe that solutions lie in the initiatives of the private sector such as paying physicians based on their performance because in providing services they attain goals of quality, in contrast to the system that reimburses doctors, hospitals, and other providers regardless of whether they provide good services or whether patients are satisfied with their care. Whatever the answers are, as of 2009 no definitive ones have been found. As already noted, by the beginning of 2006 health care spending represented about 16% of the economy and is projected to rise to about 20% by 2015, that is, $1 out of every $5 will be devoted to this economic sector. Medicare spending is projected to more than double from $309 billion in 2004 to $792 billion in 2015. Medicaid spending is projected to increase from $293 billion to $670 billion during this same period. By 2015 the nation's total health care bill is expected to exceed $4 trillion. In February 2008 economists at the CMS predicted that by 2017 health care spending will reach about $4.3 billion, almost double that of 2007, accounting for almost 20% of the national GDP.[16,17]

Table 2.1 Percentage of adults aged 19–64 with medical bill problems or accrued medical debt				
Percentage of adults reporting:	Total	Insured all year	Insured now, time uninsured during year	Uninsured now
Unable to pay for basic necessities (food, heat, or rent) because of medical bills	26	19	28	40
Used up all of savings	39	33	42	49
Took out a mortgage against your home or took out a loan	11	10	12	11
Took on credit card debt	26	27	31	23

Source: The Commonwealth Fund Biennial Health Insurance Survey (2005). Reprinted with permission of The Commonwealth Fund, New York, NY and cited at: http://www.commonwealthfund.org/chartcartcharts/chartcartcharts_show.htm?doc_id=405.

Societal impact of health care costs

The rising costs of health care pervade and affect the entire fabric of American society. In 2004 about 10% of people accounted for over 60% of spending on health services; over 20% of health spending was for only 1% of the population. At the other end of the spectrum, the one-half of the population who had the lowest spending accounted for just over 3% of spending (Table 2.1). Both within and outside the health care field rising health care costs affect wages, employment, a company's competitiveness with others in its field, domestically and internationally, family life, housing, and the economy itself. Let us look at some examples.

First, in regard to family life a study at Harvard University published in February 2005 noted that the average out-of-pocket medical debt for those who filed for bankruptcy was $12 000. The study noted that 68% of those who filed for bankruptcy had the protection of health insurance. In addition, the study found that 50% of all bankruptcy filings were partly the result of medical expenses. As already noted, every 30 seconds in the USA someone files for bankruptcy as a result of a serious health problem.[2,18]

If one member of a family does not have health insurance coverage and has an accident, a stay in hospital or an expensive medical treatment with its resulting medical bills can impact on the financial security and stability of the entire family. This, in turn, can affect a person's housing situation. Twenty-five percent of those who were in a survey said that medical debt affected their ability to pay their rent or make mortgage payments, with the resulting development of bad credit ratings.[19] The inability of a family to have money to pay rent or their mortgage or maintain their well-being physically was demonstrated by an Iowa survey in 2005 that revealed that 86% of Iowa consumers had to cut back on how much they could save in order to cope with rising health insurance costs and 44% said that they had to cut back on food and heating expenses.[20] Thus, if a family does not have the ability to save very much or must cut back on food or heating, not only might their bills like rent or mortgage be unpaid but the absence of heating or reduced food intake can affect their physical health detrimentally as well. This situation, in turn, might increase the amount of the medical bills owed if they seek medical attention for their illness and if they do not seek medical attention their physical condition might become worse, if not possibly fatal, perhaps costing them even more monies than if they had initially sought medical attention.

But it is not only families who feel the impact of health care costs: so do the businesses which employ their members. The public not only experiences the costs of health care through increased state and local taxes to pay for Medicaid but also more of its federal tax dollars are going to the federal share of Medicare and Medicaid costs, for example. The public also experiences health care costs through the premiums it pays for health insurance and through health insurance cost sharing, that is, the deductibles and copayments that it must pay at the time it receives care.

First, health insurance premiums have consistently increased faster than inflation or the earnings of workers in recent years (Figure 2.6). Between 2002 and 2007 the cumulative growth in health insurance was 76% compared with a cumulative inflation of 17% and a cumulative wage growth of 19%.

Second, although the share of total premiums that workers pay had stayed fairly stable (16% for single coverage, 28% for family coverage in 2007) over the recent past, the rapid increase in overall premium levels means that workers are paying much higher amounts than they did a few years ago.

Third, the amounts people pay out-of-pocket for health care services are affected by several factors, including the quality of their health insurance (if any) and the kind and amount of services they use. For people with health care expenses, the average share of total health costs that are paid out-of-pocket was 34% in 2004 (Figure 2.7). Because many insurance plans have limits on out-of-pocket expenses, people who experience high total spending have relatively low out-of-pocket shares. For example, in 2004 the 1% of the people with the highest health spending (total costs of $39 688) on average paid 6% of their costs out-of-pocket.

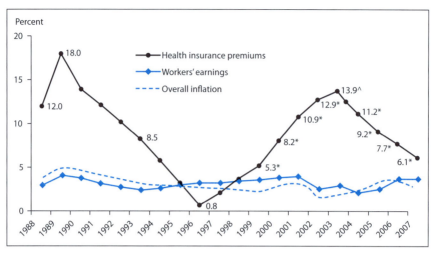

Figure 2.6   Increases in health insurance premiums compared with other indicators, 1988–2007. ^Estimate is statistically different from the previous year, shown at $P < 0.05$. *Estimate is statistically different from the previous year, shown at $P > 0.1$. Data on premium increases reflect the cost of health insurance premiums for a family of four. Historical estimates of workers' earnings have been updated to reflect new industry classifications (NAICs). Data: Claxton G, Gabel J et al. Health benefits in 2007: premium increases fall to an eight-year low while offer rates and enrollment remain stable. *Health Aff* 2007; 26: 1407–1416; Kaiser/HRET Survey of Employer-Sponsored Health Benefits, 2007, and Commonwealth Fund analysis of National Health Expenditure data. Source: Commonwealth Fund National Scorecard on US Health System Performance, 2008. Reprinted with permission of The Commonwealth Fund, New York, NY, and cited at: http://www.commonwealthfund.org/doc_img/694011.gif.

Fourth, almost one in five nonelderly individuals were in families where health care spending for premiums and cost sharing exceeded 10% of family income in 2003. This includes a third of individuals in families with incomes below poverty: that is, while about 26% of the poor spent more than 10% of their income on health in 1996, the number increased to 33% by 2003.[2,3]

It is not only the workers who are affected by the high costs of health care – so are their employers. The more employers have to pay for health insurance, the less profit they may make; the fewer employees they may be able to hire to increase the company's growth; the less they may be able to expand coverage for their workers; the more they may require workers to share more and more of the health insurance costs out of their own pocket by paying higher deductibles which, in turn. could cause employees to put off seeking necessary care and risk long-term problems later on; the less money that may be available to employers for wage increases and bonuses; the

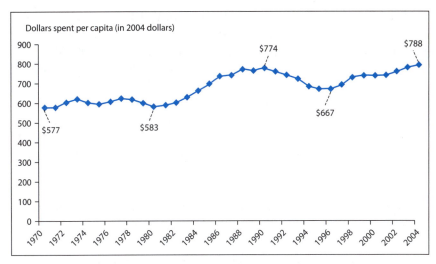

Figure 2.7   Americans are spending more out of pocket for health care. Source: Smith C et al. National health spending in 2004: recent slowdown led by prescription drug spending. *Health Aff* 25, no. 1. Centers for Medicare and Medicaid Services, National Health Expenditures Data: http://www. cms.hhs.gov/NationalHealthExpendData/downloads/tables/pdf. Reprinted with permission of The Commonwealth Fund, New York, NY and cited at: http://www.commonwealthfund.org/ chartcartcharts/chartcartcharts_show.htm?doc_id=405.

higher the costs of goods employers must charge consumers to recoup the higher cost of health insurance premiums, perhaps making the company less competitive with others in its field which, again, affects the company's profit margin as well as other factors. As examples of the latter statement, the following statistics may be of interest:

- Premiums for employer-based health insurance rose by 7.7% in 2006. Small employers saw their premiums rise 8.8% on average. Firms with fewer than 24 workers experienced an increase of 10.5%.[21]
- The annual premium that a health insurer charges an employer for a health plan covering a family of four averaged $11 500 in 2006. Workers contributed nearly $3000 or 10% more than they did in 2005.[2,3] The annual premiums for family coverage significantly eclipsed the gross earnings for a full-time, minimum-age worker ($10 712).
- Workers are now paying $1094 more in premiums annually for family coverage than they did in 2000.[2,3]
- The percentage of Americans under age 65 whose family-level, out-of-pocket spending for health care, including health insurance, that exceeds $2000 a year, increased from 37.3% in 1996 to 43.1% in 2003 – a 16% increase. The percentage of nonelderly individuals whose family

out-of-pocket expenses for health care exceeded 10% of their income increased from 16% in 1996 to 19% in 2003.[2,3]

- The average employee contribution to company-provided health insurance has increased more than 143% since 2000. Average out-of-pocket costs of deductible, copayments for medications, and coinsurance for physician and hospital visits rose 115% during the same period.[2,3]
- Health insurance premium growth has outpaced the growth in workers' earnings almost every year except for a short period of time in the mid-1990s. While premium increases have registered between 8% and 14% per year since 2000, inflation and changes in worker's earnings are generally in the 3–4% range. This generally means that workers have to spend more of their income each year on health care to maintain coverage. Again, these effects may be direct, through increased worker contributions for premiums or reduced benefits, or indirect, such as when employers reduce or limit wage increases to offset increases in premiums.[2]

However, as difficult as bearing health care costs may be for those who are working and their employers, a study published in 2008 by the Boston Center for Retirement Research at Boston College revealed that many baby boomers may have a great deal of difficulty in maintaining their standard of living in retirement, not only because they are not saving enough but also because they are confronting skyrocketing health care costs. Baby boomers are those born between 1946 and 1964, while Americans who were born between 1965 and 1974 are called the generation X'rs. As of 2008, the government estimated an individual's cost for Medicare premiums, copayments and other cost sharing at about $3800 a year for a single person and about double that ($7600) for a couple. To these figures may be added another $500 per person for dental care, eye glasses, hearing aids, and other items Medicare does not cover. To cover such costs in the ensuing decades in which most baby boomers and generation X'rs will live after leaving their jobs, the Center estimated that an individual must go into retirement with some $102 000 earmarked for health care coverage alone, with a couple requiring about $206 000. The Center estimated that 44% of baby boomers and generation X'rs are at risk of being unable to keep their standard of living in retirement and when health care costs are included that percentage rises to 61% being at risk for a lower standard of living. The Center is concerned that most Americans have savings far below the level required for health and nonhealth expenses, with the median retirement savings balance for households approaching retirement being $60 000. The Center recommends that, to improve their retirement years, people should plan on working a few years longer, increase their savings, watch their weight, and exercise more because good health reduces health care expenses.[22]

Why health care costs outpace general economy

As already noted, health care spending continues to rise more quickly than the overall economy (i.e., GDP). Since 1970 health care spending has risen at an average annual rate of 9.9% or about 2.5 percentage points faster than the GDP. In recent decades the growth rate for health spending and the GDP has slowed, but health care spending has risen from 7.2% of GDP in 1965 when Medicare and Medicaid became law to over 16% by 2006 and is projected to be 20% of GDP by 2015–2016.[23] The following are some of the reasons why the rise of health care costs outpaces the rise in GDP:

- The US population is getting older and living longer and with aging comes more health problems and the use of more health care services than young generations. Changes in disease prevalence such as increasing levels of diabetes due to obesity and the treatment of diseases such as Alzheimer's can influence cost growth as well.
- Americans pay a declining share of health expenses than they used to, that is, a smaller share of health care expenditures come out of their own pocket. Between 1975 and 2005, the portion of personal health expenditures paid directly out-of-pocket by consumers declined from 40% to 15%. Although consumers confronted increasing health insurance premiums over the period, which had an impact on their own budgets, lower cost sharing at the point where services were provided probably encouraged consumers to use more health care, leading to an increase in expenditures.
- Insurance coverage has spread. When government subsidizes health coverage, this action also has an impact on cost levels and potentially cost growth. Tax subsidies for health insurance and public coverage for certain groups such as the poor, disabled, and elderly reduces the cost of health care, encouraging consumers to use it more frequently. Some also argue that the expansion of health insurance encourages the development of health technology because those developing new technologies know that insurance will pay for a substantial share of new costs.
- The development and adoption of new medical technology (e.g., drugs, devices, treatment, and techniques) are said to be responsible for a substantial portion of the increase in health expenditures. As a nation becomes more successful and wealthier, its population wants more health care and health care suppliers, providers, and institutions have successfully provided an increasing variety of new products and services that meets society's demand. This steady improvement in medical capacity means that the nation has an increasing amount of medical interventions to treat disease that can potentially deal with a growing list of health care issues and conditions as the health care community continues to learn more about human health and health care conditions. Health care experts

point to the development and diffusion of medical technology as a principal factor in explaining the continuous difference between health spending and overall economic growth, with some arguing that new medical technology may account for about one-half or more of real long-term spending growth.[3]

Addressing rising costs

The amount of monies that the USA spends on health care per person is large, especially when compared to the smaller amounts other nations spend per person on their own health care services. In addition, the rate of increase in health care expenditures in the USA relative to other fields like education and transportation has shown rapid growth and has done so for decades. So how does the USA reduce the rate of growth in costs and spending levels or costs at a point in time, both at the same time?

Some approaches may lessen the level of health care spending but not the rate of its growth. Many policies under discussion for payers of health care services include initiatives such as increasing the use of electronic medical records and improving medical information technology; better identification and management of high cost and chronically ill patients; the introduction of wellness programs and incentives; provider pay based upon performance whereby providers are rewarded for appropriate and high quality of care; reducing payment rates to providers; instituting high cost sharing in health policies; consumer-directed health care like health savings accounts which use increased out-of-pocket responsibility, with tax incentives; more information on health care alternatives to encourage consumers to be more cost-conscious and better informed when making health care decisions; or disease management. The purpose of all of these policies is to improve the efficiency with which care is delivered.[3,5] Disease management is a system that coordinates preventive, diagnostic, and therapeutic efforts and whose purpose is to deliver cost-efficient, quality health care for a patient group that is at a risk for a specific chronic illness or medical condition.

In addition, many states have enacted laws to reduce medical malpractice judgments to reduce premium burdens on providers and lower overall costs. While these policies may reduce on average what consumers may pay for care, they are not likely to reduce in the longer term the rate at which costs are growing as a share of the economy. Assuming medical errors can be reduced to more optimal levels and may reduce the amount consumers pay for medical care, costs are likely to increase, although from a lower level, at previously observed rates. Increasing the use of medical records or reducing the differences in health practices across regions and providers may have similar effects. On the other hand, concentrating on new and expanding technologies may be successful in reducing the rate of growth and would likely require finding ways to slow the development and spread of new health care technologies and practices. Developing ways to assess and weigh the costs and benefits of new technologies is a promising approach, although such actions present serious and philosophical challenges. One example would be a policy that provides payment through insurance (public and private) only for new medical interventions that demonstrate benefits that exceed costs. On a practical basis, the very steep volume and pace of medical advances would present difficulties to judge many important challenges before they were made a part of medical practice. On a philosophical basis, medical assessment requires people to make difficult decisions about whether a medical benefit is worth the cost. As one example, the National Institute for Health and Clinical Excellence (NICE), the UK authority that is responsible for approving medical treatments, was widely criticized when it did not include beta-interferon to treat multiple sclerosis in the list of publicly covered treatments.[3,5] All these challenges in reducing the costs of medical care while reducing its rate of growth are perplexing, yet important problems to resolve. Thus far, finding even a small amount of savings in either public or private programs has been very difficult for those who work in both the public and private sectors. Steps that would lessen health expenditures by hundreds of billions or even a trillion dollars over the foreseeable future would require a fundamental change in how the USA thinks about the way health care ought to be paid for. Our length of life and the improvements in treating illnesses which were absent from the medical armamentarium decades ago cannot be overlooked as very great achievements. But developing the philosophical, ethical, and political apparatus that is necessary to weigh the benefits of future medical advances with the consumer's ability to pay for them is no less important or daunting a task if the health status of the consumer-patient, and that of the collective consumer called a nation, is to be continually improved.

References

1. US Department of Health and Human Services. *Health, United States, 2007*. Atlanta GA: US Centers for Disease Control and Prevention, 2007.
2. *Trends on Health Care Costs and Spending*. Menlo Park, CA: The Henry J. Kaiser Family Foundation, 2007.
3. *Health Care Costs: A Primer*. Menlo Park, CA: The Henry J. Kaiser Family Foundation, 2007.
4. Barry P, Basler B. Healing our system. *AARP Bull* 2007; March: 12.
5. *Comparing Projected Growth in HealthCare Expenditures and the Economy*. Menlo Park, CA: The Henry J. Kaiser Family Foundation, 2006.
6. Contiguglia C, Lovett K. The state's HMOs are a disaster, pros warn; young shun plans as prices soar. *N Y Daily News* 2008; August 24.
7. Nolte E, McKee C M. Measuring the health of nations: updating an earlier analysis. *Health Aff* 2008; 27: 58–71.
8. Schoen C, Osburn R, Doty M M, *et al*. Toward higher performance health systems: adults' health care experience in seven countries, 2007. *Health Aff Web Exclusive* 2007; 26: w717–w734.

9. Report: US health care expensive, inefficient. Reuters 2007; May 15.

10. *Health Insurance Cost: Facts on Costs of Health Care*. Washington, DC: National Coalition on Health Care, 2008.

11. Jha A K, Fisher E S, Li Z, *et al*. Racial trends in the use of major procedures among the elderly. *N Engl J Med* 2005; 353: 683–691.

12. Mead H H, Cartright-Smith L, Karenn-Jones J D, *et al*. *Racial and Ethnic Disparities in US Health Care: A Chartbook*. New York: The Commonwealth Fund, 2008.

13. Progressive health care helps older adults beat rising costs. *Erickson Tribune* 2008: 1; February.

14. Barry P, Basler B. Healing our system. *AARP Bull* 2007; March: 13.

15. Altman D E, Levitt L. The sad history of health care cost containment as told in one chart. *Health Aff* 2002; January.

16. Health care costs expected to increase rising. Associated Press 2006; February 22.

17. Big jump forecast in health spending. *Washington Post* 2008; February 26: A4.

18. Himmelstein D, Warren E, Thome D, *et al*. Illness and injury as contributors to bankruptcy. *Health Aff Web Exclusive* 2005; February 2: W5–W63.

19. The Access Project. *Home Sick: How Medical Debt Undermines Housing Security*. Boston, MA: The Access Project, 2005.

20. Seizer and Company. *Department of Public Health 2005 Survey of Iowa Consumers*, 2005.

21. *Employee Health Benefits: 2006 Annual Survey*. Menlo Park, CA: The Henry J. Kaiser Family Foundation and Health Research and Educational Trust, 2006; available online at. http://www.kff.org/insurance/7527/index.cfm; accessed on April 20, 2008.

22. Munnell A H, Soto M, Webb A, *et al*. *Health Care Costs Drive Up the National Retirement Index*. Chestnut Hill, MA: Boston Center for Retirement Research at Boston College, 2008: 8.

23. *Comparing Projected Growth in Health Expenditures and the Economy*. Menlo Park, CA: The Henry J. Kaiser Family Foundation: 2006.

3

The high costs of health care: the reasons why

Introduction

American health care is in crisis – a statement that has been made for so long and repeated so often it has almost become a saying. Yet, what is health? Essentially, it is the most valuable possession we have. It is with us every moment of our lives. We enact laws to protect it. We cannot buy it. We cannot sell it. But we can inherit and pass it on. We spend billions to keep it, billions to improve it, and billions to find it when it is lost. It is valued and accepted; it is ignored and abused. As science it is glamorized; as art it is criticized; as an issue it is politicized. It affects the private purse of each of us; it affects the public purse of an entire nation. Some enrich themselves from it. Some are impoverished by it. It is the core of our soul, our essence, our well-being – it's our health.

American health care is almost a dichotomy. On the one hand, America's capacity for the cure and prevention of disease and illness has never been greater. In the past century, even though the USA still lags behind 30 other nations, the life expectancy of Americans has been lengthened from 50 years to more than 78 years, women to almost 81 compared to about 75 for men, according to the National Center for Health Statistics.[1] In cardiovascular diseases more progress has been made in the past 50 years than in all recorded history. Cancer research has allowed millions of Americans who had a major form of cancer to lead happy productive lives. Significant declines have occurred in infant mortality, disease of early infancy, maternal mortality, and mortality rates for heart disease, accidents, and diabetes. There has also been a decline in the number of mental patients and new drugs have been developed that allow them to lead happy productive lives. At the same time new laboratory techniques, organ transplants, stem cell research, as well as new immunological techniques have been developed. As further examples of progress in the health care field, programs have been established to help the elderly and aged finance their health care services such as purchasing prescription drugs, continuation of health insurance coverage after being laid off from work or between jobs or changing jobs, and for those who prefer managed care, a variety of other managed care programs to suit the needs of those who do not wish to join a health maintenance organization.

Yet, something has gone wrong. Our ability to deliver needed health services at reasonable costs and to provide for the basic physical needs of our society is in doubt. Anxiety over providing quality care to every American is now prevalent and is termed 'the health care crisis.' It is the purpose of this chapter to examine the crisis and to explore how this nation arrived at so paradoxical a stage. Despite all its great technology and resources and its capacity to spend more than $2.1 trillion a year on health care in 2006, or $7026 per person, the USA now find itself in a position where the collapse of the health care system is predicted because of societal demands of receiving quality services at reasonable costs, unless immediate and concerted action is taken by government and the private sector of society.[2]

Evolution of health care services

The crisis in health care today besets a nation whose public and private spending in this area approximated $2.1 trillion in 2006, as already noted, and the health care portion of the gross domestic product (GDP) was 16.0%, and is projected to reach $3.6 trillion by 2014 or 18.7% of the GDP (the total market value of all the goods and services produced in the USA) in that year.[2,3] It vexes a nation which employs millions of people in this field. The institutions and organizations that constitute the health care industry include hospitals, nursing homes, clinical laboratories, home care agencies, hospices, an insurance and pharmaceutical industry, academic health institutions, health maintenance organizations, preferred provider organizations, and other forms of managed care, pharmacy benefit managers, in-store convenience care clinics, and government agencies on the local, state, and federal levels. The health problems appear in many guises: a breakdown in the delivery of health care services; the environmental implications of global warming; smog enveloping our cities; chemical and sewage polluting our rivers; remnants of prescription drugs found in sources of drinking water supply; high mortality from lung disease and chronic respiratory disease; nutritional habits that lead to an obesity epidemic among our population, especially children; severe discrepancies in health between different social classes living in the same cities; and deteriorating physical environment as reflected by housing which is substandard in many areas of the country.

The question is: how did we reach such an unfortunate position when logic indicates that the reverse should be true, especially in view of the long history of federal commitment to health progress? In fact, the involvement of the federal government can be traced as far back as 1798, when the Public Health Service was created to ensure that the health needs of merchant seamen, moving from port to port throughout the world, were being met. During the 19th century, the federal government assumed responsibility in the control of communicable disease, first through quarantine and then through the application of the newly developed science of microbiology at the turn of the 20th century. The federal health efforts changed in the 1930s, when the Public Health Service launched its programs of grants to states to assist them in attacking specific disease problems.

While spectacular federal support for research was undertaken to develop weapons to combat disease, a controversy developed over another social demand – high-quality health care as a right for all citizens. Today, federal activities direct health care to veterans, servicemen and their dependants, retired military personnel, and other beneficiaries. We award grants to health services and hospitals for rehabilitation, vaccination, technical assistance and research, as well as for specific diseases. We support programs for mental health, child health, migrant health, and Indian health. We now have major health service payment programs such as Medicare and Medicaid as well as physician peer review programs called quality improvement organizations and new health delivery systems such as health maintenance organizations, preferred provider organizations, point-of-service plans, and others.

Between 1960 and 1977, federal health expenditures increased from $3.5 billion to about $46.5 billion.[4] The reason for this enormous growth in federal spending can be found in the activities of the 88th, 89th, and 90th sessions of Congress, which passed more significant health legislation than all other Congresses combined until that time, and, perhaps, since then. During the Johnson administration, the US Department of Health, Education, and Welfare enumerated 102 pieces of legislation, many health-related, which were enacted into law. Some of the legislation has radically altered, if not revolutionized, existing concepts of health care. The programs these laws created included Medicare, Medicaid, health planning, regional medical centers to counter the risks of heart disease, cancer, and stroke, and neighborhood health centers. The implications of programs such as Medicare and Medicaid are so far-reaching that their impact on society is still being measured. For example, between 1965 and 1975 federal health spending as a proportion of our total health expenditures increased from 12% to 28% while national health expenditures (NHE) rose from $38.9 million to $122.2 billion during this same period.[5] Hence, one issue is quite clear. Health care is a basic human right. By setting up special mechanisms to support this tenet, the Johnson administration sparked a social revolution. These health reforms today are taxing to the severest limits the ability of our system to deliver quality services at reasonable costs and fulfill the purpose for which these laws were enacted.

Origins and elements in health care crisis

The crisis in health care is only one aspect of the complex problems of American life which embrace issues such as the environment, economy, energy, welfare, foreign wars on terrorism, and poverty. As health is inextricably linked with all these issues, fundamental progress in health care depends upon solving these other national problems as well.

Dr. Lester Breslow, a past president of the American Public Health Association, commented on the origins of the health care crisis as follows:

> One element in its origin was the failure to comprehend that long-term adverse health effects can result from the application of certain technological innovations. An outstanding example is cigarette smoking. Machine production of a novel, attractive form of tobacco early in this century [20th century] led to the expansion of an industry that has been highly profitable but has taken its toll in the lives of millions of consumers. We did not even recognize the consequences until four decades had passed, and it has taken us another three decades to reach the point of taking action.
>
> A second element in the health crisis is the continuing reliance on industry to find simple technological solutions to problems that are identified. If cigarette smoking is harmful, so the argument runs, simply find the harmful ingredient and remove it. If automobile exhaust results in smog, find the specific chemical responsible and remove it by changing gasoline composition or the engine.
>
> The other and unspoken side of the argument is the dangerous one: namely, while searching for the technological solution, do not interfere with the industry. Production and its profits must continue, whatever the cost in health. Just let industry alone to find the technological solution ... This blind faith in industrial technology as the only path to solution is increasingly unjustified, especially when damage to health and life as a whole lies in the balance.
>
> A third and, perhaps, more pervasive factor in the health crisis is that we have not yet developed adequate social mechanisms for the control of current health problems. This failure is manifest with respect to the environment; it is also evident in medical care.[6]

However, these comments on the origins of the problem do not effectively convey the urgency which exists in resolving it. Its consequences include long hours incurred in the 'waiting room,' hurried and impersonal attention once assistance is received, difficulty in obtaining night and weekend care, reduction of services because staff is not available, and gaps in insurance coverage or higher taxes by government to pay for the increasing cost of health services.

More specifically, the following are some of the outstanding reasons for our nation's inability to control health care costs in areas such as institutional care.

- There is a duplication of some high-cost hospital services in various geographic areas, with consequent idle capacity, as a result of improper community planning of health facilities.
- There are shortages and maldistribution in less costly alternatives to hospital care such as home health services, outpatient care, nursing homes, and extended care facilities.
- Although the nation has made many advances in medical science, it is only in the recent past that it has begun to focus its attention on improving the system through which the benefits of these scientific achievements are delivered.
- Health manpower is in short supply in various parts of the nation, due in part to the maldistribition of health personnel.
- The administration of many public medical programs is weak, and their services are fragmented with lack of coordination.

These are but a few of the problems which plague our nation in terms of health care. As examples, they dramatically illustrate the multifaceted aspects of the crisis this country must solve. If we do not solve the problem, the country may face a situation which forever denies access of adequate health care to growing numbers of Americans.

Health care costs

When the health care crisis is examined in detail, one issue surfaces more quickly than that of any other: costs. This factor becomes relevant whether these costs are incurred in the training of health manpower; the funding of public programs which pay for the health care of particular groups; the funding of research for curing disease; the costs involved in the purchasing of health insurance; or the funding of public programs such as Medicare's prescriptions drug benefit that was added to the program in 2003 when the US Congress enacted the Medicare Prescription, Improvement, and Modernization Act of 2003, and which took effect on January 1, 2006. In fact, the American Association of Retired Persons (AARP) announced on March 4, 2008 that the drug manufacturers increased their prices in 2007 by an average of 7.4% for brand-name medicines most commonly prescribed to the elderly, about 2.5 times the overall inflation rate, continuing a long-time trend.[7] The advocacy organization for the elderly noted that price increases have been slightly greater since the Medicare drug benefit began on January 1, 2006 because in the 4 years before the benefit began, wholesale prices rose between 5.3% and 6.5% a year. The issue of cost, therefore, underlies many of the problems that beset the health care field. Consequently, it is necessary to examine the issue as well as the ancillary ones which emanate from it.

Rising medical care costs are not a new dilemma. Medical care costs have generally outpaced other cost-of-living components. The roots of the problem are complex and intertwined. For example, the multitrillion-dollar-a-year health care industry has been slow in adjusting to the increasing demand by the public for its services. This demand increased suddenly and immensely, by the establishment of Medicare and Medicaid in 1965. But these programs are not the only explanation for rising costs. The industry's scientific advances have outpaced its management capability. Physicians and hospitals can accomplish much more than they once could, but they continue to be impeded by a lack of adequate space, personnel, and equipment. Additionally, rising incomes and the prevalence of private health insurance increase the ability of the public to pay for the health care they desire. Thus, the demand for health care services far exceeds the nation's capability to provide them. The availability of more expensive, state-of-the art drugs and technological services spurs health care spending not only because the development costs of these products must be recouped by industry but also because they generate consumer demand for more intense, costly services, even if they not necessarily cost-effective.

Nation's health bill

The fact that the demand for health care services has grown far more rapidly than the source of supply is clearly reflected in our nation's health bills. In 1950 the nation spent only $12 billion for health care services or 4% of its GDP. By 1960 this amount almost doubled ($25.9 billion or 5.2% GDP). By 1970 the total expenditures almost tripled the figure of 1960 ($69.2 billion or 7.2% GDP), by 1980 the amount was 20 times that of 1950 ($245.8 billion or 8.7% GDP), by 1990 it was 58 times that of 1950 ($696 billion or 12% GDP) and by 2000 the country had spent 108 times the amount of 1950 ($1299.5 billion or 12.5% GDP). In other words, the amount of money the USA has been spending on health services has been escalating with each passing decade: it was 108 times larger in 2000 than 50 years earlier in 1950. The USA now spends more of its GDP for this single service than any other country in the world. In fact, in 2006 the USA spent $2.1 trillion (16.0% of the GDP) or $7026 per person, as already noted – 10 times as much as the $737 spent for every man, woman, and child almost 30 years earlier in 1977. By 2008 the estimate was $8160 for every man, woman, and child, according to a February 2009 report of the US Department of Health and Human Services.[2,4,8–9] According to the US Department of Health and Human Services, this amount is expected to rise even more in the future. Senator

Edward M. Kennedy (D-MA) stated if health care was not so expensive, workers could take home higher wages and have better pensions.[10]

Hospital costs

Hospital care is the greatest contributing component in health care. In the financial year 2005, of NHE of $1987.7 billion, hospital care accounted for $611.1 billion or about 31%. In 1960, as a point of comparison, the USA expended $27.5 billion on NHE, of which hospital care was only $9.2 billion or still one-third.[11]

Thus, the question arises: why is there such a financial explosion in hospital care? A variety of factors have contributed to the significant rise in hospital charges and costs, but two of these determinants are unique. The first is that 90% of all hospital costs are paid by someone other than the patient – otherwise known as a 'third party' – such as Blue Cross, Medicare, Medicaid, other insurance carriers or public programs. In fact, some patients may not even know the cost of their own hospital stay because of this situation. The second reason is that, for example, until 1983 when the Congress enacted a payment system under Medicare called a prospective payment system (PPS) in response to the requirement of the Tax Equity and Fiscal Responsibility Act of 1982, hospitals under Medicare were reimbursed on the basis of the costs of the services which they provided. The budget was open-ended and there was no incentive to hold down expenses.

This reimbursement system tended to encourage hospitals to add expensive facilities and technologies like a computed tomography (CT) scanner, a technological miracle which combines a computer with an X-ray machine to produce superdetailed, three-dimensional views of any cross-section of the human body. The problem with the machine is that it costs hundreds of thousands of dollars to purchase as well as to operate. But under the prevailing reimbursement system at the time these costs were included in the hospital's charges to the third party after the costs were incurred. The third parties paid these bills from revenues which come mainly from the premiums which the American public pays at ever-increasing rates. The hospital may attempt to add equipment such as a CT scanner, even if it is not needed or underutilized, or already present in other hospitals in the community. The hospital will do so because technologies such as CT scanners not only may yield large operational profits to the medical institution but also the availability of such advanced technology will enable the hospital to compete with other institutions, attract doctors to its staff, patients to its beds, and thus stay or advance in business. But faced with sharply escalating Medicare costs in the early 1980s, the federal government completely revised the way Medicare pays hospitals for treating elderly patients. The governing agency at the time, the Health Care Financing Administration (HCFA), renamed the Centers for

Medicare and Medicaid Services in 2001, changed the way it paid hospitals from a retrospective fee-for-service system to a PPS, as already noted. Under the PPS, hospitals receive a fixed amount for treating patients who are diagnosed with a given illness, regardless of their length of stay or the type of care received. The PPS proved effective at curbing the increase in costs in hospitals and in selecting the least expensive methods of care, without sacrificing the quality being delivered.

However, the elderly are not the only patients to enter hospitals. Because most hospitals depend on government payments for about 50% of their revenues and private insurers which negotiate discounts for much of the rest, raising charges is one avenue hospitals use to bring in additional money from individuals and insurers not covered by discounts. Even increasing charges may not help much because not many insurers pay full charges. Still hospitals raise their charges to collect as many dollars as they can. Some insurers, though, pay less than Medicare, which also may not meet overall hospital costs. There is no single formula for calculating hospital charges. Hospitals take into account factors such as labor costs, the number of uninsured patients the hospital treats, and whether the hospitals contract with a lot of low-paying insurers.

Hospital charges are like any consumer good in which the person does not pay the full price that is listed on the sticker. Few pay the total amount because insurers negotiate discounts, and, as already noted, Medicare under the PPS tells hospitals what the program will pay. Still, there are instances when insurers do pay the full charges such as when a policyholder receives care from an out-of-network hospital such as in managed care, and with whom the insurer does not have a negotiated discount. Hospitals can also bill insurers for additional payments when the charges for treating a patient exceed a specified amount, which occurs more often in hospitals with higher charges. In recent years charges have risen quickly and often have little relationship to the actual cost of services. Hospitals can increase charges to any amount that the market will bear, but it is a strange market because most hospital customers negotiate discounts off the charges, as already noted. One of the reasons prices had increased in the not too distant past is that hospitals tried to increase the amount they receive from insurers, which had often used charges as the starting point for negotiations. But in recent years, as charges have risen, insurers began negotiating in other ways, basing payments on established amounts for a day of care or the treatment of a particular condition. In 2003, the national average charge was 211% higher than cost and in some states the ratio is even higher, in the low three digits.[12]

Keeping up with the latest technologies is not the only factor leading to increases in hospital expenses. Others include:

• The price of goods and services purchased by hospitals has been subject to inflation.

- Although payroll costs have lagged behind other industries, they have been catching up.
- The demand for hospital services has necessitated the hiring of additional staff.
- New approaches to less expensive health care methods have been tried on too limited a scale and are not yet commonplace.
- Health insurance coverage has been tied too closely to the requirement that the patient be hospitalized rather than an emphasis of coverage on preventive care benefits. The benefits for preventive care would pay for treating patients outside hospital in order to ward off or detect any illness in its incipient stages before it becomes worse.

In an effort to control their hospital expenses, hospitals have employed various management techniques, including more ambulatory surgery, closing down beds, reduction of personnel, better money management, more efficient use of energy, more preadmission testing, and tighter utilization review. However, hospital costs, despite their rapid rise, are not the sole factor which is contributing to the inflationary spiral besetting medical care services in the USA.

Physician services

Prices for services of physicians have behaved similarly to those of hospital care. In 1960, 5 years before Medicare became law, the USA spent $5.4 billion on physician and clinical services, which constituted almost 20% of the nation's NHE ($27.5 billion). By 1970, 5 years after Medicare was enacted, the nation spent almost three times as much as 1960 or $14.0 billion or about 19% of the NHE ($74.9 billion). By 2005, the amount spent on physician and clinical services was 30 times ($421.2 billion) that of 1970 and constituted about 21% of the NHE ($1987.7 billion), which was not much different from the 22% in 1990 ($157.5 billion in physician services versus $714.0 billion NHE) or the 21% in year 2000 ($337.9 billion in physician services versus $1602.8 billion NHE).[11] While the actual dollar amount for medical services has increased dramatically, its proportion of the NHE has been fairly uniform over the past decades. Meanwhile, during this time the creation of a new PPS for physicians who treat Medicare patients was put into place.

In 1992 Medicare implemented the Medicare physician fee schedule (MPFS) that replaced reimbursing a physician based on prevailing charges to using a resource-based relative value scale (RBRVS), which established physician service payments based on relative costs, which is adjusted by geographic region (so a procedure performed in New York City is worth more than a procedure performed in Omaha, Nebraska). When President George H.W. Bush signed into law the Omnibus Budget Reconciliation Act of 1989,

Medicare changed to the RBRVS system. It used a current procedure terminology (CPT) code for services. Not only does Medicare employ this system but almost all health maintenance organizations do as well. The goal of the MPFS was to correct distortions produced by charge-based payments and to encourage efficiencies in medical practice. Under the new system, payments to physicians are based on the number of relative value units (RVUs) assigned to each service. Total RVUs reflect three cost components: (1) physician work (or time and effort); (2) practice expenses; and (3) professional liability insurance. Costs associated with each component are given a weight, or index value, and are adjusted to take into consideration area price differences. The three index values for a service are summed and multiplied by a standard dollar amount (a conversion factor, which changes annually) to arrive at a payment amount. On average, in regard to an RVU, work represents 52% of total physician payments, practice expenses represent 44%, and liability insurance represents 4%.[13]

There are a variety of reasons for the rapid rise in physician fees. Before Medicare and Medicaid became operational in 1966, many physicians reduced their customary fees for persons with low incomes. But now physicians can, with good conscience, charge the same amount they ordinarily charge Medicare and Medicaid patients. In addition, population increases, more widespread insurance, and increasing awareness of the benefits of medicine have contributed to the growing demand for physician services by all segments of society without a corresponding supply in physicians.

The reason why an average of 19–22 cents of each dollar was spent for physician care versus an average of about 30 cents of each dollar for hospital care during the latter part of the 20th century and the beginning of the 21st century relates to the changing character of the US population. As the number of older people in our society increases, more monies are being spent on institutional services provided by a hospital or a nursing home. The monies which are being spent by or on behalf of the elderly have had a profound effect on the rise of health expenditures within recent years.

The elderly

Today, the elderly, numbering more than 35 million people, represent almost 13% of the American population. It is predicted that by 2030 this number will double to 70 million persons and one in five Americans, or 20%, will be 65 years or older. In fact, the American population is growing older and the group over age 85 is now the fastest-growing segment.[14–16] Over the years the government has established many programs to help the elderly through the financial trauma of what should be their 'golden years.' But, unfortunately, for many of the aged their 'golden years' are a time when low incomes must be budgeted to meet high personal expenses because of circumstances such as ill health. In 1965, the government established two programs, Medicare and Medicaid, which have brought financial relief to the elderly in at least one area – their personal health expenses. The necessity for such programs is underscored by the following facts. Medicare and Medicaid together serve about one in four Americans and spend about one in three of the nation's health dollars. Both programs have grown substantially in terms of the percentage of the populations served and the dollars spent. For example, Medicare alone accounts for one in five (20%) of the nation's health dollars, about twice the share of the nation's health spending, which was one in 10 (10%) in 1970. Medicaid is now the larger of the two programs, both in terms of persons enrolled and dollars spent; something that was not foreseen at its enactment or in most of the decades since. In fiscal year 2003, Medicaid had 41.4 million persons enrolled, compared to Medicare's 41.3 million and, in fiscal 2002, Medicaid spending by both federal and state governments was $259 billion, which was greater than Medicare's spending of $256 billion.[17] It should also be noted that Medicare protection does not apply to just those who are 65 years or older. In 1973 Medicare protection was also extended to certain people under 65: those who have permanent kidney failure (renal disease) or who have been entitled to social security disability benefits for at least 24 consecutive months or Railroad Retirement disability benefits for at least 29 consecutive months. Included are disabled workers and disabled widows and widowers between age 50 and 65, and people aged 18 and over who draw social security benefits because they became disabled before reaching 22 years of age. In addition, the Medicare, Medicaid, and the SCHIP Benefits Improvement and Protection Act of 2000 (PL 106-554) allowed persons with amyotrophic lateral sclerosis (Lou Gehrig's disease) to waive the 24-month waiting period. SCHIP is the State Children's Health Insurance Program which Congress created as Title XXI of the Social Security Act to address the increasing problem of children who lacked health insurance protection when Congress enacted the Balanced Budget Act of 1997.

The reasons for the large medical expenses of the elderly are varied. Compared to those under 65 years of age, the average elderly person has more costlier illnesses, is more limited by chronic health conditions, is hospitalized more often and remains longer in hospital, visits a physician more often, and as more and more of the elderly reach their 80s, 90s, and even their 100s, develops illnesses like Alzheimer's that, as of the first decade of the 21st century, have no cure and are extremely costly to treat.

The financial relief that Medicare has brought to the elderly has not been without cost to the rest of society in that Congress has had to increase the wage base and tax rate of the social security program to prevent the program from becoming bankrupt. As a result, Medicare, together with other social security programs, passes on its respective cost increases to the taxpayer, whose annual social security taxable income limit may be higher now, in some instances, than actual yearly income. These increasing costs not only affect those under 65 years of age, but also the elderly who must assume a greater share of their own medical expenses under Medicare than when the program began operations in 1966.

A number of external factors affect the costs of Medicare as well as the other programs within the social security system. Since Medicare was enacted in 1965, the nation has gone through periods of high inflation: at one time during the Carter administration, for example, interest rates were in the low double digits, approaching 21%. The country has also gone through periods of high unemployment such as during the early 1980s of the Reagan administration, when fewer persons than expected had contributed monies into social security trust funds, and had retired or claimed disability insurance. These cycles are factors which also affect the flow of monies into the social security trust funds and cause them to suffer financial shortfalls. Another major cause stems from 1972 when Congress enacted a cost-of-living adjustment to raise social security benefits automatically as the consumer price index increases. Thus, when inflation is high, social security benefits have been automatically increased to a greater extent than had been projected at the time when Medicare was enacted. In the past, changing economic and demographic assumptions that were made in forecasting the long-term projections of the social security program turned out to be wrong in regard to fertility and mortality rates in our society as well as the annual percentage increases both in the consumer price index and in average wages.[18] Consequently, because of external economic forces beyond the capability of our government to manage or foresee, the American public has had to assume a greater financial burden to protect itself and its future generations from the financial ravages accompanying aging. These can be expressed, for example, in an individual's need for disability income or the need for financial assistance under the Medicare program.

Health insurance

Today, the costs of health care have jumped so high that other groups are beginning to demand the kind of protection which programs such as Medicare provide the elderly. For example, by 2004 some New Jersey hospitals had daily room charges exceeding $5000. An appendectomy in California, including about 2 days in hospital, had an average list of charges of $18 000. Nationally, federal data showed that the median charge for treating a heart attack was more than $20 000.[12] With hospital charges this high, even the relatively affluent can have their savings and other assets wiped out by a single catastrophic or chronic illness. As the costs of health care soar, large gaps still exist in health insurance coverage. Private insurers have difficulty in keeping up with rising service charges as they attempt to cover needed services. As additional benefits are provided, the costs of insurance are inflated even more. Increasingly, requests by health insurers from state insurance commissions for rate increases are meeting more and more resistance. In fact, some decisions as to the relevancy of such increases are being brought into courts of law for review. As a result, health insurance prepayment plans, commercial insurance companies, and some state governments are beginning to support the concept of a federal national health insurance mechanism to replace, wholly or partially, private health insurance programs.

Today, the working population is not only confronted by escalating private health insurance rates, but is also faced with:

- Increased state and local taxes to pay for Medicaid
- More and more of employees' federal tax dollar going to the federal share of Medicaid and Medicare costs
- More out-of-pocket costs to cover employees' coinsurance portion of higher and higher medical charges
- More out-of pocket costs for rapidly rising charges for largely uninsured health services such as dental care when the dentist is not a member of the plan and does not accept its reimbursement schedule as payment in full.

Besieged with all these demands and with so many separate health insurance plans, how can individuals determine which plans offer adequate coverage, which is commensurate with their earnings, and which meets their particular needs? This is especially true since private health insurance does not provide complete coverage. Although private health insurers often cite the extensiveness of their coverage and the fact that the number of insured persons is constantly growing, it is important to bear in mind the limitations of the coverage. Large categories of medical expenses such as out-of-hospital physician office visits or out-of-hospital prescription drugs and dental care are still excluded from many basic health insurance policies, unlike their inclusion, for example, in major medical insurance.

As an example, let us illustrate why a physician's out-of-hospital office visit is not usually covered by private health insurance policies. If nonhospital visits to a physician's office were to be covered by private health insurance, insurers believe this might encourage patients to see their doctor for all kinds of ailments and complaints for which the patient would not ordinarily make an appointment. Such a result is feared because another party, the private health insurer, would be paying the bill. It would mean that the health insurer would have to process even more claims than at present. These administrative costs, in addition to physician payments, would cause an increase in the costs of health insurance premiums. Thus, by not providing out-of-hospital coverage for physician office visits, the insurers believe a deterrent is created. Patients will only visit a doctor's office when they feel it is medically necessary since the patients themselves must pay for the visit. Unfortunately, if a doctor must perform a procedure which can easily be carried out in the doctor's office, but is only covered by the patient's health insurance policy when it is performed in a hospital, then the physician may admit the patient to the hospital so that the patient will not have to pay for the cost of the procedure. This situation adds to the cost of hospital care which is reflected in the increasing cost of health insurance which the insurer charges the consumer. So the question arises, can these hospital costs be reduced by providing coverage for nonhospital 'ambulatory' visits to a physician's office? There is no definitive answer. Tentative evidence from health maintenance organizations seems to indicate that such a benefit would reduce the cost of hospitalization. However, the private insurance industry has not introduced such coverage on a broad population basis. Thus, no one knows whether patients will visit their physicians for minor ailments and thereby overburden the physician's office, consequently increasing the cost of health care.

Meanwhile, the costs of hospital care continue to rise and efforts to control their increases seem difficult. Needless to say, this kind of policy exclusion becomes even more critical at a time of inflationary medical care prices. And the situation is many times worse for the poor, minorities, the itinerant, and the self-employed. These groups are in the outer fringes of the health care system, not only in terms of health insurance protection, but also in terms of their accessibility to and availability of health care services (Figure 3.1).

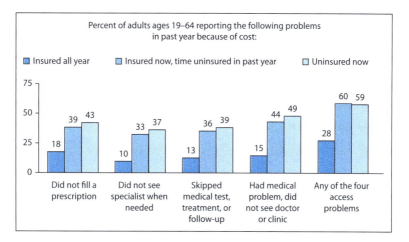

Figure 3.1   Lacking health insurance for any period threatens access to care. Source: Collins SR, Davis K, Doty MM *et al. Gaps in Health Insurance: An All-American Problem.* The Commonwealth Fund, April 2006. Reprinted with permission of the Commonwealth Fund, New York, NY and as cited at: http://www.commonwealthfund.org/chartcartcharts/chartcartcharts_show.htm?doc_id=526.

In fact, it is estimated that in 2007 at least 47 million persons in the USA did not have any health insurance coverage. And these socioeconomic conditions do have consequences, as the following case illustrates. In February 1978 a jury in Florida, which was urged by the plaintiff's attorney to return a judgment that would serve as a warning to the medical field, awarded $950 000 to the heir of a meningitis victim. The prospective patient died after she was turned away from one hospital and sent to another because of her poverty. An extreme example, perhaps, but the event did take place within the US health care system.

Medicaid and Medicare

Although the government, principally through Medicare and Medicaid, has ventured into paying some of the medical bills of those least able to pay – the elderly and the poor – many problems remain for those groups in terms of obtaining the quality of care they seek. The Centers for Medicare and Medicaid Services administers Medicare, Medicaid, and SCHIP. Together, these three public programs financed $567 billion in health care services in 2003 – one-third of the nation's total health care bill and almost three-quarters of public spending in health care.[3] Since their enactment, both Medicare and Medicaid have been subject to numerous legislative and administrative changes that are designed to improve the provision of health care services to our nation's aged, disabled, and disadvantaged. One effect of the increasing expenditures that are seen in Medicare is reflected in its monthly premium costs. In 1966, the first year of its operation, beneficiaries paid about $3.00 per month. By January 2009, the cost was almost $100 per month as total Medicare spending increased to $401.3 billion. Its acceleration of 18.7% compared to 9.3% in 2005 was due, in large part, to the introduction of Part D, which provides beneficiaries with coverage for prescription drugs. On the other hand, Medicaid spending in 2006 declined for the first time since Medicaid began, falling 0.9% to $308.6 billion, partly because Part D shifted drug coverage for dual eligibles (persons eligible for both Medicaid and Medicare programs) from Medicaid into Medicare as well as because of continued cost containment efforts by the states and slower Medicaid enrollment growth, due to more restrictive eligibility criteria and a stronger economy at the time.[3,17,19]

Medicare has traditionally consisted of two parts: hospital insurance (Part A) and supplementary insurance (Part B). A third part of Medicare, sometimes known as Part C, is the Medicare Advantage program (managed care) and was originally established as the Medicare + Choice program by the Balanced Budget Act of 1997 (PL 105-330), and subsequently renamed and modified by the Medicare Prescription Drug, Improvement, and Modernization Act of 2003 (PL 108-173). The Medicare Advantage program expands beneficiaries' options for participation in private-sector health care plans. When Medicare began on July 1, 1966, about 19 million people enrolled. In 2005, more than 42 million were enrolled in one or both of Parts A and B of the Medicare program and about 5 million of them had chosen to participate in the Medicare Advantage plans.[3] In 1965, when Medicare became law, Congress built Medicare on the foundation of private health insurance plans' payment methods. As Medicare costs escalated faster than had been predicted, the search began for ways to control its payments to providers. Over the years, the Medicare Part A providers – hospitals, skilled nursing homes, and home health agencies – were all moved from reimbursement based on the provider's costs to costs subject to PPS. Part B payments for ambulatory services also moved from a system based on a provider's charges to fee schedules for certain providers, a relative value scale for physicians, as already noted, and an outpatient PPS for hospitals.

While Medicare (Title XVIII of the Social Security law) received most of the congressional attention at its enactment and for much of the ensuing decades, Medicaid (Title XIX of the Social Security law) was not created out of whimsy as a complement to Medicare in 1965. It was built on the foundation of two earlier pieces of legislation in 1950: a state-based vendor payment program which was established to cover people on welfare, and in 1960 the extension of this program to cover indigent elderly who were not on welfare, but couldn't afford to pay their medical bills (the 'medical needy'). While some may consider that Medicaid was just an afterthought at the time of its establishment, as already noted, the program has become even larger than Medicare, which no one in 1965 could have foreseen. Medicaid is now the nation's largest health program. By 2005, it covered one in four children, one in three pregnant women, and nearly one in five Medicare beneficiaries who, without this program, could very well join the ranks of the nation's uninsured population.[17]

Since its enactment, Medicaid has expanded in scope, as has its expenditures. As examples, in 1967, an early and periodic screening, diagnosis, and treatment (EPSDT) comprehensive health services benefit for all Medicaid children under 21 was established. In 1972 Medicaid eligibility for elderly, blind, and disabled residents of a state could be linked to eligibility for the newly enacted federal supplemental security income (SSI) program. SSI is a federally funded needs-based disability program for adults and children; it provides monthly cash benefits, and, in most states, automatic Medicaid eligibility. In 1981, states were required to provide additional payments to hospitals treating a disproportionate share of low-income patients (i.e., disproportionate-share hospitals or DSH). In 1986 Medicaid's coverage for pregnant women and infants (up to 1 year of age) to 100% of the federal poverty level (FPL) was established as a state option. In 1988 Medicaid coverage for pregnant women and infants to 100% FPL was mandated, expanded again, and mandated in 1989 to pregnant women and children under age 6 to 133% FPL; and in 1990 phased-in Medicaid coverage for ages 6–18 under 100% FPL was established. In 1988, special eligibility rules were established for institutionalized persons whose spouses remained in the community to prevent 'spousal impoverishment.' In 1997 new Medicaid managed care options and requirements were established. In 2000, the Benefits Improvement and Protection Act (BIPA) created a new Medicaid PPS for federally qualified health centers and rural health clinics. Since 2003, under the Medicare Prescription Drug Improvement and Modernization Act, Medicare beneficiaries who also receive Medicaid benefits receive their drug benefits through Medicare.

The escalation of costs in Medicare and Medicaid is quite a serious problem (Figure 3.2). Unless solutions are forthcoming, whether the costs are considered on an individual beneficiary basis or in the aggregate for the nation as a whole, even programs as publicly spirited and publicly minded as Medicare and Medicaid may become too expensive for those in our society who need it the most and can afford to do without it the least.

While the federal government and the states share proportionately in Medicaid funding, the more monies a state spends on Medicaid, the less monies a state has to fund other public services such as education, transportation, and other services that are vital for all its residents. This is one way in which inflationary health care costs eat away at the very fabric of our wellbeing and standard of living. This is especially true for those who, like the elderly, must live mostly on fixed incomes and cannot cope with inflationary pressures which affect the quality and status of their personal health. Regardless of age, people become sick in good times and bad. An unemployed

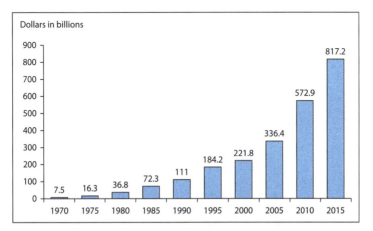

Figure 3.2   Growth in Medicare expenditures, 1970–2015. Note: Figures for 2010 and 2015 are projected. Source: The Commonwealth Fund. Data from 2006 Medicare Trustees Report. Reprinted with permission of The Commonwealth Fund, New York, NY and as cited at: http://www.commonwealthfund.org/chartcartcharts/chartcartcharts_show.htm?doc_id=479.

worker can defer the purchase of a digital camera, but he cannot defer an appendectomy if his appendix bursts. Moreover, many Americans have come to regard health care as a necessity, not as an optional expense. As more and more of post World War II baby boomers become eligible to be covered by Medicare, for example, the program's costs will continue to increase, putting pressure on the federal government to increase its spending and require more and more out-of-pocket costs by the program's beneficiaries at a time in their lives when their personal income is not as great as in the preretirement or working years (Figure 3.3) unless, like the state of Oregon and its health plan in 1994, the federal and state government devise plans to ration medical care in order to try and control program expenditures.

Some kind of resolution to this problem is needed that is equitable not only to those who expend the program's monies but also to those who require the care and health service those expenditures purchase.

Manpower

Today, the demand for health services, which far exceeds the supply of manpower, is another of the factors influencing the rising costs of health care. Yet, there is a debate as to whether there is an oversupply of physicians in the USA. Some policy experts believe that when the number of physicians is increased, for example, this situation is potentially cost-enhancing. In fact, in 1977 Robert Derzon, then administrator of the HCFA that was responsible for the Medicare and Medicaid programs and now renamed the Centers for Medicare and Medicaid Services, stated that 'over a lifetime a

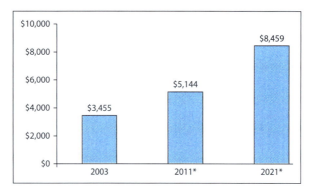

Figure 3.3   Average out-of-pocket health care spending, for all Medicare beneficiaries aged 65 and up. *Projected costs assume an annual 5.1% inflation rate. Source: Fishman E, Tamang S, Shea D (2008) *Medicare Out-of-Pocket Costs. Can Private Savings Incentives Solve the Problem?* The Commonwealth Fund, March 2008. Reprinted with permission of The Commonwealth Fund, New York, NY and as cited at: http://www.commonwealthfund.org/chartcartcharts/chartcartcharts_show.htm?doc_id=686.

doctor will add more than $9 million to health care spending.'[20] This is because great numbers of physicians can generate higher rates of utilization and higher total expenditures for health. By tradition, the physician is the centerpiece of the health care system. The physician has the principal role in the delivery of medical care, whether it is delivered in the hospital or in an office or community-based setting. The physician has the ultimate responsibility for the accurate diagnosis and treatment for diseases. When a patient visits a physician, it is the doctor who decides when the patient returns, what medical services or medical specialties the patient requires, what drugs the patient needs, and whether hospitalization or another kind of institutionalization is necessary and for how long. In addition, the physician often supervises other health care personnel, frequently is the focus of reimbursement under health insurance plans, and contributes to the formulation of our national health policies. All these factors influence the rising costs of health care.

Yet, while there is a debate whether there is an oversupply of physicians nationally, a shortage of physicians continues to persist in rural areas of the USA. In fact, as of 2005, about 20% of the US population – about 60 million people – lived in rural areas spread over 80% of the country. In counties with a population of less than 10 000 there are far fewer doctors per capita than in urban/suburban areas.[21,22] According to the National Health Service Corps, the shortage of doctors in rural America has led the federal government to designate such areas as health professional shortage areas (HPSAs) and, according to the US Office of Rural Health Policy, 10% of doctors live in rural areas.[23] Aging rural physicians, declining interest among recent medical graduates to practice in primary care (internal medicine, general and family practice, pediatrics) and in rural areas, and increases in the number of women in medicine (who are less likely to practice in rural areas) all contribute to a bleak outlook for the rural physician workforce. The Bureau of Health Professions estimates that annually 3400 physicians are needed to eliminate the most desperate needs in nonmetropolitan HPSAs and 7000 physicians annually to meet reasonable workforce targets.[24] But, overall, as of 1999 the USA had 29.1 active physicians (doctors of medicine and doctors of osteopathy) for each of its 10 000 population. By 2004 the US National Center for Health Statistics stated there were only 24 active, nonfederal patient care physicians per 10 000 population. According to the American Medical Association, as of 2000, there were an estimated 813 770 physicians in the USA. Of this number about 473 431 were in office-based practice and 157 032 in hospital-based patient care. Almost one-third practiced as either primary care generalists (33.7%) or a much smaller number as primary care specialists (6.4%). Again, according to the US National Center for Health Statistics, in 2004 there were 707 380 active nonfederal, patient care physicians in the USA.[11,25]

The reason for the debate about the supply of physicians in the USA is that since the 1980s the American Medical Association and other industry organizations have predicted a surplus of physicians and worked to limit the number of new doctors. In 1994, the *Journal of the American Medical Association* predicted that there would be a surplus of 165 000 physicians by 2000.[26] Then, in 2005 and 2006 two national reports altered these predictions. In January 2005, the Council on Graduate Medical Education (COGME), a group Congress created to recommend how many doctors the country needs, released its 186th report, *Physician Workforce Policy Guidelines for the United States, 2000–2020*, recommending an annual increase of 3000 medical school graduates by 2015 in order to meet rising demand and need. Only under the most optimistic of various supply-and-demand scenarios outlined in the report would the nation have an adequate supply to meet demand in the year 2020. While the midpoint of projected scenarios outlined in the report is used, the net result is a projected shortage of 85 000 physicians by 2020 or almost 10% of the number of physicians that the American Medical Association enumerated in 2000.[27] In 2006, the US Department of Health and Human Services, through its agency, the Health Resources and Services Administration (HRSA), released a report projecting a shortfall of approximately 55 000 physicians in 2020 if current trends continue to persist. The full-time equivalent of physician supply is projected to increase to 866 400 by 2020, while demand for physicians will increase to 921 500 due to the growth and aging of the US population.[28]

According to Richard Cooper, director of the Health Policy Institute at the Medical College of Wisconsin, there was a dramatic expansion in the number of new physicians being trained in the 1960s and 1970s, with two new physicians being created for every one who retired, and the graduation of new physicians has changed little since 1985. By 2015, the physicians licensed in the 1960s, 1970s, and 1980s will retire in large numbers and that will outstrip in large numbers the 25 000 physicians produced each year.[26] Unlike many professions like engineers, the marketplace does not determine how many physicians the nation has. This number is heavily influenced by the physicians themselves as well as others. For example, Congress controls the supply of physicians by how much federal funding it provides for medical residencies – the graduate training all physicians require. Medicare has an influence on physician supply because it reimburses hospitals for the cost of training physicians. By 2005 Medicare was already spending about 3% of its budget training physicians and may not have the resources to spend more, given the financial pressures it faces in future years to pay for the care of its beneficiaries. And very worrisome is the fact that the retirement of baby boom doctors means the number of doctors will be declining just as the first of the baby boomers become 70 in 2016. To make matters worse the USA stopped opening medical schools in the 1980s because of the predicted surplus of doctors. In February 2005 the Association of American Medical Colleges reversed this policy by recommending the number of medical schools be increased by 15%. Some worry that more doctors will drive up the costs of medical care, not make it cheaper and more accessible, because physicians can order more tests, more procedures, and more drugs, without improving the nation's health. They say doctors can create their own demand and an abundance of doctors does not necessarily mean the system is more efficient. Others believe that it is sickness, not doctors, that drives medical costs.[26]

But, as another example of manpower problems, it is not only physicians who are in short supply but also other health professionals like nurses and pharmacists who dispense the medications the physician prescribes and whose need will also rise. In regard to nurses, experts state that an estimated 116 000 registered nurse positions were unfilled in US hospitals in 2009 and nearly 100 000 jobs go vacant in nursing homes. One of the major reasons for the US nursing shortage is that there isn't a large enough pool of faculty at nursing colleges to expand nursing enrollment since nurses with a graduate degree, which is needed to teach, can earn more as a practicing nurse. Insofar as pharmacists are concerned, according to the US Department of Labor, employment of pharmacists is expected to increase by 22% between 2006 and 2016, from 243 000 to 296 000, which is much faster than the average for all occupations which the Department measures.

The increasing numbers of middle-aged and elderly people who use more prescription drugs than younger people will continue to increase the demand for pharmacists throughout the projection period, as already noted. Other factors likely to increase the demand for pharmacists include scientific advances that will make more drug products available as well as the coverage of prescription drugs by a greater number of health insurance plans and Medicare. As the use of prescription drugs increases, the demand for pharmacists will increase in most practice settings, such as community pharmacies, hospital pharmacies, and mail-order pharmacies. As the population becomes older, assisted-living facilities and home care organizations should witness especially rapid growth. Demand will also increase as cost-conscious insurers, in an attempt to improve preventive care, use pharmacists in areas such as patient education and vaccination administration. Demand is also increasing in managed care organizations where pharmacists analyze trends and patterns in the use of medication use, and in pharmacoeconomics, the cost and benefit analysis of different drug therapies. New jobs are being created in disease management – the development of new methods for curing and controlling disease – and in sales and marketing. Rapid growth is also expected in pharmacy economics – the use of technology to improve patient care.[29,30]

Whatever the answers are in terms of manpower problems, perhaps they were answered in 1969 by a distinguished Presidential Commission, the National Advisory Commission on Health Manpower. It found that the inadequacies in health manpower could not be successfully tackled outside reform of the institutional framework within which the manpower is utilized. The Commission reported:

> There is a crisis in American health care ... the crisis, however, is not simply one of numbers. It is that substantially increased numbers of health manpower will be needed over time. But, if additional personnel are employed in the present manner and within the present patterns and systems of care, they will not avert or even perhaps alleviate the crisis. Unless we improve the system through which health care is provided, care will continue to become less satisfactory, even though there are massive increases in costs and numbers of personnel ... Medicine has participated in the general explosion of science and technology, and processes cures and preventives that could not have been predicted even a decade ago. But the organization of health sciences has not kept pace with advances in medical science or with changes in society itself. Medical care in the United States is more a collection of bits and pieces (with over-lapping, duplication, great gaps, high costs, and wasted effort) than an integrated system in which needs and efforts are closely related.[31]

Similarly, Walter McNerney, former president of the Blue Cross and Blue Shield Association, stated: 'we would get more bang for the buck if we put relatively more emphasis on organization, financing, and design of the health system than simply producing professional manpower. In short, we are faced with an economic problem of organization.'[31]

Resolving the health care crisis

Recognizing the need for resolving the many health care problems which beset the nation, the federal government since the 1970s has enacted many laws to protect individuals against, and curb, the rising costs of health care. In the 1970s these included professional standards review organizations in 1972, health maintenance organizations in 1973, and health planning agencies in 1974; the Consolidated Omnibus Budget Reconciliation Act of 1986, the Health Insurance Portability and Accountability Act of 1996, part of which dealt with combating fraud and abuse in health care, and by the beginning of the 21st century there were health savings accounts for individuals and health reimbursement accounts (HRAs) for employers. Even on the state level, commissions have been established by law to control hospital costs and to have rate-making authority for various public programs within their jurisdiction. Some of the states include Massachusetts and Maryland. According to some critics, the establishment of rate-setting commissions reaches the heart of the health care cost issue – the basic philosophy of maintaining the traditional

free-enterprise system of American health care versus total government regulation, whether this control emanates from federal or state governments.
This issue underlies today's health problems because some groups feel the
conditions which led to the regulation of other industries now exist in the
health care field. It is their contention that America's medical system is not
competitive; not all hospitals are operated for profit and have little incentive
to keep prices down; and that there is little price competition among physicians. In fact Joseph A. Califano, former Secretary of Health, Education, and
Welfare during the presidency of Jimmy Carter, in 1977 was quite specific in
his analysis of the noncompetitiveness of the health care field:

- The patient may select his family doctor ... but he does not select the
  services he is told he needs.
- The physician is the central decision-maker for more than 70% of health
  care services.
- Ninety Percent of the hospital bills are paid by third parties.
- Most public and private benefit packages are heavily biased toward
  expensive in-patient care.
- The availability of price and quality information keeps patients
  dependent on the decisions of the health care provider whose financial
  well-being is determined by the prices charged.
- The ability to restrict access to competitors – hospital credential
  committees that can deny or delay privileges to health maintenance
  organizations, for example – provides special layers of market control.[32]

Secretary Califano concluded that 'doctors, hospitals, pharmaceutical companies – all inhabitants of this noncompetitive, free-spending, third-party
world – act exactly as the incentives motivate them to act: conscious of quality
but insensitive to cost. As a result, health care resources are neither well
distributed nor efficiently organized.'[32]

Reinforcing Secretary Califano's view of the lack of competition in health
care industry is Senator Edward M. Kennedy (D-MA), who has said:

> I start from the belief that health care is not like most other industries
> where free market competition operates. The consumer is not, and
> cannot be, fully informed. Risk of illness is randomly distributed,
> and risk of the cost of health care is not uniformly borne by the
> population. The economic injunction that more is better does not
> work well in health care; more may be detrimental to health. Too
> many surgeons in an area, competing with each other, produce more
> and more surgery and higher and higher fees, not lower ones. Too
> many hospital beds in a community mean too much hospitalization,
> not lower rates. Too many insurance companies in an area mean not
> better competition with premium prices, but higher premiums because
> no one insurer can control the costs of the system.[33]

In other words, the present character of the health care system fosters the direct opposite of competition.

In order to avoid a direct confrontation on this issue, many groups are seeking alternatives. One such approach is increasing consumer involvement in purchasing protection against the costs of health care. Proponents of new 'consumer-driven' health plans believe that greater price transparency would make consumers more sensitive to the costs of health care and wiser buyers and thus save consumers and employers money. One of the major forms currently available is the tax-favored HRA, to which employers contribute funds that are managed by the employee to spend on primary care as the employee wishes. Once the account is used up, a catastrophic health insurance plan begins paying for at least a portion of the expenses beyond a high annual deductible (a part of which an employee may have to pay out of his/her own pocket, depending upon how much money is in the employee's HRA). Those who criticize such plans are concerned about the potential impact that the higher cost sharing would have on lower-income people and about the potential for these new arrangements to be used far more by healthy people, shifting sicker groups to more expensive forms of insurance, and the risk that patients will not obtain important health services, especially preventive and primary care services, in order to keep money in their accounts. While mostly prevalent in the private sector, elements of consumer-directed plans, called health opportunity accounts and established by the Deficit Reduction Act of 2005 (PL 109-171), have been entering various state Medicaid programs as well.

Another solution has been government regulation. Some health experts have proposed more government regulation of the health care field, using Medicare as an example of a government program that in their opinion has been successful in controlling per-capita spending over its history. They warn that market-based approaches combined with individual financial responsibility as in consumer-driven plans can be disadvantageous to those whose financial resources are limited and, thus, present barriers to their receiving needed health care services. Promoters of a single-payer system administered by the federal government, similar to Medicare, cite significantly lower administrative costs in other such systems and argue that industry profits would have less of a role in rising prices. Critics of such government regulation state that such regulation stifles innovation and that market-based approaches are most cost-effective and will give consumers a broader range of choices.

Another approach is improving quality and efficiency. A number of initiatives are being undertaken in the USA that seek to make the health care system more efficient and higher-quality, and, thus, more cost-effective. Disease management seeks to improve and streamline the treatment regimen for certain common, chronic health conditions. Bulk purchasing of medications, like the Veterans Administration system, has been proposed for the State

Pharmaceutical Assistance Programs. Greater use of technology, such as electronic medical records, is also being researched in several demonstration projects around the country to determine its potential to share information more efficiently and reduce overhead costs.[34]

Consequently, what is seen today is a variety of proposals and experiments, advanced by public and private groups to resolve the problems which have brought the present system to its current state. Some of these actions embrace concepts of control by the private sector, quasi-public controls, while others imply total government controls. The question arises as to what kind of future lies ahead for American society with respect to a system which must continue to meet the health care needs of an ever-growing population.

The future

Despite the many problems which beset this nation today, the future resolution of these issues can be considered optimistically. Society is aware of the problems, is debating the most feasible solutions for them, and realizes that in health care, whether in the medical or environmental sense, what is at stake is the survival of society itself. Polls in 2008 indicated that health care ranks as one of the foremost concerns of the American people along with the state of the general economy, energy, and foreign conflicts. Thus, looking into the future, it may not be too long until this nation will have a national health insurance program in which all of its population, generally, will be protected against the costs and incidence of ill health. More states may follow the model of Massachusetts which, on April 4, 2006, became the first state in the nation to pass a comprehensive law that requires every resident of Massachusetts to have health insurance, and to be insured by July 1, 2007, either by purchasing insurance premiums directly or by obtaining it through their employers, with the poor being offered free or heavily subsidized health insurance coverage. Managed care will continue to expand, being stimulated by both public financing and the support of the private insurance industry, as ways are sought to reduce costs and bring a greater efficiency and coordination into the health care system.

Alternatives to hospital care, such as home care services, will continue to increase. Emphasis will be on the continuing development of institutions such as extended care facilities, assisted-living facilities and outpatient or ambulatory clinics, with walk-in clinics in retail stores gaining in popularity. Community health centers and community mental health centers will still serve and reach those who require but cannot find health services. These are not all the changes which will occur, nor will this system suddenly be developed. As some examples of the many problems this nation confronts today in the health care arena, the maldistribution or physician shortage in rural and inner-city areas must be corrected; Medicare financing in the next several decades and beyond of an increasing elderly population whose life expectancy is increasing must be resolved; and many millions of uninsured Americans must be covered against the costs of ill health. Health care, both in concept and practice, is an evolutionary process. But the public conscience that health care is a right and not a privilege has been awakened. An enlarging society demands that this basic right be applied in fact rather than in theory. Individuals now find themselves affected by health care problems, whether it be in requiring assistance in the payment of bills or the purchase of insurance they cannot afford, or the elimination of deteriorating environmental conditions which lead to ill health, or obtaining medical assistance when needed rather than when the first opportunity is available to receive it. If the present battle for maintaining this society in as good a state of health as possible is lost, either in the physical or environmental sense, then society will have lost the basic element for its future existence, namely, that of a healthful life itself.

References

1. Stobbe M. US life expectancy lags behind others. Associated Press 2008; June 12.
2. Catlin A, Cowan C, Hartman M *et al.* National health spending in 2006: a year of change for prescription drugs. *Health Aff* 2008; 27: 14–29.
3. Hoffman E D, Klees B S, Curtis C A. Overview of the Medicare and Medicaid programs. *Health Care Financ Rev* 2005; 3–5 (suppl.).
4. Gibson R M, Fisher C R. *National Health Expenditures, Fiscal Year 1977 Health Note.* Washington, DC: Health Care Financing Administration, 1978; 1: 3.
5. US Department of Health, Education, and Welfare. *Forward Plan for Health, FY 1978–1982.* Washington, DC: Public Health Service, 1976; 48.
6. Breslow L. The urgency of social action for health. *Am J Publ Health Assoc* 1970; January: 11–12.
7. *AARP Report Finds Brand Name Drug Prices Continue to Soar.* Washington, DC: AARP, 2008; March 5 (press release).
8. *Source Book of Health Insurance Data, 2002.* Washington, DC: Health Insurance Association of America, 2002; 99 (Table 5.2).
9. Health care costs to top $8,000 per person. Associated Press, 2009; February 24.
10. Kennedy E M. A bill to establish a transitional system of hospital cost containment. *Congressional Record* 1977; April 26: S6401.
11. US Department of Health and Human Services. *Health, United States, 2007.* Atlanta, GA: US Centers for Disease Control and Prevention, 2007.
12. Appleby J. Hospital bills spin out of control. *USA Today* 2004; April 13.
13. Maxwell S, Zuckerman S. Impact of resource-based practice expenses on the Medicare physician volume. *Health Care Financ Rev* 2007–2008; 29: 65.
14. 65+. *Washington Post/Health* 1996; July 23: 7.
15. Franklin MB. Elder law: saving your life savings. *Washington Post/Health* 1996; July 23: 16.
16. US Department of Health and Human Services. *CDC Fact Book 2000/2001.* Atlanta, GA: Centers for Disease Control, 2000: 53.
17. De Lew N. Overview: 40th anniversary of Medicare and Medicaid. *Health Care Financ Rev* 2005–2006; 27: 5,8.
18. Causes of Social Security's Financial Problems. *Congressional Record* 1977; October 1: S18383.

19. US Department of Health and Human Services. *National Health Care Expenditures Data*. Centers for Medicare and Medicaid Services. Washington, DC: Office of Actuary, National Health Statistics Group, 2008.
20. Eaton W J. Doctor glut seen hiking health costs. *Boston Evening Globe* 1977; June 29: 10.
21. Brown D. Recruiters offer doctors a small town 'option'. *Washington Post* 1991; October 6.
22. McConnaughey J. Doctors for rural areas are sought. *Washington Post* 2005; January 30: A13.
23. Hearn W. On the outskirts. *Am Med News* 1996; July 1: 13.
24. Physician shortages. *Health Aff* 2003; 4: 260–262.
25. American Medical Association. *Physician Master File*. Chicago, IL: American Medical Association, 2000.
26. Cauchon D. Medical miscalculation creates doctor shortage. *USA Today* 2005; March 2.
27. US Department of Health and Human Resources. *Physician Workforce Policy Guidelines for the US for 2000–2020*. Rockville, MD: Council on Graduate Medical Education, 2005.
28. US Department of Health and Human Services. *Physician Supply and Demand Projections to 2020*. Washington, DC: Health Resources and Services Administration, 2006.
29. US Department of Labor. *Occupational Outlook Handbook, 2008–2009*. Bureau of Labor Statistics, Pharmacists; available online at http://www.bls.gov/oco/ocos079.htm; accessed on March 24, 2008.
30. Dunham W. US healthcare system pinched by nursing shortage. Reuters 2009; March 8; available online at: http://www.reuters.com/article/domesticNews/idUSTRES5270VC2 0090 308; accessed on March 8, 2009.
31. Somers HM. Health economics. *Publ Health News* 1969; November: 245.
32. Counterattack launched by AMA's Dr. Sammons. *Am Med News* 1977; June 27/ July 4: 21.
33. National health care conference on health care costs. *Congressional Record* 1977; June 18: S12206.
34. An J, Saloner R, Ranji U. *US Health Care Costs: Background Brief*. Menlo Park, CA: Henry J. Kaiser Family Foundation, 2008.

4

Physician care

Introduction

By tradition, the medical profession is the centerpiece of the health care system. It has a principal role in the delivery of medical care, whether it is delivered in a hospital, an office, or a community-based setting. It has the final responsibility for accurate diagnosis and treatment of disease. When a patient visits a physician, it is the doctor who decides when the patient returns, what other medical services or medical specialists the patient requires, what drugs the patient needs, whether hospitalization or another kind of institutionalization is necessary, and for how long. In addition, the physician often supervises other health care personnel, frequently is the focus of reimbursement under health insurance plans, and contributes to the formulation of our national health policies.

As of 1999, the USA had 29.1 active physicians (doctors of medicine and doctors of osteopathy) for each 10 000 population. According to the American Medical Association, as of 2000 there were an estimated 813 770 physicians in the USA.[1] Of this number there were about 473 431 in office-based practice and 157 032 in hospital-based patient care. Almost one-third practiced as a primary care generalist (33.7%) and a much smaller number as a primary care specialist (6.4%). By 2004, according to the US National Center for Health Statistics there were 24 active, nonfederal patient care physicians per 10 000 population, whose numbers totaled 707 380.[2]

The largest number of physicians practiced internal medicine, followed by family practice.[3] Yet, millions of Americans live in communities that still lack a doctor. In fact, as of 2005, one-fifth of the US population – about 60 million persons – lived in rural areas spread over 80% of the country. In counties with a population of less than 10 000 there were far fewer doctors per capita than in urban and rural areas.[4,5] According to the National Health Service Corps, the shortage of doctors in rural America has led the federal government to designate such areas as health professional shortage areas and, according to the US Office of Rural Health Policy, 10% of doctors live in rural areas.[5,6]

The American physician in today's ever-changing health care system faces a variety of problems that affect the economics of health care as well as the quality of care Americans receive. Some of these include medical malpractice insurance, methods of physician reimbursement, shortages of physician manpower, managed care, and other issues. So let us look at some of these issues that the medical profession currently confronts and how they affect the cost of care throughout the health care system.

Manpower

The American health care system faces a potential shortage of physicians at a time when millions of baby boomers are about to reach retirement age and seek more medical care for illnesses that the aging process brings on. Some experts state that the country needs to train 3000, others say 7000, and still others state up to 10 000 more physicians each year – an increase from the present 25 000 – to meet the increasing needs of an aging, wealthy nation. Because the training of a physician can take 10 years, the USA is expected to have a shortage of 85 000 and some authorities claim up to 200 000 physicians in 2020 unless action is taken in the near future.[7] This situation is in direct contrast to predictions that were being made at the end of the 20th century. In 1994, the *Journal of the American Medical Association* predicted a surplus of 165 000 doctors by 2000.[7] It is predicted that unless the USA begins to train more medical students soon, the supply of physicians will begin to decrease around 2015, when doctors from the baby boom generation begin to retire from active practice. The Council on Graduate Medical Education, a group Congress created to recommend the number of physicians the nation needs, and its predecessor organization have been very important since the 1980s in efforts to restrict, rather than increase, the supply of physicians. Now the Council has altered its policy and recommends that 3000 more doctors a year be trained in US medical schools by 2015. In the 1960s and 1970s the USA dramatically expanded the number of doctors being trained, creating two new physicians for every doctor who retired, but the production of new doctors has not varied greatly since 1985. Today, new physicians approximately equal the number of physicians who are retiring. However, by 2015 or 2016 the baby boom physicians who were licensed in the 1960s, 1970s, and 1980s will begin retiring in numbers that will exceed the 25 000 new doctors presently produced every year, as already noted. In addition, because doctors work shorter hours today, the effective number of doctors who are available to provide care will decline even more.

The number of physicians a nation produces is not like the workforce marketplace that produces other kinds of professionals. The number of doctors available to the nation is a political decision in which doctors have a very great influence in terms of the ultimate decision. It is the US Congress that controls the supply of physicians by how much federal funding it provides for medical residencies – the graduate training that is required of doctors. To become a physician, students attend medical school for 4 years, do an internship, and then for those who wish more training, up to 7 years training as residents, treating patients under supervision at a hospital. Residents worked long hours for $35 000–$50 000 a year in 2005. Even doctors trained in other countries must serve medical residencies in the USA to practice here.

Medicare, which pays for the health care services of the elderly, also has an influence in controlling the supply of physicians because it reimburses hospitals for the cost of training doctors. In 1997, to save money and prevent an oversupply of physicians, Congress placed a limit on the number of residents for which Medicare will pay and set the limit at 80 000 residents a year. But, Medicare is going to face tremendous economic pressures in the future as baby boomers are added to its current rolls and the number of those in the workforce under age 65 who will be supporting an ever-increasing number of the elderly declines. By 2005, Medicare was already spending 3% of its budget training physicians and may not have the resources to spend more. Another 20 000 residents are financed by the US Veterans Administration and Medicaid, the state–federal health care program for the poor. Teaching hospitals also pay for a small number of residents without government assistance. The US government spends about $11 billion annually on 100 000 medical residents or about $110 000 per resident. According to estimates of the Medicare program, the portion of US income that is spent on health care has increased from 8.8% in 1980 to 15.4% in 2004 and will reach 18.7% in 2014.[8]

Even the demographic characteristics of the US medical profession have contributed to the need for more physicians. Almost one-half of new physicians are women and studies show they work an average of 25% fewer hours than their male counterparts, according to Richard Cooper, director of the Health Policy Institute at the Medical College of Wisconsin.[7] In addition, physicians who are older than age 55 work about 15% less than younger doctors, and medical residents have been limited to 80-hour weeks since 2003, ending decades of 100-plus-hour weeks. Even more of a concern is the fact that the retirement of baby boom physicians means that the number of doctors will begin declining just as the first baby boomers turns 70 in 2016, according to Ed Salsberg, a workforce specialist at the Association of American Medical Colleges.[7] Again, all these scenarios affect the availability of health care services to the general population and the quality of services they may be receiving. Worsening the shortage of physicians is the fact that the USA stopped opening new medical schools in the 1980s because of the predicted surplus of physicians. However, in 2005 the Association of American Medical Colleges recommended increasing the number of American medical schools by 15%.

Because physicians are in short supply, they tend to locate where they wish to live rather than where the greatest number of patients are. Especially in short supply are the traditional old-fashioned specialists like general surgeons, radiologists, and anesthesiologists because the newer physicians prefer cutting-edge medicine as in radiology where catheters are used to treat cancer rather than traditional radiology. But not everyone agrees that there is a physician shortage. Some medical policy specialists argue that the USA has enough doctors but their distribution, as already noted, is poor. Some attribute the poor distribution to the fact that doctors seek out higher-paying practices – such as sports medicine – that serve the wealthy and the insured at the expense of Medicare and others. Still others worry that if the nation acts upon the belief that there is a shortage of doctors, the addition of more doctors means that the costs of medical care will also rise, not make it less expensive and more accessible.

Medical care does not follow the traditional rules of the economic marketplace. When the price of an airline ticket reaches an exorbitant amount for what the consumer wishes to pay consumers have alternative substitutes such as railroads, buses, and other modes of transportation if they do not wish to pay that amount to fly. But in medicine, there really is no substitute for medical treatment. The choice is to receive it or not receive it, accepting whatever consequences may result from the latter choice. Thus, some believe that additional physicians mean that the overall costs of medical care will be greater because additional physicians will result in the ordering of more medical tests, more procedures, and more drugs – without necessarily resulting in any improvement in the nation's health. One of the reasons for higher medical costs is that some experts state that doctors can create their own demand and too many doctors may mean a less efficient system. Medicine has been described as the only business where consumers visit a physician, do not know before they visit or, perhaps, even understand the services they need to buy when in the doctor's presence, do not select the services they are purchasing, and when they leave the physician's office do not pay the whole cost of the purchase, if any, but have someone else – a third party – pay the bill for them. This latter description is not unique to the profession of medicine. Similarly, in the business model of the law clients also have the same lack of knowledge in regard to that of the lawyer, the services needed, and bear the risk of a negative outcome with no assurances guaranteed.

As examples, let us examine two important specialties, geriatricians and primary care physicians. The USA has a shortage of geriatric care physicians. One of the reasons is that salaries are lower in this field than for other specialties. As of 2007, there were fewer than 7000 geriatricians in the country – one for about every 5000 people age 65 years or older – but, according to experts, about 14 000 are needed to meet the demands of the elderly. And the shortages are expected to worsen as baby boomers age and require the care of these specialists. In addition, many medical schools have inadequate training in geriatrics because they often have assumed that students will learn about geriatrics by treating older patients on hospital rounds. As a result, some physicians do not understand the different needs of an elderly patient. With the shortage expected to worsen, geriatricians may have to be reserved for elderly persons with very complicated problems, while internists and family practice physicians will continue to serve the rest of the elderly. Geriatricians specialize in managing chronic medical conditions rather than in curing them. For example, one of the keys to taking care of the elderly is a thorough knowledge of drugs. Many older people take medications prescribed by different doctors, so geriatricians generally look for possibilities of what they can do with fewer medications rather than constantly adding more. Sometimes the best solution to a problem is no medicine at all. Most geriatric clinics affiliated with hospital centers accept Medicare payments, while some geriatricians in private practice do not. According to some geriatricians, since Medicare does not have a reimbursement code for geriatric assessments, most payments to doctors represent a portion of their costs. Basically, what this means is that, unlike many services that Medicare does cover, the program does not have a specific amount of money that will pay a physician who provides a geriatric assessment of the patient. Therefore, the payment the physician receives from Medicare may not cover the costs the physician assumes in providing this service. If the payment is less than the physician's expenses for such a service, a physician conceivably could decide not to provide the service any more, to the detriment of a patient's health.

As another example, according to the American Academy of Family Physicians, the number of medical students selecting to practice internal medicine is declining and more must be done to generate their interest. In the winter of 2007, the New York chapter of the American College of Physicians released a report that stated that 20% of third-year internal medicine residents in the USA planned to pursue careers in general internal medicine in 2005, compared with 54% in 1998.[8] In fact, by 2006, only 13% of first-year residents in internal medicine stated that they intended to pursue a career in general practice. Internal medicine, along with pediatrics and general and family practice, constitutes primary care. By 2008 at least 56 million Americans, almost one in five of the population, were 'medically disenfranchised,' having inadequate access to primary care physicians because of a shortage in their areas – according to *Access Denied*, a county-by-county study by the National Association of Community Health Centers and the Robert Graham Center,[9] a research group that focuses on primary care. Among Medicare beneficiaries, about 3% – more than 1.3 million people – have difficulty in finding a new primary care physician, a government survey found in 2007. One of the factors that distinguishes primary care physicians from others is the fact that they are the first contact for the patient. They make the initial health assessment and attempt to solve as many of the patient's health problems as possible. Moreover, they are responsible for coordinating the remainder of the health care team who serve the patient (including consultants, when necessary) and provide continued contact with the patient in acting as an adviser, confidant, and advocate. Yet, the stresses under which primary care physicians practice in the USA are very great. They earn, on average, about one-half or one-third of those doctors who practice in other specialties, yet their work days are longer and the overhead of their medical practice is higher. They must spend many hours on paperwork and telephone calls to receive prior treatment authorization which insurance companies demand – all of which reduces the amount of time they can spend with individual patients, accepting as many patients as possible to remain in practice. All these factors make the practice of primary care medicine less attractive than other medical specialties which may be less demanding of a physician's time and effort, in addition to the fact that the costs of medical education are so expensive that students feel they must specialize to pay back their loans more quickly.

As a consequence of the previous factors, despite the large number of physicians in this country, whether they are primary care physicians or other specialists, access to medical care services, which varies among different segments of our population, continues to be a basic problem. The shortage of physicians in primary care as well as other specialties in a community, as already noted, is not the only reason that affects access to medical care but also there are other factors such as the distances patients must sometimes travel to receive medical treatment and the lengthy time patients must wait before receiving a medical appointment. In addition, many patients have little or no access to the more specialized medical services they require because accurate diagnoses and timely referrals do not always occur readily or soon enough at the primary care levels. This situation may worsen in the future. In November 2008, the Physicians Foundation, founded in 2003 as part of a settlement in an antiracketeering lawsuit against physicians, medical societies, and the insurer Aetna, surveyed 270 000 primary care physicians and 50 000 practicing specialists, of whom 12 000 answered, which the group felt was representative of doctors as a whole, with the survey having a 1% margin of error. Eleven percent of the respondents said they plan to retire and 13% stated they plan to seek a job that removes them from active patient care. Twenty percent said they will cut back on patients seen and 10% plan to move to part-time work, a total percentage representing nearly one-half of the physicians surveyed.[10,11] All these access problems result from a physician shortage, whether it is due to actual numbers, a maldistribution of those numbers, or a lack of student interest in a particular medical specialty.

More than two decades of accumulated evidence reveals that having a primary care-based health system is important. People and countries with adequate access to primary care realize a number of health and economic benefits. These include reduced all-cause mortality as well as mortality caused by cardiovascular and pulmonary diseases; less use of emergency departments and hospitals; better preventive care; better detection of breast cancer; and reduced incidence and mortality caused by colon and cervical cancer. In addition, there is evidence of efficiency in having a primary care system including fewer tests, higher patient satisfaction, less medication use, and lower care-related costs. There is also evidence of equity including reduced health disparities, particularly for areas with the highest income inequality, including improved vision, more complete immunization, better blood pressure control, and better oral health.[12] All these reasons and more are why the decline in the number of primary care physicians must be reversed if the health of the US population is to be maintained and improved.

Physician reimbursement

Now whether a physician practices as a solo practitioner, in a group practice, in a health maintenance organization (HMO), preferred provider organization (PPO), or accepts the formula by which Medicare calculates his/her practice reimbursement, the manner in which the physician accepts payment can affect the quality of health care the physician delivers and whether the physician will accept someone as a patient at all. A good example is the Medicare program. As already noted, there is a shortage of primary care physicians in the USA. One of the major reasons claimed is that Medicare's payment structure has made subspecialty practices much more financially lucrative for physicians, which is one of the reasons why there is a decline in the number of students who are deciding to practice as primary care physicians. As of 2007, under Medicare, primary care physicians were paid far less than subspecialties – about $82 per half-hour for evaluation and management services compared to $683 per half-hour for cataract surgery by eye physician. According to Dr. Kevin Grumbach,[13] professor and chair of the department of family and community medicine at the University of California, San Francisco, the USA, still suffers from a maldistribution of physicians and these shortages affect rural areas and inner cities. Dr. Grumbach has noted that the supply of subspecialties has not brought about lower costs and better outcomes – rather the reverse has happened, in that higher costs have resulted and health outcomes have fallen short of what primary care physicians achieve in the geographic areas. In contrast to subspecialties, authorities state that primary care physicians contribute to a high quality of care and better health outcomes. However, despite this fact of the benefits of primary care, in September 2008 the *Journal of the American Medical Association* published the results of a 2007 survey of almost 1200 fourth-year medical students which found that only 2% planned to work in primary care internal medicine.[14] The salary gap between primary care physicians and other medical subspecialties such as cardiology or gastroenterology may be one reason, given the huge amount of debt medical students incur and must pay back (an average of about

$140 000 in 2007 according to the Association of American Colleges) but the paperwork, the demands of the chronically ill, and the need to bring work home are among the other factors that are causing young physicians to spurn careers in primary care.[13,14]

For 25 years after Medicare became operational in 1966, the physician's payment under Medicare was based on a system of customary, prevailing, and reasonable (CPR) charges. Between the mid-1970s and the mid-1980s, the US government implemented a series of CPR cost controls. A few examples include price freezes, annual price increase limits, and price incentives for primary care services and for improving beneficiary access to care. More specifically, in 1975 these efforts included the institution of the Medicare Economic Index as a limit on increases in prevailing charges; in 1984 the participating physician program began, providing incentives for physicians to accept Medicare assignment; in 1987 the maximum allowable actual charge limits began and restricted the amount nonparticipating program physicians could charge Medicare (that is, physician who did not accept Medicare fee assignment as payment in full); on April 1, 1988 the US Congress instituted the reduction in prevailing charges for a group of over-priced procedures such as hip replacement, coronary artery bypass graft, cataract extraction, knee arthroscopy, pacemaker insertion, and carpal tunnel release; and in 1989 fee schedules were instituted for radiology and in 1990 for anesthesiology. More specifically, the major effect of the price controls was to make permanent the basic pattern of Medicare prevailing charges that existed in the early 1970s.

In the mid-1980s, physicians became increasingly dissatisfied with the CPR concept. As a result, government policymakers considered several payment reform proposals, including replacing the CPR with a payment schedule which is based on relative value scale. This scale is resource-based and is also known as resource-based relative value scale (RBRVS). Prior to the passage of the Omnibus Budget Reconciliation Act of 1989 and the effective date of January 1, 1992, when Medicare's Part B fee schedule became a reality, physician payments under the Medicare program were made through a payment methodology based on the historical charges of physicians. Simply stated, Medicare's payment methodology until that date specified that the allowed charge for a physician's service is the lowest of the billed (submitted) charge, the customary charge of the physician, or the prevailing charge in the pricing locality. Customary-charge pricing screens were a major determinant in Medicare's establishment of reasonable prices for physician services. According to the Omnibus Budget Reconciliation Act of 1980 (PL 96-499), reasonable charges were determined by a fee schedule in effect on the date the service was rendered rather than the date the Medicare claim for that service was processed.

When President George H. W. Bush signed into law the Omnibus Budget Reconciliation Act of 1989, Medicare changed from the CPR to a RBRVS schedule. Medicare and almost all HMOs presently use this system. The RBRVS is a system that determines how much money medical providers should receive. RBRVS assigns to procedures which a physician or other medical providers perform a relative value which is adjusted by geographic region (so a procedure performed in Boston, Massachusetts is worth more than a procedure performed in Raleigh, North Carolina). This value is then multiplied by a fixed conversion factor, which changes annually, to determine the payment amount. The new payment system separates into three parts the resources that are required to produce physician services: physician work, practice expenses, and malpractice insurance. A distinct relative value is estimated for each of the components and the combined relative value is used to calculate the fee schedule amount. Medicare pays the lesser of the actual billed charge or the fee schedule amount. As an illustration, let us make up an example. Let us say in the year 2007 that a generic 10 000 current procedural terminology (CPT) code was worth 2.0 relative value units or RVUs. Adjusted for a geographic area of Massachusetts, let us say it was worth slightly higher, 3.0 RVUs. Using a fictitious 2007 conversion of $40.00, Medicare paid 3 × $40.00 for each procedure performed or $120. Actually, most specialties charge 200–400% of Medicare rates for their procedures and collected between 50% and 80% of those charges, after contractual and other write-offs.

Beginning in 1991, the American Medical Association constantly updates the RBRVS. Since the American Medical Association owns the copyright to the CPT codes, a CPT editorial committee develops the procedure codes by which physicians charge for their services. Another committee, the Relative Value Update Committee (the RUC), determines the resource-based relative value for each new code and revalues all existing codes once every 5 years. Again, three distinct elements determine the RBRVS for each CPT code. These include physician work (including physician's time, mental effort, technical skill, judgment, stress, and an amortization of the physician's education), the practice expense, and malpractice expenses. The RUC analyzes each new code to determine a relative value by comparing the physician work of the new code to the physician work involved in existing codes. The practice expense, determined by the Practice Expense Review Committee, is made up of the direct expenses related to supplies and nonphysician labor used in providing the service, and the pro rata cost of equipment used. In addition, there is an amount included for the indirect expense. In the development of RBRVS the physician's work, practice expense, and malpractice expenses are included in the result. As noted, the calculation of the fee is adjusted by geography but does not include adjustments for outcomes, quality of service, severity, or demand.

In 1997 the Balanced Budget Act established the sustainable growth rate (SGR) system to control Medicare physician spending. The SGR system limits the amount by which total physician spending is permitted to grow each year by establishing annual spending targets.[15] For fee-for-service physician payment Medicare assigns each type of service an RVU, and multiplies this RVU by a monetary conversion factor to arrive at the Medicare-approved fee for each type of service. By adjusting the conversion factor, Congress can manipulate total Medicare physician expenditures on an annual basis. The SGR policy requires Congress to keep the increase in total physician expenditures within the target range of spending. Each year, if the total amount of money that a physician bills to Medicare exceeds the SGR target, Congress is supposed to reduce the conversion factor for the following year to keep the Medicare physician spending at the target amount. However, pressured by the physician lobby, Congress has repeatedly overridden the SGR targets and has not permitted the conversion factor to decrease as much as the SGR formula has stipulated. Between 1997 and 2006, annual Medicare expenditures for physician services nearly doubled, increasing from $49.2 billion to $93.7 billion. If Congress had held Medicare physician expenditures to the SGR targets, Medicare physician spending from 1997 to 2006 would have increased by 66% rather than 90%. Instead, the actual 2006 Medicare spending of $93.7 billion far surpasses the $81.1 billion specified by the SGR approach.

The SGR approach has contributed to the widening gap in earnings between specialist and primary care physicians, an income gap that is a major contributor to the number of physicians not entering primary care, at the expense of the patients who need their care and treatment.[16] While all these laws may seem technical, they are true everyday concerns to the practicing physician because they have an impact on the physician's financial ability to provide medical care services to the patients who need them. Between 2006 and 2013 reductions in Medicare payments were to total 31%, although such cuts have been forestalled. But if the reductions are adjusted to practice cost inflation, the American Medical Association says Medicare payments to physician in 2013 would be less than half of what they were in 1991. 'If we can't fix this, the impact on physicians and physician practices is going to be devastating,' said Alan C. Woodward, MD, president of the Massachusetts Medical Society. Many practices are barely surviving now.'[16]

When taken together with the ongoing problem of increasing medical liability costs, Medicare reimbursement is a very important issue for the viability of physician medical practices. Failure to solve the Medicare reimbursement and cost problem will only endanger older patients' access to needed health care services, according to Dr. Woodward.[16] This is relevant not only because low payments are one of the principal reasons for the decreasing numbers of primary care physicians but also they are enhancing the shortage of geriatricians and spurring on the refusal of some physicians to accept additional Medicare patients because of the low payment rates. This scenario is occurring at a time when there is about to be an explosion of baby boomers joining the Medicare program, as already noted, and the elderly are living longer with more costly illnesses that shorter life spans did not engender. In fact, on June 12, 2008, the US government announced that life expectancy in the USA surpassed 78 years, although the USA continues to lag behind about 30 other countries in estimated life span. The numbers refer to 2006 and are mainly due to declining mortality rates for nine of the 15 leading causes of death, including heart disease, cancer, accident, and diabetes.

But in view of the problems that the current Medicare payment system engenders, Michael Leavitt, Secretary of Health and Human Services under President George W. Bush, envisioned another kind of medical practice and payment system in the future. He saw a medical marketplace in which families are able to obtain specific information about treatment success and prices of hospitals and doctors and can shop at will for the best quality and most affordable care. Under his tenure the groundwork was laid. A legislative mandate for the following demonstrations was included in the 2000 Medicare, Medicaid, and State Child Health Insurance Program Benefits Improvement and Protection Act. Ten group practices – multispecialty clinics and hospitals – around the USA have begun to measure the outcomes of alternative treatment models for common diseases and Medicare is paying them not by volume of patients or office visits but for outcomes. Medicare is linking its own evaluation results to those of the 10 groups, building a database from which national standards could be derived. Secretary Leavitt sees a system in which the best practices would be defined by national groups of physicians and business economists but it would be local committees which would perform the ratings of doctors and hospitals.

Groups of business, labor, physicians, hospitals, and other key players are beginning to be established in various communities. When there are enough of them, linked electronically in a network of networks, the USA will have, in effect, national standards for measuring the delivery of care. Secretary Leavitt's view was that the government should not own health care, but rather organize the health care marketplace and then let competition based on complete information follow.[17]

This concept of pay for performance in the 21st century has slowly begun to supersede the policy tool of choice to control rising health costs, namely managed care with capitation payments. An explicit emphasis on health care quality was basically absent, as the administrative focus was on cost per member/per month and provider organizations that competed with each other to capture market share. In the 21st century, capitation has to some extent receded as the payment tool of preference as new concepts have appeared throughout the health care marketplace. Health care is seen as entering an age in which both quality and efficiency are paramount in the purchase and delivery of this service. Taken together, the dual goals of quality and efficiency lead to a key concept, pay for performance, otherwise known as value-based purchasing.[18]

Now, as already noted, the cost control concept that pay for performance hopes to replace one day in the 21st century is managed care. Under managed care, which includes HMOs, preferred provider plans, exclusive provider organizations and others, physicians are paid by various methods. In a staff HMO physicians receive a salary. In a group HMO, the plan pays the physician group a negotiated per-capita rate that is distributed by the group among its physicians. In independent practice associations physicians maintain their own independent offices or come together as an association of independent practitioners and contract with the plan to provide services on either a fee-for-service basis or a negotiated rate per capita. In a network model, the plan contracts with two or more independent group practices and pays a fixed monthly fee per enrollee to the group, which disburses the payment among physicians.

Unlike HMOs, PPOs operate on a fee-for-service basis and patients are not locked into using the PPO physician or hospital. There is also a private fee-for-service plan (PFSP) that was authorized by the Balanced Budget Act of 1997 for physicians as an alternative to HMOs. The PFSP pays providers directly without a network. Services received under the PFSP are independent of the services received under Medicare. Patients receive services from other providers who accept Medicare. The plan reimburses doctors, hospitals, and other providers on a fee-for-service basis at a rate determined by the plan, not at the Medicare rate. Providers are also free to charge patients more than 115% of Medicare-approved charges. Again, one of the chief criticisms of HMOs relates to their method of reimbursement. Critics state that HMOs may skimp on care and encourage physicians to see patients as little as possible because physicians are paid an established annual fee no matter how many appointments the patient makes. Therefore, the fewer tests the physician orders and the fewer appointments the physician makes to see a patient, the less he/she works on the patient's behalf, is able to keep his/her expenses to a minimum, and when the payment the physician receives for the patient exceeds the costs of treatment, the health plan makes a profit. Despite such savings by a plan, of course, there are many who like HMOs because with the removal of the burden to pay for each physician office visit, people tend to seek treatment earlier, often allowing a disease to be detected at its most curable stage before it worsens and possibly requires hospitalization.

As can be noted from the previous discussion, physician reimbursement rates and their formats, whether they are public like Medicare or private like HMOs, can have a dramatic effect on the health care field. Reimbursement rates represent more than just personal income to a physician. They affect the training of new physicians to meet a possible national shortage; they influence physicians in their choice of specialty; they affect the distribution of physicians as to where they wish to practice in the country, causing a maldistribution of physicians in inner-city and rural areas; and they also create the possibility that physicians may turn away new Medicare patients because the rates are too low for the physician to maintain the economic viability of the practice in treating Medicare patients who are at stage in life where they may require medical care services the most.

Medical malpractice

As already noted, one element in the calculation of the fees a physician receives under the Medicare RBRVS system is the expense of the physician's medical malpractice insurance. This issue continues to be a festering problem for the medical profession, again affecting patient care because when physicians feels they can no longer afford the insurance, they may move to another state where the costs are lower or even in some cases close up their practice, both of which are detrimental to patients' well-being. In 1999 insurers paid out $4 billion for malpractice in the USA. An estimated 25% of practicing physicians are sued annually for medical malpractice and about 50–65% are sued at least once during their career. The majority of the cases involve misdiagnoses, diagnostic errors, or delayed diagnoses and only 10–20% of malpractice claims ever reach the trial phase.[19] According to the US Department of Justice, in 2001 nearly 50% of malpractice trials were against surgeons and 33% against nonsurgeons in 75 of the largest counties in the USA, with plaintiffs winning 27% of medical malpractice cases.[20] As of 2008, the top five diseases that receive monetary awards for malpractice, in terms of dollar value, include breast cancer, lung cancer, colorectal cancer (including colon and rectal cancer), heart attack, and appendicitis.

In order to understand the conditions that lead to malpractice litigation, it is first necessary to define it. The 1971-appointed HEW Secretary's Commission on Medical Malpractice (US Department of Health, Education, and Welfare) has offered one definition. This body stated that medical malpractice is an injury to a patient which is caused by the negligence of the health care provider. The malpractice 'claim' itself is an allegation, with or without foundation, that an injury was caused by negligence. 'Injury' implies either physical or mental harm which occurs in the course of medical care, whether or not it is caused by negligence. Consequently, compensation to patients for malpractice claims requires proof of both injury and professional negligence.

The environment in which the physician practices today is conducive to medical malpractice suits. In fact, 191 804 medical malpractice reports were made to the National Practitioner Data Bank (NPDB) regarding physicians in the USA between 1990 and 2004.[21] The NPDB is a very restricted electronic federal government file which was established by Congress as part of the Health Care Quality Improvement Act of 1986 (42 USC 11101, *et seq.*). In addition to the names of other professional health practitioners like dentists, the NPDB contains the names of thousands of physicians who, for example, have been involved in medical malpractice suit payments, were disciplined by state medical boards, or had professional society membership actions taken against them based on reasons relating to professional competency and conduct as well as certain actions restricting clinical privileges, Medicare and Medicaid exclusions, and US Drug Enforcement Administration actions. Only hospital medical boards and similar health providers can check on information in the data bank. While doctors can check on themselves, they cannot check on other doctors.

As more and more people obtain the means to finance health care, whether it is through public programs like Medicare or Medicaid or through the expansion of private heath insurance plans, a larger number of people are able to pay for their physician's medical services. The more they are able to pay for their medical care, the more they can afford to visit their physician. In fact, there were an estimated 944.1 million ambulatory care visits made in 1999. Of these visits, 756.7 million were to physicians' office, 102.8 million to hospital emergency rooms, and 84.6 million to hospital outpatient departments. Most visits were to office-based physicians, accounting for 80.2% of all ambulatory care. Visits to the emergency room represented 10.9%, followed by hospital outpatient departments at 9.0%.[22] The more patients visit their doctor, the greater is the number of patient–physician contacts. The greater the number of patient–physician contacts, the more hurried and more impersonal may be the physician's attention to each patent. In fact, physicians averaged in the USA 19.3 minutes of contact time per person during each office encounter in visits in 2000.[22] The more hurried the doctor's attention, the greater is the risk that he/she may make mistakes in diagnosis and treatment, especially given the complexity of medical technologies and the nature of the new miracle drugs. The greater these risks, the greater the chances of a malpractice suit. With the increased chances of a malpractice suit, the premium rates will be higher, or the rates the insurance carrier will charge the physician to cover the costs of the insurance will rise. Regardless of whether the physician wins or loses a malpractice lawsuit, he/she still has to pay the lawyer's fees and other expenses directly or more usually through his/her insurance carrier, which will either demand higher malpractice insurance premiums or else cancel the physician's coverage. And the higher the premiums, the more the physician has to charge the patient to cover the cost of the insurance. The higher the medical bills (of which malpractice insurance is but one of many cost items), the more the public complains that health insurance has become a service which it no longer can afford. With increased public complaint, there is more of a cry for additional government intervention into the health field. And the more the government intervenes, the more it undertakes measures such as expanding existing programs, creating new plans for those who have difficulty purchasing medical care, or increasing public regulation over health care providers in an attempt to reduce their own service costs. The more the government undertakes such measures, the more health costs increase as health care providers comply with additional government regulations and as more people are able to pay for their medical care, the more often they can visit their doctor to receive treatment and we are back to the very first step of this dilemma relating to medical malpractice suits which are factored into the payment rates physicians receive under Medicare.

On the other hand, if a physician tries to reduce the cost of medical practice by dropping malpractice insurance (also known as 'going bare'), the physician may administer medical tests for his/her own legal protection which a patient does not need. This kind of practice is known as 'defensive medicine.' In this fashion, the physician drives up the cost of the medical bill, in particular, and health care, in general. On the other hand, the physician may become more cautious in treating patients and cut back on ordering procedures, which may result in a malpractice suit being filed against him/her if such procedures are improperly administered. And even if public or private programs did not exist to help an individual purchase medical care or did not cover a wide variety of services, a patient still might need a particular medical service. If a patient has to be in nursing home, that need exists regardless of the availability of nursing home coverage which may pay for all or part of the patient's care through either public or private programs. And if patients have to pay for their medical service with their own funds, they may not be able to afford such care. So again, we have a situation where the public demands that some kind of mechanism be created to help it pay for health care. Thus, public and private programs are established to provide financial protection against the cost of ill health. And, again, the public can pay for its medical care and visit the doctor more often than when assistance did not exist. So once again we are back to the very first steps of the scenario where the increasing demand for doctor's services could lead to hurried attention, which could result in misdiagnoses or mistreatment which, in turn, could result in the patient's filing of a medical malpractice.

What does all this mean? Simply stated, the rising costs of health care services, of which malpractice suits are just one of many contributing factors, is an issue whose many components defy a singular solution. But malpractice insurance costs do contribute to the rising costs of health care. They are certainly an element in figuring out Medicare reimbursement to physicians which, in turn, affects whether a physician will continue to accept Medicare beneficiaries as patients and who need treatment at critical moments in their lives. In regard to premium costs, malpractice insurance does influence the geographic area where physicians practice, which, in turn, affects whether a jurisdiction has a shortage or sufficient supply of physicians to meet the public's needs. However, there are health authorities that believe that reorganizing and restructuring the health care system into an integrated, rationale, and coordinated whole, or establishing a universal national health insurance plan will accomplish the goals of bringing control over health care costs, improve access to health for millions who may not have it or have it with some difficulty, and improve the quality of care the American public currently receives.

Practice patterns

In providing care to the American public, physician practice has gone through many evolutions. Initially, there was the solo practitioner who evolved into group practice and prepaid group practices such as in HMOs and then into PPOs and its several permutations, and the latest evolution of convenience care clinics in retail outlets which cater to those who wish to avoid long waiting room times, problems in scheduling doctor appointments, and high medical prices. These clinics have licensed physician oversight and are managed by nurse practitioners and physician assistants and maintain their own on-site laboratory clinics as well as private examination rooms.

While convenience care clinics are beginning to develop, other physicians are returning to medicine's roots: the solo practitioner or micropractice where physicians can now spend 30–60 minutes with a patient instead of 15 minutes, as in group practice, where physicians find themselves rushed in treating patients because of having to pay for the overhead of support staff, an office manager, someone to deal with all the government regulations, and other personnel. What makes the return to solo practice manageable is that there is now computer software that allows doctors to schedule appointments online. These are largely paperless offices. Patients can also access their own health charts online. Doctors can do their insurance billings or subscribe to services that do it for them. Federally approved laboratory equipment for the basics – such as blood and liver tests – is small and inexpensive. A brand new basic electrocardiogram machine, for example, retailed for about $2500 in 2008; used ones sold for much less on eBay, the internet auction website. For doctors beginning a micropractice, it means it's just the doctors, a small office, an examination table, and basic laboratory equipment.[23]

Another form of medical practice that has become more prevalent is called 'boutique' medicine or concierge medicine. This trend began in the 1990s as a reaction to what some doctors see as the excess of managed care. Under concierge care, doctors generally reduce the size of their practice so they can expand patient visits to 30 minutes, compared to about 7–16 minutes that various studies have shown to be the average under managed care. In addition to their annual retainers, doctors also collect the usual fees-for-service or reimbursements from their patients' health insurance plans. The doctor also accepts Medicare patients. Proponents say concierge care allows doctors to provide their patients with the time and services they require, and allows them to concentrate more on preventive medicine. Critics say that the development of concierge care only worsens the inequalities in the American health care system by limiting access and increasing the workload of physicians who do not join this movement. For an annual fee to receive concierge care, let us say $1500, physicians say they offer more attention to the patient, perhaps including round-the-clock cell phone service, same-day appointments, and time to accompany their patients to specialists. In a policy statement about this movement, the American Medical Association said that, while retainer contracts offer viable options for care, 'they also raise ethical concerns that warrant careful attention, especially if retainer practices become so widespread as to threaten access to care.'[24] As of 2009, no one knows what impact the 1000 or so retainer or concierge physicians have had on medical practice because they are so few in number compared to the more than 280 000 primary care physicians nationwide.

As another example, there is beginning to emerge a form of care called 'patient-centered medical homes.' The concept was originally introduced by the American Academy of Pediatrics in 1967, evolving from a specific place where children with chronic illness can receive care to providing care for all Americans. The goal of a medical home is for patients to have a continuous relationship with a personal physician who leads a team of caregivers that coordinate care. The approach would permit more time for patients, especially those beset with multiple chronic illnesses. The physician's compensation would be linked to meeting certain standards and bundled into a 'care coordination' fee for each patient. Patients would be able to ask questions by e-mail or telephone and make appointments at short notice. That is the idealistic goal. As of 2009, Medicare, Medicaid, and some insurers were experimenting with pilot projects. In 2007, the American Academy of Family Physicians, American Academy of Pediatrics, American College of Physicians, and American Osteopathic Association – the principal primary care physician organizations – released the Joint Principles of the patient-centered medical home whose characteristics are as follows:

- *Personal relationship*: Each patient has an ongoing relationship with a personal physician trained to provide first contact, continuous, and comprehensive care.
- *Team approach*: The personal physician leads a team of individuals at the practice level who collectively take responsibility for ongoing patient care.

- *Comprehensive*: The personal physician is responsible for providing all the patient's health care needs at all stages of life or taking responsibility for appropriately arranging care with other qualified professionals.
- *Coordination*: Care is coordinated and integrated across all domains of the health care system, facilitated by registries, information technology, health information exchange, and other means to assure that patients get the indicated care when and where they want it.
- *Quality and safety*: Quality and safety are hallmarks of the medical home. This includes using electronic medical records and technology to provide decision support for evidence-based treatments and patient and physician involvement in continuous quality improvement.
- *Expanded access*: Enhanced access to care is available through systems such as open scheduling, expanded hours, and new options for communications between patients, physicians, and practice staff.
- *Added value*: Payment that appropriately recognizes the added value provided to patients who have a patient-centered medical home.

Thus, the patient-centered medical home seeks to address the issues of medical care that is disorganized, fragmented, and lacking on many measures of clinical quality by providing comprehensive, coordinated, and accessible care.

Conclusion

The profession of medicine faces many challenges not only today but in the years ahead. No one knows what kind of impact a national health insurance plan will have on the practice of medicine if such a plan is enacted in the future. While this chapter focused on physician reimbursement, it did so to illustrate how a simple effect of reimbursement can ripple out throughout the whole health care field and have an impact on so many issues of concern to the American consumer-patient. These affect the availability of physicians in their community because some fees such as those under Medicare have higher rates of payment for some physician specialties than for others; the lack of desire of some physicians to accept new Medicare patients if their Medicare fees are reduced; the influence of Medicare expenditures on the training of new physicians, influencing the shortages among various specialties such as geriatricians and primary care physicians as the number of elderly in the USA increases in future years; the emergence of new ways to pay physicians according to their outcome performance; the influence of how high malpractice insurance costs, a component in the calculation of their Medicare reimbursement, are actually forcing some physicians to close down their offices and move away to other geographical areas where the malpractice insurance costs are less expensive, and how new forms of medical practice such as boutique medicine are being developed for those who can afford it, giving them easier access to medical care, while those who have difficulties in finding access or having trouble affording medical care costs can now receive it from convenience care clinics being established in retail stores or the development of model patient-centered medical homes.

However, these are not the only issues American medicine faces in the future. Physicians have an image problem. By 2009 they were called, like many other health practitioners, providers rather than physicians. Billions of public and private dollars are spent each year on physician care. Continual improvements in technology have fostered the growth in rising medical costs so that hospitals compete with each other to have that technology, even if it may be duplicative and underutilized in a community, so doctors will seek to practice there and bring revenues into the hospital through the use of its technological resources. Doctors are under increasing pressure to perform for less reimbursement. As an example, Medicare had proposed a 10.1% reduction in physician reimbursement, effective from July 1, 2008, but this proposal was defeated by Congress. Some physicians are hurried in their treatment of patients as more and more patients visit doctors because they have the ability to pay through private health insurance and public medical care programs. Therefore, some physicians may be viewed as not taking the time to listen or appear uncaring. And, as in the case of many other occupations, there is always a very small minority of physicians whose actions violate medical ethics.

Prerogatives that were once the exclusive province of the physician are no longer so. Physician assistants, nurse practitioners, and optometrists, for example, can now prescribe medications. Nonphysician personnel now tell a physician how long the physician may keep a patient in a hospital under managed care. There are even for-profit HMOs that have disincentives for physicians, which means that a certain amount of money is held out until the end of the year.[25] So, if a doctor has not ordered many laboratory tests and other doctors have been conservative in spending money, then the doctors receive small bonuses. So if it's a question of whether a doctor orders an expensive test that may or may not be medically necessary, he/she may not do so, placing a physician in the position of being conflicted between the managed care organization which is trying to make money and the patient who is trying to get well.

But the history of American medicine is about change. The health care field is not a static entity. While it may not move as quickly as the daily pronouncements in terms of new findings of medical research, it has evolved over time through new private physician payment mechanisms, creation of public medical care programs, establishment of new health care delivery systems, efforts to control health planning in a community, to name but a few examples. The medical profession has responded to all these changes and

others, sometimes positively and at other times negatively. But in the end it
has adapted and will continue to do so because the changes are never-ending
as the nation moves forward socially, politically, and economically in trying
to find solutions to provide its citizenry access to quality health care at costs
they can afford.

References

1. American Medical Association. *Physician Master File*. Chicago, IL: American Medical Association, 2000.
2. US Department of Health and Human Services. *Health United States, 2007, with Chartbook on Trends in the Health of the United States*. Hyattsville, MD: National Center for Health Statistics, 2007: 60.
3. *Source Book of Health Insurance Data, 2002*. Washington, DC: Health Insurance Association of America, 2002: 116.
4. Brown D. Recruiters offer doctors a small town 'option'. *Washington Post* 1991; October 6: A1.
5. McConnaughey J. Doctors for rural areas are sought. *Washington Post* 2005; January 30: A13.
6. Hearn W. Health on the outskirts. *Am Med News* 1996; July 1: 13.
7. Cauchon D. Medical miscalculation creates doctor shortage. *USA Today* 2005; March 2.
8. Newspapers examine shortages in primary, geriatric care. *Med News Today* 2007; February 5.
9. Barry P. Where have all the doctors gone? *AARP Bull* 2008; September: 13.
10. US Department of Health and Human Services. *A Report to the President and the Congress on the Status of Health Professions Personnel in the United States*. Washington, DC: Public Health Service, 1978: 1V1, A6.
11. Survey: many doctors plan to quit or cut back. Reuters November 18, 2008; available online at http://www.foxnews.com/story/0,2933,453825,00.html; accessed on November 11, 2008.
12. Phillips R L Jr, Starfield B. Why does a primary care physician workforce crisis matter? *Am Fam Physician* 2003; October 15.
13. Arvantes J. Speakers say Medicare payment rates major reason for physician shortages. aafp News Now. Washington, DC: American Academy of Family Physicians, 2007.
14. Hauer K E, Durning S J, Kernan W N *et al*. Factors associated with medical students' career choices regarding internal medicine. *JAMA* 300: 2008; 1154–1164.
15. Matin M. Splitting the sustainable growth rate: a proposal to strengthen Medicare and primary care. February 14 2008, available online at: http://healthaffairs.org/blog/2008/02/14/splitting-the-sustainable-growth-rate-a-proposal-to...; accessed on June 9, 2008.
16. Walsh T. Medicare reimbursement cuts could hit physicians hard. In: *Vital Signs*. Waltham, MA: Massachusetts Medical Society, 2005.
17. Broder D S. Leavitt's healthy vision. *Washington Post* 2007; October 21: B7.
18. Thomas F G, Caldis T. Emerging issues of pay for performance in health care. *Health Care Financ Rev* 2007; 20: 1.
19. Dodge A M, Fitzer S F. *When Good Doctors Get Sued: A Guide for Defendant Physicians Involved in Malpractice Lawsuits*. Olalla, WA: Dodge Publications, 2001.
20. US Department of Justice. *Bureau of Justice Statistics*. Washington, DC: Office of Justice Programs, 2001.
21. National Practitioner Data Bank. *NPDB Summary Report*. Washington, DC: US Department of Health and Human Services. New York: Weitz & Luxenberg, 2008.

22. *Source Books of Health Insurance Data 2002*. Washington, DC: Health Insurance Association of America, 2002: 117, 118.
23. Lacitis E. Doctors going solo with micropractices. *Washington Post* 2008; May 4: A7.
24. Jenkins C L. Unwelcome surprise. *Washington Post* 2008; March: F1, F5.
25. Libov C. Connecticut Q & A: Dr. Peter Gott: the medical profession has changed. *N Y Times* 2006; September 18.

.

5

Prescription drugs

Introduction

The history of the American pharmaceutical industry can be traced as far back as 1748 when the concept of apothecary shops was imported from Europe. The first manufacturing pharmaceutical laboratory was opened shortly thereafter to provide George Washington's army with medicines in 1778. Still later, during the American Civil War, the number of pharmaceutical companies increased and quickly grew. The distribution of drugs became nationwide in scope.

The first major crisis that posed a challenge to the American pharmaceutical industry occurred in World War I when it became obvious that the USA was completely dependent upon Germany for many of the new and potent synthetics which the German drug makers manufactured. Because of the war, the importation of drugs from Germany ceased and American physicians could not receive the drugs that were important to their medical practice. Therefore, American drug manufacturers undertook the task of synthetic production. Until World War II, these companies introduced relatively few innovations and provided only modest support for research in this field. But after the USA entered World War II with the Japanese attack on Pearl Harbor on December 7, 1941, the American drug industry underwent explosive growth with the discovery of drugs such as sulfanilamide. Today, the industry leads all nations in the research, development, production, and distribution of pharmaceuticals. Since World War II drugs have included the polio, mumps, measles, and rubella vaccines as well as oral contraceptives, the statin drugs, hypertensive drugs, antibiotics, tranquilizers, steroids, antihistamines, and others. The postwar period saw the establishment of the philosophy that if enough research and development were properly directed, they would serve as the key to discovering new and better drugs, with all which that implied in regard to therapeutic and economic benefits for both the industry and the patient.

The climate for prescription drug manufacturing continues to evolve. Government programs have dramatically influenced the drug industry and the consumer-patient has become actively involved in bringing about changes in drug product selection. Since 1955, compared to earlier years, fewer new drug products have been approved by the government for marketing. Since 1963 those which are marketed must pass more rigorous animal and human tests. The Medicare and Medicaid programs and health care reform initiatives have raised the distinct possibility that in the future an increasingly large share of the drug market in the USA will be partially supported by taxes. This became more relevant when President Bush signed into law Medicare's new prescription drug program in December 2003.

The marketing of prescription drugs is quite dissimilar from the marketing of other consumer products. It is concentrated on a small homogeneous target group of physicians and is even more confined when directed at only medical specialists, which makes this marketing situation very unusual. The physician who chooses and orders a drug product is not the consumer who pays for it, and the consumer has little participation in the selection – a marketing situation almost without parallel in other consumer industries. Even if the doctor prescribes the drug, the pharmacy benefits manager which specializes in managing prescription drug benefits for employers may not cover it. As a result the patient or pharmacist asks the doctor to rewrite for a drug listed on the formulary. The physician does so most of the time. Therefore, pharmaceutical marketing must now address the physicians and formulary committees in order to sell the product. In addition, once the manufacturer has established the value of its product and its own integrity and reputation in the opinion of the physician, the manufacturer not only has a strong hold on the market for its present products but also has an opening for future products as well.

But manufacturer identification has two sides. The doctor can deny the drug manufacturer a portion of the market if the product does not meet the physician's expectations; the doctor's dissatisfaction may embrace other products as well. This possibility has increased within recent years as a result of the creation of new government drug programs and the repeal of state anti-substitution drug laws, which allows the consumer greater participation in choosing quality prescription medicines at prices the consumer can afford. Beginning in the 1990s, some prescription drug advertisements began to be aimed at consumers through television and other media formats such as celebrity personnel stating the advantages of Lipitor in lowering cholesterol levels or how they use Tagamet when they feel their ulcer acting up. Whether or not the advertising of prescription drugs to the public will increase in volume in the ensuing years remains to be seen, but the barriers to the promotion of prescription drugs to the public have been breached. Consumer advertising could play a far larger role in increasing the dialogue between patients and physicians in regard to their medication regimen than in the past, and such advertising appears to be an issue that is going to become more important over the next decades.

Although the nation has had a pharmaceutical industry for many years, there are still many questions that concern the consumer in understanding the subject of prescription medicines, such as the best way to achieve the best results from prescription drugs, what to tell and ask a doctor about prescription drugs, especially if the patient is a woman, issues about drug safety, online pharmacies, medication errors, avoiding adverse drug reactions, food and drug interactions, prescribing for the elderly, and other issues. But one of the most important questions concerns that of prescription drug costs and that is the subject with which this chapter will be primarily concerned.

Background of prescription drug costs

In 2006, US health care spending increased 6.7% to $2.1 trillion, or $7026 per person from the 6.5% recorded in 2005, but it was lower than the 9.1% when health care spending growth peaked in 2002. The health care portion of the gross domestic product (GDP) was 16.0%, slightly higher than in 2005. In 2006, the growth of health spending outpaced nominal GDP growth by 0.6 percentage point. After 6 consecutive years of slowing growth, prescription drug spending growth accelerated in 2006 to 8.5%, partly as a result of the prescription drug benefit that is available under Part D of Medicare. Prescription drug spending reached $216.7 billion in 2006. About one-half of this growth was due to the increased use of prescription drugs, again, in part, due to expenditures under Part D of Medicare as well as new indications for existing drugs, growth in therapeutic classes, and the increased use of specialty drugs. Changes in the mix of drugs (brand versus generic and therapeutic units), lower overall rebates from drug manufacturers to public and private programs which covered drugs, and increases in average units per prescription also contributed to the 2006 growth in drug spending. As noted, shifts in therapeutic mix, which can be defined as changes in the relative shares of drugs within a class or among classes or new strengths of existing drugs, contributed as well to faster growth in retail prescription spending in 2006. A higher generic dispensing rate in 2006 helped to hold down spending growth, which, despite the acceleration still remained well below the average annual growth of 13.4% per year between 1995 and 2004. The generic dispensing rate reached 63% in 2006, an increase from 56% in 2005. The generic drug trend was primarily influenced by the continued use of incentives such as tiered payment structures as in Medicare Part D, waivers of copayments, and step therapy; the loss of patent protection for a number of brand-name drugs that became available in generic form in 2006 – most notably, Zocor, Zoloft, Pravachol, and Flonase; and the lack of new blockbuster drugs. Overall prescription drug prices, as measured in the National Health Expenditures Accounts, increased similarly in 2005 and 2006, at 3.5%. By the way, step therapy, also known as step protocol, is the practice of starting drug therapy for a medical condition with the most cost-effective and safest drug therapy and progressing to other more costly or risky therapy, only if necessary.

The impact of Medicare Part D's prescription drug program on overall national health spending in 2006 was modest but Part D had a substantial impact on the source of funds used to pay for prescription drugs. The public share of drug spending increased from 28% in 2005 to 34% in 2006, while the private share decreased from 72% to 66%. The shift in funding for the Medicare and Medicaid programs was substantial. In 2002 Medicare's share of total retail prescription drug spending was 2% and in 2006 its share increased to 18%. At the same time, Medicaid's drug spending declined as a share of total drug spending from 19% in 2005 to 9% in 2006. This decline was primarily attributable to the automatic enrollment of 6.2 million dually eligible people (Medicaid beneficiaries who also qualified for Medicare) into the Medicare Part D plans and, to a smaller extent, to the continued efforts by states to contain their Medicaid drug costs. For the Part D benefit, about 87% of expenditures ($35.7 billion of $41.0 billion) were for direct drugs purchases while the remaining 13% was for government administration and other matters. Also, both out-of-pocket and private health insurance spending for drugs declined as a share of total drug spending in 2006. Out-of-pocket expenditures decreased from a 24% share in 2005 to 22% in 2006, while private health insurance spending declined from 48% share in 2005 to 44% in 2006.[1]

In March 2008, the advocacy group, American Association of Retired Persons (AARP), released a report stating that pharmaceutical companies substantially raised prices on 220 brand-name drugs which are most commonly used by beneficiaries in Medicare Part D since the implementation of this drug benefit in 2006.[2] The AARP noted that the prices of brand-name drugs most commonly used by beneficiaries in Medicare Part D rose by an average of 7.4% in 2007 – nearly 2½ times the rate of general inflation. Specifically, the AARP looked at prices charged to wholesalers and noted that, between 2002 and 2006, before Medicare Part D became operational, wholesale prices rose between 5.3% and 6.6% a year. The average treatment cost exploded from $80 per year per prescription in 2002 to $151 in 2007. A person who took three brand-name prescriptions to treat a chronic condition over this period saw an increase in the annual costs of more than $1600 between 2002 and 2007. The study found that brand-name drug prices increased far more than general inflation since 2002, with dramatic increases since 2006, the period when Medicare Part D became operational.

In 2008, IMS MIDAS Quantum, a company which is used by the pharmaceutical industry to assess worldwide health care markets in the most cost-effective way, released the following price comparisons of some American drugs versus the same drugs in other countries and as published in *Consumer Reports*, March 2008.[3] IMS MIDAS Quantum compared the average retail price for a month's supply of popular brand-name drugs in the USA with Australia, Canada, France, Germany, Japan, and the UK. The USA had the highest prices with regard to all the compared drugs. With regard to Actos (diabetes, 15 mg, 30 pills) the USA was most expensive at $86.13, second highest Canada, $62.22, and lowest Japan, $21.48; Lipitor (cholesterol, 10 mg, 30 pills), the USA $68.37, second highest Canada $48.45, and lowest France $19.53; Fosamax (osteoporosis, 70 mg, 4 pills) the USA $64.16, second highest UK $40.31, and lowest Japan $23.61; Nexium (heartburn, 20 mg, 30 pills), the USA $92.04, second highest Canada $60.69, and lowest Germany $19.26; and Singular (asthma, 10 mg, 30 pills) the USA $83.40, second highest Canada, $63.21 and lowest France $43.02. It would appear from these comparisons that Canada, America's neighbor, generally has the second highest cost in drugs while European countries appear to have the lowest.[2,3]

Brand name versus generic drugs: differences and costs

To understand drug costs, it is first necessary to know the differences between brand-name and generic drugs. First, it is important to discuss basic scientific principles. Every drug is identified by three names – chemical, generic, and brand.

- A drug's chemical name is descriptive of its chemical structure, based on rules of standard chemical nomenclature.
- A drug also has a shorter, simpler established or official or generic name. It may or may not be an abbreviated form of its chemical name. It is the name most commonly used in scientific literature, by which many pharmacists and physicians learn about a particular drug during professional schooling and training.
- The brand name is the name the company gives its product to distinguish the medicine from competitive products, which may be identical insofar as active ingredients are concerned.

As an illustration, a five-grain acetylsalicylic acid tablet (chemical name), more commonly known as an aspirin (generic name) tablet, represents a kind of class universally prescribed and used for the relief of aches and pains. Currently, aspirin is marketed under several brand names, such as Bayer and St. Joseph, and they all have the same molecular identity.

When the quality of brand-name drugs versus drugs is debated, at least two important scientific issues are raised: chemical equivalency and therapeutic equivalency. Drugs are said to be chemically equivalent if they contain the same active ingredients and are identical in strength, dosage form, and route of administration, and meet existing physicochemical standards in the official compendia.

But they may differ in characteristics such as color, taste, shape, packaging, expiration time, and, within certain limits, labeling. Drugs are said to be therapeutically equivalent when they are chemically equivalent and when administered in the same amounts, they will provide the same biological or physiological availability as measured by such criteria as their rate of absorption into the blood stream. The absorption rate can be influenced by differences among the same product in terms of particle size and the methods used in their formulation, as well as in their granulation and tablet compression pressure. Yet, each product contains the same chemical equivalents from a dosage standpoint.

The brand name is used to advertise a drug to the medical profession, although the generic name must appear in advertising and labeling in letters at least half as large as those of the brand name. It is a popular conception, though wrong, that brand-name drugs are only manufactured by large, well-known firms, while generics are produced by small, unknown companies. A small drug company can place a brand name on its product just as a large company can sell a drug under its generic name. And many large drug firms distribute, under the brand names, products that have been produced, packaged, and labeled by firms that manufacture generic drugs. Some drug makers may manufacture a drug and sell it under a trade name and a generic name. In other instances, large firms may manufacture the final dosage form from drugs purchased in bulk from other companies.

While some drug authorities claim that chemically identical prescription drugs are not necessarily therapeutically equivalent – that is, they may not have the same curative effects – Dr. Donald Kennedy, former commissioner of the Food and Drug Administration (FDA) during the Carter administration, has testified in Congress that 'we find no evidence of widespread differences between the products of large and small firms or between brand-name or generic drugs.'[4]

All drugs have a generic name. If the FDA permits the manufacturer of a newly discovered drug to market that drug and the drug is patented, that manufacturer has the sole right to sell the drug until its patent has expired. Under the present US patent law, manufacturers are granted patents that give them the exclusive marketing rights on a new drug for up to 20 years from the date a drug patent is filed, as opposed to the date on which the patent is issued, and during which no one else can copy this formula. These patents are listed in the FDA's 'Orange Book' registry. In some instances a patent holder may give other firms the right, usually in return for the payment of a royalty, to produce and sell the patented drug. While the drug is under patent protection, its manufacturer will establish a price that will allow it to recoup its research, production, and marketing costs. It should be noted that, because pharmaceutical companies obtain a patent well before the FDA approves the drug, some pharmaceutical experts believe that companies have a marketing window of about 10 years to do so. However, once the patent has expired, other firms may make and sell the drug. Since the original manufacturer's research information is now known to other firms and the generic manufacturers do not have to invent the drug, it is cheaper for the generic drug manufacturer to make the drug and sell it under its generic name or in some cases different brand names. This is why there is such a price difference between generic and brand-name drugs. Because the generic drug must be identical to the original, the FDA approval process is much simpler and less costly. The FDA does not require the generic drug sponsor to perform again the costly animal and clinical research on ingredients or dosage forms which have already been approved for safety and effectiveness. Rather, companies simply submit an abbreviated new drug application to the FDA for approval.

FDA's assurance of quality drugs

The FDA's responsibility to regulate prescription drugs includes assuring the safety and effectiveness of drugs for their claimed uses before approving them; requiring complete labeling (directed toward physicians) of all drugs; and the provision of drug information to physicians and others in the health professions. In February 2005 the FDA announced the creation of a new independent Drug Safety Oversight Board to monitor FDA-approved medications once they are on the market and keep physicians and patients up to date with emerging information on their risks and benefits through methods such as postings on the internet.

The Food, Drug, and Cosmetic Act of 1938 required that drugs be proved safe before they could be marketed. In 1962, the law was amended to require that, before drugs can be marketed, their effectiveness as well as safety must be proven. The FDA conducted an intensive review of all prescription drugs marketed between 1938 and 1962 to find out whether they are effective by modern standards. As a result of this review, thousands of prescription drugs have been taken off the market or have had their formulation or labeling improved.

Not only must each drug meet FDA requirements but so must each plant. All firms, large and small, must register with the FDA; all are subject to periodic inspection; and all must adhere to the FDA's good manufacturing practice regulations, which touch upon every aspect of manufacturing drugs, from building maintenance to quality control. These regulations apply to all producers and are intended to make sure that all drugs meet the same standards of safety, strength, purity, and effectiveness. Other FDA standards provide further assurance of drug equivalence.

Another assurance of quality stems from the FDA's monitoring programs. The FDA periodically gathers samples of all drug products, both generic and brand-name, from manufacturers and from the marketplace to test them for purity and strength. When trouble is found or suspected, the drug company is informed immediately. Faulty products are taken off the market. Batch testing and certification are required by law for insulin and for biological products such as vaccines and serums, as well as for antibiotics. When the FDA discovers particular problems with a drug, it may require that each batch of that drug be tested before it can be released for sale.

Pharmacists

While drug manufacturers research and produce the medications, it is the pharmacist who dispenses the medications to individuals. The roles of pharmacists in our evolving health care system are many. They advise their patients as well as physicians and other health practitioners on the selection, dosages, interactions, and side-effects of medications. Pharmacists monitor the health and progress of patients to ensure the safe and effective use of medications. Compounding, the mixing of ingredients to form medications, is a very small part of a pharmacist's practice, because most medicines are produced by pharmaceutical companies in a standard dosage and drug delivery form. Most pharmacists work in a community setting, such as a retail drugstore, or in a health care facility, such as a hospital, nursing home, mental health institution, or neighborhood health clinic.

When pharmacists work in community pharmacies, they dispense medications, counsel patients on the use of prescriptions and over-the-counter medications, and advise physicians about a patient's medication therapy. They also advise patients about general health topics such as diet, exercise, and stress management, and provide information on products such as durable medical equipment or home health care supplies. In addition, they may complete third-party insurance forms and other paperwork. Those who own or manage community pharmacies may sell nonhealth-related merchandise, hire and supervise personnel, and oversee the general operation of the pharmacy. Some community pharmacists provide specialized services to help patients with conditions such as diabetes, asthma, smoking cessation, or high blood pressure; others are trained to administer vaccinations. When a pharmacist sells a prescribed medicine, a fee for his/her services arises from the dispensing of the prescription, buying and stocking drugs, making deliveries to the patient's home, if this be the case, and maintaining the patient's monthly charge accounts. The fee is added to the pharmacy's cost of the dispensed medication. The fee system has generally replaced the older markup system, which, because it varied with drug prices, might have tempted a pharmacist to dispense a more costly drug. The fee varies, depending upon geographical location and other factors. However, patients can compare such fees by asking their pharmacist and other pharmacists in the community about their dispensing fees.

Pharmacists who work in health care facilities dispense medications and advise medical staff on the selection and effects of drugs. They may make sterile solutions to be administered intravenously. They also plan, monitor, and evaluate drug programs or regimens. They may counsel hospitalized patients on the use of drugs before the patients are discharged. As of January 1, 2006 a provision in the Medicare Prescription Drug, Improvement, and Modernization Act of 2003 mandates that pharmacists in hospitals or long-term care pharmacies are to be paid when they consult with patients who take multiple drugs for chronic illness.

Within the home health care field pharmacists monitor drug therapy and prepare infusions – solutions that are injected into patients – and other medications for use in the home.

When pharmacists work in a managed care environment, they are committed to ensuring that medications are used appropriately to improve a patient's health. They accomplish this by performing functions within the following categories: drug distribution and dispensing; patient safety; clinical program development; communication with patients, prescribers, and pharmacists; drug benefit design; business management; and cost management.

Some pharmacists specialize in specific drug therapy areas, such as intravenous nutrition support, oncology (cancer), nuclear pharmacy (used for chemotherapy), geriatric pharmacy, and psychiatric pharmacy (the use of drugs to treat mental disorders).

Most pharmacists keep confidential computerized records of a patient's drug therapies to prevent harmful drug interactions, Pharmacists are responsible for the accuracy of every prescription that is filled, but they often rely upon pharmacy technicians and pharmacy aides to assist them in the dispensing process. Thus, the pharmacist may delegate prescription-filling and administrative tasks and supervise their completion. Pharmacists also frequently oversee pharmacy students serving as interns.

Increasingly, pharmacists are becoming involved in nontraditional pharmacy work. Some are pursuing research for pharmaceutical manufacturers, developing new drugs, and testing these effects. Others work in marketing or sales, providing clients with expertise on the use, effectiveness, and possible side-effects of drugs. Some pharmacists work for health insurance companies, developing pharmacy benefit packages, and performing cost–benefit analyses on certain drugs. Other pharmacists work for the government, managed care organizations, public health care services, the armed services, or pharmacy associations. Finally, some pharmacists are employed full-time or part-time as college faculty, teaching classes, and performing research in a wide range of areas.

It is possible that in the future pharmacists in the USA may enjoy the same privileges as some are beginning to enjoy in the UK. Across the UK some pharmacists have been given permission to prescribe drugs for patients and provide basic care, without relying on a doctor. The move is part of the UK effort to expand its health system by permitting medical professionals like nurses and pharmacists to treat patients. Although many countries are slowly loosening the rules prohibiting nondoctors from giving out medications, none has given pharmacists as much power as the UK in its efforts to increase health services and reduce costs. In 2006 the UK expanded the powers of pharmacists to treat patients once they took a training course. The number of prescribing health professionals besides doctors remains small, but is growing as the government hopes some day this will be the norm. In the USA the role of nonphysician prescribers has been delegated to physicians' assistants, nurse practitioners, and optometrists. Pharmacists have been slow to show an interest in taking on this added duty as a general responsibility of practice.

To qualify as an 'independently prescribing pharmacist,' one pharmacist took a 9-week course and spent about 30 hours of experience treating patients under a doctor's supervision. Permitting pharmacists and nurses to prescribe medicine, according to a policy statement from the British Health Department, is part of the government's plan to modernize the health system by eliminating barriers between professions and allowing patients easier access to drugs. Some doctors state that pharmacists are especially well suited to treat patients with chronic problems, since treatment is relatively straightforward and involves lifestyle advice and coordination of drugs. But setting limits on their work is crucial, like not making diagnoses. James King, president of the American Academy of Family Practice, is worried that the British system might make it too easy for pharmacists to make mistakes. 'The whole idea of determining what medications a patient needs is the ability to diagnose a medical condition,' he has stated. 'That's where all the years of medical and residency training come in.'[5] Critics of the British system state that it is just discounted health care because nurses and pharmacists earn less than physicians. In the USA, pharmacists can write prescriptions if they have a 'collaborative' agreement with a physician. Under such arrangements, pharmacists with extra training can monitor patients on medication or make dose changes without the doctor's approval, but only according to a specific work plan supervised by doctors.[5]

Ways to pay for prescription drugs

While the cost of prescription drugs remains a primary concern of many Americans in terms of how they can pay for the medications, there are a number of programs, public and private, available to the American public that can assist them in this endeavor, aside from state Medicaid programs for those under 65 years of age and Part D of Medicare for those older than 65 years.

One public program which may not be well known became effective in August 1976 when the US Department of Health and Human Services (DHHS) initiated its new drug program, named maximum allowable cost (MAC). The program sets a price ceiling on prescription drugs at the lowest price for which that drug is widely and consistently available; for drugs whose patents have expired, which are manufactured by more than one company, and which are covered by Medicare, Medicaid, and Maternal and Child Health programs. Although MAC applies to all three programs, government savings were expected to be derived almost exclusively from Medicaid because as of 1976 Medicare did not yet have a program that paid for out-of-hospital medications and most hospitals do enforce their own cost controls on inpatient drugs. Under the MAC program, the US DHHS sends lists of drug comparisons to physicians and pharmacists in order to encourage them to reduce patient drug costs. Before a ceiling on drug payments is set forth, the FDA will study the drug to make sure there are no quality and therapeutic equivalency problems. Under DHHS regulations, manufacturers of generic drugs with known variations must match the effectiveness of the standard drug or withdraw the drug from the market. If the price of a drug product, for which a MAC limit has been established, increases or declines in the marketplace because of an increase or decrease in its supply, then, after an appropriate review by DHHS, the MAC ceiling can be adjusted upward or downward as the situation may require. Consumers who qualify for maternal and child health programs, Medicaid, or even Medicare may find that the government will pay for the entire cost of drugs their physician prescribes or, perhaps, may pay the difference between the MAC the government pays and the remaining cost the pharmacist charges.

Another source for saving money on prescription drugs is an innovation in the pharmaceutical industry called drug management companies or pharmacy benefit managers (PBMs). These PBMs serve as middlemen between health plans and drug manufacturers. Originally, the PBMs were established to process insurance company claims. Today, PBMs operate mail-order pharmacies which allow members to obtain significant discounts over standard retail pharmacies. The PBMs also contract with large employers to provide drugs at discount prices to insurance-covered employees through networks of retail pharmacies that promise savings to patients if they purchase their medications at participating stores. The drugstores are reimbursed by the drug management companies. These management companies develop lists of medicines approved for coverage based on the assessment of their cost and effectiveness. Thus, PBMs are not only drug plans but also organize the purchasing, dispensing, and reimbursement of medicines for health insurers or other large purchasers of health care such as employers and unions.

The following is how the process works. An employer issues a request for a proposal to manage its employee prescription drug benefit program. In response, prescription drug benefit managers submit their proposals. Employers assume that the chosen PBM can contract with pharmacies to reimburse the pharmacies based on a formula for each prescription dispensed. The drugstore is paid an amount equal to the employee's copayment plus the average wholesale price of the drug minus a negotiated percentage discount. Beneficiaries can trade at any pharmacy participating in the program, present their drug card, and pay a copayment to obtain a prescription. At the end of every 2 weeks, the benefit manager pays the pharmacy for the dispensed medication.[6]

Another form of cost savings is mail-order pharmacies, which use large processing centers across the country that, automated with state-of-the art computers, store information about each patient and dispense prescriptions based on that patient's insurance coverage, medical needs, and the frequency with which the person tends to use a drug. Cost savings, analysts say, come from bulk purchasing. Also, according to some analysts, to reduce the costs of prescription medicines some insurers are asking physicians in some cases to change prescriptions to less expensive generic brands or to prescribe similar brand-name counterparts. Some doctors have criticized this 'switching strategy' that some mail-order pharmacies use, stating that it can lead to drug substitutions that are not appropriate and that in some instances can cause patients to experience adverse reactions. Mail-order pharmacies state that they can often change to a generic brand without contacting a doctor but that they must receive a doctor's approval before changing to similar, but not identical, substitutes. Doing anything less, they state, could make the companies legally responsible if the substitute led to a bad reaction. That is why when comparing mail-order and retail pharmacies, consumer-patients must take into consideration which is best in terms of costs, the monitoring of drug use and drug interactions, ease of obtaining prescription refills, and other elements that constitute quality pharmaceutical services.

Still another source of assistance, if a veteran, is the US Department of Veterans Affairs health care program. In addition, if the person is a military retiree or dependant, including a widow or a divorced spouse, there is the TRICARE Senior Pharmacy Program of the US Department of Defense. TRICARE beneficiaries can receive their medicine through the national mail-order pharmacy. Beneficiaries do not have to enroll in the program. All they need is a military identification card and must send in their prescription and a patient profile registration form to the program. If they have access to a military treatment facility pharmacy, they can obtain the medication for free and they can also visit their local drugstore, as long as it is part of the TRICARE network, though their costs will increase this way.

Another way for consumers to cut their drug bills is through prescription discount cards. Hundreds of these cards are available to consumers; none of them is regulated. Many are targeted to uninsured persons or those whose health plan does not provide coverage for prescription drugs. Others target Medicare patients. Some pharmaceutical manufacturers make it relatively easy for consumers to get a card, while others make it more difficult, such as having the consumer's physician rather than the consumer submit a card or having the consumer fill out very long financial forms. Once the consumer's application has been approved, the consumer will receive a 3-month supply of medications at that time. Some companies automatically renew the medications once the 3-month supply is gone. Periodically companies will change their eligibility requirements and rules. Some cards charge enrollment fees, most a monthly fee or an annual fee, and some require both. Some companies offer free cards. Some have age or income restrictions. Some require only the consumer's name, address, and credit card numbers. But not all pharmacies accept all cards. And the cards only rarely deliver up to '65%' or greater discounts that some advertise. Many of the largest discounts are only available for certain medications at certain pharmacies in certain cities on certain days, and because prices change every day, patients rarely have the information they require to decide up front whether a card is worth the trouble, or in some instances the cost of a monthly fee. But regardless of what kind of card a consumer selects, the consumer and physician should have the option of the largest possible choice of medications, namely a card with an open formulary – an unrestricted choice of prescription drugs. If a card refers to a preferred drug list in an advertisement or a brochure, it means the consumer and the physician have less choice of prescription drugs.

Another source of coverage for prescription drugs is state Medicaid programs. Most pharmacies accept Medicaid and bill the state for the cost of the patient's prescription since they cannot bill the patient for any part of the cost. For those who have low incomes but still do not qualify for Medicaid, some states have established their own programs to assist low-income elderly and disabled patients with the cost of prescription drugs. These programs may require the patient to pay a deductible before the prescription drug coverage begins, while others may require a copayment or coinsurance and there might be a low limit on benefits. As examples, New Jersey and Pennsylvania's Pharmaceutical Assistance Contract for the Elderly (PACE) program subsidizes all prescription drugs for seniors who meet income requirements, while California, Vermont, and Florida, for example, require that most pharmacies sell drugs at a slight discount to poor seniors. State health departments or a state agency on aging are good sources of information about such programs in individual states.

To save money, some patients in the USA purchase their drugs from abroad, such as from Canada or Mexico. In Canada, pharmacies will only fill prescriptions that are written by Canadian physicians (though most pharmacies will help patients to get in touch with Canadian physicians to do so). Also, some prescriptions are available over the counter in other countries at very great savings. But it is important that the patient's personal physician has no objection to the patient buying drugs from abroad and that the patient is purchasing the correct medication at the correct dosage. Although the US government does not look upon this situation with favor, US law does permit travelers to import a 3-month supply of medicine for personal use, as long as they have valid prescriptions from their doctors at home. One factor that affects the savings that Americans can achieve in regard to Canadian drugs, for example, relates to the exchange rate of the Canadian dollar against the American dollar. Prior to 2008, the Canadian dollar used to be worth 75 cents for every US dollar so savings were greater than when the Canadian dollar currency was worth as much as the American dollar. So consumers at the time of purchase should check the exchange rate between US and Canadian dollars to learn whether they are achieving any financial savings by purchasing their drugs from abroad. Added to this factor is the emergence in 2006 of Medicare Part D, which subsidizes prescription drug sales for older Americans. Both the change in the exchange rate of Canadian dollars to American dollars and the operation of Medicare Part D has reduced by half the $1 billion a year Americans spent on drugs from Canada in 2008. However, despite the decline in savings, brand-name drugs still cost less in Canada than in the USA while generic drugs remain less expensive in the USA than in Canada. And many Americans continue to buy from Canada when generics are not available, especially those under 65 who are not insured and those who must pay the full price of drugs because they fall into that part of the Part D program known as the 'doughnut hole' where they must pay the entire cost of the medications themselves without any financial assistance from Medicare, unless other private and public non-Medicare programs help them with such costs.[7]

In an effort to help seniors who fall into the 'doughnut hole' in terms of prescription drug expenditures and who bear the entire cost of their prescription drugs out of their own pocket, the Obama Administration and the US pharmaceutical industry announced an agreement on June 20, 2009 whereby the drug industry over the ensuing decade would spend $80 billion improving drug benefits for seniors. The drug companies would pay half the cost of brand-name drugs for seniors who find themselves in the so-called 'doughnut hole,' a gap in coverage that is a feature of many plans providing prescription drug coverage under Medicare Part D. In other words, seniors would receive a 50% discount on the cost of the prescription drugs. In addition, the entire cost of the drug would count toward patients' out-of-pocket costs, meaning their insurance coverage would cover more of their expenses than otherwise would be the case. While none of the changes in the prescription drug program would directly lower government costs, several officials also said the drug industry agreed to measures that would provide the US Treasury with more money under federal health programs. In particular, officials said drug companies would likely end up paying higher rebates for certain drugs under Medicaid, the program that pays providers health care for the poor.[8]

Another source of prescription drug coverage is the Medicare Prescription Drug, Improvement, and Modernization Act of 2003 (PL 108-173) that established a new drug benefit under Medicare called Part D, as already noted. This program is described in more detail in Chapter 13. To obtain Medicare coverage, a beneficiary must join a Medicare drug plan. These plans are operated by insurance companies and other private companies approved by Medicare. Each plan can vary in costs and the drugs that are covered. There are two ways to obtain Medicare prescription drug coverage. One is to join a stand-alone Medicare prescription drug plan (PDP) that adds drug coverage to the original Medicare plan, a Medicare-subsidized employer plan, some Medicare private fee-for-service plans, some Medicare cost plans, and Medicare medical savings account plans. The other choice is to join a Part C Medicare Advantage plan (like a health maintenance organization or preferred provider organization) or another Medicare health plan that includes prescription drug coverage where patients obtain all their Medicare coverage (Part A and Part B), including prescription drugs (Part D) through these plans. These plans are sometimes called 'MA-PDs.' When beneficiaries join a Medicare drug plan, they usually pay a separate monthly premium in addition to their Part B premium.[9] Those who had third-party drug coverage before Part D took effect were covered by Medicaid, private insurance (Medigap and employer-sponsored plan), state assistance programs, Medicare managed care plans, or other governmental programs, while those without drug coverage paid for drugs directly out of their own pocket. The great majority of Medicare beneficiaries who are not enrolled in PDPs and MA-PD plans or subsidized employer plans have drug coverage through federal or military retirement plans.

Prescription drug profile

It appears for the first time that more than one-half of the American people are taking prescription medicine regularly for chronic health problems, according to data gathered in 2007 by Medco Health Solutions,[10] which managed prescription drug benefits for about one out of five Americans. The most widely used drugs are those that are prescribed to lower high blood pressure and cholesterol – problems that are often linked to heart disease, obesity, and diabetes. Experts say that the data reflect not just worsening public health problems but better medicines for treating chronic health conditions and more aggressive treatment by doctors. According to Dr. Daniel W. Jones, a heart specialist and dean of the University of Mississippi's medical school, more people are taking blood pressure- and cholesterol-lowering medications because they need them. Jones predicted, 'unless we do things to change the way we're managing health in this country . . . things will get worse instead of getting better.'[10]

Americans buy much more medicine per person than any other country. In 2007, 51% of American children and adults were taking one or more prescription drugs for a chronic condition, an increase from 50% from the previous 4 years 2002–2006 and 47% in 2001. Most of the drugs are taken daily, although some are required less often.

Medco Health Solutions examined prescription records from 2001 to 2007 of a representative sample of 2.5 million customers, from newborns to the elderly, and found that all demographic groups use medication for chronic problems; these include almost two-thirds of women 20 years and older, one in four children and teenagers, 52% of adult men, and three out of four people who are 65 years and older. Among seniors, 28% of women and 22% of men take five or more medications on a regular basis.[10]

The largest increase in the use of chronic medication was in the 20–44-year-old age group – adults who were in the prime of life – when the use of medication increased 20% between 2001 and 2007 because of depression, diabetes, asthma, attention deficit disorder, and seizures. The study also highlighted an increase in the use by children of medicines to treat weight-related problems and other illnesses previously considered adult problems. Medco estimated that 1.2 million American children are now taking medication for type 2 diabetes, sleeping troubles, and gastrointestinal problems such as heartburn. According to Dr. Jones, 'a scarier problem is that body weights are so much higher in children in general, and so we're going to have larger number of adults who develop high blood pressure or abnormal cholesterol or diabetes at an earlier age.'[10] Dr. Richard Gorman, an American Academy of Pediatrics expert on children's medicines, said more children are taking medications for 'adult conditions' partly because manufacturers now provide pediatric doses, liquid versions, or at least information to determine the right amount for a child.[10]

The Medco study also found that, among boys and girls under age 10, the most widely used medication changed from allergy drugs to asthma medicines between 2000 and 2007. Gorman stated that it is because, over the last decade, asthma care has gone from treating flare-ups to using inhaled steroids regularly to prevent flare-ups and hospitalizations.[10]

New insurance charges

As Americans take more medications per person than anyone else in the world and as they seek to cut their costs through a variety of public and private programs, insurers are very quickly adopting a new pricing system for high-cost drugs, asking patients to pay hundreds and even thousands of dollars for prescription medicines that may save their lives or slow down their disease. With the new pricing system, insurers have changed from copayments per medication to coinsurance. Under the former traditional system patients paid a fixed copayment such as $10, $20, or even $30, no matter what the drug actually cost. Under coinsurance insurers are charging patients a percentage of the cost of certain high-priced medications, usually 20–33%, that can add up to thousands of dollars per month. Thus, not only is the burden of expensive health care upon the uninsured but it also leads to a situation that even insured people may not be able to afford the treatments they require. The numbers of patients who are affected by coinsurance payments are not known, but hundreds of drugs are priced this new way. These drugs treat common illnesses like multiple sclerosis, rheumatoid arthritis, hemophilia, hepatitis C, and some cancers. These drugs have no lower-priced equivalents so that patients are forced to pay the price or do without the drugs. Insurers claim that the new pricing system holds down everyone's premiums at a time when some of the most innovative and promising new treatments for a condition like cancer, rheumatoid arthritis, and multiple sclerosis can cost $100 000 and more a year. But the result is that patients may have to pay more for a drug than they pay for their mortgages – more, in some instances, than their monthly incomes.

This system is often called Tier 4 and began in seriousness with the Medicare drug plans that became effective on January 1, 2006, and has spread very quickly. It is now incorporated into 86% of those Medicare plans. Some have even higher patient sharing for certain drugs, called Tier 5. But the Tier 4 concept is now being included in insurance that people purchase on their own or receive through their employers. It is one of the fastest-growing segments in private health insurance. In 2002, Tier 4 was virtually nonexistent in private drug plans; by 2008 10% of drug plans had Tier 4 drug categories. Private insurers began offering Tier 4 plans in response to employers who were looking for ways to hold down costs, according to Karen Ignagni, president of America's Health Insurance Plans,[12] which represents the nation's health insurers. According to the concept's purpose, when people who require Tier 4 drugs pay more for them, other subscribers in the plan pay less for their coverage. But, unfortunately, persons who are suffering from a serious illness must cope with large medical bills at the same time.[11]

Generic drugs

However, while insurers were putting Tier 4 systems into their health insurance contracts, there was an opposite trend also taking place in the pharmaceutical field. It has already been noted that generic drugs are less expensive than their brand-name counterparts, which are considered by the FDA to be therapeutically equivalent. And as more brand-name drugs began to lose their patent protection, generic drugs were becoming more available by 2008 than ever before.

The most common medical conditions – high cholesterol, depression, allergies, and diabetes – all have generics available. Changing to a generic on some company health plans can easily save the employee money on the copayment. But by 2008 the trend toward the greater use of generics had been adopted by various retailers. Wal-Mart, the world's largest retailer, and its warehouse retailer, Sam's Club, beginning in 2006, offered a 30-day supply for some drugs for just $4. The program expanded to more than 360 medications by 2008. Target offered a $4 drug program that included 315 medications. Walgreen's offered a 90-day supply of some 300 generics for $12.99. One regional grocery chain, Giant Eagle, offered 400 generic drugs for $4. For chronic conditions, most employers offer mail-order programs through a prescription benefit manager such as CVS Caremark. If a patient orders a 90-day supply, instead of enough for 30 days, not only does the provider often send the medications free, but typically the patient pays the equivalent of only two monthly copayments instead of three.[12]

Conclusion

While prescription drug costs only constitute about 10% of the total health expenditures in the USA, this particular health service is faced with many quandaries. On the one hand, the pharmaceutical industry is a business seeking to make a profit. On the other hand, the service it provides is a social one in trying to maintain a person's health in as best a state as possible through the use of medications. Brand-name drugs obviously cost more than generic drugs. To maintain as high a revenue income as possible through their sales, some companies argue that brand-name drugs are more therapeutically effective than their generic counterparts and justify the costs of their brand-name drugs on drug marketing activities as well as the desire of the pharmaceutical firms to recoup, if possible, the research and development costs of the drug so that they can continue to have the funds to conduct research and develop drugs or therapies that have yet to be discovered. Others, like the US federal government, state that the generic and brand-name drugs are therapeutically equivalent. So while public and private sectors debate the scientific merits of various pharmaceutical products on a global scale, on the most basic level paying for prescription drugs remains a personal activity between the pharmacist and the patient.

There are those who find paying for prescription drugs a great economic hardship, while others have no such problems. As a result, many kinds of public and private programs have been or are being developed to help people pay for the costs of the prescription drugs. People, with some exceptions, would basically agree that a medication is necessary for the restoration or maintenance of good health. But, the socioeconomic and political aspects of American society that result in people living longer and developing diseases that require medication on a continuous basis for longer periods of time amount to more medications being sold at a continuous cumulative cost to the patient. So those who provide health plans for their employees, for example, seek relief from high health insurance costs, of which prescription medicines are but one element, and seek financial relief by placing more of the cost burden on the employee and less on the company. Now the employee must not only bear higher personal drug costs, but also must deal with the illness that is causing the person to purchase the medications which he or she needs to fight the illness.

So everyone begins to seek relief. Businesses want financial relief by shifting the health costs, including those of prescription drugs, to their employees. Individuals want relief by asking for government intervention, as in the case of the passage of a drug benefit program under Medicare. Government wants relief because the more they spend on health care services, including prescription drugs, the less money they have to spend on other nonhealth government functions that society needs and demands. And the more everyone seeks relief and undertakes various programs, public and private, to attain it, the less it is attained. And the circular flow of increasing demand and higher costs continues and rises unabated, with all segments of society demanding relief, taking unilateral actions, not always in coordination with each other, to create programs to achieve it, only to cause the costs of health care to spiral even higher.

It is possible that some of the answers to the costs of health care may lie outside the formal health care field itself, and that perhaps when society seeks to resolve these other issues, the problems engendered by the health care field will also abate to some extent. America is an aging society whose life span continues to lengthen as never before, thanks to scientific advances of the medical field. With increasing life spans come illnesses that never had to be treated before in such numbers, and with prolonged treatment come the higher cumulative costs of such treatments for both the nation and the individuals who seek such treatments. And the costs of the medications that are applied in the course of that treatment are not only affected by the internal activities of the pharmaceutical manufacturer which produced the medication. They are also governed by outside events such as the price of a barrel of oil in a global economy over which that manufacturer has no control and from which various products are derived that go into the manufacture and packaging of a pharmaceutical. The manufacturer must take into consideration such costs when pricing its product if the manufacturer is to be profitable and remain in business. For example, some pharmaceutical products manufactured from oil include anesthetics, antihistamines, antiseptics, aspirin, bandages, cortisone, and vitamin capsules, while medical supplies made from oil include artificial limbs and heart valves. While the manifestation of these various problems, namely, the high cost of prescription medicines, is easy to discern, the answers to resolving the socioeconomic and political issues and problems that underlie the causes of these apparent manifestations are not so readily clear and the health care crisis in the USA continues on its course.

References

1. Catlin A, Cowan C, Hartman M *et al*. National health spending in 2006: a year of change for prescription drugs. *Health Aff* 2008; 27: 14–29.
2. *AARP Report Finds Brand Name Drug Prices Continue to Soar*. Washington, DC: AARP, 2008; March 5 (press release).
3. Six prescriptions for change. *Consumer Rep* 2008; March: 15 (table).
4. FDA chief says generic, brand Rx's nearly equal. *AMA News* 1973; November 21: 3.
5. Cheng M. Britain makes pharmacists first stop for treatment of some ailments. *Washington Post* 2008; April 13: A12.
6. Day K. Maryland terminates contract with drug prescription firm: Medco lacks pharmacy network to fulfill terms of deal, state says. *Washington Post* 1995; December 28: D9.
7. Canadian drug savings on the slide. *AARP Bull* 2008; May: 4.
8. Espo D. Drug companies, White House reach $80 billion prescription drug deal. *Huffington Post* June 20, 2009; available online at: http://www.huffingtonpost.com/2009/06/20/deal-reached-on-cutting-p_n_218431.html); accessed on June 20, 2009.
9. *Medicare and You, 2008*. Washington, DC: Centers for Medicare and Medicaid Services, 2007: 52.
10. Johnson L A. More Americans are taking prescription medicines. *My Way News* 2008; May 14, available online at http://apnews.myway.com/article/20080514/D90LDFNG0.html; accessed on May 14, 2008.
11. Kolata G. Co-pays soaring for high-cost drugs. *Philadelphia Daily News* 2008; April 14: 30.
12. Anderson J L. Think generic and save. *Washington Post* 2008; May 11: F3, as originally cited in *Kiplinger Personal Finance*, Washington, DC (undated).

6

Hospital care

Introduction

The word hospital, like hotel or hostel, is a derivation from the Latin *hospes*, which can mean either 'host' or 'guest.' The origin of the word may be based on the old eastern Mediterranean tradition of hospitality, which included the provision of way stations where travelers could receive meals, lodging, and if necessary, nursing care. In Greece and Egypt, the sick went to temples where priests practiced medicine along with religion. The relationship between medicine and religion remained close. European hospitals first developed as adjuncts to monasteries or abbeys; even today, many well-respected hospitals are sponsored or operated by religious orders.

It has only been in the last hundred years or so that hospitals have been looked upon as a place of healing. Until then they were the last place for the poor and friendless; people in better circumstances were treated at home. Until that time, hospitals were more dangerous than the illness because hospital-spread infections, called hospitalism, were rampant in the institutions. Then, in the 19th century breakthroughs began to occur in medical science within the environment of the hospital. In 1846 ether as an anesthetic was introduced and broadened the variety and scope of surgical procedures. Sterile techniques that employed spraying with carbolic acid were developed in the 1860s and reduced the rate of rampant hospital infections. Florence Nightingale's work in the Crimean war marked the beginning of professional nursing and in 1895 the discovery of the X-ray by Wilhelm Roentgen revolutionized medical diagnosis.

Hospitals today are multimillion-dollar institutions. The equipment necessary for their operations ranges from a Band Aid to very large computerized body scanners. Most hospitals are called general hospitals, that is, they provide a variety of services, surgical and nonsurgical care, for the treatment of acute medical problems. As health and hospital services have grown more complex, specialty institutions have also been established – hospitals for women, for children, for long-term rehabilitation, and for the treatment of specific diseases.

One way in which to judge the quality of a hospital is through accreditation. Hospitals, general or specialty, are said to be accredited when they have been given such certification by a private organization called the Joint Commission on the Accreditation of Healthcare Organizations (JCAHO) after meeting the minimum standards of the JCAHO. Accreditation involves periodic examinations of hospital services, facilities, and quality of care and is considered the generally accepted stamp of approval in the hospital field. Hospitals can also be designated by their ownership or sponsorship – nonprofit, proprietary, and governmental. Private nonprofit hospitals encompass the range from large teaching hospitals to small rural treatment centers. They may be under the auspices of educational institutions, religious organizations, or groups of private citizens. Private groups also build proprietary institutions, which are operated for profit. They are generally fewer in number or smaller in size. Governmental hospitals are tax-supported institutions under the control of cities, counties, states, or the federal government. Like private hospitals, their size varies and their quality depends upon their financial resources and their involvement in teaching programs.

Some hospitals are also schools and these hospitals are known as teaching hospitals. Four thousand years ago it was common practice in Babylon to place a sick person in his bed outside in the street. There, passersby would stop to observe his condition and give the physician advice on how to treat the patient. In today's hospitals, doctors, nurses, and other staff may question, test, probe, and discuss a medical problem with the patient. Yet, this kind of medical care attention accompanies the most advanced medical care treatment in the world. Since the teaching hospital is delivering education for graduate physicians, such an institution is most likely to provide the highest concentration of full-time staff and specialized services. The teaching hospital is the site where advances in technology and research are first made available to patients. Such hospitals generally receive the most difficult and acute patient cases. They often act as referral centers for a broad geographic area. An approved teaching hospital is an institution whose residency training programs are approved by the Council on Medical Education and Hospitals of the American Medical Association.

The level of health care provided can also distinguish hospitals from each other – namely, primary, secondary, and tertiary. *Primary care* is generally provided by a family doctor or an outpatient clinic and in the majority of cases is the only kind of treatment that is required. It often, but not always, means that the patient is hospitalized. *Secondary services* might include maternity care, an appendectomy, the treatment of a broken bone, or testing for glaucoma. *Tertiary care* is the most specialized and acute medical care that can be delivered. It often involves a patient with critical injuries or illness who is referred from a primary or secondary institution. Open-heart surgery, intensive care facilities, burn centers, kidney transplants, microsurgery – all are examples of tertiary care. As health care costs rapidly rise and medical services and facilities proliferate, health planners are seeking the most sensible ways to organize and offer these three levels of care.[1]

Character of hospitals

In some respects hospitals are not very different from any other kind of business in the hospitality field such as a hotel, a resort, or any other kind of facility in which people seek leisure and lodging. They have, for example, a manager or an administrator, an accounting department, a housekeeping department, transportation services, dietary and food preparation services. But unlike hotels or resorts, they also provide medical services to those who are ill and are seeking to become well. The medical departments that make up a hospital are many and diverse. They may include, depending upon the extensiveness of the hospital's services, nephrology (kidney disease), maternity (care of mother, child, and newborns), cardiology (the heart), dermatology (the skin), gastroenterology (digestive tract), hematology (the blood), infectious diseases, pulmonary medicine (the lungs and various respiratory problems), rheumatology (arthritis and related disorders like gout and osteoarthritis), obstetrics/gynecology (pregnancy and female reproduction), ophthalmology (eyes), orthopedics (bones), otolaryngology (ear, nose, and throat), psychiatry (the mind), physical medicine and rehabilitation, radiology, medical social service department, pharmacy department, emergency care department, and many others. In addition, hospitals can provide a variety of other medical services, again depending upon the extensiveness of the care they render. For example, a university medical center and teaching hospital would be far more comprehensive in the services it furnishes than a local community hospital. Some of the other services a hospital may provide, depending upon its nature, include a blood bank, a burn unit, physical therapy, postoperative recovery room, clinical laboratories, oral surgery, general surgery, and neurosurgery.

Hospital costs

However, when consumers think of hospitals they generally do not think initially about the various departments they may have or the services they render, but rather the cost of their whole personal hospital experience. In 2006, according to the US Centers for Disease Control and Prevention (CDC), Americans made an estimated 1.1 billion visits to physician offices and hospital outpatient and emergency departments, an average of four visits per person per year.[2] The number of visits to physician offices and hospital outpatient and emergency departments increased by 26% from 1996 to 2006, the most recent year for which complete data were available. According to the

CDC, the rise in visits can be associated with the aging of the population. In 2005, hospital care ($611.1 billion) continued to represent the largest share of personal health spending (30.8%). Hospital prices are affected by several factors, including the cost of labor and cost shifting. Often, the uninsured or the poor are treated in emergency rooms (ER) without payment. In August 2008 the US Centers for Disease Control and Prevention reported that there were 119 million ER visits in 2006 compared to 90 million in 1996. That is more than ever before and an increase of 32% in the decade between 1996 and 2006. Those most likely to go to ER are infants and the elderly. No one knows for sure what the impetus is for this increase. The study suggests that it is not the uninsured (comprising in this survey those who paid for themselves and those who did not pay) who spurred this increase and accounted for 17% and 18% of ER visits in both 1996 and 2006. Rather, in addition to population growth (the rate of ER visits per 100 people increased from 34.2 to 40.5 between 1996 and 2006), the speculation from other studies on the ER increase centers on the fact that persons who are insured are using the ER for care because they cannot receive prompt care in their own physician's offices (Figure 6.1). In the same period, the number of ERs in operation decreased from 4019 to 3833. In other words, more and more patients are visiting ERs which are declining in number, increasing the time period that patients must wait to receive treatment. Meanwhile, it is estimated that the insured bear most of the cost associated with unsponsored health care in the USA.

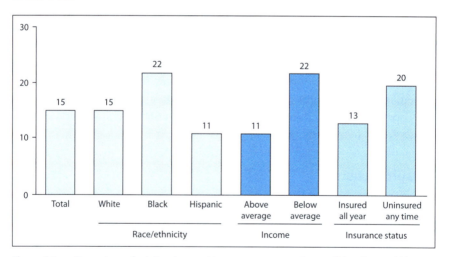

Figure 6.1 Percentage of adults who went to emergency room for condition that could have been treated by regular doctor, categorized by race/ethnicity, income, and insurance status, 2007. Data: 2007 Commonwealth Fund International Health Policy Survey. Source: Commonwealth Fund National Scorecard on US Health System Performance, 2008. Reprinted with permission of The Commonwealth Fund, New York, NY and as cited at: http://www.commonwealthfund.org/chartcartcharts/chartcartcharts_show.htm?doc_id=694.

To help relieve the burden on the public's use of hospital ERs as primary care centers when it lacks health insurance coverage or cannot access its own physician, in March 2009 President Barack Obama announced the release of $155 million to 126 community health centers under the American Recovery and Reinvestment Act (ARRA) which he signed into law as a $787 billion stimulus bill in February 2009 to help America recover from its economic recession. During 2009 and 2010 a total of $2 billion will be invested in community health centers to support renovations and repairs, investments in health information technology, and critically needed health care services. One out of every 19 people living in the USA relies on a Department of Health and Human Services (DHHS) Health Resources and Services Administration-funded clinic for primary care. They treated more than 16 million people in 2008. Nearly 40% of patients treated have no health insurance and one-third are children. Nearly 1100 health center grant recipients operate more than 7000 community-based clinics in every state and territory, giving geographically or economically distressed people access to preventive and primary care. Today, they provide more comprehensive services than ever before, including dental care, substance abuse, and mental health treatments.[3–5]

Spending on hospital care is the fastest-rising segment of the nation's health care bill. In 2004, daily room charges exceeded $5000 in some New Jersey hospitals. An appendectomy in California, including about 2 days in hospital, had an average list charge of $18 000. Nationally, federal data showed that the median charge for treating a heart attack was more than $20 000.[6] By 2005, health expenditures were about $2 trillion and hospital care represented almost 31% of that amount, as already noted. In 2005 health expenditures were 16% of gross domestic product and the percentage of health expenditures that involved public funds was 45%.[7]

Hospital costs are not just associated with what a hospital has to spend to maintain its infrastructure, whether it is the cost of labor or the acquisition of supplies or equipment; they are also related to hospital charges that are reflective of these internal costs. According to the US Agency for Healthcare Research and Quality, American hospitals charged $873 billion in 2005 – a nearly 90% increase from the $462 billion charged in 1997. The 2005 bill, which is adjusted for inflation, represents the total amount charged for 39 million hospital stays. The average annual rate of increase in the national hospital bill over the several years preceding the year 2005 was 4.5%. At this rate, researchers estimate that the annual national hospital bill may reach $1 trillion by 2008. In 2005 Medicare paid the bulk of the national hospital bill ($411 billion), followed by private insurance ($272 billion) and Medicaid ($124 billion). Uninsured hospital stays accounted for $38 billion in charges. The remaining $28 billion was for other insurers, including Workers' Compensation, TRICARE (US Department of Defense health plan for military and dependants), Title V (maternal and child health services block grants under the Social Security Act), and other government programs. One-fifth of the national hospital bill was for the treatment of just five conditions – coronary artery disease ($45 billion), pregnancy and childbirth ($44 billion), newborn infant care ($35 billion), heart attack ($32 billion), and congestive heart failure ($31 billion).[8] While the previous amounts are national totals, an insurer, Mutual of Omaha, had published in 2004 charges that represent average national costs for various conditions during a single hospitaliza-tion, acknowledging that some of these conditions might involve multiple hospitalizations over time: regular birth without complicating diagnoses ($5980), cesarean section birth without complications ($12 159), heart fail-ure and shock ($13 682), coronary bypass with cardiac catheterization ($81 334), medical back problems ($16 463), psychoses ($11 426), adult dia-betes ($10 931), adult pneumonia with complications ($14 384), and adult fractures, sprains, dislocations of the arm or leg ($9442).[9]

Hospital charges can be likened to the list price of an automobile in a dealer's showroom. Few pay the full amount because insurers negotiate dis-counts with the hospital and Medicare tells hospitals what it will pay. Yet, some insurers still pay total charges, such as when a policyholder goes to an out-of-network hospital with which the insurer has not negotiated a discount. In addition, insurers may have to make additional payments when charges for treating a patient exceed a specified amount, which frequently happens in hospitals with higher charges.

While charges have risen rapidly, they often have little relationship to the actual cost of services. Hospitals can raise charges to any amount the market will bear, but it is a strange market in that most hospital customers negotiate discounts off charges. One of the reasons why prices have risen is that hospi-tals have tried to increase the amount they could get from insurers who had often used charges as an initial point for negotiations. But in recent years, as charges have risen, insurers have begun to negotiate in other ways, basing payments, for example, on set amounts for a day's care or the treatment of a particular condition. In 1993, charges were, on average, 159% more than costs, based on data provided to Medicare. In 2003 the national average was 211% more than costs. In some states, those ratios are even higher. California, Florida, and Nevada had some of the highest hospital charges – close to 300% higher than costs, according to research conducted by Glenn Melnick, professor of health care finance at the University of Southern California.[6] There is no single formula or method for calculating hospital charges. As already noted, hospitals take into consideration elements such as labor costs, the number of uninsured patients the hospital treats, and whether the hospital contracts with many low-paying insurers. Some insurers pay less than Medicare, which also fails to meet overall hospital costs. Federal data show that in 2002 Medicare provided an overall margin of 1.7% to the hospital industry, more for inpatient care and less for outpatient. Overall, the nation's hospitals had a 4.4% margin in 2003. Since most hospitals rely on government health payments for about 50% of their revenue, private insurers who negotiate discounts provide much of the rest. The American Hospital Association says raising charges is one way hospitals can try to bring in additional money from individuals and insurers not covered by the discounts.[6]

Statistics published in 2008 on Medicare spending in the last 2 years of life at the five top teaching hospitals in the USA, as ranked by *US News and World Report* magazine,[10] revealed that the medical center at the University of California, Los Angeles, was the most extravagant, averaging $93 000 per patient; Johns Hopkins at $85 000 was next, followed by the Massachusetts General Hospital at $78 000. The Cleveland Clinic at $55 000 and the Mayo Clinic at $53 000 were the most cost-effective. The reasons for the differences among hospitals are not that one hospital has higher charges for a particular service compared to another. Instead, the high-cost hospitals deliver many more services for patients than the lower-cost hospitals: keeping patients in the hospital and in intensive care far longer, sending patients to many specialists, and performing many more tests and procedures. Also, physicians in high-expenditure institutions are typically reimbursed on a fee-for-service basis, which means that the more they do, the more income they earn. Mayo Clinic physicians, by contrast, are paid by salary and do not have the incentives to deliver more services than the patient needs. This comparison comes from the latest edition of the *Dartmouth Atlas of Health Care*, published by Dartmouth's Institute for Health Policy and Clinical Practice.[10] Researchers there for a long time have noted that there are large disparities in medical spending in different parts of the country and have demonstrated that patients usually do no better, and often fare worse, where spending is the highest. The Dartmouth researchers estimated that Medicare could save many billions of dollars annually without sacrificing the quality of care if all hospitals mirrored the practice patterns of the Mayo Clinic.[10]

As already noted, hospitals must confront the costs of health care on two fronts. They must pay for medical staff, equipment, and drugs, and, like any other organization, they must provide health insurance coverage for their own personnel. For example, in 2008 the Beth Israel Deaconess Medical Center of Boston had 6000 full-time workers. The major cost pressure on the hospital is the cost of salaries and benefits. With a shortage of nurses, pharmacists, physical therapists, and even some physicians, their salaries have been rising faster than inflation and more personnel are required to keep the hospital in operation. Since July 1, 2003 the work hours of medical residents are limited to an average 80 hours per week, with one day off in seven and a requisite 10-hour rest between on-call status and working a shift, as approved by the

Accreditation Council for Graduate Medical Education. But, a hospital must cover those remaining hours and must spend millions more on nurse practitioners, doctors, and other professionals. Hospital patients demand services, the services cost money, and with more people being covered at their workplace by some form of health insurance, they demand more services since someone else – a third party – is also paying their bills. But the provision of patient care is not free to the hospital. Added to this situation is the fact that baby boomers are going to force further increases in health care spending as they retire: according to the Centers for Medicare and Medicaid Services, this cost is expected to double to $4.3 trillion by 2017. Some of those older more demanding workers include many thousands of hospital workers around the country, which completes the circle.

Hospitals are always seeking new ways to reduce their costs, including group purchasing of supplies or changing to generic drugs from brand-name drugs. One hospital has even tried a reverse auction: vendors receive a list for operating supplies and implants and have to bid a sales price live online, which the hospital found saved it money.[11] But whatever they do, whether facing increasing health care costs to cover their own employees or trying to save money on their managerial costs, hospitals are no different than any other organizational entity in that they are not immune from the impact of the rising costs of health care simply because they are one of the resources that is also providing such services to the general public.

One possible way to reduce hospital costs is through gainsharing. According to a 5-year study that included more than 220 000 patients, giving physicians cash rewards to reduce hospital spending helps control costs without compromising quality or the patients' access to care.[12] The study compared six cardiac catheterization laboratories that established this kind of gainsharing program to 123 laboratories that did not implement such a program. The Arizona State University researchers found that gainsharing reduced hospital costs by 7.4%, or $315 per patient. That means, according to the researchers, that a national use of gainsharing could reduce hospital costs for coronary stent patients by about $195 million a year. Most of the savings from the gainsharing programs in the study resulted from lower prices for coronary stents. The gainsharing programs did not lead to any changes in patterns of patients' referrals and did not increase the overall risk of in-laboratory complications. According to the researchers, the gainsharing programs were associated with significant reductions in three specific complications. In fact, there was no evidence, according to the researchers, that gainsharing encouraged physicians to avoid existing health problems or pick the healthiest patients. Now, the gainsharing in this study refers only to one medical procedure. But, perhaps, it holds promise as another way in which physicians can make a contribution to reducing hospital costs in other medical areas.[12]

There are other ways that physicians can help reduce their patients' hospital bills. These include ordering preadmission tests to shorten hospital stays; scheduling admissions and discharges to avoid charges for extra days or weekend stays when the needed services may not be available; routinely reviewing the patient's hospital bill to determine whether there are unnecessary duplications of procedures ordered or when items are billed incorrectly for the patient and then telling the hospital administration; informing hospital administration when delayed or neglected tests or procedures require a longer hospital stay for the patient; being knowledgeable about the hospital's admitting and discharge regulations; and initiating early discharge planning when the physician knows a patient may require extended care facility or home health care after hospitalization.

One final note about hospital costs. Like any other organizational entity, hospitals are not isolated from the impact of America's general economy in terms of their viability whether the economy is improving or becoming worse. A good example of this statement is how the economic recession that beset America in 2008 and 2009 affected US hospitals. There were declines in overall admissions and elective surgery procedures, in addition to a very great increase in patients who could not pay after losing their health insurance due to unemployment, thus increasing the amount of uncompensated hospital care. Also, as the stock market declined hospitals were negatively affected by losses on their investments, which when gaining in value help set off some of the costs not covered by patients and insurers. Some hospitals had to reduce staff or services, such as those that were not making money or had high operating costs, while other hospitals had to close entirely. Many hospitals had to postpone expansions and upgrades, purchasing multimillion-dollar technology and other activities because of the lending problems which financial institutions in the USA had incurred. So while hospital costs generally continue to rise, other economic conditions like a recession can make it very difficult for hospitals to fulfill their own health care mission in providing as comprehensive a scope of care as possible because of economic conditions which are beyond their control.

Hospital utilization: a brief profile

Hospital revenues are generated from the use of the institution. In 2006, nonfederal short-stay hospitals in the USA performed 44.9 million procedures and the average length of stay of the patient was 4.8 days.[13] There were 34.7 million discharges or 1174.4 per 10 000 population. Also, 8.2% of the population stayed overnight. In addition, 90 million people visited their outpatient departments or 31.0 outpatient visits per 100 persons, while 115.3 million persons (a 2007 CDC figure later adjusted by the CDC in 2008 to 119 million) visited their emergency departments or 39.6 emergency department visits per 100 persons. Of those who visited the emergency departments only 13.9 million visits resulted in hospital admissions while even fewer, 2.2 million persons, were admitted to critical care.[7]

Diagnosis-related groups

One of the principal sources of income to a hospital is the Medicare program. With millions of people already enrolled in Medicare and with many more millions to come as the baby boomers reach retirement age, it is important to understand how Medicare reimburses hospitals. While insurers may negotiate charge rates for those under 65 years, they cannot do so for Medicare patients. Medicare has always been a flawed program due to the political compromises that were made in its enactment. Between 1966 and 1982, retrospective or cost-based reimbursement was the basis of Medicare payment. With cost-based reimbursement, the more a hospital spent, the greater its reimbursement. It has been argued that because hospitals could pass on excessive costs to third-party payers, they had no incentive to control costs and be careful purchasers of goods and services. Many economists and policy analysts believe that such a system of cost-based reimbursement encouraged inefficiency and directly resulted in inflationary health care costs. Thus, between 1967 and 1983, Medicare expenditures increased an average of 17% annually and by 1983, Medicare represented 63% of total federal outlays at a cost of $59 billion.[14] Medicare expenditures for inpatient care alone increased 10-fold, from about $3 billion in 1967 to $33 billion in 1983. By 2003, Medicare paid $82 billion for Medicare beneficiaries who were discharged from short-stay hospitals.[15,16]

The transition from Medicare's cost-based reimbursement system to a prospective payment system (PPS), commonly known as the diagnosis-related group (DRG) program, began in October 1983. In 1982 the US Congress passed the Tax Equity and Fiscal Responsibility Act (TEFRA). The purpose of the Act (PL 97-248) was to limit a hospital's reasonable costs on a per-admission or per-case basis. Less than 1 year later, Congress enacted the DRG-based PPS.

Medicare regulations require that the attending physician certify that the diagnoses and procedures performed during the hospital stay are accurate. Professional accredited personnel in the medical records department then assign to each patient's record the codes that express this information (*International Classification of Diseases Ninth Revision*, clinical modification (ICD-9-CM) codes) that lead to the DRGs. The thousands of individual ICD-9-CM codes are part of a set of mutually exclusive and exhaustive categories called 'major diagnostic categories.' Thus, in summary, DRGs are key to the PPS. By 1999, the methodology resulted in the creation of hundreds of DRGs according to the most prevalent diagnosis among patients using inpatient services. Each Medicare patient admitted to the hospital is assigned a DRG according to the principal diagnosis. Based on the patient's DRG classification a hospital receives a set reimbursement.

Under PPS, the basis of payment is a national standardized amount that represents an average payment for a typical case. DRGs based on principal diagnosis and other factors are used to group medically similar cases that require comparable resources for treatment. The other factors that account for differences in reimbursement for the DRG include differences in wages due to geographic characterizations, location of the hospital (urban or rural), whether the institution is a teaching hospital, a discretionary adjustment factor that accounts for changes in new technology and productivity, and adjustment related to treating a disproportionately large number of low-income patients.

Each DRG is assigned a weight based on its resource costs relative to the national average. These relative weights are recalibrated each year using the latest available charge data for Medicare discharges. To determine the Medicare reimbursement for an individual episode in a particular hospital, the standardized amount is adjusted, as already noted, by the relative weight of the DRG classification of the area wage level, the extent of the hospital's teaching activity, and the degree to which the hospital serves low-income patients. In addition, PPS established categories of outlier, or extremely costly, cases which receive supplemental amounts. In the years since PPS was implemented, the Centers for Medicare and Medicaid Services sought to refine the payment system to help ensure equitable payment of services and to address issues raised by the provider community.

Implicit in the PPS is the assumption that, by providing hospitals with economic incentives to be efficient, high-quality medical care can be achieved at costs far lower than it had been historically. Because Medicare's PPS concentrated on inpatient services provided in acute hospital settings, this system did not apply to all hospitals and all services. From the beginning, PPS singled out specific categories of hospitals, such as referral centers and sole community hospitals, for more generous payment. The Omnibus Budget Reconciliation Act of 1989 (PL 101-239) established another category of essential access small rural hospitals: Medicare-dependent hospitals, for which Medicare patients account for more than half of total inpatient days or discharges.

The Consolidated Omnibus Budget Reconciliation Act of 1986 (PL 99-272) established additional payments under PPS to hospitals that serve a disproportionately large share of low-income patients. This adjustment was believed necessary to ensure that low-income beneficiaries would have access to care. Certain specialized facilities – psychiatric, rehabilitation, long-term care, and children's hospitals – were excluded from the PPS. These hospitals have remained under the payment system established by TEFRA and payments to TEFRA hospitals are related to the hospital's actual allowable costs, limited by a facility-specific-cost-based target amount.[17] For those hospitals operating under the PPS, hospitals incur some financial risk if their actual costs exceed the predetermined rates of payment. Per-case payment, of which DRG is one type, was established to remove the incentives to increase length of stay or to increase the number of ancillary services provided. In an attempt to balance efficiency with quality and appropriateness of services, the Medicare PPS used a method of measuring case mix (DRGs) in order to adjust for clinical complexity and resource use.

In summary, there are three basic features of the Medicare PPS. First, all patients are classified into one of hundreds of DRGs. Second, the hospital receives a fixed payment per DRG to cover inpatient costs, with the exception of a few outlier cases in which the costs may not be fixed. Finally, as already noted, payments for the hospital's operating expenses are based on predetermined national and regional rates and hospital teaching status, but not on costs incurred by a particular hospital. These features encourage hospitals to become more efficient and provide Medicare with a mechanism to control costs.

Not surprisingly, hospitals have responded to the features of the PPS by changing their standards of operation. One method of concern to the Centers of Medicare and Medicaid Services and other interested groups has been the upcoding by hospitals to maximize their revenues. The accuracy of a hospital's Medicare DRG assignment is overseen by several agencies, including the quality improvement organizations (QIOs), the Office of Inspector General of the US DHHS, and the Medicare fiscal intermediary, such as Blue Cross. Medical record reviewers can determine when a hospital deliberately or inadvertently maximizes its DRG reimbursement. DRG 'creep' is the term used describing improper increases in case mix index (weighted average for all a hospital's DRGs). Coding more serious conditions or more intense than is documented by a medical record causes these increases. As examples, the OIG of DHHS using the weights of 1998 has documented how upcoding DRGs work:

- A patient with longstanding chronic obstructive pulmonary disease (COPD) is admitted with wheezing, rales, and a productive cough. The cause for admission is determined to be acute bronchitis (DRG 149, weight 0.59), but the physician lists this condition as secondary diagnosis and list COPD (DRG 88, weight 0.95) as the principal diagnosis. In such a situation, the admission for acute bronchitis should be shown as the principal diagnosis rather than the more highly weighted COPD.
- An elderly patient with painful joints is admitted to hospital. A workup indicates that osteoarthritis (DRG 245, relative weight 0.49) is the source of the problem, but the attending physician lists the principal diagnosis as septic arthritis (DRG 242, weight 1.04). There is no justification in the record for this diagnosis.[18]

In each of these cases, the peer review organization reviewing records would give the attesting physician the opportunity to discuss the cases and defend his or her actions. A pattern of substantial violations or a single 'gross and flagrant' (42 US code 1320c-5) case (usually one that would threaten a patient's life) would be referred to the OIG for potential sanction. Even if these cases were not chosen by the QIO for review, they might be identified by the fiscal intermediary, the insurance carrier, or the OIG during the studies, and the case would be followed up. The physician can also be involved in after-the-fact changes in the medical record in a less direct manner. The medical records department may independently change a physician's final diagnosis to reflect its reasoning for higher reimbursement without first obtaining a new physician's attestation.[18]

Unbundling the diagnostic codes

Another factor that may increase the costs the consumer-patient encounters when hospitalized is the unbundling of the diagnostic codes by physicians. The practice has many other names, including fragmentation, exploding charges, code creep, upcoding, or even multiple billing. No one really knows how extensive a problem this practice is, but when physician incomes becomes threatened by cutting physicians' reimbursement under Medicare or Medicaid programs or from contracting with managed care organizations, code manipulation is increasingly becoming more popular as one method to recoup lost income.

Code manipulation of current procedural terminology (CPT) codes by which physicians bill the third-party payer in order to obtain higher reimbursement for medical procedures than would be paid otherwise is not about which code is more appropriate for the procedure, but rather about the dollar values third-party payers assign to different CPT codes. Comprehensive multiple-procedure codes are usually given lower payment codes. Third-party payers state that most doctors usually charge less for the second procedure when more than one is performed at the same time. This is especially true for surgical procedures; more than one procedure may be performed with just one incision and one anesthetic, and the second procedure can be considered a logical follow-up of the first, depending upon the situation. For example, a total abdominal hysterectomy with a Marshall–Marchetti–Krantz procedure (CPT code 51840) is supposed to include salpingectomy (removal of the fallopian tubes) and oophorectomy (removal of one or both ovaries). But charged as a single package, the procedure pays a great deal less than if the hysterectomy with MMK, salpingectomy, and oophorectomy were billed individually. A worse example would be a bill for code 51840 (the bundled procedures) in addition to another bill for all the separate components. This would be equal to billing one patient for two total hysterectomies.

Another example of unbundling is called fragmentation of incidental procedures. Incidental procedures are generally performed as part of a larger procedure and, because they take little extra effort, are not usually paid separately. For example, an appendectomy can be incidental to the total removal of the stomach. But when done together and billed individually, each can enhance the cost of the gastrectomy by half. Another form of fragmentation is called exploding, as when a physician orders a single blood screening but bills for 17 different laboratory tests that were performed as part of that single blood screening.

Other techniques include upcoding, as already noted, that is, assigning a code that represents a more complex procedure or level of care than the one actually required or provided. Visit churning involves scheduling more than the necessary number of physician visits, usually on an outpatient basis. In contrast, an example of multiple visit coding would be when a physician who admits the patient to the hospital from the ER bills separately for seeing the patient in the ER and for a complete hospital visit following the patient's inpatient admission. The doctor has seen the patient only once but has billed twice. There are also situations in which it is the doctors who are multiplied. While more than one surgeon is needed to perform some surgical procedures, it is becoming increasingly common for co-surgeons to bill for performing a procedure that normally would only require one surgeon or one surgeon and surgical nurse.

In addition to the previous examples that can increase physician charges in the hospital, there are other more questionable procedures such as billing for procedures that are not even medically indicated or are inappropriate for the patient's age and sex. While such procedures may represent an extremely small percentage of the total claims submitted, they can add up to many hundreds of thousands of dollars not only for the third-party payer in terms of reimbursement but even for the hospitalized patients who may have to pay part of these costs, even though all of the actions might not constitute purposeful fraud in the legal sense. Another activity is called balance billing, whereby a physician will bill patients for the part of the bill the insurer won't pay even though the insurer in its contracts with patients includes harmless agreements to protect its members. But not all insurers have such an agreement in their contracts. A hold harmless agreement is a contractual agreement whereby one party assumes liability in a situation, thus relieving the other party of responsibility. Outside health care an example is a railroad sidetrack agreement with a manufacturing company under which the manufacturer is held harmless for damage to railroad equipment and tracks.

CPT stands for current procedural terminology. It is a handbook of codes like that of CPT-4, for example, which means a fourth edition of the CPT code and represents all the medical procedures that the American Medical Association publishes. Originally developed for medical research and statistical analysis, the CPT codes became popular with third-party payers as the use of so-called reasonable and customary fee schedules came into common use, especially after the introduction of Medicare DRGs. CPT, ICD-9-CM, and other coding systems are continuously being modified. Among sources of conflict is the fact that CPT-4 codes, for example, sometimes employ terminology that is not precise – called descriptors – and thus is open to interpretation by third-party payers and providers. When the descriptors are not clear, they permit much leeway in the use of the code and can lead to disputes between payers and physicians. While surgical codes are fairly exact, those for pathology, for example – especially clinical laboratory services – and for office visits are not as clear and more likely to lead to disagreements about their interpretation. For example, office visits have five distinct classifications – brief, limited, intermediate, extended, and comprehensive – and which level is appropriate for a specific visit depends upon the physician's decision. Payers differ also in how they use codes for privately insured patients as opposed to those patients covered by Medicare or Medicaid. Neither Medicare nor Medicaid gives much guidance to its intermediaries about how the codes should be interpreted. They let the carriers decide in most instances which, in turn, leads to inconsistent application of the codes, even by the same payer. All these factors can affect hospital charges and costs.

Hospital medications

Regardless of the diagnosis and treatment, medical errors, also involving medications, in a hospital setting are an increasing problem. A 1999 study that was sponsored by the US National Academy of Science's Institute of Medicine (IOM) estimated that medical errors in hospitals were responsible for the deaths of 44 000–98 000 Americans each year and were said to cost hospitals between \$17 billion and \$29 billion nationwide.[19] In 2006, HealthGrades, a leading health care ratings company, stated that among the 40 million hospitalizations covered under Medicare from 2002 to 2004, there were 1.24 million patient safety incidents in American hospitals: the incidents varied from state to state and among the best and worst hospitals and cost Medicare \$9.3 billion.[20] The patient safety incidents with the highest prevalence were decubitus ulcer and postoperative sepsis.

However, one of the biggest threats in hospitals in regard to medical errors pertains to medications. In 2006, the IOM of the National Academy of Sciences issued a follow-up report to its 1999 report titled *Preventing Medication Errors: Quality Chasm Series* that estimated that there were 380 000–450 000 hospital drug errors each year. This number rose very greatly in long-term care facilities, where almost 800 000 people suffered as a result of medication errors.[21] The report concluded that there are at least 1.5 million preventable medication errors overall each year and emphasized that the true number may be larger. Sometimes these errors take place when patients are at their most vulnerable in terms of illness and are least able to spot the problem. The US Agency of Healthcare Research and Quality studied patients admitted to two intensive care units and found that almost 10% of patients suffered a preventable adverse event, and most of these events involved medication errors.[22] To combat these medication errors a few hospitals, like those within the Veterans Administration system, have their patients wear bracelets with bar codes that match up with the bar codes on their medications. Other hospitals employ computer programs to eliminate the potential for mix-ups in the pharmacy. In February 2004 the Food and Drug Administration, in seeking to improve the safety and accuracy of in-hospital medications, issued a regulation that requires bar codes on most prescription drugs and on over-the-counter medication that is commonly used in hospitals.[23]

Yet, despite the existence of bar codes and computers, most hospitals still employ the old-fashioned approach in prescribing medications. The physician writes the prescription, the pharmacist reads the handwriting, and the patient takes the medication. Each prescription requires that the physician, pharmacist, and nurses are in perfect communication with each other that the medication and dosage are correct. Every patient is just a single misunderstanding – one illegibly written prescription, one misplaced decimal point, one misunderstood word, or one transcription error – away from a medical error. As examples, a simple mistake such as putting the decimal point in the wrong place can have serious consequences because a patient's dosage could be 10 times the recommended amount.

Drugs with similar names are another source of error, such as the pain medication Celebrex and the antidepressant Celexa or the tranquilizer Zyprexa and the antihistamine Zyrtec. Other medication errors include prescribing the wrong drug, ordering an inaccurate dosage, or administering a drug at the wrong time. Physician order entries on the computer should help eliminate illegible written prescriptions, decimal point errors, and doses outside the 'usual range.'

On November 18, 2003 the US Pharmacopeia (USP) reported that one-third of hospital medication errors that reach patients involve older adults. In 2002 there were 192 477 medication errors documented by the USP and 3213 or 1.7% of the total resulted in patient injury.[24] The USP is a nonprofit, nongovernmental, standard-setting organization that advances public health by ensuring the quality and consistency of medicines, promoting the safe and proper use of medications, and verifying ingredients in dietary supplements. These standards, that are recognized worldwide, are developed by a unique process of public involvement through the contributions of volunteers representing pharmacy, medicine, and other health professions as well as science, academia, government, the pharmaceutical industry, and consumer organizations. The information appears in the organization's 2002 MEDMARX annual data report, which analyzed the medication errors reported to the MEDMARX-USP. MEDMARX is a national, internet-accessible anonymous reporting database that hospitals and health care systems use to track and trend medication errors and is operated by the USP. As of 2003, fewer than 10% of US hospitals participated and the information collected is protected from public view. MEDMARX helps hospitals understand and ultimately prevent medication errors in hospitals. USP created MEDMARX to help health care facilities understand the causes of medication errors and the factors that contribute to them in order to improve patient care and safety.

The MEDMARX data report revealed a number of important findings about the older-adult population, including the following: more than one-half (55%) of fatal hospital medication errors reported involved older adults; when medication errors caused harm to older adults, 9.6% were prescribing errors; when the harm took place, wrong route (7%), such as tube feeding administered intravenously, and wrong administration technique (6.5%), such as not diluting concentrated medications, were the second and third most common errors involving those age 65 years and older; and omission errors (43%), improper dose or quantity errors (18%), and unauthorized medication errors (11%) were the most common type of medication errors experienced by older adults.[24]

A study published by the University of Minnesota in June 2007 indicated that the rate of medication errors skyrocketed from 5% in 1992 to 25% in 2007, with illegible handwriting and transcription errors accounting for as much as 61% of the medication errors in hospitals. But when US hospitals changed to computerized physician order entry systems there was a decline of 66% in prescription errors. However, a review of the literature also indicated that, while the number of medication errors did decrease as a whole, the incidence of one kind of error, prescribing the wrong drug, did not decrease and in five of the 12 studies, the number of adverse events from drug errors did not decrease. More than 500 000 patients suffer injuries or deaths from adverse events, costing up to $5.6 million annually per hospital.[25]

Given the number and kinds of different errors hospitals can make during a patient's stay, beginning October 1, 2008 Medicare, in addition to possibly other insurers, stopped paying for extra-cost preventable errors. Prior to this date, even when a hospital made a preventable error, it could be reimbursed for the extra treatment that the patient requires as a result of the error. Some errors can add $10 000–100 000 to the cost of hospital stay. From October 1, 2008 hospitals cannot bill the injured patient for those extra costs, with more incidents to be added in the future. These include: urinary tract infections from catheters, blood stream infections from using catheters, injury from falls, bed sores, or pressure ulcers, objects left in patient during surgery, blood compatibility, giving a dangerously wrong blood type, an infection after heart surgery called mediastinitis, and air embolism, an air bubble in a blood vessel. Medicare estimates that the move will save the government about $100 million between 2008 and 2013. Medicare's decision has led some private insurers like Aetna and Wellpoint, the nation's largest insurers, to move to make hospitals absorb the costs of serious errors and the state of Pennsylvania stated it would follow Medicare's example and stop Medicaid payments as well.[26] By the winter of 2008 hospitals in 11 states had agreed to waive fees for certain rare errors called 'never events' because safety experts stated they should never happen at all.

While it is not clear how many patients are being billed for hospital errors, the federal Medicare program has an idea. In 2006, Medicare was billed 764 times for objects left behind in surgery, resulting in an average payment of nearly $62 000 per incident. The agency was billed 33 times for patients who received the wrong blood, at an average cost of $46 000 each, and was billed nearly 323 000 times for the worst kind of pressure ulcers, a preventable problem, at a cost of $40 381 apiece. Wrong site procedures are those in which doctors operate on the wrong body part, the wrong place, and in some cases, the wrong person. According to a 2006 study published in the *Archives of Surgery*, the number of wrong site procedures performed in the USA ranges from 1300 to 2700.[27] Each year doctors and hospital administrators worry that if hospitals waive fees for errors, they'll be admitting liability that could hurt them in court, But despite the perception that most injured patients sue to recover damages, many lack the skills or resources to go to court, and many other are rejected when malpractice lawyers won't accept their cases.[27]

However, medical errors, including those involving medications, are not the only source of hospital problems. Another is the fact that the US General Accountability Office (GAO) in April 2008 issued a report titled *Health-Care-Associated Infections in Hospitals* and reported that the federal government is not doing enough to protect patients from becoming infected at hospitals, endangering many thousands of lives and costing billion of dollars, which the CDC has estimated at $20 billion a year.[28] The GAO reported that government has not established sufficient standards for hospitals to follow or pushed hospitals to follow those standards to reduce infections. About 90 000 Americans die after contracting infections in hospitals each year and 1.9 million become sick from bacteria, according to the Consumer Union, an interest group that has been advocating more action to prevent hospital-associated infections. The deaths alone account for $5 billion that is added to the nation's health care spending. Patients often receive infections through intravenous tubes, catheters, and ventilators to which they are attached. Bacteria, often meticillin (formerly methicillin: an antibiotic of the penicillin class)-resistant *Staphylcococcus aureus* or MRSA, contaminate the blood, urinary tracts, and surgical sites. As already noted, since October 2008 the

Centers for Medicare and Medicaid Services will not pay hospitals more to treat infections for patients who developed the infections at the facilities. But Medicare has established too few standards and the ones they have developed are vague. The CDC has issued 13 guidelines for hospitals and infection control but has failed to tell hospitals which of the 1200 recommended practices these guidelines contain are the most important for hospitals to follow. Physician associations do offer more specific guidelines, according to the GAO, such as requiring hospitals to offer flu vaccinations to their staff. Measures to reduce infection are known, such as making sure staff members wash their hands more often, increasing the use of medical devices coated with antibacterial agents, wearing sterile gowns and gloves, protecting patients with antiseptics, sterile drapes, and dressings, and properly ventilating operating rooms. States have assumed the lead on the hospital infection issue. Since Illinois passed the first law in 2003, by 2009 about 25 states had enacted measures to publish infection rates at hospitals. However, the collection of infection data from hospitals and using Medicare and Medicaid payments more to bring about improvements still remain a problem, even though the US DHHS states that it does collect data, cites hospitals for improper practices, and requires hospitals to solve the problems. But, the data DHHS collects through multiple databases across the federal department have not been used effectively by DHHS to provide a complete picture of the extent of the problem.[28,29]

Report cards

In view of the many problems which consumer-patients may encounter as a result of their hospital stay, how can they determine the quality of the hospital to which they are being admitted, aside from its being accredited by organizations such as the JCAHO? One of the newest innovations in judging hospital care is report cards. This effort to judge the quality of hospitals is so new that there is no standardization in writing these reports or agreement on the contents of care they should measure and include. Report cards are now available nationally, by state, and locally. But they have shortcomings. They may not be available in all parts of the country and hospitals do not routinely measure the coordination of care among various providers, error rates, the sufficiency of pain relief, or functional outcomes of medical treatments.

As a few examples, in May 2008 *Consumer Reports* released a rating system whereby almost 3000 hospitals nationwide are rated on the length of hospital stays and number of doctor visits for adult Medicare patients facing chronic diseases, including cancer, diabetes, renal failure, dementia, and liver, vascular and heart disease.[30] The ratings address complicated illnesses that affect more than 90 million Americans. As a group, these diagnoses are responsible for seven out of 10 deaths of older adults on Medicare, according to the *Dartmouth Atlas of Health Care*, the key source of data for the rating system.[31]*Consumer Reports* simplified the *Atlas* data so that consumers could better decide whether they want to fight a disease aggressively, with many doctors and specialists, or as conservatively as possible, such as in cases of late-stage cancer or when a person wishes little treatment. The rating also includes the patient's after-Medicare out-of-pocket expense for the hospital stay. The internet site is http://www.consumerreports.org/health/doctors-and-hospitals. The federal government's website (http://www.hospitalcompare.hhs.gov) now allows consumers to access information on 2500 hospitals around the USA in regard to patient satisfaction scores about a hospital. Some of the questions include the following examples: Did doctors treat patients with courtesy and respect? How often were the room and bathroom cleaned? Was the area around the room quiet? And did the patient get immediate help after pressing the call button? Since 2003 the website has helped consumers compare issues such as how quickly aspirin was given after a heart attack and how and when antibiotics were used. Consumers can compare up to three hospitals in regard to various questions. The information was collected by hospitals from a random sample of patients in October 2006 and June 2007 and the survey, developed by the government, was administered 48 hours to 6 weeks after patients were discharged. For the first time consumers can now find out and compare at the federal government's website (http://www.hospitalcompare. hhs.gov) death rates among hospitals even within their own zip code according to three criteria – death rates by heart attack, heart failure, and pneumonia – which are widely viewed as yardsticks of a hospital's overall performance. Another website is that of the US Agency for Healthcare Research and Quality that has a recommended checklist for choosing a hospital (http://www. ahrq.gov/consumer/qnt/qnthosp.htm#choosing-). One website (http://www. leapfroggroup.org/for_consumers) is a consortium of large health care purchasers that created its own survey to judge hospital quality and safety, while http://www.qualitycheck.org is the independent not-for-profit Joint Commission database of health care organizations. The Joint Commission, which evaluates and considers accreditation for more than 15 000 groups, is overseen by a board of doctors, nurses, and consumers. As a final example, the *Dartmouth Atlas* project at http://www.dartmouthatlas.org/- uses Medicare data to analyze and compare how medicine is practiced across the country and can be searched on a national and local basis.

Conclusion

Hospital costs are the single biggest impetus behind medical inflation today. This situation is forcing everyone to take another look at how hospitals will be paid and regulated. Medicare has decided not to pay for certain medical errors. Consumer organizations and others are setting up websites whereby patients can judge the quality of the hospital to which they may be admitted. Insurers are beginning to establish tiered hospital networks in which consumers pay more out of their own pockets for care in expensive hospitals. In 2004 Massachusetts state employees covered by the Tufts Health Plan, for example, paid an admissions co-pay of $200 if they chose hospitals the plan deemed lower-cost and higher-quality, but paid an admissions co-pay of $400 if they chose to go to higher-cost/lower-quality hospitals. In addition, consumers are demanding discounts for uninsured patients and individuals who have high-deductible policies while some insurers and employers are demanding that hospitals provide data on quality to justify their higher costs. Employers state that a hospital with higher initial costs may prove less expensive in the long run if it has a lower rate of infection or other complications.

While hospitals have varying sponsorships or orientations such as religious, government, profit, or nonprofit, the degree and excellence of care a hospital provides do not depend upon its ownership. All hospitals should be judged on their own merits. Proprietary hospitals, with notable exceptions, tend to concentrate on illnesses like appendectomies and tonsillectomies that can be treated relatively simply and that require a minimum of operating room personnel and equipment, unlike the elaborate equipment or highly specialized technical staff that might characterize a university teaching hospital. If hospitalization calls for routine obstetrical care or bed rest, traction and analgesics for a back disorder, a patient may do just as well medically and, perhaps, even better financially in an accredited proprietary hospital than in a more expensive accredited nonprofit voluntary hospital. Proprietary hospitals may have lower daily charges than nonprofit community hospitals because of reduced operating costs and better management efficiency since they operate on the profit motive and seek to achieve such efficiencies. On the other hand, if a person has a brain tumor and requires neurosurgery, that person would be better off in a university teaching hospital where the cutting-edge technologies are being used rather than a proprietary hospital.

Remember, regardless of costs, and today's hospitals are confronted with rising costs and staffing shortages as a result of rapid technological changes occurring in American medicine, the purpose of the hospital is and has always been the same – to preserve and prolong human life in as healthful a state as possible and that is a price that is beyond any measurable value.

References

1. What is a hospital? In: *Centerscope*. Washington, DC: Washington Hospital Center, 1977: 4.

2. Xuequan M. Americans made over 1 bln hospital, doctor visits in 2006. *China View* August 7, 2008; available online at: http://news.xinhuanet.com/english/2008-08/07/content_9005362.htm; accessed August 10, 2008.

3. *Source Book of Health Insurance Data, 2002.* Washington, DC: Health Insurance Association of America, 2002: 90–91.

4. Goldstein J. Emergency room visits hit record high. *Wall Street J* 2008; August 6.

5. US Department of Health and Human Services. *Recovery Act (AARA): Community Health Center Grants.* Rockville, MD: Health Resources and Services Administration, 2009; available online at http://www.hhs.gov/recovery/hrsa/healthcentergrants.html; accessed on March 4, 2009.

6. Appleby J. Hospital bills spin out of control. *USA Today* 2004; April 13.

7. US Department of Health and Human Services. *Health United States, 2007.* Centers for Disease Control and Prevention. Washington, DC: National Center for Health Statistics, 2007: 376, 379–380 (Tables 98–101, 121, 124).

8. Hospital bill fast approaching $1 trillion. Rockville, MD: Agency for Healthcare Research and Quality, 2007; available online at http://www.ahrq.gov/news/nn/nn121207.htm; accessed on June 16, 2008.

9. *Current Trends in Health Care and Dental Costs Utilization.* Omaha, NE: Mutual of Omaha Insurance Company, 2004.

10. Quality care at bargain prices. *N Y Times* 2008; April 10.

11. Celaschi R. Hospitals battle health care costs on two fronts. *Boston Business J* 2008; March 28.

12. Doctors can help lower hospital costs. *US News World Rep* 2008; May 13.

13. US Department of Health and Human Services. *Summary Health Statistics for US Population: National Health Interview Survey, 2006.* Centers for Disease Control and Prevention. Hyattsville, MD: National Center for Health Statistics, 2006; Table 17.

14. Sager M, Leventhal E, Easterling D. The impact of Medicare's prospective payment system on Wisconsin nursing homes. *JAMA* 257: 1987; 1762–1766.

15. Berenson R A, Pawlson L G. The Medicare prospective payment system. *J Am Geriatr Soc* 32: 1984; 843–848.

16. *Medicare and Medicaid Statistical Supplement, 2005. Health Care Financing Review.* Washington, DC: Centers for Medicare and Medicaid Services, 2006; 69 (Table 23).

17. Saunders W D. Overview. In: *Healthcare Financing Review/Winter 1993.* Washington, DC: Centers for Medicare and Medicaid Services, 1993: 1.

18. Kusserow R P, Steely B L. Pitfalls and sanctions to avoid. *Consultant* 1989; March: 94.

19. Kohn L, Corrigan J M, Molla S, *et al. To Err is Human: Building a Safer Health System.* Institute of Medicine. Washington, DC: National Academy Press, 2000.

20. Hospital errors cost Medicare $9.3 billion over three years. *Senior J* 2006; April 3: available online at: http://senior/NEWS/Health/6-04-03-MedicalErrors.htm; accessed on June 20, 2008.

21. National Academy of Sciences. *Preventing Medication Errors: Quality Chasm Series.* Washington, DC: Institute of Medicine, 2006; available online at: http://seniorjournal.com/NEWS/Health/6-04-03-MedicalErrors.htm; accessed on June 20, 2008.

22. US Department of Health and Human Services. *ICU Patients at Significant Risk for Adverse Events and Serious Errors.* Rockville, MD: Agency for Healthcare Research and Quality, 2005 (press release).

23. Traynor K. *FDA Releases Final Rule on Bar Coding.* Bethesda, MD: American Society of Health System Pharmacists, 2004.

24. *USP Releases Fourth Annual Report on Medication Errors in US Hospitals.* Rockville, MD: United States Pharmacopeia, 2003 (news release).

25. *Skyrocketing Hospital Medication Errors Can Be Reduced 66%, Says New Study.* Available online at: seniorjournal.com, June 27, 2007; available online at: http://seniorjournal.com/NEWS/Health/2007/7-06-27-Skyrocketing.htm; accessed on June 20, 2008.

26. Neergaard L. Insurers to stop paying for hospital errors. *Washington Beacon* 2008; April: 10–11.
27. Aleccia J. Patients still stuck with bill for medical errors. MSNBC February 29, 2008; available online at http://www.msnb.msn.com/id/23341360/; accessed on June 20, 2008.
28. Rockoff J D. Report calls for better hospital standards. *Sun* 2008; April 17: 2A.
29. Greider K. Battling superbugs. *AARP Bull* 2009; March: 13–14.
30. Shedden M. New ratings track hospitals' approach to chronic patient care. *Tampa Tribune* May 29, 2008; available online at: http://www.msnbc.msncom/id/24874009/; accessed on June 21, 2008.

7

Medical technology

Introduction

As the costs of American health care continue to soar, attention has focused on causes such as the price of medications and the costs of hospitalization. Other reasons that are cited include rising personal incomes, a growing share of health care costs being paid by third parties, and an aging American population, all of which have increased the demand for health care services and have contributed to the historic growth in spending. In fact, the Congressional Budget Office (CBO) has projected that, without changes in law, total spending on health services in the USA would rise from 16% of gross domestic product (GDP) in 2007 to 25% in 2025 and 49% in 2082. Federal spending on Medicare (net of beneficiaries' premiums) and Medicaid would rise from 4% of GDP in 2007 to 7% in 2025 and 19% in 2082.[1]

But a very basic question bothers health authorities as to why spending on health care consistently increases more quickly than spending on other goods and services. One of the key reasons they cite is the development and diffusion of medical technology. Some new technologies – many vaccines, for example – result in lower spending, but research has shown that, on balance, changing technologies in medicine result in increased spending and account for one-half to two-thirds of the increase in health care spending in excess of general inflation.[2] By 2004, medical technology spending exceeded $200 billion a year.[3]

History of medical technology assessment

Medical technology may be defined as the procedures, equipment, and processes by which medical care is delivered. It can range from new medical and surgical procedures like hip replacements, medications like biological agents, medical devices like magnetic resonance imaging (MRI), to new support systems like electronic medical records. A good example of how medical technology can increase the life span and improve the well-being of an individual is the treatment of preterm babies for which very little could be accomplished in 1950. But by 1990, advances in technology, including special ventilators, an artificial pulmonary surfactant to help the development of infant lungs, neonatal intensive care, and steroids for the mother and/or baby, helped lower mortality to one-third of its 1950 level, with an overall increase in life expectancy of about 12 years per low-birthweight baby.[4]

One of the major issues in regard to the development of medical technology is cost control. Related to this issue is the assessment of the treatment and the technology itself, namely, what works and what does not. Technology evaluations examine not only the clinical aspects of a technology but also its economic performance. One of the major concerns related to technology assessment, such as in regard to medical devices, is that clinical evaluations are organized to look at the safety of the devices rather than take into account their financial considerations. In addition, if examining costs, technology assessment generally seeks to analyze the cost of the technology compared to its benefit before any solid outcome studies have already been performed comparing the new technology with the existing technology. Manufacturers employ technology assessment in promoting their products, seeking approval for their use from regulatory agencies, convincing third-party payers to reimburse providers for their use, and making research and development decisions about the product. Technology assessment helps health care providers judge which set of technologies they should purchase or use in a given medical situation. Third-party payers look at technology assessments to decide whether they should cover a technology in their payment policies. When assessing a technology regulators are more concerned about its safety and effectiveness than its costs. Finally, technology assessment is important to patients because they must make decisions concerning their medical treatment and such assessments are most important in knowing what a given kind of technology can and cannot do.

The problems which concern medical technology today are that most technologies are not required to show effectiveness and most medical care predates very stringent testing. In addition, many technologies are employed in ways other than their original intent and, even if their effects on health are understood, their economic and social impact on society itself is not necessarily comprehended. The development of technology is not a process over which most governments have control. For a technology assessment to be considered successful it must be scientifically and clinically believable and the information made available to clinicians, policymakers, and the public. In addition, along with the results there should be policy recommendations in regard to the technology which are clearly understood, with the manufacturer making a commitment in regard to marketing the technology as well as educating interested parties about it.

In 2008, the Institute of Medicine of the National Academy of Sciences published a study, *Knowing What Works in Health Care: A Roadmap for the*

Nation[5] in which the Institute recommends the establishment of a national clinical effectiveness program, whose task it would be to assess treatments and technologies for clinical efficacy. If established in a way that ensures transparency, scientific rigor, and high standards for accountability and objectivity, the proposed national program would be a trusted resource for reliable information on the effectiveness of health services. With thousands of new clinical studies published each year, the amount of medical data has become so huge that it is essentially unmanageable for providers, patients, health plans, and others. Most people, including many health professionals, lack the scientific training necessary to evaluate and interpret such clinical findings by themselves. Moreover, research has shown that when reviews are financed by manufacturers or vendors – as a significant proportion of the reviews are – they are more likely to show effectiveness, which leads some to question whether, or to what extent, the cumulative body of evidence for any given health care product or service is biased.

The idea of the need for technology assessment and clinical effectiveness studies is not really new. Since its establishment in 1965, the Medicare program has been prevented by Congress from taking costs into consideration when deciding what benefits the program should include. Medicare can only consider what is medically 'reasonable and necessary.' In addition, there has been a history of federal agencies being established in the past to assess health care technology, all to no avail. One technology assessment agency whose purpose went well beyond health care was the Office of Technology Assessment, established in 1974 and eliminated by Congress in 1995. The first effort devoted to health care technology was the National Center for Health Care Technology, which Congress established in 1978. The purpose of the Center was to assess technology for its safety, efficacy, economics, ethics, and impact on society. Any effort to control costs was not in its Congressional authorization, but the fact that economics was included opened the way for considering the impact of costs. The Center had no regulatory authority but was limited to commissioning original research, setting up demonstration projects, and evaluating specific technologies – and remaining unbiased in the process. In 1981, Congress eliminated this agency. The medical profession and medical manufacturing associations opposed the agency because they believed that the agency's mandate infringed on their own prerogatives. In 1985, Congress created another agency with similar purposes: the Agency for Health Care Policy and Research, which still functions today. Renamed the Agency for Health Care Research and Quality, the organization's former authority to recommend payment decisions to Medicare and Medicaid has been eliminated.[6]

Essentially, as already noted, technology assessment evaluates not only the clinical aspects of a technology but also its economic performance. When evaluating the cost or the economic impact of health care technology, there are many kinds of cost studies that can be undertaken. These include: *an analysis of the cost of illness*: the economic impact of illness/condition; *a cost minimization analysis*: the least costly among alternatives that are assumed to yield equivalent outcomes; *cost-effectiveness analysis*: costs in monetary units as well as outcomes in quantitative nonmonetary units such as reduced mortality, morbidity, and life-years saved; and a *cost–benefit analysis*: costs and outcomes in monetary units, both of which are quantified in common monetary units.[7]

When examining the evidence from cost studies, cost study characteristics that must be taken into consideration include: the perspective of the evaluation (e.g., society, payer, provider, and patient); direct costs (medical and nonmedical); indirect costs (e.g., loss of productivity); actual costs versus charges/prices; time frame (short-term or long-term); marginal costs versus average costs; discounting; correction for inflation; and sensitivity analysis.[7]

In conducting health technology assessments, 10 steps are suggested: identify assessment topics; specify assessment problem; determine locus or responsibility of assessment; retrieve evidence; collect new primary data; interpret evidence; synthesize evidence; formulate findings and recommendations; disseminate findings and recommendations; and monitor impact.[7]

While the Institute of Medicine recommends the establishment of a national clinical effectiveness program, there are currently several federal agencies with health technology functions. Agencies within the US Department of Health and Human Services include:

- Agency for Healthcare Research and Quality (AHQR)
- Centers for Disease Control and Protection (CDC)
- Food and Drug Administration (FDA)
- Centers for Medicare and Medicaid Services (CMS)
- National Institutes of Health (NIH).

In addition, other federal agencies with health technology assessment-related activities include:

- Department of Veterans Affairs (DVA)
- Medicare Payment Advisory Committee (MedPac)
- Congressional Budget Office (CBO)
- Government Accountability Office (GAO).

One of the best sources of health technology assessment-related information is the National Library of Medicine (NLM) at the NIH, which maintains several searchable databases, including MEDLINE. Another resource is the Cochrane Collaboration Library, an international database of systematic reviews of the effects of health care interventions.

The cost drivers

In analyzing how the costs of medical technology contribute to total health care spending in the USA, there are some cost drivers which any federal agency examining such problems must take into consideration. There is a great deal of evidence that the overuse and misuse of technology lead to spending that exceeds its actual value for the patients who are receiving its benefits. In the category of diagnostic imaging, instruments such as computed tomography (CT) scans, positron emission tomography (PET) scans, and magnetic resonance imaging (MRI) scanners had grown by 2004 to a $100 billion-a-year business. This growth in spending has been fueled to a large degree by the increase in the number of machines that hospitals, physician offices, and imaging centers have been installing. This, in turn, has led to an overcapacity in many geographical areas and has given physicians the incentives to prescribe unnecessary procedures. Duplication of procedures (that is, a patient first receives an MRI and then a PET scan, even though the application of both procedures may not help the physician get closer to the diagnosis) and the overuse of high-end procedures in situations where they contribute little value has also unnecessarily increased technology spending.[3]

There are three basic reasons why medical technology is not being used in the most cost-effective manner. First, patients, for the most part, do not pay directly out of their own pocket for the health care services they receive so they sometimes can make unreasonable demands on a physician to use the medical technology when the physician is diagnosing and treating their illness. If patients know that a third-party payer will reimburse an institution for a CT scan without any cost to the patient, why not ask for it for their own peace of mind? Second, a new technology may be adopted because of its clinical superiority to existing technologies, but there is still no market mechanism to guarantee that the new technology will be used where it is clinically most appropriate or where it affords the highest value for the patient compared with other treatments. Third, because there is no market mechanism for determining the value of a medical technology, there is no generally accepted screening process to assess its value; cost-effectiveness is not a criterion for the regulatory approval of procedures, and manufacturers do not always perform studies of the economic benefits of new procedures.[3]

A 2007 study by the Center for Studying Health System Change is a good example of the use of medical technology.[8] The report noted that that the use of CT scans in the USA nearly doubled between 2000 and 2005, from 12 scans per 100 people to 22 per 100. The increase was due to the fact that the imaging machines, which can cost $1 million to $2 million a year, are useful for diagnosing more problems. Karen Ignani, chief executive officer of America's Health Insurance Plans,[9] a trade group representing the health insurance industry, has noted that when hospitals and physicians buy the equipment there is a strong incentive to use it, especially if hospitals and physicians are tempted by the income they receive from the tests, which can range from $500 to $1000 or more apiece, as they see their other sources of income shrink from government health programs and commercial insurers.

However, there are other downsides to the use of medical technology aside from the technology increasing health care costs. Insurers are afraid that some patients are being exposed to dangerous radiation levels from having repeated CT and PET scans, which use many times the radiation of a regular X-ray. Sometimes scans are repeated because the initial ones were not performed properly and because the equipment is outdated or the technicians were poorly trained. Physicians are also concerned about patients receiving excessive radiation exposure when they receive scans that are not needed or are ordered as 'defensive medicine' to protect physicians against the possibility of medical malpractice lawsuits. There is also a concern that unscrupulous physicians without adequate expertise are referring their patients for tests in their own offices or to imaging facilities in which they have a financial interest. As a result, health insurers are requiring more preauthorizations before patients can receive these scans, and setting other restrictions, including mandating that imaging equipment and the medical staff operating the equipment be credentialed in advance. This situation has also contributed to increasing health care costs.

Sometimes doctors order diagnostic tests that do not need preauthorization, even if it provides less helpful information than the ones they prefer and then seek approval for a more advanced test if the first one shows it is needed. Sometimes, the preauthorization has the potential to place the patient's life in even more danger. For example, cardiologists who want to assess blood flow and blockages inside a patient's heart arteries would prefer a nuclear cardiology test. With that, a small amount of a radioactive substance is injected in the blood and tracked using a camera. But some doctors will instead order a cardiac authorization, which does not require advance authorization but involves threading a catheter through a blood vessel up into the patient's heart and carries a 10-times-higher risk of complications such as heart attack or stroke. However, evidence has shown that, when imaging machines are used appropriately, they can hold down expenses and improve patient outcomes such as finding cardiac problems early enough to prevent a heart attack.

The Medicare program is also trying to find ways to hold down its spending on imaging services after its annual cost doubled from $6 billion in 2000 to $12 billion in 2005. By 2007, insurer limitations on the use of MRIs, CT scans, PET scans, and nuclear cardiology imaging became widespread and started a new industry of insurance consultants called radiology benefit managers.[8] Even back in 1998, medical technology was being considered as the basis of spiraling health care costs. According to Michael E. Chernow, health economist at the University of Michigan School of Public

Health, 'the reason why health care costs are higher now than they have been in the past is because of new medical technology. It's not increased waste. It's not fraud. It's not increased lawsuits. It's not the fact that people on average are older – all that may contribute, but the predominant factor relates to the development and utilization of new medical techniques of which there are an enormous number.'[10,11]

Financial impact of new medical technology

Overall, health experts believe that new medical technology has contributed to the rise in health care costs, although any medical technology may increase or decrease such expenditures in and of itself. But there are various factors involved in making such determinations. For example, is the new technology supplanting either completely or partially any existing technology that has previously been used in treating the patient or is it merely supplementing current technology that is presently being used in the patient's treatment? Depending on the use of the new technology, will it increase or lower the costs of patient treatment on an individual basis? When examining the costs of the new technology for each patient, what is the relationship between the use of the new technology and its effect on the use or costs of other health services such as hospitalization or outpatient physician office visits?

A good example of how new technology can improve the treatment of patients, yet bring about financial savings for the institution that implements the technology, relates in this instance to the barcoding of medications in a hospital. Hospitals incur $2200 in additional costs per adverse drug event, including drug–drug interactions, at a cost nationally of $2 billion per year. Instituting a barcode-assisted medication-dispensing system in hospital pharmacies can not only reduce hospital pharmacy dispensing errors that typically involve the incorrect medication strength or dosage form but also bring about a positive financial return on investment for the hospital. For example, after initiating a barcode-assisted dispensing system, one hospital pharmacy decreased the rate of adverse drug events from dispensing errors by 63% (from 0.10 to 0.07%).[12] In addition, implementation of this system resulted in a positive financial return on investment to the hospital. The study's authors performed a cost–benefit analysis of the medication barcode system within a large hospital pharmacy. They examined the net financial cost and benefit of initiating a system over a 5-year period. In inflating and time-value-adjusted 2005 dollars, total costs during the 5 years were $2.24 million ($1.31 million on one-time costs during the initial 3.5 years and $342 000 per year in recurring costs starting in year 3). The primary benefit was a decrease in adverse drug events from dispensing errors (517 errors averted annually), resulting in annual savings of $2.2 million. The net benefit after 5 years was $3.49 million. The break-even point for the hospital's investment took place within 1 year of the system becoming fully operational.[12] The problem of studying specific technologies and their impact on health care costs is that it is difficult to extrapolate them to an aggregate or national level.

Another factor relates to how extensively the new technology is being used. Can it treat patients whose illness up to that point was not treatable? Can it find new populations which might require existing treatments? Can it be used as a catalyst to expand existing treatments to new conditions, as in the case of the medication, Remicade, which was developed to treat arthritis and is now used to treat Crohn's disease as well? Are its existing capabilities undergoing continual step-by-step improvements, which can lead to improvements in the quality of care? Is it a new procedure that has been developed for discovering and treating secondary diseases within a disease, such as erythropoietin to treat anemia in patients who are receiving dialysis?

New technologies can reduce utilization, such as a new screening instrument that allows for a more focused treatment. Some new technologies, such as vaccines, may cost more initially but can cost society less over time if they lead to fewer people seeking more expensive care. New technologies can also lead to an increase in the human life span, which impacts on the kind and cost of health care that a person uses over a lifetime.

Analyzing the impact of new technology on health care costs is not simple. On the one hand, in studying a single technology it is relatively easy to illustrate the cost and the benefit of a new technology if it replaces a more costly technology and improves health care, while an analysis of health care system-wide costs may demonstrate cost increases if the new technology is used more than the old technology. For example, again in treating Crohn's disease (an autoimmune medical condition), the use of the medication Remicade, which is infused over a period of hours into a patient as opposed to the patient swallowing a tablet or pill, may stabilize the condition of the patient on a daily basis. It may ward off inflammations of the small intestine such as when the Crohn's disease becomes active and one of whose treatment choices in such a situation often involves surgery. While Remicade infusions are very expensive, at intervals of 6–8 weeks or less, depending on the patient's condition, they can easily approach $18 000–20 000 a year in costs in 2009 but are far less expensive than the combination of the costs of surgery, hospital stays, and all the other expenses that are attendant on inpatient surgical procedures. At the same time, the increased use of Remicade relative to other less expensive outpatient medication treatments can increase on a system-wide basis total health care spending in this regard.

At the present time it is not possible to measure directly the impact of new medical technology on total health care spending; innovation in the health care sector is not a sporadic event but a continual process and the impact of different changes is interrelated with each other. In addition, with the health care sector accounting for at least $2 trillion in annual expenditures and with a myriad of diverse procedures, products, and interventions, direct measurement of the impact of new technology on health care expenditures is not practical.

Economists have used indirect approaches in an effort to assess the effect of new technology on the costs of health care. In one approach the effect of medical technology on health care expenditures was initially assessed by examining the effect of factors that can be reasonably considered, such as the extensiveness of insurance, rising per-capita income, aging of the US population, supplier-induced demand, and low gains in medical sector productivity. Professor Joseph P. Newhouse of Harvard University concluded that the previous factors accounted for well under one-half of the growth in real medical spending, and that most unexplained residual increase ought to be attributed to technological change – what Professor Newhouse calls 'the enhanced capabilities of medicine.'[13]

Factors influencing growth of new technology

There are many factors that have an effect on developing innovations in medical care. One of the most significant is consumer demand for medical care services. As more and more people find themselves in a position to afford medical care services because of third-party payer coverage for their conditions, they seek out services to maintain their health status in as good a state as possible and medical technological innovations are one of the answers consumers consider. Newspapers, radio, television, the internet, and advertising are different kinds of media that inform consumers about the new technologies that are being and have been developed to treat their particular conditions. Hence, the consumer demands that they be used, especially when a third party is paying the provider for delivering the health care service. Medical treatments can be very costly and beyond the financial resources of most people unless their risk of requiring health care services can be pooled through the mechanism of insurance (be it private, such as commercial health insurers, or public programs like Medicare). Because medical researchers and suppliers know that there is insurance coverage for a particular medical condition, they are encouraged to develop new medical technologies related to the condition because they know that the public is interested in such technology, will have the economic resources to pay for it, and the financial investment in improving that particular technology can be recovered. At the same time, the possibility that an improved technology can treat a particular medical condition may entice the consumer to purchase insurance coverage in order to have the financial resources to pay for the treatment and thus increase the demand for the use of the technology.

But the consumer-patient is not the only factor spurring on the development of new medical technologies. Another source is the providers themselves, who are continually seeking out new ways not only to improve the quality of medical services they are delivering but also to compete more effectively with other providers for patients and to have available the latest and newest innovations to treat them. Other motivating factors that can spur the development of new medical technologies may be of a more personal nature. Academic or nonacademic medical researchers, for example, whose work leads to new medical technological treatments, not only receive the recognition of their peers, but also, if an academic, perhaps tenure at their professional position, as well as prestigious recognition from the public. For example, such professional and public accolades were accorded to Dr. Jonas Salk and Dr. Albert Sabin, who developed their respective vaccines against polio in the 1950s: up to that time those afflicted with this disease had been confined to machines named iron lungs to breathe. While heart transplants are commonplace today, the first artificial hearts were considered a medical breakthrough in the latter part of the 20th century. Another factor that encourages the development of medical technologies is public and private investments in basic research whose purpose is to increase human knowledge that can directly and indirectly lead to advances in medical practices.

Medical technology expenditures

In 2005, an estimated $111 billion was spent on US research. The greatest share was spent by the health care industry ($61 billion, or 55%), including the pharmaceutical industry ($35 billion or 31%), the biotechnology industry ($16 billion, or 15%), and the medical technology industry ($10 billion, or 9%). Government spent $40 billion (36%), most of which was expended by the NIH ($19 billion, or 26%), followed by other federal government agencies ($9 billion, or 8%), and state and local government ($3 billion, or 2%). Other organizations (including universities, independent research institutes, voluntary health organizations, and philanthropic foundations) spent about $10 billion (9%). About 5.5 cents of every health dollar was spent on health research in 2005, a decline from 5.8 cents in 2004.[14] How much health research money was expended specifically on medical technology is not known, though by definition most of the industry spending ($61 billion) was spent on medical technology. The medical technology industries spent greater shares on research and development as a percentage of sales in 2002 than did other US industries: 11.4% for the medical devices industry and 12.9% for drugs and medicine, compared to 5.6% for telecommunications, 4.0% for automobiles, 3.9% for electrical/electronics, 3.5% for all companies, and 3.1% for aerospace/defense.[15]

Unhealthy dilemmas

Medical technology and research in the USA rank with the best in the world. Americans have been on the cutting edge in regard to some of the boldest and most promising cancer treatments, surgical procedures, and pharmacological breakthroughs. Advanced genetic research in US laboratories has brought the medical world to a new frontier, where an understanding of the basic causes of some of the most troublesome medical conditions from acquired immunodeficiency syndrome (AIDS) to cystic fibrosis are now within reach; some inherited medical diseases may soon be prevented or reversed; and recently introduced genetically engineered medications are already saving lives. But that is only one side of the picture. There is another side. The same technology that can help in expanding life expectancy is also leading to increased demands on the health care system from an increasing population of senior citizens. Society through its government is now asking questions about when and from whom treatments should be withheld, as competition for the scarce medical resources of the health care system increases beyond the system's ability to provide care for everyone. Already, some forms of medical care rationing have been implemented, as in the state of Oregon in the 1990s, and more rationing may be unavoidable. Therefore, how does society control the costs of technology? One position is to improve its efficiency; the other to ration access to its use.

The British view

While high-cost medical technology in the USA is increasing health care expenditures and improving the health of American society, the UK has the opposite view in that it believes that low-cost technology is the key to improving health care. In a report issued by the Royal Society on December 8, 2006 and titled *Digital Healthcare: The Impact of Information and Communication Technologies (ICT) on Health and Healthcare*,[16] the Society, the independent academy of science of the UK officially called the Royal Society of London for the Improvement of Natural Knowledge, highlights that the UK has been slow to adopt even the simplest ICTs in its health care system and that by integrating these technologies now, the UK will be better prepared to deal with future challenges, including an aging population and a shortage of nurses – both problems confronting the USA today. Perhaps some of these UK ideas may be adaptable in the USA. A variety of inexpensive, existing technologies can be adapted for a health care environment, such as home security systems that could be easily enhanced to include personal monitoring to detect falls in the elderly, or mobile phones that could be modified to analyze blood sugar readings to monitor chronic conditions such as diabetes. More than 15 million people in the UK reportedly live with long-term medical conditions such as coronary heart disease or diabetes. An increasing number of low-cost personal health care devices which can be purchased over the counter or on the internet, such as heart rate monitors and infection screening kits, would permit more people to manage their own health despite a shrinking UK health care workforce. Hospitals are already text-messaging patients to remind them of appointments, saving hours of doctors' time in missed appointments. Webcam consultations could help health care professionals to monitor patients with chronic conditions like asthma in their own homes. In the UK district nurses spend hours a day traveling to visit patients when a call on a mobile phone would do the same job in a fraction of the time. Telecare is already improving the lives of some patients by permitting them to receive expert treatment from their own home, giving them access to the best care wherever they live.

Professor Peter Wells, chair of the study's working group from the School of Engineering at Cardiff University, said, 'Implementing low-cost technology would enable doctors to save time due to less paperwork and missed appointments; nurses to make best use of their home visits; and patients to leave hospitals sooner and recuperate at home as they will be able to check in with their consultants using a personal computer. Health care is a partnership. If ICTs are embraced by doctors' surgeries, hospitals, and people in their own homes, the UK's health care system will be improved for everyone.'[16] According to the report, because of the poor track record of design, implementation, and integration with existing systems, there is some feeling of resistance and skepticism towards new technology in UK health care from both patients and health care workers. This is made worse by a lack of training and involvement with those who will use the new systems to ensure their needs are met.

The future

While health technology has served as a very strong impetus for all the advances that are being made in health care and the medical fields, the question is: how much of its financial resources can the USA as a whole as well as its individual states and the localities that constitute those states afford to spend in the future in regard to health care services for its population? And since the development and spread of health technology are a significant reason why health care spending is growing rapidly, can new technology achieve cost savings or cause the spending to spiral even higher?

Some believe technology can play an important role in minimizing health care costs. Dr. Jeffrey Rideout, a physician and the leader of the Internet Business Solutions Group at Cisco Systems' health care practice,[17] has stated that the US health care industry is behind in information technology spending not only in relation to its international competitors, but also other industries domestically. For each dollar per worker a health care company spends on information technology, Rideout states, the average US company spends 7 dollars, and companies in richer industries like banking spend up to 20 dollars. US competitors overseas have also consistently outspent the US government on health care information technology investment. Rideout says the US government invests 43 cents annually per capita on information technology compared to the Canadian government, which spends $31 per capita.

One of the most commonly cited goals that could be given impetus by an increase in investment is the shift to electronic medical records. Though critics worry about privacy, digitizing patient records achieves a number of goals at once. It reduces paper costs as well as the likelihood of errors in prescriptions and in their transfer of data between hospitals – flaws that can lead to medical errors and the need for expensive ongoing care.[17] Electronic medical records can lead to a better quality of care overall. In the findings of a survey of almost 3000 physicians, published in the online edition of the *New England Journal of Medicine* of July 3, 2008, about 4% of medical practices have fully integrated electronic systems that can, for example, download a radiologist's written report as well as new X-ray images to compare with older ones on file. Another 13% of practices have more basic systems, such as online patient records. The cost of converting to electronic records, which can range from tens of thousands of dollars for small practices to tens of millions for multidoctor practices at medical centers, is the most obvious barrier, according to the study's lead author, Catherine DesRoches, a researcher at the Institute of Health Policy at Harvard.[18] Other barriers include physician worries about how much time they will require to learn the system and how fast it will become obsolete. Thus, electronic medical records, despite their obvious potential to improve medical care quality, are developing within the medical community at a very slow rate.

At present, most suggestions to slow the growth in new medical technology center on cost-effectiveness analysis. Some countries have used other approaches which might meet resistance in the USA, such as rationing, regulation, or constraints on the budget. Some approaches have been tried and found to be ineffective in significantly affecting technology-driven costs in the USA. Examples include managed care or certificate-of-need approval that no longer exists in each of the 50 states, especially when Congress abandoned the national health planning law in the 1980s during the Reagan administration. Other approaches being attempted at the beginning of the 21st century are expected to have only a limited effect on health care spending, like information technology or consumer-driven health care in the form of health savings accounts, for example.

Cost effectiveness analysis involves unbiased, well-controlled studies of a technology's benefits and costs, followed by the disbursement of the findings so that clinical practice can use them. The effort to control the use of inappropriate technology could be through third-party coverage or reimbursement decisions, by employing financial incentives so that physicians and their patients would choose cost-effective treatments. Just because a health technology has been approved for the market does not mean that it will receive approval for payment. For example, a specific technology may not fall within a covered benefit, or even if covered may not be medically necessary in certain cases. Even if a technology has gained regulatory approval, the evidence that has been collected to show its safety and efficacy for that purpose may not be enough to prove its effectiveness in a given beneficiary population such as Medicare. In addition, third-party payers may decide that, even though a technology offers a marginal health benefit for a given population, the cost of accomplishing that health benefit may not be worth the associated marginal cost and may take away from other, more cost-effective ways of using health care resources.[7,8] So, who will implement the cost-effective findings? Will it be at the health plan level or through a national health technology assessment agency, as proposed by the Institute of Medicine? Would money be saved by lessening expensive technology, which has a low marginal value? Marginal value is a term widely used in economics to refer to the change in economic value associated with a unit change in output or consumption, for example. How would the savings impact be determined and would such a cost containment approach discourage technical innovation, which again could impede progress in medical science and the health care field?

These are many of the questions to which answers are still begging as the US health care system has entered the 21st century and health care costs continue to consume more and more of the country's GDP without any kind of monetary abatement being seen in the near future.

References

1. *The Long-Term Outlook for Health Care Spending*. Washington, DC: Congressional Budget Office, 2007.
2. Ginsburg P B. Controlling health care costs. *N Engl J Med* 2004; 351: 1591–1593.
3. Beever C, Burns H, Karbe M. *US Health Care's Technology Cost Crisis. Strategy + Business*, March 31, 2004; available online at: http://www.strategy-business.com/press/enewsarticle/enews033104; accessed on June 30, 2008.
4. Cutler D M, McClellan M. Is technological change in medicine worth it? *Health Aff* 2001; 20: 11–29.
5. National Academy of Sciences. *Knowing What Works in Health Care: A Roadmap for the Nation*. Washington, DC: Institute of Medicine, 2008 (press release).
6. Callihan D. *Evidence, Technology, and Cost Control. Bioethics Forum*. Garrison, NY: Hastings Center, 2008.
7. Goodman C S. *Health Care Costs: Why Do They Increase? What Can We Do?* Rockville, MD: Agency for Healthcare Research and Quality, May 21-23 2001 *Workshop Brief,*

User Liaison Program; available online at: http://www.ahrq.gov/news/ulp/costs/ulpcosts8.htm; accessed on July 7, 2008.

8. Tynan A, Berenson R A, Christianson J B. *Health Plans Target Advanced Imaging Services.* Washington, DC: Center for Studying Health System Changes, February 2008; available online at: http://hschange.org/CONTENT/968/; accessed on June 28, 2008.

9. Johnson L A. Health insurers limit advanced scans. Associated Press, March 23, 2008; available online at http://hschange.org/CONTENT/968/; accessed on June 23, 2008.

10. University of Michigan. New medical technology may override health care costs. *ScienceDaily* August 19 1998; available online at: http://www.sciencedaily.com/releases/1998/08/980819080823.htm; accessed on June 28, 2008.

11. Chernow M E, Hirth R A, Sonnad S A *et al.* Managed care: medical technology, and health care cost growth: a review of the evidence. *Med Care Res Rev* 1998; 55: 259–288.

12. Maviglia S M, Yoo J Y, Franz C *et al.* Cost–benefit analysis of a hospital pharmacy bar code solution. *Arch Intern Med* 2007; 167: 788–794.

13. Newhouse J P. Medical care costs: how much welfare loss? *J Economic Perspect* 1992; 6: 3–21.

14. *Research! America, 2005 Investment in US Health Research.* September 2006; available online at: http://www.researchamerica.org/publications/appopriatons/healthdollar2005.pdf; accessed on June 7, 2008.

15. AdvaMed. *The Medical Technology Industry at a Glance.* September 7, 2004: 14 (Chart 3.2); available online at: http://www.advamed.org/newsroom/chartbook.pdf; accessed on July 6, 2008.

16. *Low Cost Technology is Key to Improve Healthcare Says Royal Society Report.* London, UK: Royal Society, 2006 (press release).

17. Teslick L H, Johnson T. *Healthcare Costs and US Competitiveness.* New York, NY: Council on Foreign Relations, 2008.

18. DesRoches C M. Campbell E G, Rao S R, *et al.* Electronic health records in ambulatory care – a national survey of physicians. *N Engl J Med* 2008; 359: 50-60; available online at: http://content.nejm.org/cgi/content/abstract/359/1/50; accessed on July 9, 2008.

8

Nursing home care

Introduction

As America becomes more and more of a 'graying' society and as health care costs continue to rise, nursing homes have taken on an ever more important role within American society for delivering health care services. The role arises from society's wishes to use skilled nursing homes both as institutions for providing long-term care and as extended care facilities for providing postacute short-term hospital care in order to reduce, in part, the costs of staying in a hospital. As the number of individuals who seek nursing homes increases in the future, the health care role which these facilities presently assume will continue to increase in importance.

In 1997, there were about 17 000 nursing home facilities in the USA. They had 1.8 million beds and housed 1.6 million patients. Thirteen percent of the nursing home facilities were hospital-based. Medicaid paid 68% of nursing home costs, Medicare 8%, and private pay 23%. However, nursing home care is not only for the elderly. Persons with acquired immunodeficiency syndrome (AIDS) require nursing home care during the progression of the disease and special nursing facilities devoted to the care of AIDS patients have developed since the early 1990s.[1,2] In addition, nursing homes serve patients who require hospice services, suffer from Alzheimer's disease, and need other kinds of special care. Also, there are more than 1 million children in the USA with severe chronic illnesses, some of whom require nursing care in a facility or at home.[3,4] Some of these children may have birth defects or may have learning disabilities or be dependent upon machines. Often, for these families the only course is to institutionalize the child – at great costs and heavy emotional sacrifice – or to become 'poor' enough to qualify for Medicaid to pay for home care. A major federal program for children with special health needs is known as Title V of the Social Security Act. However, it provides limited services.[5]

In fiscal 2006, the USA spent an estimated $124.9 billion on nursing home care, that is, about one out of every 20 dollars in that year expended for national health care ($2.1 trillion).[6] This increasing demand for nursing home care has led to the development of a giant new industry. In addition, the demand for this care is growing at such a rate that it threatens to overwhelm public medical care programs such as Medicaid.

In 1999 about 7 million men and women over age 65 were estimated to require long-term care. By 2020 12 million older Americans will need long-term care. According to the US General Accountability Office, estimates suggest that the future number of disabled elderly who cannot perform basic activities of daily living without assistance may as much as double from 2000 through 2040, resulting in a large increase in demand for long-term care services, especially as the estimated 76 million baby boomers born between 1946 and 1964 become elderly. Most will be cared for at home; family members and friends are the sole caregivers for 70% of elderly people. But a study by the US Department of Health and Human Services indicates that people who are 65 years of age confront at least a 40% risk in their lifetime of going into a nursing home. About 10% of people will stay 5 years or longer, with the risk much higher for women than for men.[7,8]

The American population is growing older and the group over age 85 is now its fastest-growing segment. The growth in the over-85-year population in nursing homes mirrors that of the American population in general where this group accounted for 1% of the total population in 1980 and 1.5% in 2000, a 50% increase. Today, the elderly, numbering more than 35 million people, represent 13% of the population. It is predicted that by 2030 this number will double to about 70 million persons and about one in five Americans, or 20%, will be 65 years or older.[9-11] The chances of entering a nursing home and staying there for a long period rises with age. In fact, statistics demonstrate that, at any given time, 22% of those age 85 years and older are in nursing homes and adults age 85 and older are the fastest-growing segment of the population, as already noted, with expected growth from 4 million as of 2001 to 20 million by 2050. Because women generally outlive men by several years, they face a 50% greater likelihood than men of entering a nursing home after age 65.[7,12]

Whereas once the old and sick cared for themselves as best they could, or moved in with their children, or were sent to old-age homes for custodial care, there are now nursing home companies all over the USA whose principal purpose is to care for the elderly in our society. As of 1997, about 66% of nursing care facilities were for-profit; 27%, not-for-profit, and 7%, government. Increasing age increases the chances of functional limitations.[13] One-third of elderly women age 75 and older are functionally dependent and in need of considerable assistance, while another study revealed that 9% of women age 65–69 required day-to-day assistance, including help with bathing, dressing, and eating, compared with 50% of those 85 and older.[9,13]

As in other areas of the health care field, fraud and scandal still plague the nursing home industry. Yet, there are also nursing homes in which fraud and substandard care do not exist and the elderly can receive the kind of care they require for illnesses such as arthritis, diabetes, cancer, stroke, and heart disease.

The cost of nursing home care can be a financial burden. During 2001, as a national average, a year in a nursing home was estimated to cost $54 900. By 2003, the average national cost for nursing home care was almost $58 000 a year. In some regions of the country, it can easily cost twice the amount. In April 2009 Genworth Financial, a global financial security firm, published its survey of nursing home costs[14] which showed that the national average median daily rate, with variations among states, for a semiprivate room in a skilled nursing home was $183.25 or $66 886 a year and for a private room skilled nursing facility $203.31 or $74 208 a year. Even home care can be expensive. Bringing an aide into your home just three times a week – to help with dressing, bathing, preparing meals, and similar household chores – could easily cost $1000 per month or $12 000 per year. When the cost of skilled help, such as physical therapists, is added, these expenses can be much greater. By 2004 in-home assistance averaged $18 per hour, or $37 000 a year for 40 hours per week.[7, 15–17]

Fortunately, some assistance is available to help individuals pay for part of their nursing home care. This includes public programs such as Medicare and Medicaid and private health insurance plans. Of the estimated $92.2 billion spent on nursing home care in 2000, federal and state governments paid about $55.9 billion (more than one-half the cost); the remainder was paid out of pocket by patients or their families, private health insurance, or other private sources.[1] Thus, it is very important to become knowledgeable about nursing homes.

At some point in time many health and non-health professionals interact with such facilities in providing services to the facility itself or its patients. These may include pharmacists, physicians, dentists, nurses, therapists, architects, engineers, social workers, and others. As people live longer, skilled nursing homes can fill a special need caring for people who need health supervision and daily attention but do not require a full range of hospital services. Skilled nursing homes treat young and old alike, even though most nursing home residents are senior citizens. These facilities also treat convalescents recuperating from hospital treatment as well as those who are chronically ill, as already noted, and require the kind of close nursing supervision not available in their family homes.[18]

This chapter will discuss the variety of nursing homes available to help residents or their family members or others to pay for such care, and the kinds of questions they should ask before selecting such a residence for a loved one.

Services available in nursing homes

Essentially, nursing homes offer three basic kinds of nursing services: nursing care, personal care, and residential services.

Nursing care

Certain nursing procedures require the professional skills of a registered or licensed practical nurse. These include administration of medications, injections, catheterizations, and similar procedures ordered by the attending physician. Posthospital stroke, heart, or orthopedic care is available with related services such as physical therapy, occupational therapy, dental services, dietary consultations, laboratory and X-ray services, and a pharmaceutical dispensary.

Personal care

This care includes services such as walking, getting in and out of bed, bathing, dressing, and eating, and the preparation of special diets as prescribed by a physician.

Residential services

These services involve general supervision and a protective environment, including room and board as well as a planned program for the social and spiritual needs of the residents.[19]

Classification of nursing homes

The three basic categories of care described previously can be found in a variety of facilities. A patient's personal needs will affect the kind of care a patient receives.

The following facilities provide these different levels of assistance:

Skilled nursing facilities

These nursing homes provide continuous nursing service on a 24-hour basis for convalescent patients. Registered nurses, licensed practical nurses, and nurses' aides provide services prescribed by the patient's physician. Emphasis is placed on medical nursing care with restorative, physical, occupational, and other therapies provided. This kind of facility is eligible to participate in both Medicare and Medicaid.

Intermediate care facilities

These facilities provide regular medical, nursing, social, and rehabilitative services in addition to room and board for individuals who are not capable of fully independent living. Intermediate care facilities are for residents who require less intensive nursing care than that provided by skilled nursing homes. This kind of facility may choose to be recognized for the Medicaid program. Skilled nursing facilities and intermediate care facilities that choose to participate in Medicare and Medicaid must meet the National Fire Protection Association's Life Safety Code.

Residential care facilities

These facilities provide safe, hygienic, sheltered living to individuals who are capable of functioning in an independent manner. The residential care facility stresses the social needs of the resident, rather than the medical needs provided by skilled nursing facilities and intermediate care facilities. Residents are provided dietary and housekeeping services, medical monitoring, and social, recreational, and spiritual opportunities.

Adult daycare facilities

These facilities provide nursing and nutritional services and medical monitoring in a clean and comfortable nonresidential environment. Adult daycare affords older people an opportunity for making their own decisions, while allowing the long-term care facility the opportunity to participate actively in community affairs.

Mental health care facilities

As governments reduce their support for public mental health care facilities, an increasing number of patients are entering alternative long-term care facilities for comprehensive psychosocial services with therapeutic intervention and remedial education in a homelike setting. Long-term facilities have begun to fill this social and health care need.

Childcare facilities

These facilities meet the long-term needs of chronically ill children. A close staff–parent–child relationship must be formed to guide the ill or impeded child toward normal development. Specialized nursing, social, and educational services are provided under medical supervision in close concert with all members of the family.[19]

After the kind of facility a patient needs is decided upon, there are many sources to develop a list of those which serve your community. These include the physician and social worker, if any, the state nursing home association, the local social security office, local medical society, community welfare agency, state health and welfare departments, as well as the yellow pages of the local telephone directory. Neighbors and friends are also good sources of advice as well as a church or synagogue. By telephoning the homes in advance, the field can be narrowed to two or three facilities that offer the services and location the patient and loved ones seek. They should visit each of the homes, talk with the administrators, other employees, and other patients, and tour the facilities.

Many qualified nursing homes participate in two voluntary standards programs. One is conducted by the Commission for Accreditation of Rehabilitation Facilities, which might include nursing homes. The other is the accreditation program of the Joint Commission on Accreditation of Healthcare Organizations. Their certification is based on on-site surveys of the facility's operations to determine whether they are in substantial compliance with the standards of the Joint Commission. The patient or loved ones should find out whether the nursing home under consideration has been reviewed by both the state and the national associations for accreditation and the results of such reviews.

Definition of a skilled nursing home

There are many ways to judge the quality of care in a nursing home. But in order to do so, a set of standards is needed against which to judge each nursing home that is visited. One of the best standards available at the moment in the USA is the federal government's Medicare program, which offers, among other benefits, nursing home coverage to elderly persons who qualify for it. In examining any nursing home the patient or loved ones should find out whether, as a minimum, it adheres to the following Medicare standards in its daily operation. If it does not, it is likely that Medicare did not certify the facility – in which case the prospective patient or loved ones should be careful. Find out whether the nursing home has other qualities that the patient desires. To be certified under the Medicare program, a skilled nursing home must meet the following standards:

Licensure

A skilled nursing home must be licensed in accordance with state and federal laws, including all applicable laws relating to staff, licensing and registration, fire, safety, and communicable diseases, as well as other standards required by various state and local laws. A copy of nursing home licensure standards may be obtained from the state government's nursing home licensure agency which may be located in either the state health or welfare department.

Physician services

A skilled nursing home must have a medical plan designed by a doctor. Furthermore, doctors must always be on call for routine medical examinations as well as for emergencies.

Governing body and written policies

A skilled nursing home must have a governing body legally responsible for policies and the appointment of a qualified administrator, as well as written policies established in consultation with and periodically reviewed by a professional group that includes a physician and registered nurse.

Utilization review plan

A skilled nursing home must have a utilization review plan in which a committee of medical people regularly review and evaluate the entire medical program – policies, admissions, treatment, and case histories – to determine whether Medicare coverage should be continued.

Physician's recommendation

Skilled nursing home care can be covered by Medicare only if the patient is admitted on a physician's recommendation. Each patient plan must be under the regular care of a physician.

Twenty-four-hour nursing care services

A skilled nursing home must have 24-hour nursing care services. There must be enough nurses on duty at all times, including at least one registered nurse employed full-time. There must be a registered nurse or a licensed practical nurse in charge of each tour of duty who knows about things such as medications, special feeding methods, and skin care. There must also be a continuing in-service educational program for all nursing personnel.

Hospital transfer

A skilled nursing home must have an agreement with one or more Medicare-participating hospitals for transferring patients when such transfers are medically determined by the patient's physician.

Drugs

A skilled nursing home must have appropriate methods for obtaining and dispensing drugs and biologicals according to accepted professional standards. Emergency drugs must be available and stored in an appropriate manner.

Medical records

A skilled nursing home must maintain a separate and confidential clinical record for each patient, including individual care plans and case histories.

Rehabilitation services

A skilled nursing home must provide skilled rehabilitation services in areas of posthospital care such as speech, hearing, and physical therapy to help patients maintain and improve their functional abilities.

Social services

A skilled nursing home must provide for the patient's medically related social needs (by its own staff or by arrangement with the local welfare department) but is not required to do so.

Other medical services

A skilled nursing home must have arrangements for obtaining required clinical laboratory, X-ray, and other diagnostic services such as those provided by dentists.

Food

A skilled nursing home must serve adequate food to meet the dietary needs of patients. A qualified person must prepare food in compliance with all sanitary and safety codes. Therapeutic diets, as prescribed by a doctor, must be given and meals must be served three times a day.

Activities

A skilled nursing home should encourage self-care, that is, the patient's return to normal life in the community through social, religious, and recreational activities and by visits with relatives and friend.

Building and maintenance

A skilled nursing home must be constructed, equipped, and maintained to insure a safe, functional, sanitary, and comfortable environment for patients. Fire rules must be posted.

Infection control

A skilled nursing facility must have an infection control system under the supervision of a committee composed of members from all staff departments of the facility.

Institutional plan

A skilled nursing home should have an institutional plan that is available to the public and includes information such as its personnel policies and its operating budget.

Staff education

A skilled nursing home should have an ongoing program to keep all personnel informed of new methods of patient care.

Admission policies

A skilled nursing home should have admission policies that do not discriminate against race, color, creed, or national origin.

Emergency plans

A skilled nursing home must have emergency plans for evacuation and must regularly hold fire drills involving staff and patients.[18]

Although the previous enumeration focused on the standards that skilled nursing homes must meet under US government medical care programs, patients must still careful as to the kind of facility they select, whether it be skilled, intermediate, or residential care. If Medicare and Medicaid payments are involved, the patient must make sure that the facility has been given its proper designations – skilled nursing facility for Medicare or Medicaid or intermediate care for Medicaid eligibility – and confirm that the home participates in these programs. As physicians have noted, patients do not require a higher quality of care of services than the situation demands. Choosing a nursing home according to a patient's needs not only allows the patient to hold down costs but will also allow others who are in greater need of more services to obtain them. It is best that the prospective patient, if possible, or loved ones or both tour a nursing home several times during the day and take notes about what they have observed. They should remember that nursing homes may have waiting lists and they will rarely find the nursing home's services clearly defined in the name of the facility.

Thus, the previous enumeration of standards can serve as a checklist to judge the quality as well as range of services a nursing home offers. In addition to voluntary accreditation certificates noted earlier, there are several other certificates and licenses nursing homes should have and display so the patients or their loved ones will know that the nursing home has met all the laws established by federal, state, and local governments: *current state nursing home license* (check with the state health and/or welfare department if the facility is licensed and beware of temporary or provisional licenses); *current administrator license* (required of all administrators and with a renewal period of every 1 or 2 years); *current fire safety certificate* (certificate issued by the National Fire Protection Association, indicating that the facility has met fire safety standards, as set forth by the Fire Safety Code); and *periodic nursing home inspection* (find out if the state health and/or welfare agency makes inspections and the state inspection report (CMS-2567) must be posted conspicuously at the nursing home. If not, be suspicious of the facility).

The previous licenses and certificates are required in each state. If they are not on display, the patient or loved ones should find out whether the nursing home has obtained these various seals of state approval. For their own peace of mind, safety, and well-being they should ask to see this documentation. The American Health Care Association (a national nursing home trade group) recommends that consumers do not use a nursing home that does not have a current state operating license or whose administrator is not currently licensed by the state.

In choosing a nursing home for a patient, the most important element in doing so is the patient's condition. An older patient has different needs from a younger one. A bedridden patient has different needs from an ambulatory one. It is important to choose a facility that meets the patient's needs rather than trying to make the patient fit the home.

It is also helpful to look into nursing homes long before a relative needs one.

Components of nursing home care

One of the most important aspects of a nursing home's operation is the *administrative management* policies it adopts and adheres to in its daily operation. These policies, ultimately, have a direct influence on the patient's well-being. For example, an administrator's training and education can determine how well he/she is able to understand and meet the medical, social, and psychological requirements of the patients. The kind of residents with whom the patient associates is determined by the admission policies of the facility. The adequacy of food and housekeeping operation has a direct impact on the patient's nutritional health as well as on the kind of physical environment in which the patient resides.

Another area of great concern to the patient relates to the quality of care that a nursing home can render. As of 1996, reports of abuse and neglect in the nursing home industry were widespread, according to state officials and advocates for the country's nursing home residents.[20] In 1986, a US Senate Special Committee on Aging issued the results of a 2-year study[21] in which it stated that more than one-half of the nation's skilled nursing homes fail to meet basic federal health and safety standards, and many 'resemble 19th-century asylums more than modern health care facilities.' Senator

John Heinz (R-PA) wrote in the report's preface, 'we have allowed bed, board and abuse to replace the medical and rehabilitative care the law demands.' In 1999, the Supreme Court ruled in a case known as the Olmstead decision in which two Georgia women, both Medicaid beneficiaries with mental retardation, wanted community-based services, but were refused and were treated in institutions. These older persons or those with disabilities believe they are placed into nursing homes when they are healthy enough to live at home with relatives or in other less institutional settings. The Supreme Court stated that unjustified isolation of the disabled in institutions amounted to discrimination under the Americans with Disabilities Act. The Supreme Court said that states must provide community services if patients want them, if they can be accommodated, and it is appropriate. According to Toby Edelman, an attorney at the Center for Medicare Advocacy, 'there is lot of concern that the nursing home industry is very powerful in many states and has made sure that Medicaid dollars go to institutional care as opposed to home and community based care.'[23] Nationally, state Medicaid payments have risen very greatly since the Olmstead decision, from $17.4 billion in 1999 to $42.8 billion in 2007, although spending on nursing homes and other institutions is still very much higher. In addition, in 2001 a study was published that concluded that investor-owned nursing homes, about two-thirds of the total number nationally, provide worse care and less nursing care than not-for-profit or public homes. Then, in 2002, the National Citizens' Coalition for Nursing Home Reform reported that at least one-third of nursing home residents in the USA may suffer from malnutrition or dehydration; lack of adequately trained personnel and high staff turnover are largely to blame.[21–23] About four decades earlier, in 1960, another US Senate Subcommittee stated in part, that 'every troubled son or daughter, anxious to find a good nursing home for a mother or father is dismayed and often shocked by the inadequacy, the hopelessness, inherent in most nursing homes. Those who have wandered from home to home seeking decent facilities, a therapeutic environment and a life-restoring force pulsing through its system too often have given up in frustration. Or with no other solution feasible or possible, they may consign a parent or troubled relative to an inadequate nursing home, but with a troubled conscience and feelings of guilt . . . it is this lack of medical care and restorative service in the great majority of homes labeled nursing homes which is the number one problem in the nursing home field.'[24]

Thus, when a consumer-patient is seeking nursing home care many questions must be asked in a variety of areas regarding the quality of care that is being delivered. These questions touch upon such disciplines within the health care field as medicine, social work, therapy, dentistry, and pharmacy. More specifically, these questions pertain to physician services, physical therapy, restorative care, laboratory/diagnostic activities, dental care, social services, nursing care, utilization review procedures, personal grooming services, medical records, and pharmaceutical services. In examining the patient care services of a nursing home, the consumer-patient should try to determine whether the nursing care facility provides just minimal basic services beyond this level. Basic minimal services may include a patient having a physician to care for him or her, an emergency physician available to the facility, a registered or licensed practical nurse in charge, medications only administered upon a physician's order, and medications kept in locked cabinet. Care beyond these minimal services may include the provision of physical therapy, dental, social, and laboratory services, maintenance of an emergency medication kit and the existence of in-service nursing training programs and nurse procedure manuals.

The consumer-patient should find out how much extra such services, supplies, and medications cost. For example, in regard to pharmaceutical services, an area of abuse in some nursing homes, the pharmacist should be able to answer and the consumer-patient ought to ask the following questions. The importance of these questions was underscored in February 2008 when the Centers for Medicare and Medicaid Services released a list of 131 poorly performing nursing homes in the USA. They were cited as 'special focus facilities,' so designated by the states because, while most nursing homes upon inspection have on average six to seven deficiencies upon inspection, these 'special focus facilities' generally have double that number and continue to have problems over a long period of time. One of the major problems they have typically involves the unnecessary use of medication for elderly residents, or inadequate safeguards to protect residents such as those with Alzheimer's disease from day-to-day hazards in the nursing home. Thus, in examining the pharmaceutical service component of nursing homes pharmacists and patients should find out:

- Are pharmaceuticals only dispensed on the order of the attending physician or dentist?
- Are medications stored in a locked cabinet?
- Are medications that are poorly labeled or damaged returned to the pharmacy for disposal or relabeling?
- Does the medication label include the patient's name, pharmacy, prescriber, date, directions, dosage unit, and prescription number?
- Does the patient have the freedom to purchase medicines outside the home?
- If a medication is prescribed for a specific patient, does the nursing home allow it to be administered to another?
- Is the patient's medication stored and kept in the original container unless otherwise authorized by a physician?
- Can a prescription order be renewed without a physician's permission? If so, why? Under what conditions?

- Does a qualified pharmacist maintain and monitor a record of each resident's drug therapy?
- Is there an excessive use of drugs and tranquilizers? Many listless and drowsy patients may be an indication.
- Does the nursing home keep poisons and medications 'for external use only' in a locked cabinet and separated from other medications?
- After the expiration date, is the prescription medicine removed from use? If not, why?
- Are medications requiring refrigeration kept in a refrigerator?
- If patients are discharged or die, is the unused portion of their medication destroyed by the nursing home? If not, what happens to it?
- Can nurses package or repackage, bottle, or label, in whole or in part, any medication?
- Does the nursing home prohibit unlabeled medications or medications with illegible labels?
- Does the nursing home have automatic stop orders for dispensing medication after a given time has passed, unless otherwise authorized by a physician?
- Does the nursing home make an inventory of narcotics that is signed and recorded by the nurse in charge, and on what basis – daily, weekly, monthly?
- Does the nursing home maintain a record of the use of narcotics by the patient?
- Are unused narcotics destroyed according to state/federal government regulations?
- Does the nursing home maintain first-aid supplies?
- Does the nursing home maintain a pharmacy whose operation permit is approved by the state board of pharmacy? Does the nursing home have a room for storing drugs and other pharmaceutical items?
- Is a state-licensed pharmacist in charge of the pharmacy?
- If the nursing home has no pharmacy on the premises, then does it have contractual services with a pharmacy outside the facility? Does the pharmacy deliver drugs promptly?
- Are residents allowed to choose their own pharmacist?
- Can prescribed medication be dispensed only by a licensed pharmacist/ pharmacy?
- Does the nursing home keep an emergency drug kit on the premises? Is the kit kept in a locked box? Are narcotic drugs kept in the emergency drug kit? Does a pharmacist or physician inspect the drug kit to account for and replace used drugs? Can emergency medications in the kit be used only on the orders of a physician or a dentist? If not, who else has the authority to order their use? When medication is used from the kit, does the pharmacist replace the medications and is the kit resealed? If not,

why not? Are emergency medications issued only in the name of the patient?[25]

The answers to these questions are most important for both the pharmacist and patient in judging, in part, one aspect of the quality of care in a nursing home. For example, the nursing home should prevent drug abuse by not allowing a prescription order to be renewed without a physician's permission and by prohibiting the administration of one patient's medication to another. Without these prohibitions, a problem is created whereby a patient can receive a continuous dosage of medication at a level and at a time of treatment when it is no longer needed. As another example, the registered or licensed practical nurse should have the responsibility for supervising the administration of a drug. If not, the possibility exists that an individual of lesser skill or knowledge or training may be supervising such activities. Unless such individuals have the rudimentary knowledge of the characteristics of a drug for which they are responsible, dire consequences may befall the patient upon the receipt of such a drug.

The nursing home can also prevent drug abuse within the facility by making sure that it takes appropriate safeguards with a correctly labeled medication by safely storing and keeping it in its original container unless otherwise authorized by the patient's physician, The nursing home must also make sure that it keeps poisons and medications which are marked 'for external use only' in a locked cabinet and separated from other medications.

It is also important for the pharmacist and consumer-patient to find out from the local or state health department whether it has had reports of drug abuse in regard to the facility; whether the nursing home keeps an emergency kit or even first-aid kit; and whether the charge nurse or someone of similar authority makes an inventory of narcotics on a daily basis, which she/he records and signs so that the facility's narcotics are not abused and improperly administered. All these responsibilities and others, as implied by the questions, are important for the pharmacist to assume in the administration of drugs, overseeing their disposal and their inventory control so that the nursing home provides the highest quality of care to its patients in terms of drug therapy in order to prevent its abuse.

A third important aspect of nursing home administration is related to the issue of whether or not a *favorable environment* exists in the facility for the physical and emotional well-being of the patient. In its certification requirements for extended care facilities, the US Department of Health and Human Services recognizes this fact by requiring extended care facilities to be equipped and maintained to provide an environment that is functional, sanitary, and comfortable. The presence or absence of recreation areas, dining rooms, adequate bedroom furnishings, special care, and physical examination rooms as well as a safe and sanitary electrical-mechanical system can enhance or detract from the functional aspects of the facility's operation – also they can affect the spirit, attitude, and, ultimately, the basic health of the patients themselves.

A fourth important aspect of nursing home administration relates to the *patient's physical safety* which, in turn, results from both the protective fire measures a facility adopts and the physical construction of the facility. All too often public attention is focused on the nursing home field for the wrong reasons: an example is when fire strikes a facility with the ensuing loss of human life, sometimes owing to the fact that improper measures were taken initially to protect the facility residents such as the nursing home not meeting the National Fire Codes of the National Fire Protection Association. Thus, both fire safety and construction are interrelated in the sense that the quality and extent of construction can determine the spread or magnitude of fire or other disaster.

Medicare's Nursing Home Compare

The federal government has made it slightly easier for consumers to judge the quality of care a nursing home provides. In November 2002, the Centers for Medicare and Medicaid Services established a new feature on Medicare's Nursing Home Compare website (http://www.medicare.gov/nhcompare/home.asp) that provides quality indicators on nearly 17 000 nursing homes in the USA. For each nursing home, Medicare, as of 2009, established as many as 14 long-term performance categories that show the percentage of long-term residents in physical restraints, with weight loss, with the inability to perform basic daily tasks, and receiving pneumococcal vaccination and influenza vaccination during flu season. Other categories show the percentage of patients with bedsores, pain, urinary tract infection, worsening of ability to move in or around their room, most of their time spent in bed or on a chair, catheter inserted and left in bladder, depression or anxiety, and bowel or bladder problems. Some of the short-term stay measures (five) as of 2008 include patients with delirium, moderate to severe pain, pressure sores, and receiving influenza vaccinations and pneumoccocal vaccinations. As of 2008, the site also reports on the results of fire inspections of facilities and information on the number of registered nurses, licensed practical nurses, licensed vocational nurses, and certified nursing assistants (who work under the direction of a licensed nurse to assist residents in activities of daily living such as eating, grooming, hygiene, dressing, and other activities after completing a competency evaluation program) in each nursing home such as the hours they spend on residents per day compared to other facilities nationally and in their area. But some words of caution: the measures do not address quality-of-life issues such as activities for patients in the nursing home, its overall environment, or the quality of its staff – all important measures in a good nursing home.

If consumers do not have access to a computer or the internet, they can telephone Medicare at 1-800-633-4227 for information. Also, be aware that the nursing home is responsible for reporting its own quality indicators – for example, the percentage of patients in pain. Also, the General Accounting Office, now renamed the General Accountability Office, has stated that 17% of the nursing homes listed online had four or more positive indicators and no highly negative scores – all apparently good homes. Yet, the General Accountability Office has stated that all those homes have been cited by state authorities for practices that physically harmed the patient. So when using these various tools, another note of caution must be raised. The data at this site are just another tool to judge the quality of the home but are no replacement for visiting the facility itself, talking to its staff and the families of patients. Also, be aware that the US government has a system called the Scope and Severity Index, which rates the seriousness of violation of federal minimum standards for patient care. For each violation, a state inspector determines the harm to a resident and how widespread the problem is within the nursing home. Each violation is assigned a letter grade A–L. The letter A is the least serious. Ask the state if these results are available to the public in a report so that the consumer can determine the quality of care a nursing home delivers.

Financing nursing home care

Nursing home care is expensive. In September 2006, MetLife, a leading commercial health insurer of long-term care policies, published the results of a survey of nursing homes and home care in conjunction with LifePlans, a risk management and consulting firm that provides data analysis and information to the long-term care insurance industry.[26] The study showed that the national average daily rate for a *private room* in a nursing home is $206 or $75 190 annually. The national average daily rate for a *semiprivate* room in a nursing home is $183 or $66 795 annually. Given the magnitude of these costs, how can the average consumer finance such long-term care since over one-half (58.2%) of current residents have been there at least a year, with 13.8% staying 5 years or more? On the other hand, the discharge of residents with stays of 3 months or less has doubled between 1977 and 1999, reflecting the increased role of nursing homes in rehabilitation or post acute care.[27] Well, there are a number of ways to pay for such care in the USA.

Medicare

Under certain limited conditions, Medicare will pay some nursing home costs for Medicare beneficiaries who require skilled nursing or rehabilitation services under Part A, the hospitalization plan under Medicare. To be covered, a patient must receive the services from a Medicare-certified skilled nursing home after a qualifying hospital stay. A qualifying hospital stay is the amount of time spent in a hospital just prior to entering a nursing home. This is at least 3 days. In 2009, for the first 20 days of confinement in a skilled nursing home, the Medicare patient does not pay anything. From the 21st to the 100th day, the patient pays each benefit period $133.50 per day and pays all the costs for each day beyond the 100th day in the benefit period unless the patient has insurance coverage, sometimes called Medigap or Medisupp, that pays for the benefits Medicare does not cover.

Although the hospital insurance program (Part A) of Medicare does not cover physician services while the patient is in the skilled nursing home, it does pay, as already noted, for up to 100 days of care in each benefit period while the patient is in such a facility. A benefit period begins the first day the patient receives covered services in a hospital. It ends after the patient has been out of the hospital or skilled nursing home for 60 consecutive days (including the day of discharge). Again, the hospital insurance program under Medicare pays all the covered services for the first 20 days while the patient is in the skilled nursing home, as already noted, and all but $133.50 per day for up to 80 more days if all of the following conditions are met:

- The patient has been in the hospital for at least 3 consecutive days (not counting the day of discharge) before the patient is transferred to a skilled nursing facility.
- The patient is transferred to the skilled nursing facility because the patient requires care for a condition that was treated in the hospital.
- The patient is admitted to the facility within a short time (usually 30 days) after leaving the hospital. If the patient leaves a skilled nursing facility and is readmitted within 30 days, Medicare covers the patient without the patient having to return to the hospital for a new 3-day stay. In some instances, the patient may exceed the 30-day criterion if for some reason the patient is discharged from the hospital but cannot undergo treatment within 30 days because of the nature of the patient's condition.
- A doctor certifies that the patient needs and actually receives skilled nursing or skilled rehabilitative services on a daily basis.

Medicare's hospital insurance program (Part A) pays for the following major services when the Medicare patient is in a skilled nursing home:

- a semiprivate room (two to four beds)
- all meals, including special diets
- regular nursing services
- rehabilitation services, such as physical, occupational, and speech therapy
- drugs, furnished by the facility during the patient's stay
- medical supplies such as splints and casts
- use of appliances such as a wheelchair.

Medicare's hospital insurance program (Part A) cannot pay for the following services when the patient is in a skilled nursing home:

- personal convenience items a patient requests, such as television, a radio, or a telephone in the patient's room
- private duty nursing by skilled nurses and medical social workers
- any changes above the hospital's semiprivate room rate unless the patient needs a private room for medical reasons
- the first three pints of blood a patient receives in a *benefit period*. If a patient needs blood while an inpatient of a hospital or a skilled nursing home, the hospital insurance program under Medicare pays the full cost of the blood starting with the fourth pint in a benefit period. If the patient is covered by a blood donor plan, it can replace the first three pints of blood for the patient. A hospital or other facility may not charge the patient when it arranges for the replacement of the *first three pints of blood for which Medicare does not pay*. Also under the voluntary medical insurance program (Part B) of Medicare, the medical insurance pays, after the patient pays the annual deductible, 80% of the reasonable charges for blood starting with the fourth pint in the calendar year. Again, medical insurance does not pay for the first three pints in each calendar year.

Medicare supplemental insurance

This is private insurance. It is often called Medigap or Medisupp, as already noted, because it helps pay for gaps in Medicare coverage such as deductibles and coinsurance, including hospital deductibles, doctor's deductibles, and coinsurance payments or what Medicare considers excess physician charges, but it is not long-term care insurance. Most Medigap plans will pay for skilled nursing home care but only when that care is covered by Medicare. Some people use employer group health plans or long-term care insurance to help cover nursing home costs.

Under Medicare, beginning in 1998 and mandated by the Balanced Budget Act of 1997, Medicare payments for skilled nursing care following hospitalization are based on a prospective payment system. Hospitals have been paid under a prospective payment system for inpatient services since 1983. Under this system, each facility receives a base payment amount adjusted for local wages and the care needs of individual patients. The payment rates to skilled nursing facilities cover the costs of furnishing most covered nursing home services, including routine services such as room, board, nursing services, and minor medical supplies; related costs such as therapies, drugs, and laboratory services; and capital costs including land, building, and equipment. The payment is designed to ensure better patient care by relating payments to the condition of the patient, recognizing that some patients need more services or more expensive care than others. Under the previous system, which based its payment on the nursing homes' reported costs, the skilled nursing facility benefit was one of the fastest-growing components of Medicare spending.

Personal resources

About one-half of all nursing home residents pay nursing home costs out of their own savings. After all these savings and other resources are spent, many people stay in nursing homes for long periods, eventually becoming eligible for Medicaid.

Medicaid

Medicaid is a state and federal cost-sharing program that will pay most nursing home costs for people with limited income and assets. The program is designed to meet the cost of financing medical care for the poor and 'medically needy' – persons who do not qualify for welfare but still cannot pay for medical care. Although states design their Medicaid programs within broad federal guidelines, eligibility varies by state. Medicaid will only pay for nursing home care provided in a facility certified by the government to provide services to Medicaid recipients. State Medicaid programs use the same definition of a skilled nursing home to which it will make payments under certain conditions that Medicare uses. However, unlike Medicare, Medicaid also pays for care in intermediate care facilities, which were described previously. The intermediate care facility caters to those who need some health services in addition to nursing supervision along with assistance in eating, dressing, walking, and other similar essentials. For those patients who qualify for both Medicare and Medicaid, the Medicaid program may pick up the charges after the first 100 days of skilled nursing home care are used up under Medicare. Many people who begin paying for nursing home care from their own funds soon discover that their savings are not enough to cover lengthy stays. If they become impoverished after a nursing home stay, they turn to Medicaid to pay their bills.

Using Medicaid once meant impoverishing the spouse who remained at home as well as the spouse in the nursing home. Recent changes in the law, however, allow the at-home spouse to keep a specified level of assets and income.[7] Thus, in 1988 Congress enacted the spousal impoverishment reforms in the Medicaid program that allows a spouse who remains in the community when the other spouse is in a nursing care facility to keep one-half of the couple's assets up to a maximum of $76 000, in addition to the family home and automobile. In some states the healthy spouse can keep $76 000 even if it represents more than one-half of the couple's savings. This so-called amount is subject to annual increases to keep pace with inflation. While most government Medicaid offices tell their applicants for nursing home care that they must 'spend down' their assets until there is only $2000 (varies by state) remaining to qualify for nursing home benefits, this is true only for individuals but does not take into account a special provision for married couples when one spouse is at home.[28] Medicaid allows individuals to reduce their assets in various ways such as paying off debts, prepaying burial expenses, modernizing their home, or purchasing an automobile.

On February 8, 2006 President Bush signed into law the Deficit Reduction Act of 2005 (PL 109-171), part of which is designed to prevent wealthy senior citizens from qualifying for Medicaid by transferring money to their children so that seniors appear poor and thus have Medicaid pay their nursing home bills. As already noted, only seniors with $2000 or less in assets, excluding a car or a house, can qualify for Medicaid (married couples are allowed more resources). In addition, they had to prove under the former law that in the previous 3 years they had not tried to defraud Medicaid by giving away assets. The new law in 2006 extends the previous 3 years to 5 years and limits the value of the excluded house to $500 000. However, each state has the option of raising that equity to $750 000. Gifts to a spouse or disabled child are permitted. If seniors have transferred money improperly, they are not permitted to be covered by Medicaid for months or years, depending upon how much they transferred. The new rules strengthen that penalty.[29–32]

Managed care

A managed care plan will not help pay for care unless the nursing home has a contract with the plan. If the home is approved by the plan, the consumer-patient should find out whether the plan also monitors the quality of nursing care the nursing home provides.

Long-term care insurance

This is a private insurance policy. The benefits and costs of these plans vary widely. But there are certain basics or standards in such a policy that the National Association of Insurance Commissioners recommends:

- At least a year of nursing home or home care health care coverage, including intermediate and custodial care. Nursing home or home health care benefits should not be limited primarily to skilled care.
- Coverage for Alzheimer's disease if the policyholder develops the disease after buying the policy.
- An inflation-protective option. The policy should offer a choice between automatically increasing the initial benefit level on an annual basis; a guaranteed right to increase benefit levels periodically without providing evidence of insurability; and covering a specific percentage of actual or reasonable charges.

- An outline of coverage that systematically describes the policy's benefits, limitations and exclusions, and also allows the consumer to compare it with others.
- A long-term care insurance shopper guide that helps the consumer decide whether long-term care is appropriate for the consumer.
- A guarantee that the policy cannot be canceled, nonrenewed, or otherwise terminated because the consumer becomes older or suffers deterioration in physical or mental health.
- The right to return the policy within 30 days after the consumer has purchased the policy (if for any reason the consumer does not want it) and to receive a premium refund.
- No requirement that the policyholder first be hospitalized in order to receive nursing home benefits or home health care benefits; or first receive skilled nursing home care before receiving intermediate or custodial care; or first receive nursing home care before receiving benefits for home health care.[5]

Other ways to finance nursing home care

Additional resources to finance nursing home care may include social security payments, a person's own funds, assets in escrow or as an endowment, assistance from the local welfare department, or assistance from private organizations such as veterans groups, trade unions, fraternal organizations or, as already noted, private health insurance plans.

The USA and the UK

The problems of finding and judging the quality of nursing home care is not unique to the USA but is common to many countries.. While those in the USA can compare various nursing home criteria on the Medicare website (http://www.NursingHomeCompare.com), residents of the UK may visit the following website (www.ucarewecare.com) in seeking and comparing nursing home information. The UK website suggests questions prospective patients may ask when deciding to enter a nursing home and the questions are as applicable to patients or their loved ones in the USA as they are in other countries when seeking nursing home care. These questions include:

- How regularly do doctors visit the nursing home?
- Does the home cater to nursing as well as residential care? It is best to find out, depending upon the patient's needs, before the patient moves in so that the patient would not have to move elsewhere at a later date.
- Do the homes retain key staff? Familiarity with the patient's condition and needs can improve the quality of care the patient receives.

- Does each home on your shortlist have space available at the time of expected admission?
- Does the home have a care plan or a particular philosophy?
- What emphasis does the home give to caring for the resident?
- What makes this particular home different from others you have inquired about?
- Does the home offer any special activities that will interest your loved one?
- Does the nursing home's geographical location make visiting by family and friends possible at any time? Regular visits are the best way to make sure that your loved one is doing well and is receiving the kind of care the patient's loved ones desire.
- Are there sufficient local transport options available?
- Are residents' religious denominations and cultural needs catered to?
- Are special dietary requirements catered to?

Just as there are many questions a consumer may have prior to choosing a nursing home, whether it is in the USA, the UK, or other countries, there are also many complaints a person may have after a loved one is admitted to the facility. Within the USA, in particular, consumers have many sources to obtain corrective action about their grievances. These include: *nursing home officials,* including the head nurse on a unit (who may be called the charge nurse), the director of nursing, the nursing home administrator, and the facility's resident council, if any; *government officials*, including patient's caseworker or the county welfare office, state Medicaid agency (if the patient is covered by Medicaid), US Congressman or Senator (address Congressmen at the US House of Representatives, Washington DC 20515; Senators at US Senate, Washington DC 20510), state house and locally elected representatives like a city council, or private organizations such as local Better Business Bureau, Chamber of Commerce, and/or a reputable lawyer or legal society.

In addition to the previous sources, the following US sources are available not only to file grievances but also to obtain information about nursing home care:

- The American Health Care Association (1201 L St. NW, Washington DC 20005), if the nursing home is a member: http://www.ahca.org.
- The American Association of Homes and Services for the Aging (2519 Connecticut Ave., NW, Washington, DC) if the nursing home is a member: http://www.aahas.org.
- The National Coalition for Nursing Home Reform (1828 L St. NW, Washington, DC 20026): http://www.nursinghomeaction.com.
- The American College of Health Care Administrators (300 North Lee St., Alexandria VA 22314), if the nursing home administrator is a member: http://www.achca.org.

- The Joint Commission on the Accreditation of Healthcare Organizations (One Renaissance Blvd, Oakbrook Terrace, IL 60181), if the nursing home has received accreditation from this organization: http://www.jacho.org.
- A local hospital association and medical society.
- The nursing home ombudsman if such an office has been established in your community or in your state Office of Aging. The federal Older American Act requires each state to have an ombudsman program to serve as an advocate for residents of nursing homes, board and care homes, and assisted living facilities. For the telephone number of your state and local long-term care ombudsman program, telephone 1-800-677-1116 or visit http://www.aoa.dhhs.gov. The ombudsman may have a directory of facilities in your area and information about problems particular facilities may be having, including your own facility.

Whether the individual is a patient, relative, or friend, all these sources exist to help everyone who has nursing home problems and to serve as a source of information about such care. Remember, nursing home administrators who operate homes of quality will welcome such queries. The stay, treatment, and physical well-being of a loved one will ultimately be affected by the answers given to these queries.

References

1. *Source Book of Health Insurance Data*. Washington, DC: Health Insurance Association of America, 1995: 98 (Table 5.1), 121.
2. *Nursing Home Care. Vital and Health Statistics*. Hyattsville, MD: National Center for Health Statistics, 2000: 147.
3. Ross N L. The long-term care-care tangle. *Washington Post* 1989; January 31: D5.
4. US Department of Commerce. *Statistical Abstract of the United States: Resident Population by Age and Sex: 1980–2002*. Washington, DC: Bureau of the Census, 2003: 13.
5. Wasik J F. Can you afford to take care of a loved one? *Parade* 1990; December 16: 14–25.
6. US Department of Health and Human Services. *National Health Expenditure Accounts, 2006, Highlights*. Washington, DC: Centers for Medicare and Medicaid Services, 2008.
7. *Guide to Long-Term Care Insurance, 1999*. Washington, DC: Health Insurance Association of America, 1999: 3–5, 13–14.
8. *GAO Issues Report on LTC Financing*. Washington, DC: US General Accountability Office, 2005: 2, 4.
9. *65+*. *Washington Post/Health* 1996; July 23: 7.
10. Franklin M B. Elder law: saving your life savings. *Washington Post/Health* 1996; July 23: 16.
11. US Department of Health and Human Services. *CDC Fact Book 2000/2001*. Atlanta, GA: Centers for Disease Control, 2000: 53.
12. *Fact Sheet: The American Geriatrics Society (AGS)*. New York: American Geriatrics Society, 2001.
13. US Department of Health and Human Services. *Online Survey, Certification, and Reporting Date*. Washington, DC: Health Care Financing Administration, 1997.

14. *Summary of 2009 Finding Table. Genworth 2009 Cost of Care Survey.* Richmond, VA: Genworth Financial, 2009.
15. Nursing home costs top $80,000 a year. *Silicon Valley/San Jose Bus J* 2002; March 4.
16. 2003 GE [General Electric] nursing home cost of care survey, conducted by Evans Research July 31 2003, as cited in long-term care insurance material sent to author January 2005, from General Electric Capital Insurance Company.
17. Be prepared for long-term care. Cox News Service 2004; March 15.
18. Illinois Department of Health. *What Everyone Should Know about Skilled Nursing Homes.* Springfield, IL: State Health Coordinating Council, 1977: 2–3, 5–10.
19. *Thinking about a Nursing Home?* Washington, DC: American Health Care Association, 1979: 2–5.
20. Nursing homes in area, nationwide plagued by reports of abuse. *Washington Post* 1996; October 13: B1, B6.
21. Third of US nursing homes faulted on care. *Washington Post* 1986; May 21: A15.
22. Sedensky M. Medicaid recipients seek community care. *Washington Post* 2008; September 28: A5.
23. Harrington C, Woolhandler S, Mullan J *et al.* Does investor ownership of nursing homes compromise the quality of care? *Am J Publ Hlth* 2001; 91: 1452.
24. *The Condition of the American Nursing Home: A Study.* Washington, DC: US Senate Subcommittee on the Problems of the Aged and Aging of the Committee on Labor and Public Welfare, 1960: 1–2.
25. Braverman J. *Nursing Home Standards: A Tragic Dilemma in American Health.* Washington, DC: American Pharmaceutical Association, 1970: 44–49.
26. *The MetLife Market Survey of Nursing Home and Home Care Costs.* New York, NY: Metropolitan Life Insurance Company, 2006: 4.
27. Decker F H. *Nursing Homes, 1977–1999.* Hyattsville, MD: National Center for Health Statistics, 2005.
28. Franklin M B. Elder law: saving your life savings. *Washington Post/Health* 1996; July 23: 17–18.
29. Crenshaw A. Long-term care is hot topic in insurance. *Washington Post/Health* 1996; June 18: 10.
30. Dembner A. Medicaid proposal could hurt seniors. *Boston Globe* 2006; January 30: Your Life section.
31. Weisman J. Budget cuts pass by slim margin. *Washington Post* 2006; February 2; A1, A7.
32. House B J. *House Approves Medicaid Reform, Digital TV.* US House of Representatives: Committee on Energy and Commerce, 2005.

9

Home care and hospice care

Introduction

One of the 'newest' solutions to rising hospital costs and escalating health insurance premiums today is home health care services, but in actual fact they are one of the oldest programs within America's health care system. Unlike nursing homes, which have received a great deal of federal and state financial support over the years for long-term care, this situation has not necessarily been true for in-home care programs. Yet, various assessments have shown that many hospital and nursing home patients could be cared for in their own homes. Care at home has many benefits: financial, emotional, and psychological. No one can measure the value of peace of mind when patients receive care at home, upon their physician's recommendation, rather than in an institution.

Home health care agencies provide a broad spectrum of services to the public, including blood tests, home kidney dialysis, medical social services, and skilled nursing care, as well as intravenous, inhalation, physical, and occupational therapy. In addition, some agencies provide a variety of personnel, including nurses, social workers, and speech, physical and occupational therapists, as well as home health aides who attend to housekeeping, marketing, and personal patient needs such as bathing and grooming. Other agencies are more specialized.

The services that home health agencies provide vary widely. Some of the more sophisticated agencies provide services similar to those of hospitals, including nurses with advanced training in chemotherapy and pediatric nurse practitioners as well as specialists in nutritional therapy or in caring for surgery patients. Some agencies can set up traction in a patient's home; others provide medical supplies or equipment and intravenous drug therapy as well as arrange transportation to the hospital or doctor's office for periodic treatments or follow-up examinations. However, most agencies are not so elaborate in regard to their services. Most have only three or four nurses, a few home health aides, and usually a physical therapist.

During 2000 more than 1.3 million patients received home health care services (acute and long-term) from 7200 agencies. Seventy percent of patients (70.5%) were 65 years of age or older and almost 22% of home health patients (21.9%) were 85 years of age or older. Two-thirds of home health patients were women. Most of the patients received skilled care (75%), with 44% receiving personal care and 37% receiving therapeutic services. Fifty-one percent received assistance with at least one activity of daily living and the average length of service was 312 days.[1,2]

Among home health patients in 2000, almost 48% (47.5%) of the admission diagnoses were composed of the following six conditions: diseases of the heart (10.9%), diseases of the musculoskeletal system and connective tissue (9.8%), diabetes (7.8%), cerebrovascular diseases (7.3%), malignant neoplasms (4.9%), and respiratory diseases (6.78%).[2] Home care has no restrictions on age or illness. Everyone from babies born with severe birth defects or other illnesses to elderly persons injured in automobile accidents is eligible to be treated at home. Home care can be for anyone, not just for the sick and the elderly. Aside from short- or long-term illness, individuals and families who may have a variety of health and social problems such as an injury, mental disorders and learning disability, alcoholism, and physical and social handicaps, among others, can be treated at home. In some locales, hospital discharge planning teams, which might include a public health nurse, suggest when patients might be discharged to their home and recommend the kind of care the patients will require when they get there. In most places, however, the patient or family is responsible for investigating the possibility and availability of home care and then asks the physician to order it. Often good care at home can prevent the patient's need to enter a nursing home and spare the family the ordeal of visiting the patient in an institution, operating the household, and working at several jobs at the same time.[3]

Basic services

Home care is not just a solitary service but a wide spectrum of services with a common purpose: to maintain the home and improve the quality of life by providing assistance in the home. These services include the following:

- *Social services* to identify and overcome specific problems within the home, supervise services, and coordinate home care with other community programs. These services involve: medical care; nutrition services; personal care (bathing, dressing, eating, taking temperatures, changing dressings, helping with exercises); and skilled nursing services (giving drugs and other prescribed treatments); therapy for specific problems: speech therapy, respiratory therapy (breathing), physical therapy (movement), and occupational therapy (managing household and work tasks).
- *Homemaking services* to improve or maintain the home, including environmental care (light housekeeping, doing the laundry, grocery

shopping, planning and preparing meals) and teaching home management (budgeting, home safety) and parenting (children skills and family relations).

- *Supplemental services* to improve the quality of life.
- *Pastoral counseling* to provide comfort and advice to individuals and families, especially the seriously ill.
- *Meals on wheels* to deliver nutritious meals to the homes of those unable to make or obtain their own meals.
- *Chore services* to aid with or perform heavy-duty household tasks and to maintain safety in the home, including minor home repairs (step, rail, or electrical repair); heavy cleaning (outside window washing and cleaning attics or basements); and yard tasks (lawn cutting or snow removal).
- *Friendly visiting* to provide regular visits for companionship, at least once a week, to the homebound who are lonely. Visitors converse, write letters, read, or often just listen.
- *Telephone reassurance* to link the homebound to the community via a 7-day-a-week call system. Telephone reassurance diminishes loneliness, depression, and fear common to those living alone and assists in emergency situations.
- *Transportation and escort service* to help those needing assistance to leave the home. Minibuses, cars, or public systems may be used as transportation to medical or community services. Escorts provide physical assistance, support, or protection needed to encourage elderly and disabled individuals to go into the community. Often these two services work hand in hand.
- *Equipment services and loan closets* to provide needed health care equipment such as hospital beds or wheelchairs. Equipment services rent or sell equipment; loan closets lend health care devices as needed at little or no cost.

Today, many health professionals help or counsel those who need home care such as those who provide equipment services such as pharmacies. So how can a health professional or lay person determine who might need home care? The following are some signposts:

- The person has trouble caring for himself/herself or family at home because of age, health, or social problems.
- The person can provide adequate care at home for another but feels angry, frustrated, or exhausted at the end of each day and as a result family relationships are deteriorating.
- The person may be homebound, living alone or feeling depressed, fearful, or lonely.

- The person may be in hospital or about to go home without a satisfactory plan for care following discharge.
- The person is missing days at work to care for a family member.

If any or all of these conditions are present, home care may be a service that ought to be considered.

Financial advantages of home care

In locale after locale where home care programs have been founded, organizations that established and offered these programs to the public have achieved financial savings. In a Connecticut home care program, a Blue Cross plan study of 991 patients showed a reduction of 8919 days (an average of 9 days per case) and money savings of $801 511. And in Philadelphia in just 2 years another longstanding plan saved an average of 12 days per patient and reduced hospitals bills by $2.5 million or an average of $869 per case.[4] The potential savings that home care programs can accomplish in reducing unnecessary hospital stays, health insurance premiums, and individual health expenses, perhaps, are without limit as our population's life expectancy increases and begins to age in future years. Because chronic illnesses such as diabetes, hypertension, malignancies, and other long-term partially disabling illnesses are widespread and can be treated at home, the value of home care programs to society is beyond measure.

Availability of home care

When the US Department of Health and Human Services certifies agencies to provide health care services under the Medicare program, it means that the home care agency meets minimum federal standards and qualifications to receive Medicare reimbursement. When an agency has no such certification, this is not a reflection of an agency providing poor services. Rather, the agency may only wish to provide services to non-Medicare patients and not become involved in the federal government program.

Definitions of bonded, licensed, and certified health personnel

As already noted, certain terminology is used in regard to home care personnel. These include bonded, certified, and licensed.

Bonded, a term agencies use, almost always refers to the agencies and claims against it, not to their employees. Although agencies could bond employees, not many do because of the expense involved. It is not common practice for individual employees to bond themselves but, if they do, bonded personnel, like bonded agencies, have some protection or 'insurance' against consumer claims. So if a consumer has a problem with a bonded employee – for example, personal property damage – and takes court action and wins, the bond can pay the damages. The term 'bonded' does not mean that the employees are qualified to provide safe and satisfactory care.

Licensed health personnel pass a state test, upon which the state department of health or education issues a license that permits them to work. Every state licenses doctors, dentists, registered nurses (RNs), pharmacists, licensed practical nurses (LPNs), and physical therapists. Some states license social workers, dental hygienists, occupational speech, and respiratory therapists, and laboratory personnel. States do not generally license homemaker/home health aides.

Certified health personnel must meet the specific standards established by the national organization representing the profession. For example, the American Dietetic Association represents and certifies dieticians. The standards usually require passing a national test and/or providing proof of work experience. Social workers and therapists are among the health personnel who are generally certified. Homemaker/home health aides are not certified by a national organization.

State licensure and certification help protect the public against unqualified health personnel working in home care, health facilities, and private practice. But standards vary from state to state, and in all instances a person's best defense is to screen carefully and supervise workers themselves, or rely upon a good home care agency.[5]

How to find home care agency services

The most common form of home care assistance in many communities is an informal system of friends, family, or individually hired help who earn their living by performing work in the home, including childcare, home nursing, homemaking, or chore work. However, more and more assistance is provided through a variety of agencies, public and private. As a health professional or as a lay person, you can find their names and addresses from your physician, the public health department of your community or state, which can refer the patient to Medicare/Medicaid-certified home health agencies, your state or local welfare department, a hospital social service department, or the visiting nurse association in your community. A place of religious worship may also be able to help in finding home care agencies.

Home care agencies may be listed in the yellow pages of a telephone directory under 'nursing,', 'nursing services,' 'homemaker/home health aide agencies,' 'home health care,' 'social service organizations,' or 'home health services.'

In addition, there may be area agencies on aging in the community that sponsor home care and other community programs to assist those aged 60 and older to stay independent. Although such programs are established for services to older citizens, they will often help people of any age trying to find community home care. The Elder Locator, financed by the US Administration on Aging, may also be able to provide information about services available in a community (telephone: 1-800-677-1116, toll-free, or visit http://www.aoa. dhhs.gov). The American Association of Retired Persons (AARP) may provide information to its members (write to AARP Department P, 601 E St., NW, Washington DC 20039 or visit http://www.aarp.org). If home care services are needed in regard to specific problems such as cancer, blindness, mental retardation, or other illnesses, then the local offices of the appropriate community agency such as the American Cancer Society should be contacted. Most agencies have 'patient services' divisions that may be of assistance in locating services. Finally, do not ignore city, county, or state officials. Check with the mayor's office, the board of supervisors, if any, state senators or congressional representatives.[5] The following are common home health agencies.

Voluntary tax-exempt agencies

Voluntary agencies are locally funded, community-based, usually operated by a volunteer board of interested citizens, usually offer a sliding scale of fees, good sources for information and referral, and, mostly, are visiting nurse associations.

Public health agencies

About one-half of the Medicare-certified home health agencies are government-sponsored and are usually supported by a city or county health department. Most charge for their services but can arrange reduced rates or free care for those who cannot pay. Some may limit services to the poor or the elderly, but most serve a broad-based clientele. Even if public health departments do not provide direct home care, they can usually refer to agencies that do.

Hospital-based agencies

A small number of hospitals operate home health agencies. They provide many of the clinical services available in the hospital, such as laboratory work and physical therapy. Nearly all limit themselves to providing follow-up care for patients released from the hospital so it is in the consumer's interest to ask whether a hospital provides such a service.

Proprietary agencies

A number of profit-making organizations offer home health services in cities throughout the USA. Consumers should ask whether their agency qualifies for Medicare benefits because not all proprietary agencies are eligible for Medicare reimbursements. More commonly, though not universal, private insurance plans reimburse proprietary agencies. While private agencies do offer skilled services, many agencies emphasize nonskilled care, such as homemakers, companions, and home health aides.

Private nonprofit agencies

These are usually small organizations owned by families or individuals who technically earn a salary, rather than take a profit. This situation makes such agencies eligible for Medicare reimbursement, regardless of state licensing procedures, and Medicare patients represent a high percentage of their clients. The majority of private nonprofit agencies operate in urban areas where there are large numbers of elderly persons.

Employment agencies and nurses' registries

These agencies refer and place health personnel in a home for a fee. The resident of the home assumes the responsibility of an employer. In general, although employment agencies and nurses' registries furnish a referral system that helps locate and employ individuals who are willing to work in a home, they do not supervise them once they have been placed. Thus, an agency concerned with good quality of care – whether profit making, nonprofit, or government – and which supervises its employees provides additional services that are not available otherwise to the person seeking assistance.[3]

If contacting a home health agency, it is important for patients to explain the kind of health problems for which they are seeking help and to select an agency that seems most likely to meet personal needs. A good agency carefully evaluates the home situation and works with patients to develop a plan of service that corresponds to their health, social, and financial needs. This is very important. A good agency will only provide those services that the patient requires. For example, it will not provide round-the-clock services when a few hours a day is all that is necessary. It would not provide assistance for tasks patients would and could do themselves. This can help patients maintain or regain their independence and help lessen home care costs. A good home care agency supervises all personnel coming into the home, including volunteers, so problems are prevented or corrected as soon as possible if they occur.

Medicare's Home Health Compare

Regardless of the sponsorship of a home health agency, Medicare has made available a tool to the public to judge the quality of care a home heath agency provides. It is called Home Health Compare, is available on the Medicare website (http://www.Medicare.gov), and provides quality-of-care information about home care agencies throughout the country. These measures offer information about patients' physical and mental health and whether their ability to perform basic daily activities is maintained or improved. The quality-of-care measures are grouped into four categories, and include:

- four measures related to improvement in getting around
- four measures related to meeting the patient's activities of daily living
- two measures related to patient medical emergencies
- one measure related to improvement in mental health.

The quality measures are based on data collected about home health patients whose care is covered by Medicare or Medicaid and provided by a Medicare-certified home health agency. Anyone of any age can access the website. To reduce the chance that the home health agency which serves sicker, older, or frailer patients may look worse in the quality measures, the quality measures are risk-adjusted. That means that some of the percentages have been changed to take into consideration the fact that agencies treat sicker people. In more specific terms, the website informs patients of the following quality-of-care measures:

- percentage of patients who get better at walking or moving around
- percentage of patients who get better at getting in and out of bed
- percentage of patients who get better at getting to and from the toilet
- percentage of patients who have less pain when moving around
- percentage of patients who get better at bathing (improvement in ability); percentage of patients who stayed the same or don't get worse at bathing (stabilizing measures of maintaining ability)
- percentage of patients who get better at taking their medicine correctly (by mouth)
- percentage of patients who get better at getting dressed
- percentage of patients who had to be admitted to the hospital
- percentage of patients who need urgent, unplanned medical care
- percentage of patients who are confused less often.

These various tools can help consumers make the kind of decision as to what agency will best meet their personal needs. Again, to access the comparative information consumers can log on to the Medicare consumer website, http://www.Medicare.gov, and click 'Home Health Compare.' Once on the site, consumers can search home health care information by state, county, zip code, or name of agency. Consumers can also obtain the information via Medicare's 24-hour-hotline at 1-800-Medicare (telephone: 1-800-633-4227).

Home care personnel

There is a wide variety of personnel who provide home care services. These include the following major categories:

- *Physicians* (doctors of medicine and osteopathy) may prescribe home care for their patients. They outline specific health or other services that are needed and the level of care. Sometimes doctors provide medical care at home.
- *Social workers* provide counseling and find and coordinate resources and supervise home care services.
- *Registered dieticians* or nutritionists plan special diets to hasten recovery from illness or injury or to manage health conditions such as high blood pressure or diabetes.
- *Speech therapists* help those with communication problems, such as learning to speak after a stroke.
- *Respiratory therapists* help patients with breathing difficulties so that their lung function is restored or kept at its highest possible level.
- *Physical therapists* use exercise, heat, light, water, or other methods to treat patients with problems of movement.
- *Occupational therapists* teach people how to manage daily activities at home and/or work despite physical or mental disabilities: for example, carrying out housekeeping from a wheelchair.
- *Nurses*: RNs provide skilled nursing care and LPNs also provide nursing care.
  - RNs are the most highly skilled and educated. RNs are best prepared to manage the critical needs of patients who may require complex treatment. The RNs often act as home care supervisors. RNs with public health education may be employed to coordinate agency services with other health and social services available in the community.
  - LPNs have less education in nursing than RNs. LPNs are equipped to take care of patients with simpler nursing needs who usually require more routine treatment and care.
- *Homemaker/home health aides* may provide one or more services: homemaking services (environmental care and home management), personal care, and others. When delivering personal care services, they may be called 'nursing assistants,' 'health aides,' 'home health aides,' and 'attendants.' When employed primarily to perform household duties, aides may be called 'homemakers,' 'housekeepers,' or 'home helps.'

- *Case manager* is a professional, usually a nurse or social worker, who will thoroughly review the patient's needs and coordinate services. To learn the names of qualified case managers in a local community, contact the National Association of Professional Geriatric Care Managers in Tucson, Arizona at 1-520-881-8008 or click on its website at http://www.caremanager.org.

In addition to the previous personnel others may provide home care services. These include the clergy, laboratory technicians, and others.

Cost of home care services

As far as fees and visit charges are concerned, most home health care agencies charge for professional services by visit. Bringing an aide into a home just three times a week (2–3 hours per visit) to help with dressing, bathing, preparing meals, and similar household chores can cost $1000 a month or $12 000 per year. In 2004 the national average cost for home care provided by a home health aide was $18 per hour or $37 000 per year for a 40-hour week of assistance: in or near cities the charges would probably be higher, but less in rural areas. When the costs of skilled help such as physical therapists are added, the costs can be greater. In comparison, nursing home care during 2001 as a national average cost more than $54 900 per year and by 2003 almost $58 000, and much more than this amount in some regions of the country. In its April 2009 survey report Genworth Financial, a global financial security firm, noted that the national average median daily rate, with variations among states, was $183.25 for a semiprivate room in a skilled nursing home or $66 886 a year, and $203.31 for a private room in a skilled nursing home or $77 208 per year.[6–11] As already noted, an official home care agency is an organization sponsored by a unit of the government such as a city or county, while nonofficial agencies are all nongovernmental home health organizations, whether they are operated for profit or on a nonprofit basis. Proprietary agencies require a minimum stay of 2–4 hours (thus, sometimes raising the cost per visit), although this is subject to negotiation. Therefore, when consumers employ the service of a home health care agency they should ask about its fees and minimum-stay policy in advance so that they can compare public versus proprietary costs. Some services such as meals on wheels, friendly visiting, and telephone reassurance usually operate at little or no cost because of volunteer help. The same may be true in some cities where transportation and escort services operate as community services.

How to finance home health care services

In determining whether consumers can afford home care services, they should know that a variety of private and public sources are available to help them pay for such care, including Medicare, Medicaid, other public programs, private health insurance, health maintenance organizations (HMOs), as well as charitable funds. However, consumers should be aware that government and private financial assistance may not be sufficient to pay for all home care services. Some of the funding is too limited in the type of services covered. As a result, patients can sometimes pay more out of their own pocket when they stay at home than if they were hospitalized and an insurance plan paid for the hospital stay. Moreover, some people who could be cared for at home must enter an institution or give up the home care because they cannot meet all the third party's (insurance or government assistance program) requirements for payment. Consequently, if a consumer needs home care, the following sources may help pay for such care. But it is very important to learn in advance what restrictions home health agencies impose in order to receive their services. Consumers will then know what kind of financial burden they may have to assume in deciding whether they can afford to receive care at home.

Medicaid

All states and the District of Columbia are required to provide Medicaid payments for three home health care services: nursing, home health aides, and medical supplies and equipment. As an option of the state, Medicaid may also provide other services such as physical therapy, occupational therapy, and speech and hearing services. Consumers should ask their local or state public assistance or welfare departments, their local department of social services, or local social security office whether Medicaid in their state pays for these additional services.

Blue Cross

Many Blue Cross plans provide some form of home health benefits. A majority no longer require prior hospitalization. If consumers have Blue Cross coverage, they should find out from their plan or insurance agent whether this waiver applies to them. Many plans also pay for comprehensive home care services: drugs, medical/surgical supplies, transportation, nutritional guidance, counseling, social services, rental of equipment in addition to visits by medical professionals. Homemaking services are not usually covered.

Private insurance

Many Americans who have major medical insurance may have home care benefits included in their insurance coverage plan. Except for prior hospitalization and coverage of prescription drugs, the restrictions of the insurance coverage are similar to those of Medicare. Many private health insurance plans require the patient to pay a deductible and a percentage (usually 20%)

of any charges beyond the deductible. Except in some states where home health care coverage is mandatory, private hospitalization plans will probably not cover home care. Consumers should check their policy carefully or contact their private insurer. In some instances, consumers will not find home care listed specifically in the policy, but they may be covered under 'miscellaneous' or 'other' clauses.

Federal programs

Aside from Medicare and Medicaid, for persons who qualify there may be other federal program funds available for home health care services. Homemaker services may be provided to needy persons under Title XX of the Social Security Act which is block grants to states for social services. When these programs are available, they are usually administered by the local welfare agency. Money for home care for the elderly is available on a limited basis under an Administration on Aging program or the Older Americans Act. Consumers should check with their local agency or state Agency on Aging. Disabled persons may qualify for home health services under the Developmentally Disabled Assistance Act. An agency that deals with rehabilitation of handicapped individuals may be able to help.

Health maintenance organizations

The Health Maintenance Organization Act of 1973 requires that a federally qualified HMO provide home health services to its members. Others may include some aspects of home care in their consumer health plans.

Charitable funds

Nonprofit home health agencies such as visiting nurse associations often receive United Way Funds to help offset the costs of home care when patients cannot pay the full cost of service.[3]

Special insurance

Special insurance, including workers' compensation, disability, home liability or care insurance, may cover home care services under specified conditions, for example, if care is needed as a result of an injury at work or in a car.

US Department of Veterans Affairs

This federal agency provides home care benefits for military-related illnesses or injury.

Medicare

Under Medicare home health care was originally conceived as a way to bring about early hospital discharge. In the 1980s, due to litigation, the Medicare manual for home health agencies was revised so that coverage could no longer be denied just because a patient has a chronic disease, and a physician's prescription for home care could no longer be rejected unless objective evidence was found that contradicted the order. To qualify for home care under Medicare, a beneficiary must be 65 years or older, or have been entitled to social security disability benefits for 24 consecutive months, under a physician's care, and certified by a physician that he/she needs a specified home health service which can be provided by a home health agency participating in the Medicare program.

The Medicare program provides home health care services under its hospital insurance program (Part A) and its voluntary medical insurance program (Part B). Coverage under the hospital insurance to which all social security beneficiaries are automatically entitled pays the reasonable cost of unlimited home health visits during a benefit period. A benefit period begins with the first day a beneficiary receives covered inpatient services in a hospital. It ends when the beneficiary has been out of the hospital or the skilled nursing home for 60 consecutive days (including the day of discharge). There is no limit to the number of benefit periods a person may have. The payment for the home health care visits may be made for a noncalendar year (365 days) after the start of each benefit period. Therefore, the beneficiary qualifies for home health visits under the hospital insurance (Part A) of Medicare if the beneficiary meets the following conditions:

- The beneficiary is in a Medicare program-participating hospital. Effective from July 1, 1981 and as a result of the enactment of the Omnibus Budget Reconciliation Act of 1980 (PL 96-499), the beneficiary can qualify directly for home care under Part A of Medicare without first being hospitalized for 3 days.
- A home health plan is established by a physician within 14 days after the beneficiary leaves the hospital or the skilled nursing home if the beneficiary needs such services before receiving home care.
- The home care program is for further treatment of a condition for which the beneficiary received treatment in the hospital or the skilled nursing home if the beneficiary required such prior care or can receive home care directly without first being hospitalized. The beneficiary is confined to his/her home.
- The beneficiary's condition is such that the beneficiary needs skillful nursing care on an intermittent basis or physical or speech therapy.

In addition to the home health care benefits of the hospital insurance plan (Part A), additional home health benefits are available under the insurance plan (Part B) of Medicare for which a beneficiary can sign up on a voluntary basis. The home health services under the supplementary voluntary medical insurance program of Part B are without limit within a calendar year, unlike Part A, which is within a noncalendar year. The benefit period does not apply in the Part B program as it does in Part A. Also, like Part A, no prior stay in a hospital or a skilled nursing home is required in the Part B program of Medicare before these home health benefits become effective. Consequently, a beneficiary can become eligible for home health benefits under Part B of Medicare if the beneficiary voluntarily signs up for this insurance (it will pay 100% of the reasonable costs of the covered services), is confined to his/her home, a doctor orders and reviews periodically the plan for home health care, and the beneficiary's condition is such that he/she will need skilled nursing care on an intermediate basis or physical therapy or speech therapy. If the beneficiary qualifies for any of these home health benefits, his/her eligibility for home health services may be extended solely on the basis of continuing need for occupational therapy.

Home care services provided under the Medicare program are delivered by home health agencies that qualify for participating in the Medicare program. Such agencies have policies established and supervised by physicians and RNs, are licensed under state and local laws, and are approved for participation in the Medicare program. The agencies retain clinical records of all patients and carry out the orders of the physician. In addition, services may be performed outside the patient's home if the patient requires special equipment that cannot be brought to the home.

Medicare pays for the following services which home care agencies provide: professional skilled nursing (part-time); practical nursing care; physical therapy services; speech therapy services; occupational therapy services; medical social services to understand the social and emotional problems or personal difficulties related to the beneficiary's recovery and health; home health aide services such as assistance with personal grooming and bathing; exercises under a physician's orders and under the supervision of a nurse or therapist; and medical supplies like surgical dressing, oxygen, gauze, cotton, rubbing alcohol, and intravenous fluids. The services do not include: drugs or biologicals; medical appliances like wheelchairs, crutches, hospital beds, oxygen tanks, trapeze bars, and air pressure mattresses as prescribed by the physician; and physician services.

However, while many services are covered under Medicare's home health program, many are not. Medicare does not cover the following health services: full-time nursing care; drugs and biologicals, as already noted; personal comfort items; general housekeeping services; meals on wheels (meals delivered to the patient's home); and ambulance or special transportation to and from a patient's home when the patient receives covered services on an out-patient basis.

In looking for home care services, beneficiaries can find out whether the agency is approved by Medicare by asking their local Social Security Office, their physician, or the home health agency itself. If the beneficiary qualifies for the hospital insurance program (Part A) under Medicare and voluntarily purchases the supplementary medical insurance (Part B), the beneficiary will not have to decide whether to receive home health care services under the hospital insurance (Part A) or the medical insurance (Part B). If the beneficiary meets the hospitalization requirements of Part A, he/she will automatically come under the hospital insurance plan and its home health benefits.[12] If the beneficiary does not meet Medicare hospitalization requirements, the home health benefits will automatically come under the medical insurance plan (Part B). After beneficiaries receive their home health visits, they do not have to pay the home health agency directly and then collect the cost of service from Medicare. Rather, the home health agency will collect from Medicare directly. And if beneficiaries are living in a rest home, they are still eligible for home health care benefits because the rest home is their place of residence. In addition, the home health agency provides services for the treatment of mental illness if the beneficiary meets all the qualifications for receiving home health care under Medicare.

Now when Medicare reimburses the home health care agency they use a system that went into effect in the year 2000, called a prospective payment system (PPS). Under this system Medicare pays a fixed, predetermined rate for services and supplies bundled into 60-day episodes of home health care. The episode payment rates vary, depending on the characteristics of the patient's clinical, functional, and utilization of services, that is, the payment rates vary depending upon the home health resource groups (HHRGs) to which Medicare patients are assigned. Reduced or additional amounts are paid when certain conditions exist. The six home health disciplines are: home health aide services, medical social services, occupational therapy, physical therapy, skilled nursing care, and speech language pathology. All payments are subject to medical review adjustments reflecting beneficiary eligibility decisions, medical necessity determinations, and HHRG assignments. The new approach is expected to redistribute Medicare payments among home health agencies, achieve cost savings, improve the coordination of services, and reduce the number of unnecessary home health visits.

Prior to the establishment of the PPS, Medicare paid home health agencies at a rate reflecting either their reasonable costs or their per-visit cost limit that was applied in the aggregate, whichever was lower. The lower-rate test gave home health agencies the financial incentives to continue furnishing care as long as a visit's revenues exceeded the costs involved in producing those revenues, regardless of whether the benefits to the patients were noticeable.

These inflationary underpinnings contributed to the rapid increase in home care service expenditures over the years. For example, during the calendar year 1999, about 2.7 million Medicare enrollees received over 113 million home health visits. Total program charges were almost $11.4 billion, of which payments of $7.9 billion were made. In contrast, a decade earlier, in 1988, 1.6 million Medicare enrollees received 37.7 million visits, for whom total program charges were almost $2.5 billion, of which $1.9 billion in program payments were made. This growth was the result of the 1988–1989 liberalization and standardization coverage for home health care services, which, in turn, spurred a substantial increase in the number of home health agencies certified by Medicare. Between 1989 and 1999, the number of agencies increased by almost 40% (from 5676 to 7857).[13]

Thus, home care has proven to be a very important alternative within the health care field to other forms of more expensive delivery systems such as hospitals and nursing homes in attempting to control the rapid rise in the overall costs of health care services. Its role in the health care system of the future will become ever more important as our aging population grows and home health agencies are asked to provide needed services to this group as well as others in ways that will have to be financially and organizationally more efficient because of systems such as PPS, in contrast to the more open-ended reimbursement system that existed before the establishment of the PPS. If the past is any indicator of the future, then home health agencies should be able to meet these challenges successfully as American society has placed health care reform as one of its top priorities in the years that lie ahead.

Hospice care

One form of care that can be delivered at home, in a nursing home, in a hospital, or in any kind of inpatient facility is a relatively new addition to the US health care system in regard to the services it provides, the illnesses it treats, and its method of financing. Its name is hospice care. The focus of the hospice movement is so basic that most people prefer not to think about it – namely, our death.

The concept of hospice care began when a group of Catholic widows founded a hospital in Lyon, France, in 1842 for young women with incurable disease and inoperable cancer. In the mid-1800s, the Irish Sisters of Charity established a hospice for the dying in Dublin, Ireland. The beginning of today's modern hospice movement started in England in 1967 when Dame Cicely Saunders began St. Christopher's in London to provide care for terminally ill patients. This hospice served as a model for a movement that has migrated to northern Europe and the USA. In 1974 the first hospice in America was established in New Haven, Connecticut.[14] The National Hospice and Palliative Care Organization (NHPCO) estimates that, as of 2007, there were about 4700 hospices in the USA and that 1.4 million patients received hospice services during 2006 compared to 495 000 in 1997. The hospice organization further estimated that about 930 000 patients died while receiving hospice care in 2006 (or about 38.8% of all deaths in the USA in that year).[15]

Hospice care is a notion, not necessarily a physical place. The concept is based primarily on the relief of pain so that the dying patient may make more complete use of the final stages of life. If a patient's condition so warrants, medication is administered on a regular basis before the patient feels the need. Pain is something to be prevented and controlled and the dosage of narcotics is always concentrated downward to get the minimal effective dose to alleviate the pain without making patients into drugged zombies. Although some hospices may provide care in discrete units of hospitals or other free-standing facilities, it is the nature and the underlying philosophy of hospice care rather than its setting which distinguish it from other approaches to terminal care treatment because hospice care provides pain management and symptom control, as already noted, as well as psychosocial support and spiritual care to patients and their families, before a patient's death and even after. In 2006 while 44.1% of hospice admissions were for the primary diagnosis of cancer, the next highest four admissions were noncancer diagnoses. These include heart disease (11.8%), debility unspecified (11.2%), dementia, including Alzheimer's disease (10.3%), and lung disease (7.9%).[15] In 2006, the average length of stay for patients receiving hospice care held steady at 67.4 days. The median length of service – a more accurate measure in understanding the experience of the typical patient – was 20.0 days. This means that one-half of hospice patients received care for less than 3 weeks and one-half received care for more than 3 weeks.[15]

The shift in the patient mix in hospice care has created a very difficult problem for the federal government. Since about 2000 through 2007, the federal government has begun to demand that some hospices begin to repay hundreds of millions of dollars to the Medicare program since the hospices have exceeded their reimbursement limits because some patients do not die according to the actuarial tables. Unlike those with cancer, patients with Alzheimer's disease and dementia have less predictable trajectories in regard to a terminal illness and the latter patients now form the majority of hospice consumers. Their average stay is far longer – 86 days for Alzheimer's patients, for example, compared with 44 days for those with lung cancer, according to the Medicare Payment Advisory Commission, which analyzes Medicare issues for Congress. This situation, where the money has already been spent, may force some hospices out of business, at a time when the demand for hospice care services is increasing and when research indicates that hospice care actually saves money for the Medicare program. Medicare has now issued disease-specific guidelines for certifications, which must be made by both a personal physician and the hospice medical director. In the initial days of the Medicare hospice benefit, which was designed for those with less than 6 months to live, nearly all patients were cancer victims who tended to die relatively quickly and predictably once curative efforts ceased.

As already noted, hospice care is palliative, unlike other institutions such as hospitals which are oriented toward curative cases and the rehabilitation of the patient; that is, hospice care is aimed at pain relief and symptom control for the patient, not a cure for the illness. To ease the dying process, the hospice program focuses on helping the patient live as long as possible; providing support for the entire family as the unit of care; making it possible for the patient to remain at home as long as home care is appropriate; supplementing rather than duplicating existing services; and keeping expenses down.[16] Providing hospice care involves a broad range of disciplines and skills, including physicians, psychologists, nurses (RN, LPNs, and nurses' aides or visiting nurse), nutritionists, pharmacists, occupational and physical therapists, social workers, home health aides, clergy, administrative personnel, and volunteers.

An indepth analysis of all Medicare beneficiaries aged 65+ who died in 2002 was published in 2007 and conducted by researchers at Harvard University in cooperation with NHPCO. The analysis validated what previous smaller studies have shown about this age 65+ population. Female decedents use hospice services more than their male counterparts (30% versus 27% in 2002). White decedents use hospice services more than blacks (29% versus 22% in 2002); and overall, about one out of three older Americans use hospice services (28.6% in 2002).[17] The same study also reported that hospice use was higher for diseases that impose a high burden on caregivers, or diseases that predictably lead to death. The three causes of death with highest hospice utilization rates (malignancies, nephritis/kidney disease, and Alzheimer's disease) correspond to diseases that commonly impose high burdens of caregiving on family caregivers and/or that make it easier for decision-makers to predict the time frame of death.

Financing hospice care services

The Medicare hospice benefit, enacted by the US Congress in 1982, is the dominant source of payment to hospice providers. A hospice's total annual reimbursement cannot exceed the product of the number of patients it serves and a per-patient allowance set by the government each year ($21 410 in 2007). In 2005 Medicare spent about $8.2 billion on hospice care services, almost triple the amount in the year 2000.[18]

Under this hospice benefit, a patient may be asked to pay 5% of the cost of outpatient prescription drugs or $5 for each prescription, whichever is less, and 5% of the Medicare rate for respite care (short-term care given by another caregiver, so the usual caregiver can rest). The beneficiary may also have to pay room and board if the beneficiary receives hospice care in a facility other than for short-term general inpatient care or respite care. The Medicare hospice benefit does not pay for treatments or services unrelated to the terminal illness. In order to be eligible for this benefit, beneficiaries must be entitled to Medicare Part A and be certified by their medical doctor and the hospice medical director as having a terminal condition with a prognosis of 6 months or less to live if the illness was to follow its natural course, and the care is provided by a Medicare-certified hospice program. To be certified a hospice must provide 24-hour staffing, medical and nursing care, home health services, access to patient care, social work services, counseling, including bereavement counseling, medications, medical supplies, and durable medical equipment.

Twenty-six years after Congress enacted the hospice care benefit under Medicare, the federal health program issued a new rule in June 2008 that became effective on December 2, 2008. The rule requires hospice providers to be more closely accountable on the quality of care they provide by implementing a quality assessment and improvement system, and guaranteeing that hospice care patients have an input into their treatment plans. The rule also requires hospice care providers to demonstrate to the Centers for Medicare and Medicaid Services that they are improving areas where they have been found to be deficient. Initially, data about quality will only be available to each hospice organization and Medicare. Eventually, providers and advocates of hospice care expect that the data will be made available to the public just as the federal government has shared such information about nursing homes, hospitals, and home health agencies. On their own volition, hospices are working on quality care issues. NHPCO members have already been voluntarily following performances through its Quality Partners program, while most hospices use family surveys to measure how well they have handled a case. In 2006 Medicare spent about $10 billion on hospice care, an increase from about $3 billion in 2000. According to the Medicare Payment Advisory Commission, for-profit hospices, which represented about one-half of the hospices in 2005, made annual profits of about 12% from 2001 to 2005.[19]

Presently, there are two initial 90-day benefit periods with one additional 30-day period, followed by an unlimited number of 60-day periods (each period requires physician recertification). Under Medicare the patient may stop hospice care at any time and return to cure-oriented care. Any remaining days in a benefit period are forfeited once the hospice care is stopped. The percentage of patients covered by the Medicare hospice benefit (versus other payment sources) is presently 83.6%. Most agencies (93.1%) have been certified by the Centers for Medicare and Medicaid Services to file for reimbursement under the Medicare hospice benefit. There also exists a small minority of all-volunteer programs that do not seek federal reimbursement for patient care, but instead rely on community donations for support.[15] In addition to Medicare, private health insurance policies as well as many state Medicaid programs cover hospice care services.

In 2007, a Duke University study found that hospice care reduced Medicare costs by an average of $2309 per hospice patient when Medicare beneficiaries who used hospice care were compared to those who did not. In addition, hospice care cost would have been reduced for seven out of 10 hospice recipients if a hospice had been used for a longer period of time. For cancer patients hospice care decreased Medicare costs up until 233 days of care. For noncancer patients, the savings were observed up to 154 days of care. Beyond these periods hospice use costs Medicare more than conventional care.[20]

Finding hospice care

There are a number of sources to find hospice care in a community. Patients or their loved ones can check with their physician, local Blue Cross and Blue Shield plan or other local insurance company, a church or synagogue, the hospital administrators in the community or the social service department, the visiting nurse association, local public health or welfare department, state hospice organization, local social security office, and the county medical society. Since hospices include care at home, home care agencies may be listed in the yellow pages of the local telephone directory under 'nursing,' or 'home health services.' Or an individual may telephone the NHPCO help line (1-800-658-8898) or visit the website at http://www.nhpco.org.

Conclusion

To die with dignity is a phrase that many people hope will one day apply to themselves. The fact that hospice care is an ever-growing part of the health care system reinforces that hope. Hospices are hard at work helping people live their lives as fully and as completely as possible during their remaining days by emphasizing the fullness and quality of life, rather than death. Hospice care tells people that perhaps in their final days they do not have to die in the sterility of a hospital environment or in pain, shunned by friends who are reminded in their presence of their own mortality or surrounded by loved ones who, at this special time, do not know how to act around them. Through hospice care they can now have the support of many kinds of professionals, be they pharmacists, physicians, nurses, bereavement counselors or others, who can ease the transition for a person who is dying and those who survive the deceased. Only time will determine whether hospice care will succeed in changing society's attitude toward the process of dying as the treatment becomes an ever-important part of our health system. Given the increasing number of persons who are turning toward and using this special health care service, perhaps it has begun to achieve such a goal.

References

1. *The MetLife Market Survey of Nursing Home and Home Health Costs.* New York, NY: Metropolitan Life Insurance Company, 2006: 8.
2. US Department of Health and Human Services. *Health United States, 2003 with Chartbook on Trends on Health of Americans.* Hyattsville, MD: National Center for Health Statistics, 2003: 268 (Table 87).
3. Scott M, Mantz B. A guide to home healthcare. *Better Homes Gardens* 1978; September: 71, 74, 78.
4. Porter S. Home care plans cut expenses of illnesses. *Washington Star* 1978; May 17.
5. *All about Home Care: A Consumer's Guide.* New York, NY: National Homecaring Council, 1982: 9–10, 12–13.
6. *Guide to Long-Term Care.* Washington, DC: Health Insurance Association of America, 1999: 5.
7. Nursing home costs top $80,000 a year. *Silicon Valley/San Jose Bus J* 2002; March 4.
8. Home care agencies: understanding your option. *AARP Healthcare Options* 2004; October: 14.
9. Be prepared for long-term care. Cox News Service 2004; March 15.
10. *2003 GE [General Electric] Financial Nursing Home Cost of Care Survey*, conducted by Evans Research, July 31, 2003, as cited in materials sent to author from General Electric Capital Assurance Company, January 2005.
11. *Summary of 2009 Findings Table: Genworth 2009 Cost of Care Survey.* Richmond, VA: Genworth Financial, 2009.
12. *Medicare and You, 2008.* Washington, DC: Centers for Medicare and Medicaid Services, 2008: 13, 21.
13. *Medicare and Medicaid statistical supplement, 2001. Healthcare Financing Review* Washington, DC: Centers for Medicare and Medicaid Services, 2002: 217 (Table 50), 218 (Table 51).
14. Wald ML. Hospices give help for dying patients. *N Y Times* 1979; April 22.
15. *NHPCO Facts and Figures: Hospice Care in America.* Alexandria, VA: National Hospice and Palliative Care Organization, 2008: 4, 5, 8, 10.
16. Abbot JW. Hospice. *Aging* 1979; November/December: 382.
17. Connor EF Sr, Spence C, Christakis NA. Geographic variation in hospice use in the United States in 2002. *J. Pain Symptom Manage* 2007; 34: 277–285.
18. Sack K. In hospice care, longer lives means money lost. *N Y Times* 2007; November 27.
19. Ault A. For hospice, a higher authority. *Washington Post* 2008; July 1: HE01.
20. Taylor DH Jr, Ostermann J, Van Houtven CH *et al.* What length of hospice use maximizes reduction in medical expenditures near death in US Medicare program? *Soc Sci Med* 2007; 65: 1466–1478.

10

Health care planning

Introduction

The year was 1974, another period of economic crisis in the health care field. Health care spending had risen from $26.7 billion in 1960 to $41.8 billion in 1965, the year Medicare and Medicaid had been enacted into law. A year earlier Congress had enacted the Health Maintenance Act of 1973 to create a new form of health care delivery and, hopefully, reduce health care costs that in 1975 amounted to $132.9 billion, almost triple the figure of 10 years earlier.[1] In 1974 Congress was considering another law to address health care costs. This law aroused so much fear and opposition that Dr. James Sammons, then executive vice president of the American Medical Association, made the following comments: 'It is the single most dangerous piece of legislation ever enacted by a US Congress ... it will totally restructure the practice of medicine, make the HEW [Department of Health, Education, and Welfare] Secretary an absolute czar of the delivery of health care and give nonmedical people the power to decide whether a service to be rendered in a hospital is the appropriate one.'[2] With this strong denunciation, Dr. James Sammons gave his view of the National Health Planning and Resources Development Act of 1974 (PL 93-641).

Ironically, as time was to demonstrate, it was actually the Health Maintenance Law of 1973 that gave nonmedical people the power to decide whether a service to be rendered in hospital was the appropriate one. Rather than slowing down the rise in medical costs, America's national health expenditures while this health maintenance organization (HMO) law was on the books rose rapidly from $132.9 billion (8% of gross domestic product in 1975) to almost $2 trillion ($1987.7 billion) or about 16% of gross domestic product by 2005.

A decade earlier the Comprehensive Health Planning and Public Health Service Amendments of 1966 were enacted into law. At the time, Dr. William H. Stewart, then Surgeon General of the US Public Health Service, stated that 'the people shall be served and new social instruments, institutions, and patterns of operation shall be developed to serve them.'[3] That statement has proven to be quite prophetic. In the ensuing decades, as America entered the 21st century the US health care system has seen the creation of new payments systems for hospitals, nursing homes, and home care agencies called prospective payment systems; resource-based relative value scales that affect physician and other providers' payments under Medicare and HMOs; the evolvement of managed care into new organizational formats like preferred provider organizations; convenience clinics being established in retail stores; the rapid increase in ambulatory surgical centers; physician payments being based on the quality of their performance; the creation of consumer-driven health financing mechanisms like health savings accounts which make consumers more responsible than ever before for paying for their own health care services; the development of report cards on judging the quality of care provided by hospitals and nursing homes; the enactment of federal laws like the Employee Retirement Income Security Act of 1974, the Consolidated Omnibus Budget Reconciliation Act of 1986, the Health Insurance Portability and Accountability Act of 1996, as well as the creation of new pharmacy payment systems like the federal government's maximum allowable cost program; and the development of pharmacy payment intermediaries called pharmacy benefit managers.

So what is health planning? Why did and does the nation need to have such a law even today? When we hear about the costs of health care today we listen to numbers that can boggle the human mind. We hear about billions of dollars spent for this social service each year and health professionals who themselves number in the millions. We hear about scientific advances in health fields whose technology and subject matter have become so complex that consumers have little everyday understanding of their nature. Under these circumstances, basic questions arise. How can ordinary consumer-patients have any influence over such a complex health system which keeps absorbing more and more of their personal income? How can consumers exert any control over the prices they must pay for their health care services? How can they make any input which ensures that they will receive quality health care at reasonable costs and not inferior care at expensive prices? After all, it is their out-of-pocket expenses, their personal income taxes, and their insurance premiums which are supporting the health care system. How can they be assured that the decisions which the health professional is making are for their best interest as a patient rather than for health professionals' personal self-interest? Where is the entrance into the health care system that everyone keeps talking about? How can consumer voices be heard and their rights and interests, as consumers and patients, be protected and respected? These are some of the legitimate questions which consumers have begun to ask as they realize that it is becoming terribly expensive to become sick in America today.

From a practical point of view, a single consumer cannot affect the billions of dollars which are being spent on health care nationally. Nor can the single consumer specifically affect the national costs of pharmaceutical care, hospital care, or physician services, nor the costs of the other health services and problems which are discussed or heard about on a daily basis. But a single consumer can have a significant influence on the costs and quality of health care where the consumer lives. This was the original intent of the health planning law in 1974. Wherever a consumer lived – in urban or rural areas, north or south, east or west – at that time from the mid-1970s through the mid-1980s there existed across the country an organization called a health systems agency (HSA) which represented their health care interests and geographic area. This agency, along with others at higher levels of government, was established in accordance with requirements of the Health Planning Act of 1974. In the ensuing years health planning agencies encountered severe funding problems as the 1974 health planning law under which they were created was repealed by the Reagan administration in 1986 so that by 2009 only 14 HSAs on the local level were still operating in the country. There were five in Virginia, two in New York, and seven in Florida. At least in these local agencies a consumer can still sit on the agency's governing board as part of majority representation while the providers of health care services, such as physicians or pharmacists, constitute the minority representation. Consumers can have their voices heard as they consider how health care services ought to be delivered in their local community. By participating in the processes of this agency consumers can create a dialogue with the members of their community upon whom their health care depends – their doctor, their pharmacist, their hospital administrator, or health insurer, to name but a few. They can now decide whether their hospital should build a new wing or purchase various kinds of expensive equipment. It is not only their judgment which is involved but also their money. Their decision will be reflected in their hospital's daily charges, their physician's fees, and their health insurer's premiums.

But health planning not only involves consideration of costs, but also the quality of care which consumers receive from those who provide the services. There were many who negatively viewed the role which HSAs assumed in the health care system, although today their role on the local community level has been severely diminished numerically from their original conception in the 1970s. These opponents consider HSAs to be a potential evil rather than a positive good. These detractors have many reasons for their beliefs. In view of this dichotomy of opinions, let us examine the issue of health care planning: what it is, how it has evolved, the conflicts it has created within the health care field, and what it has meant thus far and for the future.

Definition of health planning

Health planning is part of an evolving process called creative federalism – a term used to describe a pluralistic approach to solving problems of urban society. Creative federalism encompasses an environment which Nelson Rockefeller, former governor of New York State and Vice President under

President Gerald Ford, described as 'the free play of individual initiative, private enterprise, social institutions, political organizations, and voluntary association.'[4]

As a concept, there are various forms of planning. But they have the common basis, that planning is the opposite of improvisation. Planning is a process of developing alternative courses of action and predicting foreseeable results. Planning is not just a decision-making process. It is also a process of projecting and documenting choices of action. The selections are made through the political and social decision-making system of society. Dr. William H. Stewart, former Surgeon General of the US Public Health Service, gave a good explanation of the planning process when he stated:

> there are at least two kinds of planning, interrelated but distinct from each other, that need to go on simultaneously if we are to fulfill the expectations of the society we serve. One type is largely operational – it is directed toward day-to-day and year-to-year decisions on specific activity directed toward a specific objective. It is the kind of planning done by a program manager to carry out his program mission. The other type of planning is truly comprehensive. It is less concerned with targets and more concerned with directions. Ultimately, it must be tuned to values – the changing aspirations of society that require translation into changing goals for health and changing patterns of relationship among target-oriented activities.[5]

In a further refinement of this working planning concept, certain questions may be asked when attempting to accomplish the objective of comprehensive health planning. They include:

- What is the problem for which the plan is being developed?
- What information is required for developing a comprehensive plan?
- Who has the information, including the experience and judgment, required as an input into the development of the plan?
- What groups and agencies are expected to act on the plan?[5]

In seeking the answers to these questions, planning embraces essentially four basic steps: the survey, its analysis, the plan, and its implementation. In more specific terms:

- The survey: the problems are defined, resources located, and the facts obtained.
- The analysis: this includes the forecasting of anticipated conditions and the relation of the central issue to those either influencing or influenced by it.
- The plan: directed toward goals, based on the needs and standards, and elaborated with cost estimates and time schedules for implementation.

- The implementation, which most planners are not inclined to ignore. They approach it by stimulating community participation in the planning process.

These steps are the basis upon which the principles of health planning are carried out. Although these principles seem quite simple and direct in their approach, the process of health care planning has slowly evolved and has been characterized as much by failure as it has by success.

The historical development of planning

The evolution of health planning in the USA has several phases, the first of which evolved during the early 1920s. During this period the public became cognizant of the planning effort. In 1921, the New York Academy of Medicine issued a report which found that there was one hospital bed for every 200 persons in New York and concluded this ratio was sufficient. At the time, under the prevailing standard of the US Public Health Service, it was estimated that about 2% of the population would be sufficiently sick at any given moment to require hospital care. However, during the ensuing decade, the realization developed that the method for determining a community's need for hospital beds had to be refined. Separate criteria had to be established for hospital beds in a general hospital, beds for contagious diseases, maternity beds, and beds for mental and tubercular patients. By the 1930s, local socio-economic conditions were the primary criteria for making these hospital bed determinations. These criteria included the economic status of the community, the character of housing and industry, education, morbidity levels, and caliber of the local profession.[6] In addition to the US Public Health Service, other estimates of ideal bed size were made at this time. In the late 1920s, both the Duke Endowment and American Hospital Association's Committee on County Hospitals agreed upon a ratio of five general hospitals beds per 1000 population. In addition, the Duke Endowment established bed ratio standards for contagious, children's, and tubercular disease.[7] In 1945, the US Public Health Service sanctioned a ratio of 4.5 beds per 1000 population which, with slight refinement, became the national standard for the Hill–Burton law of 1946.

As the number of planning agencies increased during the 1930s, there was a general belief that the quality of health services would be greatly improved if hospitals began to work more closely with each other. Thus, planning agencies became interested not only in hospital beds, but also in the organization of health facilities. However, by the 1940s a general shortage of hospital beds, their uneven distribution throughout the nation, and a lack of coordinating operations among hospitals were observed. Rural areas especially faced a crisis not only in terms of a supply of hospital beds but also in regard to the availability of medical personnel. These situations led to the second period of health planning which began when the US Congress passed the Hospital Survey and Construction Act of 1946 (PL 79-725, also known as Hill–Burton). This law offered federal funds to states for the construction of hospitals and related facilities, pending a survey by each state of its existing institutions and submission of a state plan to meet its needs.

Although the Hill–Burton Act did not contain any reference to the coordination of facilities on a regional basis, the Act did provide limited acknowledgment to planning and regionalization by means of area-wide planning councils.[7] As a result of Hill–Burton, all states between 1946 and 1961 developed plans and established priorities. A total of $1.6 billion in federal monies and $3.4 billion in state funds was spent on the construction of 239 000 general hospital beds. One-third of these beds were in communities of less than 50 000 population. Although hospital design and construction were improved during this period of time, no real progress was achieved in terms of the coordination or integration of facilities on either a regional or local level.[6]

However, interest in the subject did not disappear. It was rekindled by a series of meetings which were held in 1958, under the co-sponsorship of the American Hospital Association and the US Public Health Service. These meetings developed a joint report which assisted in the organization and operation of planning agencies. In 1961 the planning process received a further boost by the passage of the Community Health Service and Facilities Act which authorized grants for area-wide planning and the development of hospitals and related facilities. This Act became part of the Hill–Burton program and, together with the 1964 amendments to the Hill–Burton Act, provided financial impetus for health planning agencies. With these changes came a resurgence of interest in planning for other health services as well. For example, the enactment of the Community Mental Health Center Act (PL 88-164) in 1963 encouraged the planning of mental health services.

By 1966, there were about 60 voluntary health planning agencies operating in the country. These agencies focused on the supply and geographic distribution of hospital beds; on controlling the duplication of services and facilities; and on encouraging activities and programs of coordination between institutions. Thus, the agencies were involved with institutional planning such as that related to hospitals. Physicians were not the subject of the planning process at this time. Consequently, they were not directly affected by the decision of the agencies. Agency planning was more technologically oriented than systems-oriented.[8]

As the concept of health planning evolved during this period together with the establishment of planning agencies and the federal funding of such programs, Congress became increasingly aware that the changing character of American health care demanded new government initiatives. These included comprehensive health planning for health services, health manpower, and health facilities at every level of government; revitalized administration of health agencies at the state level; and broader and more flexible support of health services at the community level as well. This perception led, in part, to the enactment of the Regional Medical Program (RMP) in 1965 (PL 89-239). The original purpose of this program was to encourage regional planning and the transfer of medical technology for the categorical illnesses of heart disease, cancer, and stroke from university medical centers to the community providers of health services. Over the years the program shifted its focus toward regionalizing health care delivery, facilitating cooperative action among health care providers, and designing as well as testing innovative ways to improve health care services.

Despite the passage of the Regional Medical Program in 1965, health planning activities were still not considered broad enough nor sufficiently oriented toward the problems of upgrading the health status of the public, improving the environment, and raising the quality of life of the American people. Therefore, Congress enacted the Partnership for Health Act (PL 89-749) in November 1966 and then amended the law in 1967. It was passed to correct the earlier flaws of health planning and to undertake once again the rationalization of our health care delivery system. The Comprehensive Health Planning (CHP) program established gradations of agencies within state and local government, including the 314(b) agencies which were named after the authorizing section of the Act. The CHP(b) agencies were charged with the responsibility of planning the total needs of their region. They were expected to build on the activities of the area-wide Hill–Burton agencies, whose federal support was phased out with the passage of Partnership for Health Act in 1966. However, in some states, Hill–Burton continued to exist with local funding.

The legislative purpose of the Regional Medical and the CHP programs was to improve the health care system without interfering with existing patterns of medical practice.[9] However, the concerns and focus of the new agencies were at times so broad that the planners went from problem to problem, never quite solving one before another became of immediate concern. Too often they spent more time debating what should be done rather than doing anything. But by the late 1960s, despite these problems, CHP agencies received some powers to influence health activities through their role of reviewing and commenting on statewide certificate-of-need (CON) programs, where they existed, and through their participation in the award process of federal grants for some Public Health Service programs. One of the important ways in which CHP influenced the health system was by participating in Section 1122 of the Social Security Amendments of 1972 (PL 92-603).[9] Under Section 1122, a hospital or other health care institution cannot recoup any major financial capital investment by adding charges to the bills of Medicare or Medicaid patients unless an authorized state authority permitted the improvements first. However, despite having the authority to make these reviews, both the Regional Medical and CHP programs still remained dependent upon whatever persuasive powers they could muster to encourage the development of health resources among their regional constituencies.

Also, by the late 1960s, the emphasis on delivering health services began to shift toward other nonhospital organizations such as neighborhood health centers, community mental health centers, and HMOs. By the early 1970s, the rise in the cost of medical care, growing concern about the quality of care which was being delivered, and the re-emergence of national health insurance as a major policy issue gave further impetus for designing a more effective health planning system. By about 1972, there was general agreement that comprehensive health planning had been a failure. After a brief flirtation with substitute experimental health delivery systems, the US HEW (since renamed the US Department of Health and Human Services) began to look for a wholly new approach to health planning. This search ultimately led to the passage of the National Health Planning and Resource Development Act of 1974 (PL 93-641). The act was signed into law on January 4, 1975.

The 1974 legislation combined aspects of the Hill–Burton, Regional Medical, and CHP programs into a new generation of agencies. These organizations took over the health planning and resource development functions previously performed by the CHP and Regional Medical programs which were phased out under the 1974 health planning law. Also, the experimental health service delivery systems, which HEW was testing for the purpose of public demonstration, were terminated upon the enactment of the 1974 legislation.

Health Planning Act of 1974

The National Health Planning Act of 1974 (PL 93-641) not only established a new program of comprehensive health planning but also empowered a system of local planning agencies to oversee the use of some federal funds, including funds for new hospital construction. The goals and purposes of the law were increased accessibility, acceptability, continuity, and quality of health services; restraint of the rising costs of health services; and the prevention of unnecessary duplication of services. The law thus created a prospective national framework for reviewing the funds which would be spent under any future national health insurance plan.

A network of local health planning agencies called HSA was at the core of the new program. A total of 205 geographic areas throughout the country had been designated for such agencies. To the maximum extent possible their boundaries were approximately coordinated with professional standard review organizations (PSROs), which evolved into the peer review organizations of the 1980s, which, in turn, became the quality improvement organizations as the 21st century began as well as existing regional planning areas and state planning administrative areas. Each of these agencies was to serve, except in special cases, a specific population of between 500 000 and 1 000 000 people. These local agencies could be either a nonprofit private corporation or public agency operating under the auspices of a unit of general-purpose local government or public regional planning body. The Secretary of HEW (now the US Department of Health and Human Services) had to certify these agencies according to criteria laid out in the law. In addition to the HSA, there were planning bodies at the state level and the national level which formed policy and supervised the work of these local agencies. These included the National Council on Health Planning and Development, which assisted the Secretary of HEW in developing national health planning guidelines; the Statewide Coordinating Council, which developed the state health plan, which, in turn, could supersede the plan developed at the local HSA, and monitored the activities of HSAs, reporting to Washington on its importance; and the State Health Planning and Development Agency, which could enforce the HSA's decisions on major equipment purposes and new construction since the state agency administers the state's CON laws. The State Health Planning and Development Agency (often called the 'state agency'), for example, provided the enforcement for carrying out the HSA's decisions on major equipment purchases and new construction. They administered the CON laws (that all states had to enact under the penalty of losing federal funds). State agencies were designated by the governor from one of the existing agencies, such as state health department, which had previously operated the CON program.[2]

On the local level, the HSA is required to:

- gather and analyze data
- establish area-wide long-range health system plans and an annual implementation plan
- provide planning assistance to organizations seeking to develop plans
- review and approve or disapprove applications for federal grant funds for health programs in the health service area
- assist states in reviewing capital expenditures under Section 1122 of the Medicare Act
- assist states in their mandated CON programs
- recommend to states projects for modernizing, constructing, and converting medical facilities.[10]

The HSA develops a health systems plan for its geographic service area. This plan, in turn, is approved at the state level. When established, the HSA directly controlled the federal grant monies which were spent for health projects in their areas under the Public Health Service Act, the Community Mental

Health Centers Act, and the Comprehensive Alcohol Abuse and Alcoholism Prevention, Treatment and Rehabilitation Act of 1970. Even though federal regulations guided the HSAs, the organizations are very important to organized medicine and the rest of the health care field. Their plans and recommendations may determine which new hospital, nursing home, or even physician's office, receives the all-important building permit – the CON from the state agency.[2]

Before the passage of the 1974 planning law, there were very few constraints to control the costs of health care. Until this law mandated that all states enact CON laws, only slightly more than one-half had done so on their own volition. Also, only a small number of states have attempted to regulate costs through the establishment of state rate-setting commissions such as Maryland and the law provided monies for up to six states that had wished to do so in the future. Before this new law, if a group of doctors in a hospital wished to add a service or increase their rates, they only needed the approval of the hospital board of directors – bodies which are not known for contradicting the wishes of their physician staff. But under the 1974 law, both the local HSA and the state planning agency were to conduct at least every 5 years elaborate reviews of existing facilities, services, and of any proposed construction to determine the need or lack of need for these additions. There were no sanctions in regard to an HSA's findings. Even the Hill–Burton hospital construction program was affected by the 1974 law. Rather than concentrating on the building of new facilities, as in years past, the 1974 planning law gave the Hill–Burton program new directives. These include concentrating on the construction of ambulatory care centers and improving and converting existing facilities, but only in areas of rapid population growth.

A final example of the new planning law's orientation is its emphasis on the consumer movement within the health field as well as the greater voice it gives to planning professionals in directing the course of health delivery. At the state and local levels, governing boards oversaw health planning activities. These boards were carefully constituted so that a majority of their members would be consumers, professionals, and government officials. The providers of health care – the doctors, hospital administrators, and others who have a vested interest at stake – were legislated to form a minority on these boards.[11]

Aftermath of the 1974 Planning Law Certificate of Need laws

Health planning is not the only method that has been tried to control health care costs in the USA. There has also been government and industry regulation, provider incentives, 'free market' incentives, and educational efforts. Some of these include:

- limitations on physician referrals to facilities in which they or a family member have a financial interest
- supervision by insurers to make sure a treatment is necessary (precertification, concurrent, or retrospective medical necessary review)
- prepayment for insured or covered services
- fixed payment for defined services such as diagnostic-related groups in hospital care
- providing information to patients about the costs and necessity of certain tests and treatments (including transparency and disclosure program)
- providing information to patients about the quality of outcomes at certain facilities.[12]

Aside from these methodologies to control health care costs, states have used another way to restrain the rising cost of medical care. This tool is called CON programs. As already noted, these programs, authorized by law, are aimed at holding down health care facility costs and to permit the coordinated planning of new services and construction. Many CON laws were established across the country as part of the National Health Planning and Resources Development Act of 1974. These laws were supposed to help the country achieve several health care goals. These included keeping down skyrocketing health care costs, preventing the unnecessary duplication of services, and achieving equal access to quality health care at reasonable cost. When Congress required CON laws, it sought to reduce the total cost of health care in the USA. Despite numerous changes in ensuing decades, as of 2009 about 36 states and the District of Columbia still retained some kind of planning law. Health planning agencies in states without CON programs include Arizona, California, Colorado, Idaho, Indiana, Kansas, Minnesota, New Mexico, North Dakota, Pennsylvania, South Dakota, Texas, Utah, and Wyoming. In contrast, from 1945 to the mid-1980s, virtually all states had significant health service planning operations. As of 2009, as already noted, only 14 HSAs at the local level in the USA remained in operation – five in Virginia, two in New York State, and seven in Florida. In a 19-state survey, at least 10 states have sustained a health services planning operation at the state level. These states appear to be concentrating on traditional health care facilities and equipment issues directly related to the CON process.

In 1964, New York became the first state to pass a statute giving the state government the power to make sure whether there was a need for any new hospital or nursing home before it was approved for construction. Four years later the American Hospital Association expressed an interest in CON laws, and began a national campaign for states to initiate their own CON laws. The 1974 federal Act required that all 50 states have a mechanism that, before any major capital projects could begin, such as building expansions or ordering high-tech devices, proposals had to be submitted and approved by the state planning agency. Many states established CON programs, in part because they had the incentive of receiving CON federal funds.

In 1986, as already noted, the federal CON mandate was repealed, along with its federal funding, as the Reagan administration wanted to cut federal spending and regulation. After repealing the 1974 Health Planning Act and its CON requirements, Congress did not abolish CON throughout the nation. Congress only repealed the legislation mandating CON laws. States were still free to continue regulating health care facilities with CON even after Congress repealed the mandate itself. In the decade that followed 14 states discontinued their CON programs. However, 36 states maintain some form of CON programs, as already noted, and even the 14 that repealed their state CON laws still retain some mechanisms whose purpose is to regulate costs and duplication of services. Puerto Rico and District of Columbia also have CON programs.

States that have kept CON programs currently tend to concentrate their activities on outpatient facilities and long-term care. This is largely due to the trend toward free-standing, physician-owned facilities that constitute an increasing segment of the health care market. The basic assumption underlying CON regulations is that extra capacity (in the form of facility overbuilding) directly brings about health care inflation. When a hospital cannot fill its beds, fixed costs must be met through higher charges for the beds that are used. Larger institutions have higher costs, so the CON supporters state that it makes sense to limit facilities to building only enough capacity to meet actual needs.

Statistics, called the 'Roemer effect' after the person who developed the theory, have shown that when there are more beds open in a hospital, more beds will be filled. Thus, if a hospital has excess beds due to unnecessary construction and additions, the hospital will begin to manufacture demand to fill all the beds because it is widely accepted by hospitals that an empty bed costs the hospital about two-thirds as much as an occupied one. The original purpose of the CON programs was to regulate the number of beds in hospitals and nursing homes, and to prevent the purchase of more expensive equipment than was necessary. This was based on the belief of health care consumers, providers, and hospitals that the quality of a facility can be directly related to the institution having the biggest, most elaborate, most modern facilities and equipment. Again, it was the belief that if these hospitals had all of this space and new equipment, the hospital would want to put it to use in order to begin paying it off. Doctors would want to practice in hospitals with the newest technologies, with the ensuing hospital revenues, while a hospital without the same equipment might lose revenues if the doctor decides for the benefit of his/her practice that the institution's equipment is not as up to date as the competing hospital which has it. A doctor could prescribe procedures which a patient did not require and use the equipment in order to generate income because the doctor knows the insurance company will pay the bill no matter its amount. In addition, hospitals would be able to fund these unneeded new pieces of equipment and unnecessary construction projects by passing on the cost of the construction projects to consumers in the form of higher costs for their services, which would be paid by third-party insurance companies. This would permit health care facilities to spend freely on new construction and equipment without giving any thought to the public's requirements for such expenditures or the efficiency of the system. These activities would again transfer the actual costs of such needless construction and spending on to consumers indirectly in the form of higher premiums to be paid to their insurance companies and which the insurers would charge to recoup their own costs.

The previous scenarios were the economic conditions that existed when Congress passed the 1974 Health Planning Act and its CON requirements. Mandatory regulation through health planning agencies determined the most urgent health care priorities that required resolution and attempted to manage the fluctuations in prices often caused by a competitive market. The concept was that new or improved facilities or equipment would receive approval based only on a genuine need in a community. Statutory criteria were often created to help planning agencies decide what was necessary for a given location. By reviewing the activities and resources of hospitals, the agencies judged what was required to be improved. Once need was established, the applicant organization (corporation, not-for-profit, partnership, or public entity) was granted permission to begin the project. As already noted, these approvals are generally known as CON.[12]

Proponents of CON programs

Proponents of CON programs argue that health care cannot be viewed as a 'typical' economic product. They state that many market forces do not obey the same rules for health care services as are applicable to other products. In support of this argument, CON advocates point out that, since most health services (like a blood test) are ordered for patients by physicians, patients do not shop for these services the way they do for other goods and services. If individuals require transportation and find that gasoline is too expensive to drive their automobile, they can find substitutes like subway trains, buses, taxis, bicycles, walking, or other means of cheaper transportation. But what less expensive substitute is there for a needed blood test? This makes the hospital, the laboratory, and other services insensitive to market effects on price, and suggests a regulatory approach based on public interest.

The American Health Planning Association (AHPA) is the professional organization of state agencies responsible for regulation and planning. The AHPA points out three factors that suggest the necessity for CON programs.

The principal argument is that CON programs place limits on health care spending. CONs can promote appropriate competition while maintaining lower costs for treatment services. The AHPA argues that, when construction and purchasing are controlled, state governments are able to oversee what expenditures are needed and where monies will be used most effectively. This situation helps to get rid of projects that take away attention from more urgent and useful investments and lessens excessive costs. AHPA also states that CONs have a valuable impact on the quality of health care. When facilities and equipment are under scrutiny, hospitals and other treatment centers can acknowledge what kind of services are in demand and how effectively patients are being taken care of. In addition, CON proponents state that the programs can distribute care to areas that new medical centers might ignore. Policymakers can also use CON programs as a resource. CON regulations are described as a reliable manner to put into effect basic planning policies and practices, and help in distributing health care to all demographic areas. The CON process can highlight areas that are in need because planners can follow up and evaluate the requests of hospitals, doctors, and citizens and determine which areas are underserved or need to be improved and developed.[12]

A good example of a new and expensive technology that could easily proliferate throughout the USA in the future, whether a community needed it or not, is the rush by medical centers to turn nuclear particle accelerators, formerly used only for exotic physic research, into the latest weapons against cancer. Some experts state that this rush reflects the best and worst of the nation's market-based health care system, which tends to pursue the latest, most expensive treatments – without much evidence of improved health – even as rapidly rising costs add to the nation's economic burden. The machines accelerate protons to nearly the speed of light and shoot them into tumors. Scientists say proton beams are more accurate than the X-rays generally used for radiation therapy, meaning fewer side-effects from stray radiation and, possibly, a higher cure rate. But a 222-ton accelerator – and a building the size of a football field with walls up to 18 feet thick in which to hold it – can cost more than $100 million. That makes a proton center, in the words of one equipment vendor, the world's most expensive and complex medical device. Until 2000, the USA had only one hospital-based proton therapy center. By 2009 there were five, with more than a dozen others announced. Still more are being considered. While some experts say such proton centers are needed, others argue that an arms race state of mind has taken hold as medical centers seek to be the first to take advantage of the prestige and profits a proton site can bring.[13] 'I'm fascinated and horrified by the way it's developing,' said Dr. Anthony L. Zietman, a radiation oncologist at Harvard and the Massachusetts General Hospital, which operates a proton center. 'This is the dark side of medicine.'[13] Once hospitals have made such a huge investment, experts like Dr. Zietman say, doctors will be under pressure to guide patients toward proton therapy when a less costly alternative might exist. And, of course, the question arises: would there be a possible proliferation of proton centers throughout the USA if HSAs were still in operation in the other 47 states and CON laws were still in force in all 50 states rather than just 36? As examples of the latter concerns, some of the planned proton therapy centers will be very near each other, raising the odds of overcapacity. Two proton centers are planned for Oklahoma City and two more in the western suburbs of Chicago. Dr. Zietman stated that, while protons were vital in treating certain rare tumors, they were little better than the latest X-ray technology in dealing with prostate cancer, the common disease that many proton centers are counting on for business. Dr. Zietman noted that you could hardly tell the difference between them except in price. Medicare pays about $50 000 to treat prostate cancer with protons, almost twice as much as X-rays.[13] Proponents insist, however, that proton centers provide better treatment. Companies have been established to help finance, build, and operate the proton centers. In some cases, local and state governments, seeking to attract medical tourists, have contributed to their costs. Such financing is permitting proton centers to be built even by community hospitals and groups of physicians. In the past, the issue of the development of these proton centers might have been decided by the deliberations of the local HSA. But, as already noted, for the most part these agencies are now part of past health care history in the 47 states in the country where, as of 2009, they no longer operated.

Critics of CON programs

In addition to their advocates, CON programs have had their share of critics, even when they were initially established in the 1970s. Their critics state that it is not so obvious that these state-sponsored programs have actually controlled health costs. For example, they note that by limiting new construction, CON programs may lessen price competition between facilities and may actually keep prices high. Impediments to new building were seen as unfair restrictions, sometimes by both existing facilities and their potential new competitors. A Federal Trade Commission and Department Justice report noted that CON programs contribute to rising prices because they inhibit competitive markets that should be able to control the cost of health care and guarantee quality and access to treatment and services.[14] Some critics believed that changes in the Medicare payment system (such as paying hospitals according to diagnostic-related groups) would render external regulatory control unnecessary because health care organizations would be more subject to market pressures. Some noted that CON programs are consistently administered. A flexible program could permit development, to the dismay of competitors. A restrictive program could limit competition, with the same impact.

Many argued that health facility development should be left to the economics of each institution, in view of its market analysis, rather than being subject to political influence. Some evidence suggests that absence of competition paradoxically encourages construction and additional spending. Some opponents of CON programs believe that an open health care market, based on quality, rather than price, might be the best principle for containing rising costs. Advocates of CON programs do not agree. Theoretically, CONs are issued based on objective analyses of community need, rather than economic self-interest of a single facility. However, critics of the CON program claim that the programs have not worked in this manner. They note examples in which CONs were apparently granted on the basis of political influence, institutional prestige, or other factors apart from the interests of the community. In addition, it is sometimes a matter of debate what kind of development is in the community's interest, with people having the best of intentions sharply divided on how to determine this objective.[12] As already noted, between 1960 and 1975, national health care spending increased fivefold from $26.7 billion to $132.9 billion. Between the period of 1975 and 1985, after the enactment of the health planning law in 1974, national health expenditures rose from $132.9 billion to $428.2 billion, or slightly more than three times as much.[1] But then, as already mentioned, in 1986 the Reagan administration, in cutting budget costs, basically ceased funding state health planning and repealed the CON mandate for the states. So it would appear that most states have not sustained health services planning on the local level in the absence of federal financial support. In contrast, from 1945 to the mid-1980s, virtually all states had significant health service planning operations. By 2005, as already noted, national health expenditures had ballooned from $428.2 billion in 1975 to slightly more than $1.9 trillion. While this almost fivefold increase in health care expenditures cannot solely be attributed to the absence of HSAs on the local level or the repeal of the CON mandate on the state level, certainly some portion of it, however small, may be attributed to the absence of health planning.

The future

When the Reagan administration repealed the 1974 health planning law in 1986, health care expenditures represented only 10% of gross domestic product. By 2015 national health expenditures are expected to reach almost $4 trillion or 20% of national health expenditure, twice the percentage recorded when President Reagan had the 1974 health planning law repealed in 1986. Also, in 2008 there was a great deal of discussion in the presidential election about establishing a national health insurance program in the USA. Will health planning be revived and return nationally as part of such a national health insurance plan in the form of HSAs or something akin to those organizations on the local level or will CONs be mandated at the state levels for all jurisdictions since 36 states still retain such programs? After all, on the local community level some HSAs continue to operate in several states. US Congress was considering a national health insurance plan in the summer of 2009. As of August 2009, no one knew for certainty what the details would contain.

The following national set of health care initiatives were outlined as part of the 1974 Health Planning Act which local communities, through the activities of HSAs, were to try to incorporate into their health systems. They are still as relevant today when reform of the US health care system is being discussed:

- Provide primary care for medically underserved population.
- Develop 'multi-institutional systems' to coordinate obstetrics, pediatrics, emergency medicine, intensive and coronary care, radiation therapy, and other services.
- Develop group practice, especially those linked to institutional health services, as well as HMOs and other organized systems for the provision of health care.
- Train and use more physician's assistants, especially more nurse clinicians.
- Develop multi-institutional sharing of support services; promote improvements in the quality of health services, including those identified by PSROs that, as already noted, evolved by the 21st century into quality improvement organizations.
- Provide various levels of institutional care on a geographically integrated basis, including intensive acute general and extended care.
- Promote prevention of disease, including studies of nutritional and environmental factors.
- Get health services institutions to adopt a more uniform and simplified form of cost accounting, better management procedures, reimbursement arrangements, and utilization reporting in order to improve the management of health care programs.
- Develop effective methods of personal health education for the general public.[2]

Whatever the future may hold for health care planning in the USA, given the fact that health care costs are becoming an increasing segment of the gross domestic product, the more the USA spends on health care the less money that is available to meet the nation's other domestic and foreign policy goals, be it education, transportation, defense, or other matters. But at least one point is certain. It was once a national tool for helping to control health care costs no matter how controversial it was at the time of its enactment and enforcement in seeking to achieve the objectives for which it was created.

Whether health planning has had a positive impact on health care costs or not in the past, some facts cannot be denied: America's population is growing, its population is living longer and succumbing to more diseases which were not as prevalent in prior generations whose life spans were shorter; also treatment costs like those for Alzheimer's are very expensive. The postwar baby boomers will soon be joining the Medicare program, swelling the number of Americans aged 65 years or older to about 70 million in the next several decades. New hospitals, nursing homes, home care programs, assisted living facilities and other institutional arrangements as well as additional professional manpower like geriatricians will be needed in ever greater numbers to accommodate America's growing health care needs. Health manpower is not evenly distributed throughout the USA, and the development of new medical technologies is a continuous and ever-present fact. All of these factors will require some kind of health planning, whether it be under governmental jurisdiction or not. There is an old saying, 'If you are not part of the solution, you are part of the problem.' HSAs at the local level gave the consumer of health services on its board of directors an opportunity to be in direct dialogue with health professionals as part of the solution. Only time will tell whether another mechanism will arise to afford consumers the same opportunity to determine how health care services in their local community are to be provided at costs which are reasonable for them to afford. But the socioeconomic trends in regard to evolvement of American society are already in motion, and that is one certainty those both within and outside the health care field cannot deny. Someone, whether it be on local, state, or federal levels, will have to deal with these issues in such a way that they are part of the solution and not part of the problem. Only the future will determine whether health care planning will be one of the tools America turns to again to resolve the many issues that lie ahead, as the concept had attempted to do when it was enacted into law in 1974.

References

1. *Source Book of Health Insurance Data, 2002.* Washington, DC: Health Insurance Association of America, 2002: 100 (Table 5-3).
2. That blockbusting health planning act: how will doctors fix it? *Med World News* 1976; April 5: 54–55.
3. South Carolina State Board of Health. Community health planning. *J South Carolina Pharm Assoc* 1969; September: 16.
4. Kane D A. Comprehensive health planning: an organizational means in creative federalism. *Am J Publ Health* 1969; September: 16.
5. Williams J D. Comprehensive health planning: an organizational means for transition. *Am J Publ Health* 1969; January: 50.
6. Health Insurance Council. *Community Health Action-Planning, Problems and Potentials.* New York, NY, Health Insurance Council, 1969: 2.
7. Froh R B. The evolution of community health planning. *J Am Pharm Assoc* 1969; June: 255.

8. May J J. Will third generation planning succeed? *Hosp Progr* 1976; March: 60.
9. Werlin S A, Walcott A, Joroff M. Implementing formative health planning under P.L. 93-641. *N Engl J Med* 1976; September 23: 699.
10. Phillips D F. Health planning: new hope for a fresh start. *Hospitals* 1976; April 5: 54.
11. Health planning: new program gives consumers, Uncle Sam a voice. *Science* 1975; January 17: 152–153.
12. *Certificate of Need: State Health Laws and Programs.* Washington, DC: National Conference of State Legislatures, 2008: 2–3.
13. Pollack A. Cancer fight goes nuclear, with heavy price tag. *N Y Times* 2007; December 26 (Health Section).
14. The Federal Trade Commission and the Department of Justice. *Improving Health Care: A Dose of Competition.* Washington, DC: Federal Trade Commission and Department of Justice, 2004.

11

Private health insurance

Introduction

The health insurance industry has arrived at its moment of truth! The higher costs of health care services for the American consumer have resulted in a demand for relief. Americans want the protection that the word insurance implies. But, they find, the more they spend, the less protection they receive!

> I doubt that health insurance as we know it and as you design it and sell it will survive the changes that government and consumers are going to bring about. For the past 20 years, the insurance industry and the 'Blues' have watched a bad situation get worse and have not developed the machinery to cope with the problems. The health insurance industry has not earned the confidence of working man. You have a big task ahead of you, which is to demonstrate that in a rapidly changing industry you are socially responsible and economically relevant. I believe you must either find new products and shape them for better informed, more critical consumer markets or face obsolescence as an economic institution.[1]

Almost four decades after these words were spoken to the commercial insurance industry by a vice president of the International Brotherhood of Teamsters in 1970, the situation for those purchasing private health insurance has not improved in the products they are buying. Even though in 2006 employers provided health benefits to more than 160 million working Americans and their families,[2] by 2008, according to the Bureau of the Census, more than 47 million nonelderly Americans (16% of the population) could not afford health insurance. About 37% of the uninsured live in households with an income over $50 000 a year. Researchers at George Mason University in Virginia and the Urban Institute, Washington, DC, reported that Americans who did not have health insurance coverage for any part of 2008 (about 28 million went without coverage for some part of the year, compared to the 47 million Americans who lack health insurance coverage whatsoever) spent about $30 billion out of their own pocket for health care services and received $56 billion worth of free care. Government programs paid about three-fourths or about $48 billion of these bills for these uninsured persons. In addition, on average, uninsured Americans paid $583 out of their own pocket toward average annual medical expenses of $1686 per person (35%) while the annual medical costs of Americans with private insurance averaged far greater, $3915 with $681 or a smaller percentage of 17% out of their own pocket. Thus, not only are the uninsured receiving less care than those who have insurance coverage but they are spending a greater percentage of monies out of their pocket to pay for it.

In addition, the Commonwealth Fund, a New York City health research organization, published a paper in August 2008 that noted that the share of US adults who reported that the costs of health care prevented them from obtaining needed care increased from 29% in 2001 to 45% in 2007. Reports of cost-related access problems increased among all income groups and among insured and uninsured adults alike. One of the leading causes of personal bankruptcy filings in the USA is the inability to pay medical bills. The Commonwealth Fund stated in the same issue paper that in 2007 more adults were struggling to pay their medical bills and were accumulating medical debt over time. Forty-one percent of working-age adults, or 72 million people, reported a problem paying their medical bills or had accrued medical debt, up from 34%, or 58 million, in 2005 (Figure 11.1).

An additional 7 million adults aged 65 and older also reported bill or debt problems. This increase took place across all income groups but families with low and moderate incomes were particularly hard hit: more than one-half of adults with incomes under $40 000 reported problems with their medical bills in 2007. Underinsured adults or those with gaps in their health insurance reported the highest rates.[3–5]

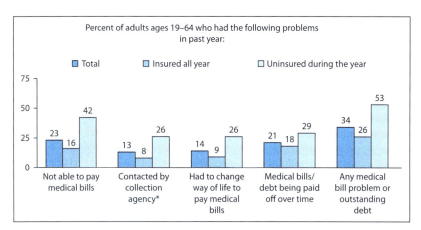

Figure 11.1   Many Americans have problems paying medical bills or are paying off medical debt. *Includes only those individuals who had a bill sent to a collection agency when they were unable to pay it. Source: The Commonwealth Fund Biennial Health Insurance Survey (2005). Reprinted with permission of The Commonwealth Fund, New York, NY and as cited at: http://www.commonwealthfund.org/chartcartcharts/chartcartcharts_show.htm?doc_id=405.

Again, remember that the words of the union official quoted above were spoken in 1970, when the country's national health expenditures were $69.2 billion or 7.2% of the gross domestic product and by 2008 America's national health expenditures exceeded $2 trillion or double the gross domestic product in 1970. National health insurance as a panacea for our nation's health cost crisis was one of the main issues being debated during the presidential elections of 2008, as it was in the 1970s as well. Since the previous words were spoken, as examples, the health insurance industry has introduced health maintenance organizations (HMOs), preferred provider organizations (PPOs), point-of-service plans, pay-for-performance reimbursements, and other programs to stem the tide of rapidly increasing health care costs, thus far all to no avail. In 2007, the following words were heard:

> It's an outrage that any American's life expectancy should be shortened simply because the company they worked for went bankrupt and abrogated health care coverage and now we have a company like Ford [Motor Company] virtually being bankrupted by the problem of rising health care costs, and yet you've got tens of millions of people with no health insurance.[6]

These words were not spoken by another labor union leader but by Wilbur L. Ross, Jr., a billionaire, and the former chairman of the International Steel Group and a major investor in US textile, coal, and auto parts companies.

While the private health insurance industry claims that its coverage has been greatly broadened in recent years to keep pace with inflation, not everyone agrees with this view. In 2005, money-losing General Motors spent $5.3 billion to cover the costs of 1.1 million employees, retirees, and dependants. According to Wilbur Ross, on a per-capita basis General Motors was spending more money on health insurance than on steel. The cost of health insurance is climbing rapidly, according to the Henry J. Kaiser Family Foundation, but wages show only modest growth. From 2001 to about 2007 premiums for family coverage had risen 78% nationally but wages had increased only about 19%. The average annual premium for family coverage in 2007 was $12 106 and workers paid an average of $3281 out of their pay checks to cover their share of the cost of a family policy. Employers and employees are being squeezed by the price of health care. The effort to control health costs is viewed as extremely important to improving wages and living standards for working Americans. Employees are paying more for health care and other benefits, leaving less money for pay raises. In March 2008, the US Labor Department reported that benefits now account for 30.2% of an employer's compensation costs, with the remaining money going to wages. That is an increase from 27.4% in 2000.[7–9]

Officials of various companies have stressed that the bulk of extra dollars have gone to pay for the higher costs of old benefits rather than the purchase of new ones. While companies can pinpoint the exact causes of the increase in health care costs, they express little agreement on how to reduce them. Some try one thing, like HMOs, and some try another, like health savings accounts (HSAs), and most apparently feel helpless. The question which immediately arises is: why? What has happened to the private health insurance industry in this country? What has made it so incapable of completely protecting the individual against the costs of ill health at prices which are reasonable for the public to afford? Why do many voices, both public and private, declare that a new social mechanism, as exemplified by national health insurance, is needed to afford all individuals their right to comprehensive health care? Part of the answer lies in a convergence of a variety of forces at work in our society. They include the facts that the demand for health care is increasing along with the cost of providing it; consumers' voices are becoming more militant as their frustrations and expectations in regard to this service continue to increase; shortages of health manpower and facilities continue to persist; America's population had already reached 300 million by 2008 and continues to increase as well as age. As more and more Americans reach 65 years and beyond, their life expectancy also increases due to medical advances and with this increased longevity comes illnesses that were not as a prevalent in shorter life spans and are very costly to treat. Meanwhile, consumer groups criticize hospitals and physicians for charging too much for services; for building hospitals in areas where they are not needed and adding unnecessary technology that is duplicative with other institutions in their geographic locality with the demise of national health planning law in the 1980s, one of whose purposes was to control the growth of medical facilities on the community level; and for allowing the costs of health care to skyrocket because they know they will be reimbursed by health insurance programs. In reply, some hospital administrators and physicians state that the huge sums of money which are available from government programs are among the reasons why health care costs have risen so rapidly. For example, in 2003 Medicare, Medicaid, and State Children's Health Insurance Program financed $557 billion in health care services – one-third of the country's total health care bill and almost three-quarters of all public spending on health care.[10] Since their enactment into law, both Medicare and Medicaid have been subject to numerous legislative and administrative changes designed to make improvements in the provision of health care services to America's aged, disabled, and disadvantaged. Another cost-inducing factor, they say, is physicians who feel pressured into ordering more and more tests, expensive laboratory tests, and other patient services in order to protect themselves against the possibility of malpractice suits. And health insurance, both public and private, underwrites the cost of all these activities.

Because of the existence of health insurance our whole philosophy and attitude toward seeking medical treatment and paying for such care have also

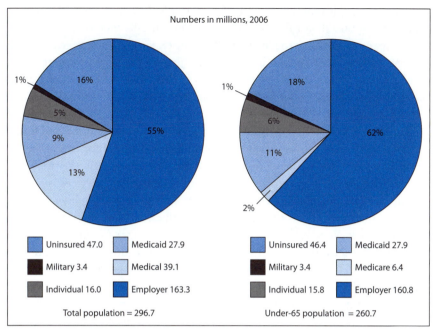

Numbers in millions, 2006

Figure 11.2 Employers provide health benefits to more than 160 million working Americans and family members. Data: US Census Bureau, Current Population Survey, March 2007. Source: Collins S R, White C, Kriss J L (2007) *Whither Employer-based Health Insurance? The Current and Future Role of US Companies in the Provision and Financing of Health Insurance.* New York: The Commonwealth Fund, 2007. Reprinted with permission of The Commonwealth Fund, New York, NY and as cited at: http://www.commonwealthfund.org/doc_img/653659.gif.

changed. By enabling millions of Americans to finance their personal medical expenses, health insurance has severely distorted the sensitivity of both the patient and provider toward the cost of medical treatment. As individuals, patients can now say that as long as other groups – the third parties like Blue Cross and commercial insurers – are paying the bills, why shouldn't they seek out the best care possible, meaning the most expensive? Why worry about cost? It must be borne in mind that only a very small percentage of all policies are written for individuals. In 2006, 16 million Americans purchased individual polices while 160 million had employment-based coverage (Figure 11.2).[2]

Also, it is only at the turn of the 21st century that new health insurance vehicles like HSAs and similar programs were created that have enabled consumers to become more responsible in terms of saving for and purchasing their own medical care, thus making consumers more sensitive to these costs. These corporate health contracts put consumers at financial risk because consumers must decide what they are willing to pay for and what they are not. These company plans reduce the company's medical expenses by putting more of the burden upon the worker. What they have in common is a high upfront deductible that workers pay. For example, in a family plan the worker might be responsible for the first $4000 in medical bills each year. After that, the company might have to pick up 90% of the expenses. The employer might also contribute some money into a special health care savings account that workers can use, tax-free, for bills paid out of their own pocket. On the other hand, workers might be left to fund the savings account themselves, through payroll deductions.

Supporters of these plans state they will encourage competition and lower national medical costs, because everyone will shop around for care at better price. However, for that to happen, consumers need to know the price and decent price and quality information regarding health care services is not yet readily available to the American public. In addition, the Employee Benefit Research Institute reports that having a big deductible plan does cause workers to cut back on care.[11] They are more likely not to seek treatment or even delay such a decision, especially if they are in poor health and earn less than $50 000 a year. In other words, to avoid the upfront cost of the deductible they allow themselves to become more sick and eventually use more care, because they did not take care of themselves. But by and large, most consumers do not have consumer-driven plans and, by not being responsible individually for large portions of their medical expenses since someone else is paying the bill, they become responsible collectively as a nation. We have to pay higher insurance premiums to cover the rising costs of health care and, thus, take home less personal income from our work; we have to pay higher taxes under public programs such as social security to cover the rising costs of government medical programs in which we might not even be qualified to participate; and we observe government intervening more and more in the health field in an attempt to control costs and frequently driving up these costs as a result of increasing regulation and intervention. By developing a product called health insurance which enables consumers to pay their medical bills, thereby performing a social service, the private health insurance industry now finds itself ironically accused of abetting our present health crisis.

Consequently, it is the purpose of this chapter to explore the issue of private health insurance: what it is, why it has problems protecting consumers fully against the costs of ill health, the economic impact which health insurance has upon society, and the programs government has created to ease the costs and increase the protection of its citizenry through health insurance.

History of private health insurance

The origin of private health insurance in the USA can be traced to the middle of the 19th century when a few insurance companies answered the public's need to be protected against rail and steamboat accidents. As the 19th century progressed, mutual aid societies, which started in Europe, began to be established in the USA. Workers came together in these membership organizations and made small contributions, in return for which they received a promise that they would receive a cash benefit if they suffered a disability as a result of an accident or sickness. Therefore, not only did fraternal organizations provide health insurance at that time but mutual benefit associations, named establishment funds, composed of workers and sometimes partially underwritten by employers, also made small payments for death and disability. In addition, toward the conclusion of the 19th century not only did accident insurance companies enter the field, with the subsequent growth of health insurance coverage, but also when life insurance companies made accident and health insurance available to the public the growth of this coverage was spurred on even more. Thus, between the mid 19th and mid 20th centuries – the private health insurance system evolved. During this period, the number of people protected by policies steadily rose.

In general, the protection afforded by private health insurance encompasses five broad categories: hospital expenses, surgical costs, regular medical expenses, major medical, and earnings lost because of illness or accident.

When health insurance protection first began, its principal emphasis was not on hospital and surgical benefits. Rather, the insurance sought to offer the individual beneficiary protection against any lost wages the individual might endure as a result of contracting any one of a limited number of diseases, such as typhus, typhoid, scarlet fever, diphtheria, and diabetes. Although subsequent plans increased the number of diseases covered, got rid of medical examinations, and included surgical fee schedules, this emphasis on the earnings aspects of insurance continued until the beginning stages of the Depression in 1929. As the Depression deepened, the public became increasingly conscious of the fact that better methods were necessary for sharing the expenses of medical care. On the other hand, hospitals were confronted with empty beds and decreasing revenues. As a result of this situation, a number of teachers and the Baylor Hospital in Dallas, Texas, devised an arrangement that both found mutually advantageous, in which teachers could receive hospital care on a prepaid basis. This is how the Blue Cross service concept for financing hospital care began. Its impact on the insurance industry was quite significant for it heralded the development of reimbursement policies for hospital and surgical care.

At the same time, another form of prepayment service was being established in Los Angeles, California, where a group of health care providers began combining group practice with prepayment. This physician-sponsored organization, operating today as the Ross-Loos Medical Group, served as the predecessor of such well-known programs as the Kaiser Foundation Health Plan of California and the prototype for today's medical care foundations and HMOs.

During World War II, the health insurance industry underwent a significant change. The freezing of industrial wages made fringe benefits a very important part of collective bargaining and one of these fringe benefits was group health insurance. After World War II, three powerful forces interacted and gave modern health insurance its strongest impetus for growth. First, the US Supreme Court in 1948 held that fringe benefits, including health insurance, were a legitimate part of the collective bargaining process.[12] The second factor was the rapidly increasing costs of medical care. The third element was the capacity of private health insurers to create new kinds of coverage and expand existing benefits.

Thus, as the nation left behind the Depression economy in the postwar years, insuring organizations began to create more expansive benefits and in the early 1950s introduced the most comprehensive insurance program yet devised – major medical expense coverage. This kind of insurance has been defined as protection especially designed to offset the very large medical expenses resulting from catastrophic or prolonged illness or injury. The policy is often superimposed or supplements basic protection, that is, its benefit coverage does not start until regular hospital/surgical or medical insurance benefits are exhausted, or the policy can be provided as comprehensive protection where both the basic and extended benefits are a single unit. From its beginning, major medical has grown quickly in response to a family's need for protection against rapidly increasing hospital, medical, and surgical costs.

In addition, the rapidly expanding economy of the postwar years not only witnessed the creation of major medical insurance but also led to the reemergence of yet another form of protection, namely, long-term disability benefits, which again emphasized the concept of replacing income during times of disability and other financial emergencies.[13] Thus, it appears that the health insurance has returned to its origins when the industry emphasized replacing income rather than just providing health care service benefits in its insurance policies.

Between the mid 20th century and early 21st century, private health insurance offered the public a whole host of new health insurance products, such as HMOs, PPOs, dental expense insurance, vision care insurance, long-term care insurance, Medicare supplemental insurance, HSAs and other products, some at the behest of federal law. By the beginning of the 21st century new programs, called pay-for-performance, began to emerge, in which providers like physicians are being reimbursed on the basis of their performance because in providing services they are attaining goals of quality of care, in contrast to a system that reimburses doctors, hospitals, or other providers regardless of whether they provide good services or not or whether patients are satisfied with their care. As a result, doctors are being reimbursed at higher fees, those in the middle with standard payments, and the worst providers receive a reduction in fees.

Federal laws and programs

In offering the public a diverse scope of health insurance products the private health insurance not only has to operate under state laws and rulings of the state insurance commissions, but also has to adhere to federal laws and programs. These laws allow companies to offer health insurance protection to their employees without meeting all the requirements that private health insurers usually must meet: they allow workers to take their health insurance from one company to another when changing job; they allow workers to keep their health insurance for a period for time after they are separated from their jobs for whatever reason, while looking for another position; and they have created new ways for workers to pay for their medical bills outside the traditional health insurance policy. That is why it is necessary to be knowledgeable about such federal laws and programs that have been passed and created since the latter part of the 20th century.

The Employee Retirement Income Security Act of 1974 (ERISA)

ERISA (PL 93-406) was enacted in 1974 and spurred companies to develop self-insurance plans in which employers pay their employees' doctor and hospital bills themselves, giving companies significant cost advantages in view of rising health care costs. The US Department of Labor rather than the states regulate self-insurance plans. Originally, the law was aimed at protecting workers' fringe benefits such as pensions. But over the years the courts have interpreted the law as overriding state regulation of employee health insurance in situations where employers insure themselves. The advantage of self-insurance is that it allows companies to insure those ailments it wishes to cover rather than the wider variety of benefits state laws require of traditional insurance. At the time of its enactment the ERISA law stated that if employers wanted to act as their own insurers – to pay premiums and pay out benefits themselves rather than using an insurance company – they would be exempt from all state taxes and regulations that govern insurance. The original intent of the ERISA health section exemption was to permit companies with dispersed operations to offer uniform health packages from state to state.

In November 1992, the US Supreme Court ruled that self-insured companies have the right to discriminate on the basis of disease on the kind of health insurance coverage they provide to their employees. Companies do not have to cover a particular disease if they do not wish to do so since they are not subject to state laws that would have prevented such actions. Also, large companies have begun to combine their self-insurance system with the delivery of general medical services by their in-house medical clinics that are staffed by their own doctors or provided by contract medical firms, in order to lower their own medical bills even further. Besides savings on drugs and tests, companies can also save money by avoiding unnecessary hospitalizations through careful case monitoring and negotiating low fees with hospitals, which may be likely if a firm can guarantee a hospital many patients.[14]

It is not always obvious that the health insurance plan that protects the worker at work is self-insurance. The worker's health insurance documents and claim forms may carry the name of a well-known insurance company, yet still be a self-insured plan. The reason for this is that companies often contract with insurance or other organizations known as third-party administrators or TPAs to process the claims. In addition, the health insurance plan is not subject to state regulation if it has entered into a TPA arrangement. The TPA receives the claims, evaluates whether they meet the plan's terms, and send out the checks. However, it is the employer who is paying the money: the TPA is not insuring workers. Therefore, if a worker wishes to know what benefits are being covered or not, depending upon the person's individual needs, the employee should find out from the company whether it self-insures, that is, pays claims out of its own pocket, or buys coverage from an insurer. In general, ERISA does not cover group health plans established or maintained by governmental entities, churches for their employees, or plans which are maintained solely to comply with applicable workers' compensation, unemployment, or disability laws. ERISA also does not cover plans maintained outside the USA primarily for the benefit of nonresident aliens or unfunded excess benefit plans.

Consolidated Omnibus Budget Reconciliation Act of 1986 (COBRA)

COBRA is a federal law that was enacted as public law 99-272 on July 1, 1986. This law amends ERISA to gives workers and their families who lose their health insurance benefits the right to choose to continue their group health benefits which are provided by their former company's group health plan for limited periods of time. They can do so under certain conditions such as voluntary, or involuntary, job loss, reductions in the hours worked, transition between jobs, death, divorce, and other life events. Qualified persons may be required to pay the entire premium for coverage up to 102% of the cost of the plan. In other words, they must pay the portion of their premiums for which they had been responsible, in addition to the portion that their employers previously paid as well as an extra 2% of this combined premium. Thus, while COBRA gives people the right to continue health insurance coverage at their own expense, depending upon an individual's economic circumstances the availability of COBRA does not mean that the person will find that the coverage is necessarily affordable.

As of January 1, 1997 COBRA generally requires that group health plans that are sponsored by employers with 20 or more employees in the prior year offer employees and their families the opportunity for a temporary extension of health coverage (called continuation coverage) for up to 18 months in certain instances where coverage under the plan would otherwise end. Also, as of January 1, 1997, a COBRA-qualified beneficiary may extend the original 18 months of COBRA eligibility for up to 29 months if the qualified beneficiary is determined to have been disabled at any time during the first 60 days of COBRA coverage, rather than the coverage requiring that the disability exist as of the date of the qualifying event. COBRA outlines how employees and their family members may choose continuation coverage. Also, effective January 1, 1997 COBRA participants may be eligible to change their coverage status if a child is born or adopted during the COBRA period so that child is also covered for the balance of the continuation period. If an employer goes bankrupt, there is no group health insurance, and, therefore, no COBRA. Once a company's group health insurance plan is canceled, it does not have to provide a plan that connects the worker to COBRA coverage. COBRA also requires employers and plans to provide notice about COBRA.

Health Insurance Portability and Accountability Act of 1996 (HIPAA)

HIPAA (PL 104-191) also amended the ERISA Act in that it provides important new protections for working Americans and their families who have preexisting medical conditions or might otherwise suffer discrimination in health insurance coverage based on factors that relate to an individual's health. Basically, the law protects workers from losing their health insurance when they change jobs. Named portability, this means that if workers are insured in their current job and go to work for a new employer, they have the right to sign up for whatever coverage their new employer offers without undergoing a waiting period. As long as the worker had a policy for at least 12 months, their insurability is guaranteed if they join a new plan within 30 days of becoming eligible. Some insurers will require employees to wait 18 months for coverage if they enroll late. The workers obtain immediate coverage under their new employer's plan, including coverage for illnesses they have already had – that is, the company would be required to issue the policy without it containing exclusions for preexisting conditions. This protects workers who have heavy medical expenses. In addition, workers can be charged higher premiums than someone in good health.

However, this does not mean that workers can take a more generous health plan with them when they go to work for a new employer, nor does it guarantee insurance. If the new employer does not offer health insurance coverage, portability will not assure the worker group coverage. HIPAA allows insurers to charge what they want, even if it prices people out of their so-called guaranteed coverage. Also, workers may not receive every benefit that their new plan offers. Employers can limit workers to the kind of coverage they had before. If their old plan did not cover maternity benefits, for example, their new plan is not required to offer it, even if other employees do have it. Nothing mandates what benefits the plan has to cover. The employer could exclude certain illnesses or put a cap or ceiling on benefits. As long as premiums are paid, health insurers must renew benefits. Finally, state and local governments can choose not to participate in HIPAA, freeing them to exclude a worker's preexisting illnesses.

Other ERISA amendments

Other important amendments were made to the ERISA law in the 1990s, including the Newborns and Mothers' Health Protection Act of 1996, the Mental Health Parity Act of 1996, and the Women's Health and Cancer Rights Act.

The Newborns' and Mother' Health Protection Act of 1996 (Newborns Act) was signed into law by President Clinton on September 26, 1996, effective January 1, 1998. It includes important protections for mothers and their newborn children with regard to the length of the hospital stay following childbirth. The Newborns Act requires that group health plans that offer maternity coverage pay for at least a 48-hour hospital stay following childbirth (96-hour stay in the case of cesarean section).

The Mental Health Parity Act of 1996, PL 104-204, was signed into law on September 26, 1996, effective January 1, 1998, by President Clinton and approved parity in the application of aggregate lifetime and annual dollar limits on mental health benefits with the dollar limits of medical/surgical benefits. A plan that does not impose annual or lifetime dollar limits on medical and surgical benefits may not impose such a dollar limit on mental health benefits offered under the plan. The Mental Health Parity Act does not apply to benefits for substance abuse or chemical dependency. Health plans are not required to include mental health benefits in their benefit packages. The Mental Health Parity Act only applies to those plans that do offer mental health benefits. On October 3, 2008 Congress enacted the Paul Wellstone and Peter Domenici (US Senators) Mental Health Parity and Addiction Equity Act, which closed loopholes that existed in the 1996 law. While the law does not mandate that health insurers cover mental health, if insurers do, they must provide coverage and treat psychological and addictive disorders just like any other physical condition. Thus, insurers are not permitted to minimize the number of outpatient visits or allowable days in the hospitals or charge higher deductibles or copayments. Mental health care must be equal to the benefits an insured individual receives for any other disease, also including, in addition to the previous equalities, day limits, dollar amounts, coinsurance, and out-of-pocket maximums. Just like the 1996 mental health law, the 2008 law applies to health plans covering more than 50 employees, preserves state mental health parity laws which typically do not govern large corporate health plans as covered by federal and consumer protection laws, and extends protection of mental health services to millions of Americans not protected by state laws. The law ensures coverage for both in-network and out-of network services.

The Women's Health and Cancer Rights Act of 1998, signed into law on October 21, 1998, includes protections for individuals who elect breast reconstruction in connection with a mastectomy. The Women's Health and Cancer Rights Act provides that group health plans and health insurance that provide coverage for medical and surgical benefits with respect to mastectomies must also cover certain postmastectomy benefits, including reconstructive surgery and the treatment of complications.

Health savings accounts

Beginning January 1, 2006, as a result of the Medicare Prescription Drug, Improvement, and Modernization Act of 2003, a new HSA was established for persons under 65 who have high deductible health insurance policies (at least $1050 for singles and $2100 a year for a family) and who can shelter income from taxes. Persons under 65 years of age, employers, or family members would make pretax contributions equal to the deductible, up to a maximum of $2700 for an individual and $5450 for a family in 2006. The insurance plan must limit the person's out-of-pocket expenses to no more than $5250 for an individual or $10 500 for family. No one can deposit money after age 65. In addition, so-called out-of-network charges do not count toward out-of-pocket expenses. After age 65, earnings and distribution would also be tax-free, provided the money is used for qualifying health expenses, defined as costs that arise to diagnose, cure, treat, or prevent disease, including health insurance premiums, doctor visits, prescription drugs, laser eye surgery, and long-term care, but not cosmetic surgery, except when it cures an ailment such as reconstructive surgery after an accident or operation. Money in HSAs can also be used for dental expenses and orthodontia. Otherwise, funds withdrawn from the account and not used for medical expenses would be subject to income taxes with an additional 10% penalty. Money in the HSA can accumulate from year to year. The money saved in the HSA can be provided by the worker, the employer, or both. Whoever makes the contribution can take the tax deduction. If a worker dies with money left in the HSA and there is a surviving spouse, the account can be transferred directly to the survivor without distribution or immediate tax implications. Either employers or individuals can establish the HSA. Employers can establish HSAs for workers in conjunction with a health insurance plan. Or, individuals with a high deductible plan can establish an HSA separately.

Private health insurance industry

Health insurance is a contract between an insurance company and an individual. Underlying the development of private health insurance programs, whether reinforced by federal laws or not, are three basic principles which are used in making actuarial determinations from which the premium rates are derived. They are as follows. First, the unpredictability of risk for the individual. Simply stated, no one can predict with certainty which persons will suffer an illness or an injury. Nor can anyone predict the effect of a disability on a particular person. Second, a reasonable predictability of the degree of risk for a group – the larger the group, the more accurate the prediction can be. As an example, studies of persons with high blood pressure reveal an extra hazard for the group, even though particular individuals in the group have a favorable outlook clinically. Thus, by drawing on the past experience of groups, risks can be evaluated. Third, transfer of risk from the individual to the group, through the traditional pooling of resources.[15]

However, premiums are not the only financial obligations that a person may incur in a health insurance policy. Others include a *deductible*, which is the amount that policyholders must pay from their own pocket before the plan pays its share; a *copayment*, which is the amount the policyholder must pay out of pocket before the health plan pays for a particular service, such as $30 for a doctor's visit; *coinsurance*, which is a percentage of total cost rather than a fixed dollar amount upfront, like 20% of the cost of surgery while the health plan pays 80%; *exclusions*, which are services for which the health plan does not pay; *coverage limits*, such as when some plans pay for health services up to a certain dollar amount and the policyholder may be expected to pay any charges exceeding the health plan's maximum payment for a specific service; and *out-of-pocket maximums*, which refer to the fact that members' payment obligations end when they attain the out-of-pocket maximum and the health plan pays all further covered costs.

The industry which operates on the previous principles is comprised of three broad categories: Blue Cross and Blue Shield, commercial insurance companies, and independent plans. These independent plans include plans which offer health services on a prepayment basis or insuring basis to the subscribing public of their general area. Also included are benefit programs of welfare funds, employers, employee benefit associations, or unions. The diversity and array of plans and benefits available were best described by one health authority which stated:

> To begin with, we have not even made up our minds about the name of the game. Some call it insurance and seek to replace financial losses that people incur when they need medical care. Others call it prepayment and seek to share the predictable expenses of care. From there on, the dichotomies proliferate. We have plans that regard their

responsibilities as essentially financial and believe that once they have paid the amount prescribed by their policies their responsibility is discharged. We have plans that believe that their responsibilities go further into a concern with the availability, cost, and quality of care they finance. We have plans that cover specified segments of care. We have plans that reimburse people a level of expenditure.

We have plans that regard the degree and content of protection the province of the patron – he wants less, he gets less; if he wants to invest in extra accident benefits instead of laboratory services, that is his choice. We have plans that believe that it is their duty to provide all subscribers with a constellation of benefits designed to maximize their health. We have plans that believe in preventing illness and intervening if possible before a disease becomes grave. We have plans, on the other hand, that do not believe in the inclusion of provisions for the prevention of disease and the maintenance of health insurance We have plans that pay the physician a separate fee for each person on the theory that such fee-for-service payment is essential to good care and that it rewards the physician only for what he does. We have plans that pay a physician a set amount over a period of time for each person in his care, believing that this encourages the physician to keep people well or at least diminishes the pecuniary incentive in prescribing more service. We have plans that regard it as their mission to preserve the conventional methods of practice. We have plans that regard it as their function to change the mode of practice. We have plans that serve a closed constituency. We have plans that try to cover as many people as possible. We have plans that believe that no one should make a profit in providing health protection. We have plans that expressly seek profit, although many, in fact, have not found it in the health field.

These are but some of the major differences in approach that have thus far shaped our plans.[16]

In view of the variety and complexity of health insurance plans presently in existence, it is not surprising that even the most sophisticated purchasers of this product can find themselves shortchanged, in terms of benefit protection which they thought they had purchased originally, when the time comes to use the insurance.

Shortcoming of insurance

There are many reasons why insurance carriers have problems in providing the kind of broad protection the public seeks but cannot obtain, regardless of the kind of insurance which may be purchased. One is that the general public does not always clearly perceive its own health insurance requirements. Thus, there may be little demand for a particular kind of coverage which, in turn, causes comprehensive health insurance to grow slowly. Another reason relates to the method by which health insurance is developed. Before a new coverage can be widely sold, administrative techniques, methods of reimbursing providers of services, and feasible benefit packages must be developed. Experimentation is required and this takes time. A third reason relates to custom, tradition, and inertia. Certain health insurance has become well accepted by the public, and health insurance companies have become accustomed to offering this. Only gradually are the limitations of these coverages recognized, and only slowly are new and broader coverages offered and accepted. There are other reasons why insuring organizations may sell restricted coverages. They do not do so because they are not willing to offer comprehensive benefits. Rather, individual employee groups, business corporations, or unions have only so much money available to purchase health insurance and thus are limited in the scope of the coverage they can obtain.

In some instances, existing legislation can also hamper or slow down an insuring organization from developing and offering new health insurance benefits to the public. For example, Blue Cross and Blue Shield have generally operated under enabling acts which defined the benefits they could offer; amendments of such legislation have been required before new kinds of benefits could be sold to the public. However, once the plans determined that they really wished to offer these new benefits and obtain endorsement of groups representing hospitals and physicians, for example, the desired legislation could be achieved.

Present state laws are almost completely silent on the adequacy of the benefits which private health insurers should offer the policyholder. As a result, insurance carriers are presently writing an infinite variety of policy combinations, as already noted. Because of the silence of states on benefit adequacy, it is easy to see why benefit coverage may be inadequate in terms of basic services such as hospitalization, the promotion of one-disease-only policies like that for cancer coverage, the lack of uniform standards in regard to areas such as length of stay and surgical schedules, and allowing the combination of health service benefits with other benefits such as income coverage for loss of time incurred because of accident or illness. It is extremely difficult, if not impossible, for purchasers of health insurance to compare benefits and costs and shop intelligently among those policies which are available. And, even if they had time to shop around, they might be overwhelmed by the fact that there are probably thousands of kinds of insurance policies being written in the USA, while the combinations of these policies are infinite.[17]

Costs and inadequacy of insurance protection

In view of the problems in providing, determining, and purchasing adequate health insurance protection, it is not surprising to learn that there are not only gaps in health insurance today but there are also a significant number and percentage of Americans who have no health insurance at all. As already noted, the US Census Bureau reports that more than 47 million Americans went without health insurance in 2006. That is 2.2 million more than the previous year and about 16% of the total population. Nationally, this is the sixth year in a row that the number of uninsured has grown.[18] The number of children nationwide not protected by health insurance also increased in 2006 to 8.7 million, or about 12% of all children. When the estimated 16 million people nationally who have inadequate insurance coverage is coupled with those who have none, then what results is millions (about 63 million people) who do not receive regular checkups, do not receive screening for life-threatening diseases, and don't receive rapid treatment that can prevent an injury turning into a disability.[18,19] To combat this situation, the state of Alabama has undertaken a plan, which if it works could spread to other jurisdictions, or perhaps even to the private sector itself. By 2010 each state employee will be confronted with a $50 per month health insurance premium, $25 more than in 2008. Beginning in 2009, each employee will be offered a free screening for health factors such as high blood pressure, high blood glucose, and body mass. If the employee chooses not to take the screening, the health insurance premium remains at $50. If the screeners discover something of concern, the employee will be offered a doctor's office visit free of charge, and if the employee decides not to take the free visit, the premium remains at $50. On the other hand, if the employee takes the free screening and is found to be healthy or is unhealthy, but decides to see a doctor, the premium is discounted to $25. Thus, Alabama is trying to make its state employees monitor their own personal health for their own well-being and hopefully cost the state less monies in terms of health care expenditures.

When the inadequacy of health insurance coverage is analyzed according to population demographics, 36% of Hispanics are uninsured, compared with 22% of African Americans, 17% of Asian/Pacific Islanders and 13% of whites, according to a Henry J. Kaiser Family Foundation analysis of census data.[9] The situation for the working poor on Medicaid is especially bad. The Center for Studying Health System Change has been studying 12 metro areas since 1995.[11] In a 2005 report the Center concluded that, for the underprivileged, access to basic health care is becoming worse. Because of cutbacks to Medicaid payments to providers, more physicians are ceasing to treat the working poor. State-of-the art hospitals and clinics are not opening downtown where they may live, but in the affluent suburbs. States are reducing their Medicaid rolls, and if individuals are uninsured, they are less than half as likely as the insured to receive any medical care. Strong cutbacks in services to the mentally ill are increasing homelessness, increasing costs of shelters, jails, and emergency rooms. Fewer specialists are even serving emergency rooms, never mind providing follow-up care.

Americans believe that everyone can receive health care services if they really need it. But except for real emergencies, such as traumatic injuries, physicians and hospitals may turn the prospective patient away if the person cannot pay upfront and that is why the fact that millions of Americans lack health insurance coverage is very bad and a serious problem not only to their personal health but also collectively to the nation's health as well.[11]

Even those with health insurance protection are beginning to find that in some instances their health insurance coverage is not sufficient, especially in regard to a provision called lifetime limits. An annual survey by the Henry J. Kaiser Family Foundation found that 55% of workers with employer-based coverage had lifetime limits in 2007, including 23% with a cap of $2 million or less. This was an increase from the 50% who had a cap in 2004. Those who require an organ transplant or who have hemophilia, Gaucher disease, or other costly chronic illnesses can easily build up medical bills that can exceed the lifetime benefits cap of $1 million or more that is a standard part of many insurance policies. This has left some very ill people confronting health care costs of hundreds of thousands of dollars or more, forcing families to turn to government for help or try to change jobs or even divorce for no other reason than to qualify for new health insurance. Advocates state the amount of many caps has not changed in decades, or at least has not kept up with health care inflation, and the very high costs of life-saving new therapies are making it more likely that people will reach the limit and then have to find some other way to pay for their expensive health care costs, aside from insurance.[20]

Impact of health costs on US business

Since millions receive their health insurance protection through their place of employment, businesses are being hard hit by the rising costs of health care. The percentage of employers offering health insurance is shrinking and employers with fewer than 200 employees are leading the way out. Hardest hit are construction, service, and agricultural workers who are least likely to have health insurance through their jobs. Health care costs also threaten the international competitiveness of US manufacturers which spend more than twice as much as their trading partners. In the 21st-century global economy, US industries must compete internationally. Health care costs would not be a burden to firms if the costs could be shifted to consumers through higher prices. But with globalization and increased competition in international markets, this is not possible. Therefore, health care impacts the profitability of US businesses and job stability. Businesses find themselves at a competitive disadvantage with foreign competitors who have their operations in countries with universal health insurance programs for their own citizenry and slower health care cost inflation. American companies compete against other businesses in developed countries (Germany, Japan, and France) where the government funds health care, and against developing countries (China, India) where neither business nor society at large is responsible for health insurance. Either way, American businesses that provide health insurance are at a competitive disadvantage. This disadvantage becomes more noticeable when it is realized that the average worker contribution for family health insurance coverage in the USA between 2000 and 2007 has increased 102%. When out-of-pocket medical costs are added to the annual health insurance premium costs, the portion of American household income that went toward health care in 2008 was approaching one-fifth of the average household's spending, according to the consulting and accounting firm Deloitte.[18,21,22] In more specific examples, by 2006 AK Steel, a US manufacturer, spent $230 million for the health care costs of 54 000 employees, retirees, and their dependants. Retiree health expenditures in this company have risen 50% since 1999, led by prescription drugs costs, which have more than doubled. In 2006, Starbucks spent $200 million for 80 000 workers in health insurance costs; that is, the company spent more on health insurance than on coffee beans. Howard Shultz, chairman of Starbucks, has stated: 'It's completely unsustainable.'[23] Ford Motor Company spent $3.5 billion in health care costs for 550 000 employees and retirees. In the first 9 months of 2006, Ford lost $7.24 billion. The company is closing plants and eliminating thousands of jobs to cut future costs.[23]

How bad is the Ford situation? In the late 1970s Ford purchased health care services for nearly 1 million hourly and salaried employees, retirees, surviving spouses, and their dependants. In 1965, Ford's health bill totaled $65 million. By 1977, Ford projected costs were over $450 million or $2100 per active employee and almost 30 years later Ford's health care costs were almost nine times as much as 1977 and covering almost half as many workers.[24] The cost increases must be recovered through either higher prices or increased productivity.

In fact, the consumer is paying. By 2005 one of Ford's competitor's, General Motors, was adding $1500 on to each and every car and truck that it produced because of health care costs.[25] In 2005, as already noted, money-losing General Motors spent $5.3 billion to cover the health care costs of 1.1 million employees, retirees, and dependants, spending more money on health insurance than on purchasing steel.

How burdensome was this situation for US automakers? By the end of 2008, General Motors, Chrysler, and the Ford Motor Company told the US Congress that unless the US government loaned them billions of dollars they would face bankruptcy by 2009. In December 2008, General Motors and

Chrysler accepted such government loans, while Ford declined for the moment. While health care costs were not the only economic reasons for the automobile manufacturers' financial problems, they certainly were one of them.[23] Finally, on June 1, 2009, unable to maintain its financial solvency, despite government loans of slightly more than $19.4 billion and after being in business for an entire century, General Motors had to declare Chapter 11 bankruptcy, as had done one of its US competitors, Chrysler LLC, on April 30, 2009. Not only did General Motors' manufacturing plants and automobile dealerships have to be closed, and many thousands of workers were laid off, but more than 650 000 retirees and family members saw their health insurance coverage shrink, which they depended upon in their retirement years. On June 10, 2009 most of Chrysler's assets were purchased by Italy's Fiat automobile company.[26] On July 10, 2009 General Motors came out of bankruptcy.

When health insurance premium costs reduce the operating margins of American business, they are lessening the ability of business to grow by investing in research, capital spending, product development, and marketing because monies that would normally be allocated to these other functions are being spent on health insurance premiums. When health insurance is high, large firms hesitate to add new jobs. Since about 2003 through 2007 smaller firms have been experiencing larger annual increases in premiums (15–20% annual increase) compared to large firms, making it more difficult to add new jobs. There is no question that health insurance costs are the fastest-rising business expense for companies. In more specific terms, health insurance premiums for employers increased nearly 100% between 2000 and 2007, compared to wages, which have increased by only 24% during the same period, and inflation, which increased 20%.[27]

But the costs that businesses sustain in higher premium costs which affect their competitiveness with other firms both domestically and abroad as well as impact on their economic expansion and viability are affected by economic situations in American society that are not directly within the sphere of control of US business entities. Employers are also paying in their premiums for the added costs of treating the uninsured when hospitals and physicians provide medical care to patients who have no health insurance. A 2005 study reported that costs for family health insurance coverage provided by private-sector employers include an extra $922 annually in insurance premiums due to the cost of the uninsured population.[28] In addition, the lack of insurance leads to losses to businesses as a result mainly of lower productivity of the uninsured (and, on average, less healthy and functional) workers. The HR Policy Association, which represents senior human resource officers at 200 of America's largest companies, puts the annual cost of reduced productivity alone at between $87 billion and $126 billion.[27] Even America's National Academy of Sciences' Institute of Medicine estimates that the economic value of the healthier and longer life that an uninsured adult loses because the adult lacks health insurance could be as much as $3300 for each additional year spent without coverage. The Institute of Medicine projects that the annualized cost of diminished health and a shorter life span of Americans who lack health insurance reaches almost $135 billion for each year of health insurance forgone.[29]

Private business cost initiatives

Businesses are using a whole variety of approaches in an effort to control their health care costs. These include the establishment of HSAs; chronic disease management; ban on smoking; investing in in-house-corporate health education programs relating to personal health maintenance; providing employees with preventive care programs such as health screening examinations and annual physical examinations in order to detect illness as early as possible; and the use of second-opinion surgical programs as well as investing in technology to control their expenses. Some small businesses are hiring professional employer organizations that combine dozens of small firms into big employee groups for discounted rates. They may be likened to off-site personnel departments. For an annual fee of 2–7% of the dollar value of annual payroll, a professional employer organization manages everything from recruiting and hiring to managing health benefits for many small businesses that cannot afford or need a full-time human resources department.[30]

Some businesses are also establishing health reimbursement accounts (HRAs) which are a sum of employer-provided money that workers can use to pay medical costs that are not covered by health insurance or they can let the HRA monies accumulate over the years, and the funds would be available in retirement for the workers to supplement Medicare. In general, employers allocate to workers an annual allowance (for example, $2500) to spend on medical expenses. The employer's contribution can be without limit, only defined by how much the employer can afford. Thus, the key difference between HSAs and HRAs is that the HRA is financed by the employer rather than the employee and any unused money belongs to the company. The health reimbursement arrangement remains with the originating employer and does not follow employees to their new employer. The employer can deduct the cost of the insurance plan as a business expense under internal revenue code section 162.

Of course, corporations are using HMOs and PPOs to reduce their health care costs, as well as derivatives of PPOs called an exclusive provider organization (EPO), in that it attempts to avoid the middle agent such as health insurers (including HMOs), who may take 25% or more of the health care dollar. In this arrangement, the health care providers deal directly with buyers of health care services. Providers are typically reimbursed on a fee-for-service basis according to a negotiated discount or fee schedule. Medical services that are delivered by providers who are not affiliated with EPOs are not covered, so people belonging to an EPO must receive their care from affiliated providers or pay the entire cost themselves. In this latter sense, an EPO resembles an HMO. Usually, at the beginning of the plan year, individuals must decide whether they wish to use an EPO-type organization.

Another plan that employers are implementing to help reduce their health costs is called flexible spending accounts (FSAs), through which employees, not employers as in HRA, put aside their own money to pay unreimbursed health care costs. An FSA is a benefit plan that allows companies to give their workers the opportunity to pay for their out-of-pocket health (medical/dental) and dependent care costs on a pretax basis. Over time, this lowers payroll-related taxes for both employer and employees: the money which employees deposit in their account, which they set up each year, is deducted from their salary before it is taxed, giving them the benefit of immediate tax relief. The FSA only applies to family members who qualify as dependants under Internal Revenue Service rules for income tax purposes. While there is no legal limit on the size of the FSA account, most employees establish their own maximums. The principal drawback of the FSA is the fact that employees must use the money or lose it. Employees decide at the beginning of the year how much they think they may need, but if they fail to use it all up by the end of the year, they will lose the money. This often leads to a splurge of late-year spending on health-related items as workers realize they have put aside too much money and consider buying something they don't need or totally lose their money.

Next to these kinds of plans, claims monitoring is another corporate device for controlling health care costs. Monitoring seeks to ensure that health providers actually give the care they billed for, that both the care and bill were appropriate, and that the company policy covered the care in question. Its single most important task is spotting excessive hospital stays and reporting them to utilization committees. Sometimes the insurance carrier will serve as the monitor, while sometimes an outside consultant will perform the services. Also, as already noted under ERISA, many corporations use the concept of self-insurance in which they set up a benefit plan which does not pay premiums to an insurance company for health coverage but pays the bills directly to health providers. The concept can save costs, such as taxes – which an insurance company must pay but a benefit plan need not – and other relatively small administrative costs. It also gives benefit plan administrators direct control of reimbursing health care providers and thus puts the administrators in a position to work with the providers in controlling costs.

Conclusion

No industry is more aware of the limitations of its product and the distance it must travel to make it more effective than the health insurance industry, despite the efforts of health insurers to broaden their benefit plans and provide more protection to more people than ever before in history. Yet, as of 2009, about 47 million Americans lack health insurance coverage in a country of 300 million. Based on census data, 13.7 million people aged 19–29 had no health insurance, up from 13.3 million in 2005. Men and women in this age group accounted for 17% of the population under age 65, but they made up almost 30% of the uninsured, according to a report of the Commonwealth Fund, a private foundation that researches health issues.[31] Children are dropped from pubic insurance programs at age 19 or from parents' private insurance policies once they finish their education, either graduating from high school or college. Many jobs available to young adults tend to be below-wage or temporary, the type unlikely to provide health coverage.[31] Yet, in 2009, as almost 30 years earlier when the Democratic Party in its election-year platform espoused the enactment of national health insurance, the issue has once again come to the fore of the nation's domestic agenda.

The question remains: does private health insurance still have time to demonstrate that it is far more capable of controlling health care costs than the federal government under a national program? What is being witnessed once again in a free-enterprise society is an industry whose concept of operation is under attack. Its large consumers, namely labor and management, are expressing doubt as to its future viability. The US Congress is expressing deep concern over the industry's inability to control the costs of its premiums, and social planners are seeking to demonstrate the inability of the industry to deal effectively with the health care problems which beset the nation. The task ahead will be difficult. Since the 1970s the private insurance industry has used HMOs, PPOs, EPOs, point of service, and other devices to slow down the rise of health costs, yet by 2009 Americans are spending slightly more than $2 trillion a year on health care services.

The social and economic conditions which are pressuring society to call for a change in the manner by which the nation finances and provides health care are not giving any group or organization much time to reflect philosophically upon the course of action. Consumers in the 21st century have become increasingly aware of what constitutes adequate health care and are questioning the kind and cost of care they are now receiving. Report cards are being published on the quality of various institutions like hospitals. The internet now hosts a whole series of websites that provide consumers with medical information. Medicare has established sites where consumers can compare hospitals, nursing homes, and home care agencies throughout the country and within their own locality concerning the quality of care these organizations provide.

Thus, the situation which confronts the private health insurance industry is but one element of the larger health care picture in which other providers of services are confronted by similar issues of varying degree. The health care field, in turn, is but one element of the larger picture of the social and economic revolutions which are sweeping the USA. What makes the insurance element of special significance is that the industry, as a representative of the American free-enterprise system, is being given notice that if it cannot sufficiently and economically meet and serve society's needs, then the public will turn to and seek assistance from its own representative – namely, government – to perform private industry's function. Private health insurance versus national health insurance is the battlefield upon which the issue will be settled.

References

1. Crisis and health insurers. *Life Assoc News* 1970; June: 1.
2. US Census Bureau. *Current Population Survey*. Washington, DC: Bureau of the Census, 2007.
3. Uninsured pay $30 billion for health care. Reuters 2008; August 25.
4. Collins S R, Kriss J L, Doty M M, *et al*. *Losing Ground: How Adequate Health Insurance Is Burdening Working Families*. New York: The Commonwealth Fund, 2008; August 20: 2 (issue brief).
5. US Department of Commerce. *Income, Poverty and Health Insurance Coverage in the United States: 2006*. Washington, DC: Bureau of the Census, 2007.
6. Gross D. Health care for all: big business makes a case. *AARP Bull* 2007; January: 20.
7. Lack of health insurance a threat to nation's health. *AARPDC* 2008; winter: 4.
8. Fletcher M A. Rising health costs cut into wages. *Washington Post* 2008; March 24: A01.
9. Singletary M. Lack of insurance hits us all. *Washington Post* 2008; March 16: F4.
10. Hoffman E D Jr, Klees B S, Curtis C A. Overview of the Medicare and Medicaid programs. In: *Health Care Financing Review/2005 Medicare Supplement*. Baltimore, MD: Centers for Medicare and Medicaid Services, 2006: 3.
11. Quinn J B. Health care's new lottery. *Newsweek* 2006; February 27.
12. Inland Steel *v*. National Labor Relations Board, 170 Federal Second to 47, Court of Appeals, 7th Circuit 1948, Denial of Certiorari (Denial of Review), 336-U.S. 960.
13. *1971-1972 Source Book of Health Insurance Data*. New York: Health Insurance Institute, 1971-1972: 8.
14. Gladwell M. When health plan changes leave employees vulnerable. *Washington Post* 1992; April 20: A1, A4.
15. *Modern Health Insurance*. New York, NY: Health Insurance Institute, 1969: 9, 36.
16. Pollack J. New approaches to healthcare plan, as cited in *Proceedings of a Seminar on Prepaid Group Practice Plans*. Denver, CO: University of Colorado, 1968: 1.
17. US House of Representatives. *National Health Insurance Resource Book*. Washington, DC: Committee on Ways and Means, 1974: 214.
18. Lack of health insurance a threat to nation's health. *AARPDC* 2008; winter: 4.
19. Sloane M. Alabama to link premium costs to workers health; available online at: http://www.cnn.com/2008/HEALTH/diet/fitnmess/09/19alabama.obesity.insurance/index.html; accessed on September 19, 2008.
20. Lee C. More hit cost limit on health insurance. *Washington Post* 2008; January 27: A1, A5.
21. *New Report Shows Impact of Employer Health Care Costs on Global Competition and US Jobs*. Washington, DC: New American Foundation, 2008: 1.
22. Abelson R, Freudenheim M. Even the insured feel strain of health costs. *N Y Times* 2008; May 4.
23. Gross D. Health care for all: big business makes a case. *AARP Bull* 2007; January: 21.
24. GM's outlays for national health insurance exceeds $1 billion; Ford undertakes pilot programs on health care. *Review* 1977; December: 27, 28, 30.
25. Appleby J, Carty S. Ailing GM looks to scale back generous health benefits. *USA Today* 2005; June 24.

26. Isodore C. GM bankruptcy: end of an era. CNNMoney.com June 2, 2009; available online at: http://money.cnn.com/2009/06/01/news/companies/gm_bankruptcy/; accessed on June 10, 2009.
27. *The Impact of Rising Health Costs on the Economy.* Washington, DC: National Coalition of Health Care, 2008: 2.
28. *Paying a Premium: The Added Cost of Care for the Uninsured.* Washington, DC: Families USA, 2005.
29. Institute of Medicine. *Hidden Costs, Value Lost – Uninsurance in America.* Washington, DC: The National Academies Press, 2003.
30. Hopkins J. Putting a Band-Aid on small firms' health costs. *USA Today* 2006; April 19.
31. Number of uninsured young Americans grows from 2005. Reuters 2008; May 30.

12

Managed care

Introduction

It is the panacea to our health care problems! It is new! It will reduce the costs and change the delivery of health care services in this country! All these exclamations and more might have been proclaimed back in 1973. At that time the US Congress established a new program to function as an alternative to the private health insurance industry. The law was the Health Maintenance Organization Act of 1973 (PL 93-222). Only 2 years before, the Nixon administration, in advocating its passage, proclaimed that by the mid-1970s more than 1000 of these new delivery systems would blanket the USA, serving 45 million Americans. Moreover, the administration asserted that by 1980 about 1700 health maintenance organizations (HMOs) would be operating throughout the country, covering 90% of the population.

The predictions have not matched the reality. As of July 2006, there were only 539 HMOs in the USA, serving 71 million persons among a population of almost 300 million.[1] Even in the late 1970s, instead of 1700 HMOs blanketing the country, there were only 175 HMO-like organizations operating in the USA, serving slightly more than 6 million persons. At that time even the enthusiasm of Dr. Paul Ellwood, one of the fathers of the HMO movement, seemed to be waning as he talked about altering the approach of the HMO concept:

> We're not abandoning it but broadening it [the approach]. The key to lowering costs is to reduce hospital use and established HMOs like Kaiser have proven their ability to do this. However, we have been seeing more and more evidence that group practice doesn't necessarily have to be on a capitation basis to hold down costs. Individuals enrolled in the HMO program were found ... to be experiencing greater hospital use than their fee-for-service counterparts. But both groups showed outstanding low rates of hospitalization.[2]

What has happened? How did a concept which was being proclaimed as one of the salvations of the health care delivery system begin to create so much doubt and negativism that has remained with it into the 21st century? Why were these HMOs so strongly advocated by the Nixon administration and others? In view of these and other questions let us examine the HMO movement in this country and later managed care derivatives from the movement, such as preferred provider organizations (PPOs) and point of service (POS) plans. Each of these forms of managed care has great significance for the American consumer.

What is managed care?

Before discussing HMOs and other forms of managed care such as PPOs and POS plans, it is first necessary to discuss the concept of managed care. In contrast to fee-for-service medicine, managed care is a planned and coordinated approach to providing health care services. Its goal is to reduce health costs without suffering the loss of the quality of care. Under managed care the patient no longer can go to any doctor or hospital the patient wishes if the patient wants the health insurance plan to pay the bill. It also means that people besides the patient and his/her doctor decide what treatments the patient receives in health plans, which closely monitor and often limit treatment, both to save money and, it is stated, to improve the patient's health.

Managed care is being applied in two forms. One is case-by-case review and the other, 'approvals' and 'denials' in traditional health insurance. This is called utilization review. It really means the patient, for example, must obtain a second opinion before surgery, and a doctor or nurse on the telephone at a review company must give his or her approval before the patient goes to the hospital, except in an emergency. The reviewer usually limits the number of days the plan will pay for hospital or mental health or other care, if it will pay at all. It may say a doctor or dentist has charged more than the plan will pay, leaving the patient the rest of the bill. But more formally *utilization review* is a collective term for the following activities:

- *Preadmission certification*, in which elective hospitalizations are assessed against standard criteria prior to admission. The purpose of the review is to determine whether the admission, diagnostic testing, or surgical procedure is appropriate.
- *Concurrent review,* or the formal review of an ongoing hospitalization to determine whether the length of stay and any subsequent medical intervention is appropriate and consistent with good medical practice.
- *Discharge planning*, in which, to keep hospital stays to the shortest appropriate length, the HMO prearranges for care to be received after discharge.
- *Case management*, in which systematic reviews take place to identify patients who, because of the severity of their illness, are likely to require prolonged hospitalization or intensive therapy. These patients are

carefully monitored to insure that the most appropriate and cost-effective care is being delivered.[3]

Another form of managed care is enrollment in various kinds of restricted groups of doctors and hospitals, for example, HMOs. Thus, managed care organizations do not actually decide about a patient's medical care treatment: the patient's doctor still has that responsibility. But the organization does decide whether a particular service will be covered and in that way affects the kind of care the patient receives. The managed care organization decides which doctors, hospital procedures, and sometimes which medicines are covered by the patient's insurance plan. Managed care companies today are developing specialty networks for mental health, vision, dental, chiropractic, podiatric, and physical therapy care. Sophisticated managed care principles are also being applied to other fields like long-term care, as well as medical bills associated with auto liability and workers' compensation claims.

Most managed care plans have a sufficient number of physicians and hospitals to deliver comprehensive care and some degree of choice. If a patient desires a particular physician, hospital, or medical procedure, then it is important to select an insurance plan that includes the one the patient wants. The problem is that some people receive their insurance through their place of employment and, thus, do not have that choice. So patients must make sure that they thoroughly understand the details of their managed care contract to ensure that it is the kind of health insurance protection they want for themselves and their loved ones. Thus, in managed care the insurer or employer does more than pay the bills. The payer becomes involved in selecting the physician, hospital, or other provider and in deciding what care will be provided. Patients who demand to visit a different physician or undergo an unapproved procedure will have to pay more.

Health maintenance organizations

Although HMO premiums in some instances may be higher than those of private health insurance, membership in an HMO may lessen the costs of medical bills over the long term. Unlike the usual arrangements between the patient and the doctor (or the insurance company) under which a physician is paid for each service he/she delivers, the HMO receives a flat or fixed fee or premium for all medical and hospital services. The HMO's fee for that year does not increase, no matter how much care or how many tests, including hospitalizations, the patient requires. In addition, HMOs, as multidisciplinary medical groups, provide a broad spectrum of benefits. Private health insurance does not cover some services like preventive care to any large degree. Preventive care tends to identify illness early, treats it efficiently as possible, and hopefully avoids the necessity for more expensive treatment later, such as hospitalization. Again, such a process saves money. With a typical health insurance policy, the family has to pay for regular preventive care, office visits, well-baby care, immunizations, and sometimes a certain amount of hospital expenses and a portion of a surgeon's fee. HMOs cover all of these services.

HMOs as a concept had been in operation for half a century prior to the enactment of the HMO Act of 1973. The term *health maintenance* in the title of this organization derives from its basic purpose, to maintain the patient's health by emphasizing *preventive* medical care, as already noted. Because an HMO receives a fixed premium for all medical and hospital services, regardless of the amount of services used, it has the rationale to deliver high-quality preventive care and not engage in excess hospitalization or perform duplicative or unnecessary tests. Prior to their redefiniton as operational entities by Congressional law these organizations were known as prepaid group practice plans. It is of interest to know what these organizations are, how they have evolved, and what services they offer.

Definition of prepaid group practice

However, before examining these and other issues, it is first necessary to define the concept of an HMO. Prior to the enactment of the Health Maintenance Organization Act of 1973, group practice plans such as the Kaiser Foundation Health Plan on the west coast functioned in this country for many years. In terms of definition, prepayment plans are those to which payments (premiums) are made beforehand or in advance into a fund which is used to pay for an individual's health services as the need arises.[4] Such services may be provided, for example, by a medical group practice.

Group practice, on the other hand, is more difficult to define. The term has various meanings to different people, depending upon the aims which they believe the group should seek. To some individuals group practice means nonmedically controlled, closed panel, and prepaid medical care by physicians on a salary.[5] To others, group practice has other meanings. The difference in meanings centers around the concept of who controls and administers the multispecialty groups. In its most basic form, group practice is a systematic relationship between physicians or dentists who are organized for the conduct of group practice. A variety of group practices exist, depending upon the scope and content of the relationships. The US Public Health Service has defined group practice as:

> Any group of three or more physicians (full-time or part-time) formally organized to provide medical services with income from medical services distributed according to a prearranged plan. Comprehensive

group practice may include the provision of preventive, diagnostic and curative services by family or personal practitioners, specialists and other professional and sub-professional technical staff working as a team in a center, pooling their knowledge, experience and equipment as well as their income.[4]

The previous description covers what is meant by a closed panel group. A *closed panel* of physicians is the more traditional type of prepaid group practice in which physicians work together as a group, typically as a professional corporation or partnership, pool their income, and share common facilities, support staff, and medical records. On the other hand, an *open panel* of physicians refers to independent solo practitioners or small group practices who maintain their existing fee-for-service practices and individual offices while agreeing to provide prepaid care to HMO plan subscribers in much the same way that they provide such services to Blue Shield (physician services) subscribers.

However with the passage of the Health Maintenance Organization Act of 1973, the concept of prepaid group practice was refined even further. An HMO was now defined as a legal entity which provides a prescribed range of services known as basic services in return for prepaid, fixed, and uniform payment. An HMO also had to provide its members with an equal opportunity, on a prepaid basis, to contract for certain prescribed optional health services, known as supplemental services, if the HMO found it feasible to make such services available.[6] HMOs have several variations:

- A *staff HMO* provides services through physicians who receive salaries from the HMO. In some cases physicians may receive incentive payments in addition to a salary. Services are provided in a clinic setting with the number of service outlets dependent upon number of enrollees and their area of disbursement.
- The *individual practice association* is sponsored by the state or county medical association. Enrollees pay monthly premiums to the HMO which contracts with physicians to provide services on a fee-for-service basis.
- *Network (direct contract) model*: A network model HMO contracts directly with two or more independent (single or multispecialty) group practices to provide services, rather than work through an intermediary, and pays a fixed monthly fee per enrollee. The group decides how fees will be distributed to individual physicians.
- A *group practice* is an HMO which contracts with a medical group, partnership, or corporation composed of health professionals to provide health services. All physicians are usually located in one facility and are paid a salary or are remunerated on the basis of the number of persons for whom they are responsible.[7]

In the previous enumeration, the individual practice association would be thought of as an open panel of physicians engaged in group practice. The physicians retain their own existing fee-for-service practices and individual private offices. They agree to provide prepaid health care to HMO members in much the same manner they deliver services to their other patients who are covered by Blue Cross/Blue Shield or commercial health insurance. Such is the conceptual nature of the HMO.

Evolution of HMOs

In terms of history, great controversy has accompanied the development of prepaid group practice in this country since the 1920s. Medical society opposition on local and national levels often led to bitter litigation. These lawsuits involved whether physicians with closed panel groups had the rights of membership in medical societies and the rights-of-hospital privileges. Yet, despite these obstacles, a number of plans have survived and the concept of prepaid group practice received renewed impetus, as already noted, with the passage of the Health Maintenance Organization Act of 1973.

For purposes of discussion, again, two kinds of group practices must be delineated. Some groups are primarily made up of specialists and act as referral centers. Examples of such groups include the Mayo Clinic of Rochester, Minnesota, and the Lahey Clinic of Boston. In the other category, groups include a substantial number of personal physicians and provide not only a referral service but also comprehensive care for the patient or for the patient and family. In addition, such group practices may be organized as prepayment plans to which the patient and/or family is a subscribing member. Examples of the latter organization are the Group Health Cooperative of Puget Sound in the state of Washington and the Health Insurance Plan of Greater New York.

Many pressures have contributed to the expansion of prepaid group practice. According to W.P. Dearing, former director of the Group Health Association of America (now renamed America's Health Insurance Plans), the educated desire for more health services, together with the economic capability of purchasing more services, has been accompanied by a demand for efficiency and quality control of the more costly product. Not only are consumers, like individuals and as groups such as labor unions, demanding more and more comprehensive care with quality controls, but also business management is increasingly demanding efficiency, quality, and cost controls.[8] Prepaid group practice is becoming widely recognized as an effective means of accomplishing these goals.

These attitudes have taken a long time to develop, for the very early era of group practice plans predates the large-scale growth of voluntary health insurance. Most of the early attempts at group practice came from the labor unions and industrial organizations as the only viable means of bringing a minimum of health services to workers. Typical industrial developments include the early health service programs of the railroad, lumbering, and mining industries while medical centers of the International Ladies Garment Workers Union were large-scale prototypes in this field. But these programs were not financed very well. They never really succeeded in developing the kind of popularity and appeal which voluntary health insurance has had since the end of World War II.[8] Yet, despite their lack of universal appeal, these organizations did develop excellent reputations as being providers of high-quality care through an organized system. They emphasized ambulatory care and preventive service, as opposed to the private health insurance system, which stresses inpatient hospital care rather than outpatient preventive care treatments: HMO members are hospitalized at a rate of 30–40% less than non-HMO members.[9] As already noted, the preventive care emphasis of HMOs allows an illness to be detected early in its more curable stages, thus reducing the need for hospital care. Because of this mode of operation, the evidence indicates that HMO-type systems significantly lessen the cost of care without lowering its quality. Through a combination of management and provider incentives, HMOs can reduce costs below unmanaged fee-for-service by about 20% and below managed fee-for-service by about one-half that amount.[9]

There are various reasons why many prepaid group practice plans did not succeed since their beginnings in the 1920s. Some people have perceived these organizations as being impersonal, inconvenient, and involving long waiting periods prior to the delivery of health services. Others felt that there was a clinic or charity atmosphere in the health care facilities. In addition, it was difficult to get doctors interested in practicing in these plans. Many did not wish to practice in a prepaid group practice setting. Even today these problems remain and continue to impede the development of HMOs in this country. Yet, various studies have shown that the operation of a prepaid group practice system in this country reduces the number of days of inpatient hospital care by as much as 50%, while its members receive more outpatient and preventive care services than in the traditional fee-for-service system.[10] Thus, despite some negative impressions, the evidence has pointed to the fact that the HMO-type system significantly lessens the cost of treatment without lowering its quality.

Consequently, when health care costs began to increase dramatically in the period following the implementation of Medicare and Medicaid in the mid-1960s through the 1970s, a reexamination of the health care system seemed urgent. The Nixon administration conducted such a study. In the course of analyzing the system, the administration considered HMOs as one way to control spiraling health care costs.

After studying the concept thoroughly, the administration decided to promote HMOs as a major federal initiative. Thus, a series of bills was

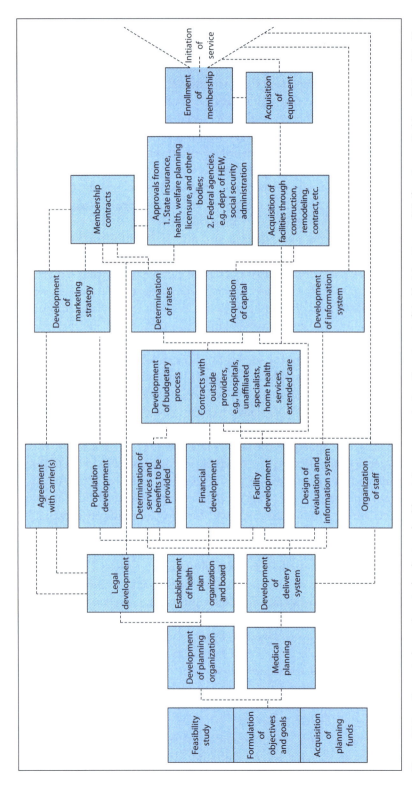

Figure 12.1 Suggested procedures in developing a health maintenance organization. Department of Health, Education, and Welfare. Source: *Building a National Health-Care System*. New York, NY: Committee for Economic Development, 1973:54–55. Reprinted with permission of Committee for Economic Development, New York, NY.

introduced into Congress in the early 1970s – one by the Nixon administration, another by Senator Edward M. Kennedy (D-MA) and still another by Congressman William R. Roy (D-KS). Public hearings were held on the bills and discussions took place with various elements of the health care industry. Legislative language was revised, compromises achieved, and finally, in the late fall of 1973, Congress passed the Health Maintenance Organization bill and President Nixon signed the bill into law (PL 93-220) in December of that year.

Managed care today, especially HMOs, continues to be one of the country's most important responses to escalating health care costs. In addition to private-sector enrollment, government programs such as Medicare and Medicaid also began enrolling their members in HMOs. By January 1998 the majority of HMOs were using a variety of measures to control health care costs: home health care, preventive care, and preferred provider negotiations (Figure 12.1). Other cost control measures include risk management programs, durable medical equipment monitoring, retrospective review admissions, discharge planning, and the usual inpatient and outpatient utilization review.

Health Maintenance Organization Act of 1973

In order to understand the broad appeal of HMOs to the public, especially employers who wish to cut their medical bills, a brief description of the law is necessary. The law contains several sections which allow the American public to have serious choices about the way they wish to receive their health care services in future years. One section stipulates that every employer, subject to section six of the Fair Labor Standards Act, who employs 25 or more persons to whom a health benefit plan is offered, must, under certain specified circumstances, offer those employees the option of membership in a qualified HMO. Another section supersedes certain restrictive provisions in state laws which would have prevented the operation of otherwise qualified HMOs. Another section of the Act defines an HMO in terms of the services which it must provide and the manner in which the HMO must be organized and operated.[6]

Then, the HMO Amendments of 1976 (PL 94-460) were signed into law on October 8, 1976. The new legislation corrected several aspects of the 1973 law which made the certification of HMOs a difficult problem. In order to qualify as an HMO under the 1973 Act, an organization has to provide its members with the following set of basic benefits without limitation as to time and cost: physician services, including consultation and referral; outpatient services; inpatient hospital services; medically necessary emergency services; short-term outpatient evaluative and crisis intervention mental health care services; diagnostic laboratory and diagnostic and therapeutic radiological services; home health services and preventive services, including voluntary family planning services, infertility services, preventive dental care for children and eye refractions for children; and medical treatment and referral services for abuse of or addiction to alcohol and drugs.[10]

The 1973 law required that, in addition to the offering of basic benefits, an HMO provide certain supplemental benefits if the HMO had the manpower to do so and if its members wished to purchase such services. The supplemental benefits include the services of intermediate and long-term care facilities; vision, dental, and mental health care; long-term rehabilitative services; and prescription drugs. The payment for basic health services is on a community-rated basis, that is, everyone, regardless of individual health status, pays the same premium rate. The cost of the premium payments is different in one respect. A single person pays a higher but uniform rate. In this fashion community rating spreads the cost of illness evenly over all HMO members rather than charging the sick more than the healthy for health insurance coverage. On the other hand, an HMO could provide supplemental services on both a community-rated and fee-for-service basis. In addition, the 1973 law allows an HMO member to make a copayment as long as this cost sharing does not prevent an individual from receiving health services. A copayment means that the insured patient pays a fixed amount for a unit of service, such as $15 for a doctor's visit or for a unit of time, such as $30 per day in a hospital, and the insurer pays the remaining amount.

As far as federally qualified HMO organizations and operations are concerned, the HMO must:

- show fiscal soundness and provide safeguards
- take full financial risk with only limited reinsurance
- enroll persons broadly representative of the service area
- provide for open enrollment periods
- not expel any member because of health status
- have a policy-making body, of which at least one-third consists of members of the HMO
- provide meaningful hearings and grievance procedures
- show that it has satisfactory quality assurance arrangements
- provide medical social services and health education to its members
- provide continuing education for its health professionals
- report to the Secretary of Health Education, and Welfare (HEW, now renamed the US Department of Health and Human Services (DHHS)), to the public, and to its members data relative to the cost and utilization of its services.[10]

There are many HMOs operating in the country that provide comprehensive care services and which have not received federal qualification.
The difference between a federally qualified HMO and one that has not
been so certified is that the qualified HMO must meet standards mandated by federal law. The nonqualified HMOs determine their own requirements and, for reasons of their own, have not chosen to obtain federal
qualifications.[11]

While some harbor negative feelings for HMOs as a conceptual and operational entity, many do not find their services inferior to the traditional fee-for
service system of medicine. Certain aspects of HMOs still have appeal for
potential enrollees, including: one-stop medical care when services are available for all family members and for all conditions; 24-hour service; convenient
location; more benefits, including preventive care services for the same
money; a physician who is the total health manager; and a physician who is
backed up by a range of specialists.[12] Prospective members view the HMO as
the kind of organization where it is easy to receive the care they need, when
and where they need it. Patients enrolled in an HMO know their entry point
into the health system – they do not have to seek out a specialist or worry
where to go after hours or on a weekend. The HMO provides full-time
coverage and arranges necessary referrals. From the HMO's viewpoint this
situation makes its own planning more efficient. At the beginning of the year
the HMO can estimate the number of patients to whom it will be delivering
care and, accordingly, can arrange for hospital beds and specialists. At the
other end, the consumer knows in advance the total cost of the HMO's
services.

On the other hand, HMOs also have their critics. In terms of its disadvantages, critics state that in an HMO patients cannot choose their own
doctor, can only see those doctors who belong to the group, and the HMOs
may encourage physicians to see the patient as little as possible. This is
because physicians are paid an established annual fee no matter how many
appointments the patient makes, so the fewer appointments the patient
makes with a physician, the less the physician works on the patient's behalf
and keeps his/her expenses to minimum, so that the HMO's revenues exceed
its expenses. Other criticisms include inconvenient location; impersonal
attention is given to the patient; long waiting periods before delivery of
services; patients must sever relationships with their private physician if
the doctor is not a member of the HMO; hospitals affiliated with the
HMO do not have the best reputation; patients must terminate their private
health insurance policy; and HMOs do not always save the employer money
because they do not have enough patients to reduce costs over traditional
fee-for-service medicine. However, each of these attributes, positive or negative, must be examined in terms of each specific HMO. Each HMO is

different and should be judged upon its individual merits and demerits in terms of a patient's personal health needs.

Other forms of managed care

However, HMOs are not the only forms of managed care in the USA. Beginning in the early 1980s new forms of managed care appeared in the USA, aside from HMOs. Two such organizations are PPOs and POS.

Preferred provider organizations

The general difference between an HMO and a PPO is that the HMO contracts with or employs a group or groups of doctors, hospitals, and other health care providers in a limited number of locations to deliver services to member patients under a fixed premium rate. A PPO is a health plan that negotiates with providers of care to give the purchasers of care lower rates if their member patients use doctors from a selected list. However, it is important to examine such organizations in more detail. In more specific terms, there are several other important differences between a PPO and an HMO.

As already noted, a PPO is a group of doctors and/or hospitals that provides medical care only to a specific group or association. The PPO may be sponsored by an insurance company, by one or more employers, or by some other kind of organization. The PPO physicians provide medical services to the policyholders, employees, or members of the sponsor(s) at discounted rates and may set up utilization control programs to help reduce the cost of medical care. In return, a sponsor(s) attempts to increase a provider's patient volume by creating an incentive for employees or policyholders to use the physicians and facilities within the PPO network.

Rather than prepaying for medical care, PPO members pay for services as they are provided. The PPO sponsor (employer or insurance) generally reimburses the PPO member for the cost of treatment, less any copayment percentage. The physician also may submit the bill directly to the insurance company for payment. The insurer then pays the covered amount directly to the health care provider and members pay their copayment amount. The price of each type of service is negotiated in advance by the health care providers and the sponsor(s).

The advantages of PPOs compared to HMOs are that PPO members are not required to seek care from PPO physicians. However, they generally have strong incentives to do so. For example, members may receive 90% reimbursement for care obtained from network physicians but only 60% for nonnetwork treatment. In order to avoid paying an additional 30% out of their own pocket, most members choose to receive their health care within the PPO network. Thus, if the patient's long-time physician is outside the PPO network, the patient may choose to continue seeing the physician, but it will cost the patient more.

The disadvantages of PPOs is that there is less coverage for treatment provided by a non-PPO physician. In addition, as a PPO member, patients may have to fill out paperwork in order to be reimbursed for their medical treatment. Also, most PPOs have larger copayments than HMOs and the patient may be required to pay a deductible.

Point of service plans

Another form of managed care, aside from HMOs and PPOs, is a POS plan. POS is a type of managed health care system that has the characteristics of a PPO and HMO. Like an HMO, the patient does not pay any deductible and usually only a minimal copayment when the patient uses a health care provider within the network. The patient must choose a primary care physician who is responsible for referrals within the POS network. If the patient chooses to go outside the network for health care, POS coverage functions more like a PPO. The patient will likely be subject to a deductible and a higher deductible for a family. And the patient's copayment will be a substantial percentage of the physician's charges (usually up to about 40%).

POS coverage has the advantage of allowing the patient freedom of choice. Like a PPO, a POS has a mix of the kinds of care patients and their family can receive. For example, a child could continue to use a pediatrician who is not in the network, while the rest of the family receives the rest of their care from network providers. The freedom of choice encourages the patient to use network providers but does not require it, as with HMO coverage.

As with HMO coverage, the patient pays only a nominal amount for network care. For example, as an illustration the payment could be about $15 per treatment or office visit. Unlike HMO coverage, however, the patient always retains the right to seek care outside the network at another level of care.

Generally, there is no deductible when a patient chooses to use network providers. Coverage begins from the first dollar the patient spends as long as the patient stays within the network of physicians.

There is also no gatekeeper, as in a HMO, for nonnetwork care. If patients choose to go outside the POS network for treatment, they are free to visit any doctor or specialist they choose without first consulting their primary care physician. Of course, the patient will pay substantially more out-of-pocket charges for nonnetwork care.

The disadvantage of a POS plan is that there is a substantial copayment for nonnetwork care. As in a PPO, there is generally a strong financial incentive to use POS network physicians. For example, a patient's copayment may only be $15 for care obtained from network physicians, but, as already noted, the patient could be responsible for up to 40% of the cost of treatment provided by nonnetwork doctors. Thus, if a patient's long-term family care is provided outside the POS network, the patient may choose to continue seeing the physician, but it can cost the patient more.

In most cases, a patient must reach a specified deductible before coverage begins for out-of-network care in addition to any copayments the patient must make for any copayment care.

The POS also administers tight controls to receive specialized care. As in a HMO, the patient must select a primary care physician. The primary care physician provides general medical care and must be consulted before the patient seeks care from another doctor or specialist within the network. However, the screening process can also lead to complications if the primary care physician does not provide the referral the patient needs.

Prescription drug coverage

One of the benefits that HMOs and POS provide is prescription drug coverage. In 2002 the trade association, America's Health Insurance Plans, surveyed its members regarding a variety of services, one of which concerned prescription drugs.[13] There were 194 plans eligible to participate in the survey and they provided information on nearly 50 million covered individuals – 64% of the total HMO/POS enrollment. The following is a profile of the prescription drug benefit which they provided. The percentage of enrollees in HMO/POS plans that:

- cover prescription drugs: 99%
- manage the prescription drug benefit in-house: 56%
- manage the prescription drug benefit through a vendor: 43%
- offer a mail-order pharmacy service: 96%
- have a drug utilization program: 99%
- cover the following drugs in formulary:
  - protease inhibitor drugs: 92%
  - alcohol dependency drugs: 80%
  - chemical dependency drugs: 54%
- report the top three classes of drugs prescribed based on total health plan expenditures (weighted by plan enrollment):
  - cardiovascular/renal drug class: 81%
  - central nervous system drug class: 75%
  - gastrointestinal drug class: 68%
- report the top three classes of drugs based on the number of prescriptions (weighted by plan enrollment):
  - cardiovascular/renal drug class: 79%
  - central nervous system drug class: 52%
  - hormone drug class: 31%.

In addition, as of December 31, 2001 the HMO/POS plans had the following characteristics:

* The average (mean) number of commercial HMO/POS enrollees per health insurance plan was 161 186, while the average number of Medicaid HMO enrollees was 93 698 and the average number of Medicare HMO enrollees was 58 822.
* Among responding companies, the independent practice association was the predominant HMO/POS model type (74.9% of enrolled).
* The majority of respondents (61.9%) were affiliated with a national or regional health insurance plan (other than Blue Cross/Blue Shield).
* The vast majority of responding health insurance plans were for-profit and publicly held (71.1%), with the remainder either nonprofit (18.0%) or for-profit and privately held (10.8%).[13]

Impact on the pharmaceutical industry

Managed care, especially HMOs, has had many ripple effects throughout the health care industry. As examples, it has affected the manner in which the physician practices medicine and the way some want to practice it. It has affected the profit margins of American businesses. It has affected patients' perception of the US health care delivery system, their perception of the way medicine is practiced, and how they wish it might be practiced. As another example, it has affected the pharmaceutical industry. As an illustration of the impact of managed care today, let us briefly examine how it has affected this important segment of the health care system.

Since HMOs have become an integral part of the health care system in the 21st century, past evidence has indicated that these plans provide a prescription dispensing service at a lower cost than the community retail pharmacy, and the pharmaceutical manufacturer will be directly affected by any potential HMO–retail pharmacy competition. At the time of the enactment of the HMO Act of 1973, the current author, Jordan Braverman, in his study *Pharmaceutical Payment Plans: An Overview*, laid out the following scenario.[14] Although it may be commonplace to think of an HMO in terms of a single physical health care institution, this is not always the situation. In fact, at the time HMOs were without any specific organizational definition, and, hence, could assume many guises. An HMO may indeed be a single physical structure but also may operate as a group of hospitals that have integrated their services with each other. Or it may be a hospital with satellite clinics that has, as one criterion for enrollment, the requirement that HMO members reside within a given number of miles or minutes from the HMO center, as was true of Harvard University Community Health Plan at that time.

HMOs may also be a group practice 'without walls.' This concept is amenable in terms of operation to rural areas where a single physical institution is not convenient in terms of transportation for a scattered and low-density population. In many of our rural and western states physicians throughout such relevant areas would still conduct their practices out of their private offices, rather than being grouped together in a single institution in a specific community, and would provide care to those patients who may wish to prepay for a given set of health care services. In addition, the physicians as a group might contract for the services of their local pharmacies to effect an integration of medical and pharmaceutical services without causing the geographic relocation of either professional practitioner from his or her community. Similarly, HMOs within an urban area might contract with local pharmacies or elect to develop their own in-house pharmacy if they believe it to be more efficient in terms of administration and economics.

Consequently, *Pharmaceutical Payments Plans: An Overview* noted in 1973 that pharmaceutical manufacturers will be confronted in the future with a heterogeneous rather than a monolithic health care delivery system.[14] In some instances, the marketing strategy of the manufacturer may be concentrated on a mix of institutions within a given geographical area such as community hospitals and nursing homes existing side by side with HMOs that serve a given subscriber population, optimally estimated at that time at 20 000–30 000 persons. The HMO may purchase its pharmaceuticals on an individual basis if it is a single institution maintaining its own in-house pharmacy or on a group-purchasing and centralized basis if the HMO consists of a central health care institution with satellite clinics or health centers. As a result of this institutional mix, the marketing of pharmaceuticals will become more intensive than at present among manufacturers since they may have to concentrate their sales on a smaller group of health care institutions compared to today's number. This will be especially true if HMOs successfully compete with the community pharmacy in developing pharmaceutical services at lower costs. In turn, if the number of community pharmacies declines over time and HMOs adopt a formulary system that follows the operational guidelines of today's hospital formularies, allowing brand–generic name substitution of a prescription drug, a narrowing of price ranges among drug products competing to get on the HMO formulary could result. In addition, more intensive detailing of HMOs is likely to occur so as to educate the HMOs on the relative quality and efficacy of one drug product versus that of another, especially if the HMO engages in centralized purchasing for the health care institutions with which it is associated.[14]

A few years earlier, in the late 1960s the National Association of Retail Druggists (NARD) issued its own dire predictions regarding community pharmacies and manufacturers. Looking at the Group Health Cooperative of Puget Sound, a prepaid group practice plan, where the cost per enrollee was about 45% less than the average per-capita costs of prescription drugs in the USA, the NARD wrote:[15]

The Group Health Cooperative of Puget Sound provides services for 95 000 persons in the Seattle area. If costs similar to the group health level could be achieved for most of the population ... it would require about 2105 such group health plans for the entire 200 million civilian population. At four pharmacies for each health group, only 8420 pharmacies would be needed to serve all the prescription needs in the country instead of the approximately 52 000 currently operating. This could mean the discontinuance of about 43 500 pharmacies ... This squeeze would not only affect pharmacists and the community pharmacy segment of US business but manufacturers as well who would still be producing and selling the same volume and would be selling competitively in bulk and by generic name. The total dollar volume of sales and the profit margin would be substantially reduced, but production costs would not be proportionately reduced. Profits would be less and even a loss could result.[16]

These were the predictions that were being put forth by the late 1960s and early 1970s. So, what has happened since that time to the pharmaceutical industry? During the 1990s more than 11 000 independent pharmacies went out of business. Managed care was probably not the only reason for their numerical decline but it certainly has to be considered at least as one of the elements. By 2001, independent pharmacies numbered about 25 000 and accounted for 4% of the retail prescription market. While the decline of independent pharmacies began to reverse itself by the beginning of the 21st century, it was due to the increase of prescription sales. Spurred on by an aging population and array of new drugs, prescriptions were expected to rise from 2.7 billion in 1999 to 3.7 billion in 2004. Prescriptions represent about 83% of average independent revenue, compared to only half of the income of chain drug stores like Walgreens or CVS Caremark, which depend more heavily on the sales of convenient items. Another factor is that many independent pharmacists have developed successful health care specialties. Some, for example, serve as nursing home consultants or make house calls to patients with specific illnesses or needs such as human immunodeficiency virus (HIV)/acquired immunodeficiency syndrome (AIDs) or intravenous drug infusions. Others still offer compounding, a method of combining different drugs in custom doses and forms. All of these specialties are very labor-intensive and uniquely oriented to the local market for chain pharmacies to be concerned with.

Purchasing cooperatives have also helped independents. Most locally owned pharmacies have now joined one of about 30 local and regional purchasing groups which negotiate with drug manufacturers for volume discounts. Although pharmacy buying groups have been in existence since the 1980s, they are now more important than ever. HMOs have dramatically lowered the reimbursement rates for pharmacies. On most drugs, pharmacists net extremely thin margins and the added cost savings that purchasing co-operatives provide have become especially critical. Some buying groups are now operating as third-party networks, which negotiate with large employers to provide pharmacy benefits through their network of stores in much the same way as major chain stores.

The biggest threat facing independent pharmacies is not so much the chain stores as much as it is mail-order companies. In 2000 mail-order companies captured about 15% of prescription spending and 96% of the HMOs offer a mail-order service. In addition, pharmacy benefit management (PBM) companies, which contract with HMOs to provide pharmacy benefits, often create economic incentives to shift consumers to purchase from mail-order companies. They may, for example, require a substantially smaller copayment if the consumer purchases by mail rather than through a retail store. As motivation, the three top PBMs, which covered two-thirds of all insured Americans, own their own mail-order companies.[17]

But the changes have not only occurred in regard to pharmacies. Pharmaceutical manufacturers have also been affected by the development of managed care since the 1970s. Historically, pharmaceutical companies have operated in a relatively stable and certain environment that was characterized by good profits, little (if any) pressure to change the way they price their products, and large barriers to entry.[18] These barriers included patent-protected drugs, research and development programs that required a great deal of money and time to bring new drugs into the marketplace, and the ability of their large sales forces and expensive marketing campaigns to deter new companies from entering the market as additional competitors.[18] In addition, there was little product overlap across manufacturers, which divided the market by therapeutic class of drug. There was not a great deal of price pressure from buyers. Physicians were generally not cognizant of the prices of the drugs they prescribed. In addition, insurers and employers began offering benefit packages that covered prescription drugs, so that individuals generally didn't shop for the lowest-priced drug. Even when out-of-pocket payments were built into insurance coverage, many persons did not look for less expensive sources for their prescription drug purchases other than at their local pharmacy.

However during the late 1980s and early 1990s three factors began to erode the profitably of the industry: the growth of managed care and managed pharmacy benefits; the emergence of firms named PBMs that administered benefit programs for employers; and development of mail-order pharmacies.[18] Managed care in the drug industry has generally concentrated on the monitoring of the utilization of prescription drugs. Managed care firms created information systems whose purpose was to track the prescribing patterns of physicians and pharmacists and the utilization of prescription drugs by patients. In addition, restrictive formularies were designed that had the impact of increasing the awareness of physicians and pharmacists about the actual costs of drugs.

PBMs, as a separate organizational structure, emerged in the late 1980s and early 1990s and represent one form of managed care in the drug industry. They specialize in managing prescription drug benefits for employers and for other managed care organizations by employing mechanisms that verify subscriber/employee eligibility for benefits, process claims, and manage communications with retail pharmacies. The services they offer can include: claims processing, prescription education for users and physicians, concurrent and retrospective utilization review, formulary review/management, monitoring of physician prescribing patterns, mail-order drug plans, assistance with retail pharmacy networks, and consulting services regarding the design of pharmacy benefit plans.[18] The PBMs may be owned by drug manufacturers, or some form of managed care or insurance company, chain or retail pharmacies, by various types of other enterprises, or be independent. They offer three core information reporting mechanisms: prescribing patterns/physician profiling, generic versus brand-name utilization, and patient/employee utilization reports. They also offer employers a mix of reimbursement methods, including fee/claim, volume discounts, negotiated rates, and capitated rates.

Also, during the late 1980s and early 1990s, mail-order pharmacies began to develop. Pharmaceutical experts expect mail-order pharmacies to continue to grow as copayments and other incentives motivate patients to use their services. Experts believe that it is possible that the ability of mail-order pharmacies to centralize operations and achieve economy of scale might result in a great reduction of community pharmacy practice. These organizations have tended to serve specific groups such as the elderly, who needed to have prescriptions refilled regularly. As a result of these various movements, as well as federal legislation, such as the Waxman–Hatch Act of 1984 that simplified the requirement of approval of generic drugs by the Food and Drug Administration and made it easier for generic drugs to enter the marketplace at a lower price than brand-name drugs, pharmaceutical firms began to experience a decline in profits, failed to secure needed resources, that is, customers, and began operating in a turbulent and uncertain environment. One way they began to counter this situation, and to gain some kind of operational stability, was to merge not only with PBMs but also with other pharmaceutical companies and a consolidation of the field followed. As examples, the British firm Zeneca merged with Swedish firm Astra to become Astra-Zeneca. Pharmacia, a Swedish firm that merged with US-based Upjohn, bought out Monsanto, another US company which is not only a drug manufacturer but also makes genetically modified seed. In 1989 SmithKline, a US firm, merged with Beecham, one of the oldest UK drug companies, to become SmithKline Beecham, while Glaxo Laboratories merged with Burroughs Wellcome to become Glaxo Wellcome in 1995; they, in turn, eventually merged to become GlaxoSmithKline, said to be the largest drug company in the world and the largest in the UK. Meanwhile Pfizer merged with Warner Lambert in 2000 and the consolidation within the drug industry continued.

These mergers have also occurred because the development and marketing of drugs has become a very expensive business experience. Health services throughout the world are demanding that drug companies reduce their prices and supply them with the cheapest pharmaceuticals. It is now a common scenario for the UK National Health Service to refuse to prescribe a drug because it is too expensive. Rising research and development costs have meant that drug companies have been unable to 'go it alone' and have had to use the expertise and resources of other drug companies in order to survive in a very competitive market.

PBMs have also become very important in fostering the growth of managed care in the pharmaceutical industry. By merging with pharmaceutical companies they may gain more bargaining power with employers as they unite pharmaceuticals with insurance services.[19] This feature could make them more appealing to managed care organizations, hospitals, and employers who may more likely enter into contracts with them. On the other hand, pharmaceutical manufacturers also benefit. First, PBMs collect data on physicians' and pharmacists' prescribing patterns as well as the utilization of drugs by patients. These data can be used to develop information about drug effectiveness, which, in turn, can be used to market drugs to physicians who prescribe drugs. Second, PBMs can promote the parent/manufacturer's comparable products that are sold at competitive prices, thereby expanding the parent's customer bases.[18] Finally, PBMs provide drug manufacturers with an opportunity to engage in product development that they might not otherwise have done. For example, PBMs can develop new approaches to risk-sharing such as capitation and disease management programs. Through approaches such as disease management, information about the characteristics of individuals who require specific pharmacologic intervention can be learned. The PBM could then use this information to create new marketing strategies for its parent's products.

For its part, the drug manufacturer can market its drug more efficiently, such as by using a smaller sales force. When Merck and Medco Containment Services merged in 1994, the Federal Trade Commission became concerned about the integration and merger of PBMs with pharmaceutical manufacturers and required the merged firms to institute two structural changes. First, they required that PBMs which merge with drug manufacturers keep their formularies open to other drug manufacturers' products. In addition, the Federal Trade Commission required PBMs which obtain price information from manufacturers in the course of administering pharmacy benefits plans keep that information separate from their parent/drug manufacturer's information database.[18] This was designed to prohibit a parent/manufacturer from obtaining information on competitors' bids for pharmacy contracts. Thus, while mergers have occurred in the drug industry for a variety of reasons and have certain advantages when drug manufacturers merge with PBMs or other drug manufacturers, the major concern still remains whether the mergers will result in levels of market concentration that will ultimately reduce competition in the industry and raise the price of their products for consumers.

Conclusion

Managed care is an excellent example that illustrates that, even though the health care field is composed of distinct industries such as hospitals, nursing homes, home care, pharmaceuticals and others, that seem like self-contained industries unto themselves wholly and separately apart from others and from the events occurring in these other industries, they are truly interlocked with each other. In the late 1920s the Kaiser Foundation Health Plan was established to help people obtain as many health care services as possible for one fee rather than pay separate fees for each service so they could maintain their health in as best a state as possible before the illness became worse. In this fashion, they would not have to worry whether they could afford to pay for one service relative to another, each with a separate fee when the services were required and received. Over 80 years later, the prepaid group practice plans of the 1920s, now renamed as managed care, are seeking to achieve the same goals, yet its influence has spilled into other fields like the pharmaceutical industry. It has contributed to many independent retail pharmacies going out of business. It has also helped create mergers among many independent drug manufacturing companies, as their numbers shrink and their size becomes larger as they feel the effects of this managed care concept on their bottom line in terms of profitability and as they seek to maintain their economic viability within turbulent and uncertain times as the health care industry continues to evolve into an uncertain future. John Donne once wrote: 'no man is an island entire of itself; every man is a piece of the continent, a part of the main.' The same is true in the health care industry. What happens in one segment of the health care field will eventually have repercussions on other aspects of the industry and that is why it is important to understand the health care field in general, as well as the specific roles of the various industries within it, such as hospitals, nursing homes, managed care, and other various groups, because each industry does impact on others in ways that no one can foresee.

References

1. *The Interstudy Competitive Edge, Part II: Managed Care Industry Report.* Table 15 March 2007; available online at: www. healthleaders-interstudy.com; as cited on the Kaiser Family's www.statehealthfacts.org; accessed on May 15, 2008.

 2. The biggest HMO advocate backs off prepayment. *Med Economics* 1976; August 9: 29–30.
 3. *The Fundamentals of Managed Care*. Washington, DC: Health Insurance Association of America, 1991: 9.
 4. American Public Health Association. *A Guide to Medical Care Administration: Concepts and Principles*. Appendix II: 81.
 5. Universal 'group practice' prepayment plans – a clarification and economic implications. *J Natl Assoc Retail Druggists* 1969; May 19: 21.
 6. US Senate Committee on Labor and Public Welfare. Health Maintenance Organization Act of 1973, S. 14. Washington DC: Subcommittee on Health, February 1974 (explanation of Act and text of Public Law 93–222): 1.
 7. Judge M. HMOs stimulate competition; bring hospitalization rates down. *Forum* 1977; September–October: 3.
 8. Braverman J. Group practice prepayment plans – universities give new impetus to old concept. *J Am Pharm Assoc* 1969; November: 564–565.
 9. Wallack S S. Managed care: practice, pitfalls, and potential. *Health Care Financ Rev* 1991; suppl.: 28.
10. Seubold F H. HMOs – the view from the program. *Publ Hlth Rep* 1975; March–April: 99, 102.
11. Porter S. Health maintenance organizations groups gain support. *Washington Star* 1978; December 26.
12. Galiher C B, Costa M A. Common acceptance of HMOs. *Publ Hlth Rep* 1975; March–April: 108.
13. *2002 AHIP Survey of Health Insurance Plans: Chartbook of Findings*. Washington, DC: America's Health Insurance Plans, 2004.
14. Braverman J. *Pharmaceutical Payment Plans: An Overview*. Washington, DC: Pharmaceutical Manufacturers Association, 1973: 61.
15. McCaffree K M, Newman H F. Prepayment of drug costs under a group practice prepayment plan. *Am J Publ Hlth* 1968; 58: 1215.
16. Universal 'group practice' prepayment health plans – a clarification and economic implication. *J Natl Assoc Retail Druggists* 1969; May 10: 21.
17. Independent pharmacies on rebound. In: *The Hometown Advantage*. Washington, DC: Institute for Local Self-Reliance, 2001: 1–3; available online at: The New Rules Project: www. newrules.org; accessed on May 24, 2008.
18. McGahan A M. Industry structure and competitive advantage. *Harvard Bus Rev* 1994; November–December: 115–124.
19. Kihistrom L K. *Mergers and Alliances*. Richmond, CA: Institute for the Study of Healthcare Organizations and Transactions, 2000.

13

Medicaid and Medicare

Introduction

The concept embodied in the Medicaid program, namely, that government is accountable for the medical care of the needy and medically indigent, can be traced as far back as the colonial period when common law established that the care of the poor, including the provision of medical care, was essentially a function of local government. Common law held that no government should permit its citizens to die from starvation, sickness, or exposure just because they were poor and, generally, assigned the responsibility of relief for the poor to the smallest political unit, whether it was the village, town, city parish, or county. When America became an independent nation, this idea was included in its state constitutions and statutes.

In the 19th century, state government gradually began to assume some administrative responsibilities for aiding the impoverished and began to provide care, based on need, to certain groups of the poor who, until then, had only been the responsibility of local government. Thus began government assistance that was based on a category of need. It was not only humanitarian motives that inspired this activity but also the very high costs of providing special care to only a few persons in any one special category in a single locality. These categories generally embraced the sick, the deaf, and insane.

The division of responsibility between state and local government essentially continued until the 1930s. State and local governmental responsibility for the medical care of the poor was undertaken either by public institutions which employed salaried physicians or by purchasing medical care from private physicians. In most of the larger local jurisdictions, however, city or county hospitals usually delivered such medical services. In addition, a large number of physicians and voluntary hospitals provided the indigent with free services or reduced-payment care.

As far as Medicare is concerned, the idea of a government-sponsored health insurance plan can be tracked as far back as the early 1900s when interest developed in creating a national compulsory health insurance program in the country. In fact, Theodore Roosevelt's Progressive 'Bull Moose' Party platform in 1912 advocated such a concept as one of the political planks of its party platform. In the 1930s the government renewed its interest in the subject when President Roosevelt appointed a committee to explore the issue of government health insurance. Although the committee eventually recommended health insurance legislation in 1935, President Roosevelt did not include any such proposal in the Social Security Act. The president and some members of the committee believed that the inclusion of such legislation would harm the prompt passage of the social security legislation with its other extremely important provisions of old-age and unemployment insurance.

The Social Security Act of 1935 created a categorical public assistance system in which the federal government shared with the states the expense of providing maintenance to the aged who were needy, blind, families with dependent children, and, subsequently, the permanently and totally disabled. The Social Security Act did not incorporate any special provision for medical assistance, but it included the cost of medical care in the individual's monthly assistance payment for which federal participation was available. Without any limitations on how to spend their payments, many welfare recipients ignored their personal medical care – often because states set the payment so low that it was not enough even to pay for basic food and shelter. This situation continued until the 1950s when congressional legislative action attempted to correct it. Beginning in 1950, Congress passed a series of amendments to the Social Security Act that expanded the definition of public assistance to include money for 'vendor payments' – that is, states directly paid physicians, nurses, and health care institutions, rather than send the payment to the welfare recipients themselves.

This change established an administrative framework for a welfare medical program. By 1958 the federal government was sharing not only in cash payments but also in a separate category of medical payments to those who met a state's definition of being 'needy.' As of 1960 most of the states made vendor payments in federally aided categorical assistance programs, and many states, in determining their cash payments to welfare recipients, also allowed for the purchase of some items of medical care.[1] Despite this expanded federal and state effort, however, states could only finance a few services.

Efforts continued through the Kennedy and Johnson administrations during the early 1960s to improve the financing of medical care for the elderly and the poor through the social security system. Then, Congress enacted the Social Security Amendments of 1965. President Lyndon B. Johnson signed this new legislation into law on July 30, 1965, thereby adding two new titles to the Social Security Act – Title XVIII, known as the Medicare program, and Title XIX, known as Medicaid.

Medicaid

Medicaid and Medicare help many older Americans with their medical bills. Nearly all persons aged 65 years and older are eligible for Medicare, while needy, low-income elderly persons may also be eligible for Medicaid – a *public assistance program* financed by federal, state, and local governments. All states, as well as the District of Columbia, Puerto Rico, and the Virgin Islands, have Medicaid programs. Medicare is a federal government program that is the same all over the country. Medicaid is a federal–state partnership under which the program's benefits differ from state to state. Whether or not a low-income older person is enrolled in Medicare, that person may also qualify for Medicaid. For senior citizens not eligible for Medicare, Medicaid helps pay for a wide variety of hospital and other medical services. For elderly persons already enrolled in Medicare, Medicaid often pays for services not covered by Medicare, such as eye glasses and long-term nursing home care. Thus, Medicare and Medicaid are linked with each other. State governments can also buy into the hospital insurance plan of Medicare (Part A) for the medically needy by paying its coinsurance and deductible amounts as well as buy into the voluntary supplemental medical insurance of Medicare (Part B) by paying its monthly premium.

A state determines whether an individual or family is eligible for Medicaid according to the state's definition of need, within certain federal government limits. However, in general, low-income people in the following categories qualify for Medicaid coverage: the aged (65 years or older), the blind, the disabled, and families with dependent children.

In addition, some states provide coverage for other groups of low-income people who do not qualify for public assistance programs but still cannot pay for medical care. These people are known as the 'medical needy.'

In August 1996 President Clinton signed into law the Personal Responsibility and Work Opportunity Act of 1996 (PL 104-193), otherwise known as welfare reform. The welfare reform law continues Medicaid as an entitlement to families on welfare and continues to cover for 1 year people who leave welfare to go to work. However, the law does change Medicaid in one major aspect since it replaced the categorical program of Aid to Families with Dependent Children (AFDC) with the Temporary Assistance for Needy Families (TANF) program, effective July 1, 1997. In place of AFDC, states establish their own assistance programs, funded by annual federal payments, instead of open-ended federal funds they have received in the past. States can determine who is eligible and for how long, although federal benefits cannot be used to provide benefits for more than 5 years over a lifetime. The law reduces food stamps and supplementary security income (SSI) to legal immigrants who have not become citizens. SSI is a federally funded needs-based disability program for adults and children which provides monthly cash benefits, and in most states, automatic Medicaid eligibility. States must decide whether to continue Medicaid and cash payments to poor immigrant families.[2] On February 8, 2006, the president signed the Deficit Reduction Act of 2005 into law (PL 109-171). The new law is expected to push states to tighten work requirements for women on assistance under the TANF program.

Medicaid pays the full cost of covered services, which, as a minimum, include the following: inpatient hospital care; outpatient hospital services, prenatal care, physician services, other laboratory and X-ray services, family planning services, rural health clinic services, pediatric and family nurse practitioner services, home health care services for persons eligible for skilled nursing services, certain federally qualified ambulatory and health center services, services furnished by nurse midwives to the extent authorized by the state, skilled nursing facility services for persons over 21 years of age, and early periodic screening, diagnosis, and treatment services of children under age 21.

Also, in many states Medicaid pays for additional services such as dental care, prescribed drugs, intermediate care facility services, optometrist services and eyeglasses, clinic services, hearing aids, and prosthetic devices, as well as other diagnostic screening and rehabilitative services. As a result of the president signing the Deficit Reduction Act of 2005 (PL 109-171) into law on February 8, 2006, Medicaid is reducing payments for prescription drug benefits to combat inflated prescription drug markups and is requiring its recipients to pay new copayments and deductibles for expensive drugs and emergency room visits for nonemergency care. In addition, the Deficit Reduction Act of 2005 established a new mechanism for financing Medicaid called the health opportunity account which is being tested as a demonstration program from 2006 to 2011, in up to 10 states. These accounts would be similar to the health savings accounts that are attached to high-deductible health insurance plans, which were created with the passage of the Medicare Prescription Drug, Improvement, and Modernization Act of 2003. In general, once beneficiaries have met the deductible, Medicaid coverage would begin, and Medicaid recipients would be required to pay the regular copayments and other cost-sharing charges that Medicaid requires. States would contribute specified amounts for adults and children into these accounts with matching funds from the federal government in order to help Medicaid beneficiaries pay for the health care costs that they would incur before the Medicaid coverage begins. However, states would not be required to offset these Medicaid costs fully.

Medicare

Almost everyone who is 65 years or older can qualify for Medicare (exceptions: certain aliens and criminals, in addition to a few federal government workers for whom benefits are limited). In 1973 coverage for Medicare was extended to certain groups under age 65. These include those who have permanent kidney failure (renal disease) or who have qualified for social security disability benefits for at least 24 consecutive months or railroad retirement disability benefits for at least 29 consecutive months. Included are disabled workers and widows and widowers between 50 and 65 and people 18 and over who receive social security benefits because they became disabled before they reached 22 years of age.[3] Like Medicaid, the Centers for Medicare and Medicaid Services, an agency of the US Department of Health and Human Services, administers Medicare.

Medicare consists of four parts. *Part A* is the hospital insurance program that helps beneficiaries pay for medically necessary inpatient hospital care, and after a hospital stay, skilled nursing home care as an inpatient, as well as for care of a beneficiary at home by a home care agency. *Part B* is the voluntary medical insurance that pays for physicians' services and a whole array of other medical services. *Part C*, known as Medicare Advantage, is managed care such as health maintenance organizations (HMOs) provide, and *Part D* is the prescription drug coverage if a beneficiary qualifies for the Medicare program because of social security or railroad retirement eligibility. The protection the beneficiary receives lasts as long as the beneficiary lives. If individuals do not qualify for Part A (the hospitalization insurance) but decide they wish to purchase it, they can do so but must also purchase Part B (the voluntary medical insurance plan). On the other hand, if they only want to purchase Part B and not buy Part A, the hospitalization plan, they can do that as well.

It is not the purpose of Medicare to cover every health expense of the elderly. It is not a comprehensive health insurance program but rather was created to relieve persons aged 65 years or older of the major aspect of the medical costs that result from their hospitalization, surgery, and lengthy periods of recovery.

Part A: hospital insurance

Part A's hospital insurance plan automatically covers beneficiaries who are entitled to retirement, survivor, or disability benefits under social security or the railroad retirement system and is free except for various deductibles and coinsurance charges. Others may purchase this insurance. Persons who are over 65 years of age who do not have at least 10 years of work experience that is covered by social security, the railroad retirement system or Medicare-covered government employment do not receive automatic Part A coverage, such as state, local, and municipal workers and teachers who have access to other health care plans through their unions or former employers (Table 13.1).

Table 13.1 Medicare 2009 hospital insurance program, Part A

Program benefits Part A	Medicare coverage Part A	Patient pays Part A (2006)	Remarks
Hospital care	First to 60th day	First $1068 in costs	Recalculated each year
	61st to 90th day	$267 per day	Recalculated each year
	91st to 150th day	$534 per day	Recalculated each year: after 90 days in hospital. Medicare patient has 60 reserve hospital days that can be used at any time, but once used are gone for a lifetime
	Ends after 150th day of hospital care	For all hospital care services	
Psychiatric hospital care	First to 190th day	Initial deductible and daily cost sharing	Limited to 190 days of care in patient's lifetime
Skilled nursing home care	First to 20th day	Nothing	Must be Medicare-participating hospital for at least 3 consecutive days before transfer to nursing home
	21st to 100th day	$133.50 per day	
	Ends after 100th day	For all nursing home care	Custodial care, private duty nursing, and first 3 pints of blood in nursing home not covered
Home care	Unlimited home health visits in 365-day noncalendar year. Medicare pays entire cost of visiting nurses (part-time), physical therapy and speech therapy services, medical supplies, and appliances (but not physicians)	For other home health care services such as housekeeping and full-time nursing care	Patient can qualify directly for home care without previous hospitalization
Hospice care	Up to 210 days or more	Up to $5 per prescription drug and 5% of inpatient respite care	Covers some non-Medicare benefits

Adapted from Braverman J. *Your Money and Your Health: How to Find Affordable, High Quality Healthcare*. Amherst, NY: Prometheus Books, 2006: 242, 248, and data based on US Department of Health and Human Services. *Medicare and You 2009*. Baltimore, MD: Centers for Medicare and Medicaid Services, 2008: 125–126.

On being admitted to a hospital that participates in Medicare, the patient becomes responsible for the first $1068 in costs (the deductible as at January 1, 2009). From the first through 60th day Medicare pays all of the following services above $1068 deductible. These include a semiprivate room (2–4 beds); all meals, including special diets; regular nursing service; costs of special care units such as intensive care and coronary care; drugs furnished during a hospital stay; laboratory tests included in hospital bill; X-ray and other radiology services, including radiation therapy billed by the hospital; medical supplies such as splints, casts, and surgical dressings; use of appliances such as wheelchairs; operating room and recovery room costs; and rehabilitation services such as physical therapy, occupational therapy, and speech pathology services.[4] On the other hand, the hospital insurance plan does not pay for the following services: private duty nursing; a private room unless medically necessary; a television or telephone in the room; and the first 3 pints of blood, but a hospital will not charge the patient for the first 3 pints of blood if the patient has arranged for their replacement through a blood donor plan, a friend or other sources.

If a patient's hospital stay exceeds 60 days, then the patient must pay, effective January 1, 2009, $267 per day from the 61st through 90th day and Medicare pays the rest. If a patient must stay in the hospital for more than 90 days, then each Medicare beneficiary has 60 reserve hospital days that can be used at any time. Effective January 1, 2009, the patient pays $534 per day and Medicare pays the rest. Once used, reserve days are gone forever. However, 60 days after being discharged from the hospital or other qualified facility such as a skilled nursing home (including day of discharge) the patient is qualified for a new benefit period and can begin again with the previous health coverage. Under Medicare patients can have as many benefit periods as they need. Again, a benefit period begins when a patient enters a hospital and the benefit period ends when the patient has been out of the hospital or skilled nursing home facility for 60 consecutive days.

Other benefits included under Part A are 190-day limit for psychiatric care in a Medicare-participating psychiatric hospital during a patient's lifetime as well as hospice care, skilled nursing home care, and home care. Medicare does not pay for long-term care or custodial care in a nursing home such as assistance with bathing, dressing, eating, taking medications or having dressings changed for noninfected conditions but it does pay for meals and semiprivate rooms. As far as skilled nursing home care is concerned, the program functions in the following manner. After a patient stays in a Medicare-participating hospital for at least 3 consecutive days, not including day of discharge, Medicare helps pay up to 100 days of extended care in a skilled nursing home, provided that the skilled nursing care is certified as being connected to the illness that caused the hospitalization. Skilled nursing care, like intravenous injections or physical therapy, is defined as that which 'can only be performed by, or under the supervision of, licensed nursing personnel.' As with hospital coverage, the nursing home benefit pays charges normally associated with these facilities. Medicare pays the first 20 days of nursing home care in full. For the remaining 80 days, the patient, as of January 1, 2009, pays $133.50 per day for days 21–100 during each benefit period. Patients pay all costs for each day after day 100 in the benefit period.

Part B: voluntary medical insurance

Part B of Medicare is the voluntary medical insurance program in which a beneficiary pays a monthly premium. As of January 1, 2009 the Part B premium was $96.40 a month for those earning $82 000 or less a year. As a result of the Deficit Reduction Act of 2005, which President Bush signed on February 8, 2006, beginning in 2007 the highest-income seniors, those whose incomes begin at $82 000, will pay a higher premium than those earning less than that amount. The size of the premium would increase on a sliding scale, topping out at 80% of Part B costs for people with incomes over $200 000 and which in 2009 ranged from $134.90 to $308.30 per month for the wealthier beneficiaries, depending upon their annual income.

Part B helps pay for physician and other services both in and out of hospital. The voluntary medical insurance plan pays 80% of the Medicare-approved amount for specified medical expenses. The patient pays the remaining 20% plus an annual deductible which, as of January 1, 2009, was $135. The deductible is not paid more than once a year and Medicare establishes the deductible each year. Beginning in 2005, the deductible began to be increased annually, indexed to the growth in Part B spending. One way patients can control their Medicare bill is finding out whether their physician accepts Medicare assignment. This means the physician will accept as his or her fee what Medicare will pay without charging the patient any additional amount. Thus, patients can limit themselves in 2009 to the $135 deductible plus 20% of the doctor's charges. If the physician does not accept Medicare assignment then the patient's medical expenses in 2009 will include the $135 annual deductible, plus 20% of the physician's Medicare charge plus that part of the physician's Medicare charge that exceeds Medicare's definition of an approved amount. Thus, most nonparticipating Medicare physicians can charge a patient 115% of the Medicare fee schedule, which really means the physician can charge the patient an additional 15% higher than Medicare's approved amount. This is federal law.

Medicare Part B covers many kinds of benefits as well as preventive care services (Table 13.2). Some of the services it covers include physician services anywhere in the USA (in the doctor's office, hospital, at home, or elsewhere); outpatient hospital services for diagnosis and treatment in an emergency room; diagnostic tests and clinical laboratory procedures that

Table 13.2 Medicare 2009, voluntary medical insurance, Part B

Program benefits Part B	Medicare coverage Part B	Patient pays Part B (2006)	Remarks
Physicians' and surgeons' services as well as other medical services	80% of reasonable charge as determined by Medicare or its agent	First $135 of expenses (not charged more than once per year) plus 20% of all charges above $135	Voluntary monthly Part B recalculated each year Other medical services include outpatient hospital services such as X-rays and tests; outpatient physical therapy and speech therapy; outpatient dialysis treatments; artificial limbs and eyes; limited dental surgical care and chiropractic care; certain colostomy care supplies; rental or purchase of medical equipment; and approved ambulance services if other modes of transportation are a potential health hazard
Home care	Unlimited visits per calendar year – pays 100% of reasonable charges	All services not covered by the program	Like Part A of Medicare (hospital insurance) no prior hospitalization is required to qualify for benefit
Independent physical therapists	$1840 maximum per year	Rest of charges	
Outpatient psychiatric services	50% per year	Rest of charges	

Adapted from Braverman J. *Your Money and Your Health: How to Find Affordable, High Quality Healthcare.* Amherst, NY: Prometheus Books, 2006: 242, 248, and data based on US Department of Health and Human Services. *Medicare and You 2009.* Baltimore, MD: Centers for Medicare and Medicaid Services, 2008: 125–126.

are a part of medical treatment, like blood tests, urinalysis, and more; medical supplies like splints, casts, and surgical dressings; home and office services by licensed and Medicare-certified physical therapists, with certain payment limitations; hepatitis B, flu, and pneumococcal vaccine shots (PL 96-611), and many others. Among its preventive services are cholesterol and bone mass measurements for certain people who are losing bone mass; glaucoma screening; mammogram screening, Papanicolaou (pap) tests and pelvic screening, and colorectal screening for all people age 50 and older, with no age limit for having a colonoscopy; diabetes self-management, and prostate cancer screening for all men age 50 and older, including a digital rectal examination (once very 12 months) and a prostate-specific antigen test (once every 12 months), and others. Some of the tests Medicare does not cover include custodial care, routine dental care and dentures, acupuncture treatments and cosmetic surgery, supportive devices and routine foot care, hearing aid and examinations, and other services.

Supplementary Medicare insurance

Since Medicare is not comprehensive, given the fact that the program includes deductibles and copayments and omits some health services and supplies which the beneficiary has to pay out-of-pocket, commercial insurance companies and Blue Cross and Blue Shield sell supplementary Medicare insurance known as 'wraparound coverage' because it is designed to fill in such Medicare gaps. But supplementary insurance rarely pays physician fees that exceed Medicare limits. In 1990, Congress passed a law to regulate the sale of Medicare supplemental (Medigap or Medisupp) insurance. Under the law, all companies that offer insurance to supplement Medicare must offer a core package of basic benefits and they must provide consumers with an understandable outline of coverage that is comparable in language and format to help in comparative shopping. The law also limits insurance carriers to a maximum of nine additional coverage packages that exceed the core package or a total of 10 packages.

In 1995, Congress passed another law that requires that when a person is sold a policy that duplicates some Medicare or Medigap benefit, the insurance company has to tell the buyer of that fact. Also, such policies must pay all the stated benefits regardless of coverage. This rules out what is called coordination of benefits, the practice of having one insurer refuse to pay in cases where there is multiple coverage. Coordination of benefits is widely used to keep policyholders from double dipping and collecting more than their costs, but in the past it also meant that sometimes consumers got little or nothing from a policy that duplicated Medicare.[5]

Other forms of Medicare coverage

Medicare also pays for second and even third opinions if beneficiaries want to make sure that a specific treatment, like surgery, is required. Under very restrictive conditions it also helps pay the services of chiropractors, podiatrists, dentists, and optometrists. Medicare also pays for a variety of services provided at special kinds of health care facilities like ambulatory surgical centers, rural health clinics, comprehensive outpatient rehabilitation facilities, community mental health facilities, certified medical laboratories, and federally qualified health centers like community health clinics, Indian health clinics, migrant health centers, and health centers for the homeless. They are generally located in inner-city and rural areas and are open to all Medicare beneficiaries.

Quality improvement organizations (QIOs)

QIOs are chosen and paid for by the federal government to review the hospital treatment of Medicare patients. Each state has a QIO to oversee the review of inpatient services in its area. These organizations have been given the authority to conduct reviews of patient cases before, during, and after hospital admissions. QIOs use physicians and nurses to provide this review service. A US Court of Appeals has upheld a 2001 review finding that doctors used by the QIO cannot block the release of the review findings.[6]

QIOs make determinations about hospital care and ambulatory surgical center care. A main function of a QIO is to review records seeking elective nonemergency surgery. QIOs also try to reduce admissions for procedures that can be performed safely and effectively on an outpatient basis, such as cataract operations and certain types of foot surgery. The QIOs decide whether care provided to Medicare patients is medically necessary, is provided in the most appropriate setting, and is of good quality.

When patients disagree with a QIO decision, they can appeal by requesting reconsideration. Two things can happen with a QIO reconsideration: either the QIO will decide that Medicare will pay for some or all of the services, or it will confirm that the initial decision was correct and appropriate. If a person disagrees with a QIO decision upon its reconsideration and the amount in question is $200 or more, a person can request a hearing by an administrative law judge of the Social Security Administration. Cases involving $2000 or more can eventually be appealed to a federal court. Appeals of decisions on most other services covered by Medicare hospital insurance Part A (skilled nursing facility care, home health care, hospice services, and few inpatient hospital matters not handled by a QIO) are handled by Medicare intermediaries. If patients disagree with the intermediary they can appeal to an administrative law judge of the Social Security Administration in cases of $100 or more within 120 days and again eventually to a federal court in cases of $1000 or more. Under Part B patients can also appeal their claims to insurance carriers. If the amount is $500 or more they can appeal the carrier's decision within 60 days to an administrative law judge and cases involving $1000 or more can eventually be appealed to a federal court.

Thus, Medicare not only covers a vast array of benefits but also reimburses a wide spectrum of institutions and professional providers who deliver health care services. It also has the infrastructure to determine the quality, necessity, and appropriateness of care that is being delivered to beneficiaries as well as afford beneficiaries the right to appeal the decisions that third-party payers are making in regard to their cases.

Part C: Medicare Advantage

In addition to receiving Medicare benefits under Parts A and B, beneficiaries can also receive care through coordinated care plans that have contracts with Medicare under the Medicare Advantage program or Part C, such as competitive medical plans (CMP) and traditional HMOs. The Tax Equity and Fiscal Responsibility Act of 1982 created the CMPs to facilitate the enrollment of Medicare beneficiaries into managed care plans. CMPs are organized and financed like HMOs, but they do not have to meet all the regulatory requirements which bind HMOs.

To receive care under Part C, beneficiaries must be enrolled in Medicare Part A (hospital insurance) and Part B (voluntary medical supplementary insurance) and continue to pay the monthly Part B premium as well as live in the service area of the Medicare managed care plans, which are not available in all parts of the country. In addition, beneficiaries cannot have end-stage renal disease to enroll in Medicare Part C – that is, permanent kidney failure requiring kidney dialysis or a kidney transplant – or be receiving care in a Medicare-certified hospice. Under Part C there are various kinds of arrangements that beneficiaries can make to receive care. These include:

- An HMO is an organization that provides a broad spectrum of comprehensive health care services for a specified group at fixed periodic payments that are made in advance by or on behalf of each person or family. Sponsors of an HMO can include hospital medical plans, insurance companies, consumer groups, labor unions, medical schools, government, and others.
- A preferred provider organization (PPO) is a financing and delivery system that brings together aspects of standard fee-for-service indemnity plans and HMOs. Essentially, a PPO is a group of doctors and hospitals that negotiate with a company, labor union, or insurance firm to provide medical services for reduced fees. Unlike HMOs, PPOs operate on a fee-for-service basis and patients are not compelled to use the PPO physician or hospitals. They can visit any provider they wish, but personal out-of-pocket expenses are less if they visit a preferred provider.
- A provider-sponsored organization (PSO) is affiliated hospitals and doctors who operate a plan and take on the financial risk. The PSO, which does not include an insurance company, receives a fixed monthly fee from Medicare to assume the risk in providing such care.
- A private fee-for service plan (PFSP) is an insurance plan that pays providers directly without a network. Services that are received under the PFSP are independent of the services received under Medicare. In addition, patients can receive services from providers who accept Medicare. Doctors, hospitals, and other providers are reimbursed by the plan on a fee-for-service basis at a rate the plan determines, not at the

Medicare rate. Providers can also charge beneficiaries more than 115% of the Medicare-approved charges.

- Medical savings accounts (MSAs) were established by US Congress in the 1990s and enrollment was limited to 750 000 persons. Individuals purchase a health insurance plan with a deductible. After the person's or family's medical expenses exceed the deductible, the MSA pays 100% of Parts A and B expenses. In addition to the monthly tax-deductible premium, which the individual pays, Medicare pays the MSA plan the difference between the monthly premium and the beneficiary's capitation rate (the amount that would be paid to an HMO). Funds can be carried over to the next year.

Disease management plans

Medicare is also working on developing new ways to provide focused health care for some people. These are called disease management plans and are designed to give beneficiaries not only their Medicare health care but also more focused care to manage a disease or condition like congestive heart failure, diabetes, or end-stage renal disease.

Regional Medicare Advantage plans

Beginning in 2006, a new regional Medicare Advantage plan program was established that allows regional coordinated care plans to participate in the Medicare Advantage program. Between 10 and 50 regions were to be established, and plans wishing to participate musts serve an entire region.[7]

Risk versus cost managed care plans

When discussing managed care under Part C of Medicare, it is important to distinguish between risk versus cost contracts with Medicare.

Risk plans have lock-in requirements, which means that beneficiaries are committed or locked into receiving all their covered health care services through the plan or through referrals by the plan. In most cases if beneficiaries receive care that the plan does not authorize, neither the plan nor Medicare will pay for the services. The only exceptions recognized by the plan are emergency services anywhere in the USA and for services the beneficiary urgently requires when temporarily outside the plan's service areas. A third exception offered by a few risk plans is called the 'point-of-service' (POS) option. Under the POS option, the plan permits the beneficiary to receive certain services outside the plan's provider network and the plan will pay a percentage of the charges. In return for this flexibility, beneficiaries may expect to pay about 20% of the bill.

On the other hand, cost plans do not have any lock-in requirements. Medicare pays them based on the enrollee's use of an HMO's services. When a beneficiary enrolls in a cost plan, the beneficiary can visit with a health care provider affiliated with the plan or go outside the plan. If the beneficiary goes outside the plan, the plan probably will not pay for the services but Medicare will. Medicare will pay its share of the charges it approves. The beneficiary will be responsible for Medicare's coinsurance, deductibles, and other charges just as if they were receiving care under the fee-for-service system. Because of this flexibility, a cost plan is good for beneficiaries who travel frequently, live in another state part of the year, or want to visit a physician who is not affiliated with the plan.

Thus, most plans serving Medicare beneficiaries must provide all Medicare and hospital benefits available in the plan's service area. Some plans also provide benefits beyond what Medicare pays, such as preventive care, prescription drugs, dental care, hearing aids, and eye glasses for little or no extra fee. And the beneficiary does not have to pay Medicare's deductibles and coinsurance. So, if a beneficiary is a member of an HMO or competitive plan, these plans will make decisions about the beneficiary's coverage and payment of services and, as in the case of Parts A and B, the appeal rights of Part C beneficiaries are similar to the rights of Medicare beneficiaries under traditional fee-for-service Medicare.

Part D: prescription drugs

On November 25, 2003, the US Congress enacted legislation that added a drug benefit to the Medicare program beginning January 1, 2006. President Bush signed the bill into law on December 8, 2003, as the Medicare Prescription Drug, Improvement, and Modernization Act of 2003 (PL 108-173). This insurance program is voluntary. All Medicare beneficiaries can join no matter what their income may be if they are enrolled in the original Medicare program (Parts A and B), or in a Medicare cost plan, or in a Medicare private fee-for-service plan that does not cover prescription drugs. No physical examination is required to obtain this coverage, nor can the program turn down any beneficiary for any reason. Again, if a beneficiary does not want to sign up in the program, the beneficiary is not required to enroll.

For purposes of definition, a Medicare cost plan is a kind of HMO. In a Medicare cost plan, if patients obtain care outside the plan's network without a referral, the original Medicare program (Part A or B) will pay their Medicare-covered services, except the cost plan does pay for emergency services or urgently needed services outside the service area. A *private fee-for-service plan* is a kind of Medicare Advantage plan (Part C) in which a patient may visit any Medicare-approved physician or hospital that accepts the plan's payment. The insurance plan, rather than Medicare, determines how much it will pay and what the beneficiary will pay for the services the beneficiary receives. The beneficiary may pay more or less for Medicare-covered benefits and may also obtain extra benefits that the original Medicare plan (Parts A and B) does not cover. Despite the establishment of this Part D prescription drug program, as in the past, Medicare Part B does continue to cover drugs such as those administered in a doctor's office or in a hospital.

Enrollment penalty

Although the Part D program is voluntary insurance (January 1, 2006 was the first month of coverage), coverage begins the first month after the date of enrollment. Thus, if a person enrolls in March, coverage should begin in April of that same year. May 15, 2006 was the last day a beneficiary could sign up without being penalized with a high premium. For each month beneficiaries delay enrolling in Medicare Part D an extra 1% of the initial monthly premium is added to their own premium and the increase is permanent as long as the beneficiary has Part D coverage. For example, if the monthly premium in a particular state or region was $50 a month in 2006, and rates do vary throughout the country and by plan, and a beneficiary waited 8 months to enroll, the beneficiary would pay an extra 8% penalty, or an extra $4 per month (8% × $50) added to the premium. So instead of paying a premium of $50 a month, as an example, assuming the premium has not changed 12 months later, the beneficiary would be paying $54 ($50 + $4) a month. But whether or not the premium increased, the $4 added to the initial premium is a permanent increase or penalty. Each year there is an open enrollment in November–December when beneficiaries have the chance to change their plans, such as if they moved from one area to another or their plan ceased to provide prescription drug benefits.

There is one exception to the 1% penalty increase. If individuals had already been enrolled in a prescription drug plan that was creditable, that is, as good as or even better than the new Medicare program benefit, they can enroll in the Medicare Part D program after May 15, 2006 without the 1% monthly benefit penalty being added to their monthly premium as long as they sign up for the Medicare drug coverage within 63 days of losing their previous prescription drug coverage. This nonpenalty rule is also true for persons who are enrolled in the US Veterans Administration's health program and the US Department of Defense's TRICARE-for-Life program for military retirees and dependants, because both programs are considered creditable or better than Medicare's standard plan coverage.

Also, if working, employees had to be told by their employer, union, or other third party whether Medicare affected their current prescription drug coverage with the organization. The organization had several options at the time: maintain their current drug coverage, but employees had to find out whether it was creditable, that is, as good as or better than Medicare; offer employees new drug coverage which employees had to sign up for if they wanted to be covered for prescription drugs; offer employees drug coverage that supplements the Medicare drug program by paying all of part of their out-of-pocket expenses; or drop their drug coverage, maybe assisting employees to pay part of the cost of their insurance premium or maybe not helping them at all.

Medicare drug benefit administration

Beginning on January 1, 2006, multiple private insurance companies approved by Medicare administer the Medicare prescription drug benefit. In addition to standalone plans, Medicare beneficiaries can also choose to enroll in an HMO or PPO plan (Medicare Part C, called Medicare Advantage) that offers prescription drug coverage in addition to other health benefits, if beneficiaries want to receive their health care services through managed care. All Medicare Advantage managed care plans must offer at least one choice that includes prescription drug coverage. On the other hand, if a beneficiary prefers fee-for-service plans, which offer diverse benefits, and wishes to remain or change to a traditional Medicare fee-for-service plan, then the beneficiary may wish to consider joining a standalone plan if the beneficiary decides to enroll in a fee-for-service plan that does not cover prescription drug coverage. But, beneficiaries have to remember the following rule. They can only select a combination of both a managed care plan and a prescription drug standalone plan if the managed care plan does not provide prescription drug coverage. If a beneficiary is already enrolled in a Medicare Advantage plan (Part C) that covers the beneficiary for prescription drugs, and if by mistake the beneficiary also then enrolls in a standalone plan (Part D), then the beneficiary is automatically transferred out of the Medicare Advantage Plan (Part C) and returns to traditional Medicare (Parts A and B). No beneficiary can join a Medicare Advantage plan (Part C) as well as remain in traditional Medicare at the same time.

While all prescription drug plans meet or exceed a Medicare-established standard, as defined by Congress and, depending upon the plan, require written disclosures, each plan can vary in its coverage options, how it establishes costs (different premiums, different drug prices, different copayments, which are defined as a specific dollar amount for each prescription, or coinsurance, which is defined as a percentage of the prescription price), and will also vary in where beneficiaries can buy their prescription drugs since the pharmacies that accept the plans will also differ.

Payment according to drug levels or tiers

Most plans will have three or four levels (known as tiers) of copayments or coinsurance, beginning from the least expensive generic drugs at the lowest level or tier, through 'preferred' brand-name drugs (on the formulary) at the second level, to 'nonpreferred' brands (drugs listed on the formulary but at a higher copayment than the preferred drugs' tier) at the third level, to rarer high-cost drugs on the fourth level, for which the beneficiary may pay a coinsurance amount rather than a copayment. In the context of the discussion about the Part D prescription drug program, a formulary is a list of certain kinds of prescription drugs that a Medicare drug plan will cover subject to limits and conditions. Plans cannot alter the premium or deductible amount a beneficiary pays between January 1 and December 31 of each year. But the copayment the beneficiary pays can be different during the year if a drug is moved from one tier to another tier. Plans can also change all charges for a year and each future year. Also, beneficiaries may receive more coverage and pay less out of their own pocket through a special segment of the Medicare drug coverage program called Extra Help (full coverage) if their income and personal savings are limited, or if they are in a state pharmacy assistance program or if their employer or union coverage supplements Medicare. If they live in the US territories – Puerto Rico, Virgin Islands, Guam, American Samoa, and the Northern Mariannas – the Extra Help program is different from that in the USA and they will also have fewer Medicare drug programs from which to choose.

Selection of pharmacy

It is important for beneficiaries to find out whether the pharmacy where they shop will be part of their drug plan's preferred or nonpreferred network (preferred pharmacies offer lower prices). Many plans also use mail-order services that will deliver drugs to the beneficiary. Plans must make 90-day supplies of medications available through pharmacies in their network as well as through mail order. Because of possible conflicts of interest, pharmacies cannot help beneficiaries select a Part D plan because they could suggest a plan favorable to their own pharmacy rather than to the beneficiary.

Design of prescription drug benefits

The various insurers which are seeking to sell beneficiaries their prescription drug plan may vary from each other in the way they design their benefits, but the overall value of their benefits cannot differ from the basic benefits of the Medicare standard prescription drug plan. For example, a plan may offer a lower deductible ($100) rather than the standard Medicare's plan's $250 deductible and higher copayments than does the basic standard benefit.

A plan must cover at least two drugs in each class of medications (a group of drugs, e.g., similar drugs addressing a similar problem or used to treat the same condition, like statins for high cholesterol) and most of the drugs in six classes: antidepressants, antipsychotics, anticonvulsants, antiretrovirals to treat human immunodeficiency virus (HIV) and acquired immunodeficiency syndrome (AIDs), cancer drugs, and immunosuppressants. But the plans won't have to provide coverage for all drugs, and they will be allowed to alter the drugs they cover at any time. However, the plans must tell beneficiaries of these alterations at least 60 days in advance of the changes if the changes involve prescription drugs that the beneficiaries currently take.

Each plan maintains its own list of preferred drugs (a formulary), and the list of drugs varies from plan to plan since not every drug is available on every plan. The prescription drug plan does not provide coverage for over-the-counter drugs as well as those medicines that the law forbids Medicare to cover, such as drugs for weight problems. Each plan itself, rather than the federal government, works out the prices of drugs with pharmaceutical companies on the beneficiary's behalf. When the beneficiary pays for drugs within the plan, the beneficiary has access to discounted drugs. Medicare prescription drug plans cover both brand-name and generic drugs.

People who sign up for the Part D plan can change plans once a year, as already noted. Monthly premiums will also differ. The premiums can be deducted from a social security check or the beneficiaries can pay the premiums themselves directly to their Part D Medicare drug plan. Married couples are not given any special benefits under this program. Each spouse pays his or her own premiums, copayments, deductibles, and other personal out-of-pocket costs for medications and will attain each level of coverage according to the rate each incurs prescription drug expenses over each calendar year.

It is important that when beneficiaries enroll in Part D they choose a plan that covers the drugs they are taking. If the plan does not cover the drugs a beneficiary uses, the beneficiary can ask the doctor to change prescriptions. If the doctor decides there is no substitute for the current medication, he or she can ask the Medicare drug plan to cover the prescription drug(s). All plans must have an appeals process. However, before giving the beneficiary an exception, a plan may require the beneficiary to try a drug on its formulary (drug list) that is similar to the prescription drug the beneficiary is now taking and that is included on the formulary in order to determine whether the prescription drug on the formulary is equally as effective in treating the beneficiary's medical condition as the medication he/she is now taking.

Drug plans and employers

The federal government will subsidize employers who continue to provide drug coverage to their workers and retirees, as long as their plan is as good ('creditable') as Medicare's. If employees who receive a statement from their employer that says that its drug plan is as good as Medicare – again, meaning it meets Medicare's standards – then employees don't have to enroll in Medicare's Part D but, if they must, can do so at a later time without a late enrollment penalty. But if the employee joins Medicare Part D while still working for his/her current employer, the organization will remove the employee from the company's drug insurance plan and possibly may even cancel the person's health insurance. Thus, employees must check with their company's human resources department to find out whether they would lose their health insurance coverage if they enroll in Part D.

Employers that offer equivalent drug coverage for retirees would secure tax-free subsidies. Employers could also offer subsidies for premiums and cost-sharing assistance for retirees who enroll in Medicare drug plans. But be aware that the employer has the right to change or drop retiree health and drug benefits at any time.

Out-of-pocket drug costs for Medicare beneficiaries

When Medicare became effective January 1, 2006, the average national monthly premium under the standard Medicare prescription drug was $32 a month, or $384 per year, with some plans offering premiums below that amount and others above that amount for their drug coverage. After the beneficiary meets the $250 deductible for the program, Medicare would pay 75% of the drug costs up to $2250 (or $1687, with the patient paying the remaining $563 out of pocket). If the beneficiary then incurs annual drug costs between $2250 and $5100, the patient will pay the total amount of $2850 out of pocket under the national standard Medicare drug plan because the Medicare program does not cover this cost gap, also known as the 'doughnut hole.' That is a gap that is built into the program. When the annual drug costs or expense reach $5100 or more, the Medicare program will pay 95% of the beneficiary's drug bill and the beneficiary will pay the remaining 5% out of pocket at this catastrophic cost level. In other words, once beneficiaries accumulate $3600 in annual drug bills out of their own pocket, the catastrophic drug coverage begins under the Medicare program. The $3600 expense limit does not include the cost of their monthly premium for the Part D prescription drug program but does include deductibles, copayments, any out-of-pocket expenses beneficiaries pay for drugs while they are in the $2850 gap, and any payments a friend or member of their family made in buying drugs, as well as any charitable groups or state pharmacy assistance plan that did the same. But in instances, only payments for those drugs that the beneficiary's plan covers, including exceptions the beneficiary receive, count toward the $3600 limit. Payments that are not involved in the $3600 out-of pocket expense limit include the beneficiary's premiums, as already noted, personal costs for drugs that the beneficiary's plan does not cover; payments an employer, union, or other third-party payer like the federal government or the beneficiary's own insurance plan makes; and drugs the beneficiary buys from Canada or other foreign countries which are not considered 'creditable.'

In August 2008, the Henry J. Kaiser Family Foundation released a study that noted that in 2007 about 3.4 million Americans enrolled in Medicare Part D reached the gap in the prescription drug coverage also known as the 'doughnut hole,' with the result that some stopped taking their medications. Of the 26% of the Part D enrollees from which the 3.4 million figure was estimated and who reached the coverage gap in 2007, 22% remained in the gap for the remainder of the year while 4% eventually received catastrophic coverage. Beneficiaries who reached the coverage gap confronted very great increases in out-of-pocket costs. For example, among Part D enrollees who reached the coverage gap, but did not reach catastrophic coverage, average monthly out-of-pocket costs nearly doubled from $104 to the coverage gap to $196 in the 'doughnut hole.' The study found that enrollees who were pre-scribed drugs for chronic conditions had a much higher risk of a gap in their coverage under Part D. For example, 64% of enrollees taking medication for Alzheimer's disease reached the coverage gap, along with 51% of those taking oral antidiabetic medications, and 45% of those taking antidepressant med-ications. The study also found that some patients changed the use of their drugs when they reached the Part D coverage gap and had to pay the full cost of the prescription drugs.

In an effort to assist seniors who fall into the 'doughnut hole' in terms of prescription drug expenditures and bear the entire cost of their prescription medicines out of their own pocket, the Obama Administation and the US drug industry announced an agreement on June 20, 2009 whereby the drug indus-try over the ensuing decade would spend $80 billion improving drug benefits for seniors. The drug companies would pay 50% of the cost of brand-name drugs for seniors who find themselves in the 'doughnut hole.' a gap in cover-age that is a feature of many plans providing prescription drug coverage under Medicare Part D. In other words, seniors will receive 50% discount on these drugs. In addition, the entire cost of the drug would count toward patients' out-of-pocket costs, meaning their insurance coverage would cover more of their expenses than otherwise would be the case. While none of the changes in the prescription drug program would directly lower government costs, several officials also stated that the industry agreed to measures that would provide the US Treasury with more money under federal health programs. In partic-ular, officials stated that drug companies would likely end up paying higher rebates for certain drugs under Medicaid, the program that pays providers health care for the poor.[8]

Eight classes of drugs that are used to treat a variety of common conditions were examined and the study found that 15% of enrollees who reached the gap stopped their drug therapy, 5% changed to another medication in the same class, and 1% reduced the number of drugs they were taking in the class. The study analysis did not include beneficiaries who receive low-income subsidies, because they did not confront a gap in coverage under their Medicare drug plan. According to Drew Altman, Kaiser chief executive offi-cer and president, 'the Medicare drug benefit has produced tangible relief for millions of people, despite the unusual coverage gap that was created to make the benefit fit within budget constraints. But if a new president and Congress consider changes to the drug benefit, it will be important to keep in mind that the coverage gap has consequences for some patients with serious health conditions.'[9]

Other sources of drug payment assistance

If a person is receiving free drugs from a pharmaceutical drug manufacturer's patient assistance program, the person can continue to obtain them and still sign up for the Medicare prescription program but only as long as the drug manufacturer keeps operating the program for Medicare beneficiaries. The federal government will make certain that there is drug coverage in any region of the country that does not have at least one standalone drug plan and one private health plan like an HMO or PPO. In other words, if a region lacks one or both kinds of plan, the government will still make certain that drugs are covered in that particular region.

Medigap policies with prescription drug coverage

If individuals have a Medigap plan that pays for prescription drug coverage, they can: (1) retain their current Medigap plan but get rid of its prescription drug coverage and sign up for the Part D plan; (2) select another Medigap plan that does not include drugs so that they can sign up for the Part D plan; or (3) keep their current plan with prescription drug coverage. After January 1, 2006 no new Medigap policies covered prescription drugs, but people who already have such policies will be allowed to continue them indefinitely.

Medicaid prescription drug coverage

If Medicaid was paying for a patient's prescription drugs, after December 31, 2005 Medicaid no longer covered the patient's drugs if a prescription drug plan covered the same drugs. Rather, the person's prescription drug benefits are now the responsibility of Medicare Part D. If any elderly Medicaid recipient did not choose a Part D plan by December 31, 2005 then Medicare selected a plan for that person. But the problem with this process is that the selected program may not cover the drugs the person is being prescribed and the person would have to return to his/her own doctor to obtain a prescription for a different drug or change the prescription drug plan to another Part D plan that does cover the patient's drugs. If a person decides to go into a new plan, the person has to fill out a new application and that will take time to get into a new plan.

Dual eligibles for Medicare and Medicaid

If a person is eligible for both Medicaid and Medicare, also known as a 'dual eligible,' the person will be transferred into the Medicare program, though he/

she will have very low copayments and low costs on premiums or no premiums at all. Also, dual eligibles will receive continuous treatment all year and avoid the $2850 gap in the program for which others have to pay the $2850 out of their own pockets.

Conclusion

As can be noted from the previous discussions, Medicare and Medicaid are extremely complicated and complex programs whose costs in 2004 were $299.6 billion for Medicare and $276.8 billion (federal and state) for Medicaid.[9] As more and more expenditures are devoted to state Medicaid programs, the state has fewer economic resources to devote to its other financial responsibilities for its residents, like transportation and education. This has caused states like Oregon in the 1990s to begin rationing medical care services under its Medicaid program and through rationing some people who require certain services can no longer receive them, perhaps to the detriment of their own health status. This situation became more acute as the year 2008 ended and 2009 began, with the USA in an economic recession. Other states also began to reduce their own Medicaid coverage. With revenues declining at the same time as more persons were becoming unemployed and losing private health insurance coverage, states began to look for even deeper cuts than in the past. By the end of 2008, the District of Columbia and 19 states had lowered payments to hospitals and nursing homes, eliminated coverage for some treatments, and compelled recipients out of Medicaid altogether. Many states are stopping payments for health care services not required by the federal government such as physical therapy, eye glasses, hearing aids, and hospice care. A few states are requiring poor patients to contribute more to their own care. 'It's not a pretty list at all,' said Michael Hales, Medicaid director in the state of Utah. According to Diane Rowland, executive director of the Kaiser Commission on Medicaid and the Uninsured, the states 'have taken the cuts that were making the program more efficient . . . Now they are making . . . cuts into the core.'[10]

In April 2009, the National Conference on State Legislatures in a survey of state budgets found the situation of the states was becoming very dire. As unemployment rose, tax collections became smaller, and revenue shortfalls increased, the state budget gaps were expanding – in some instances to enormous amounts. Except for Alabama, Michigan, New York, and Texas, the 46 remaining states as well as the District of Columbia begin their fiscal year on July 1, 2009 where they will confront a budget gap of $121 billion from July 1, 2009 to June 30, 2010 versus $102.4 billion for the fiscal year that ended June 30, 2009. In California a $24 billion budget deficit was the nation's worst. Meanwhile, Maine planned to add taxes on candy and ski tickets, Wisconsin on oil companies, and Kentucky on alcohol and cellphone ring tones.

Washington State is laying off thousands of teachers, Idaho reduced aid to public schools, forcing pay reductions for teachers, while in June 2009 Illinois announced that it would temporarily cease paying about $15 million for about 10 000 funerals for the poor. Susan K. Urahn, managing director of The Pew Center on the States, has stated that, even if the recession ends, unemployment could keep rising through 2010, continuing to hurt tax collections and increasing the demand for Medicaid, one of the state's most burdensome expenses. She noted that stress on Medicaid tends to appear later in a recession so that for the next couple of years the states will be struggling with this issue as well.[11]

On the other hand, Medicare is a national program. Its description herein with all its complicated sections, Parts A, B, C, and D, each with different financing mechanisms, demonstrates how complicated the financing of health care services has become in the USA. That is why the chapter is devoted to a detailed description of the program because how can solutions be offered to resolve a problem if it may not be understood in the first instance? For example, when discussions center on controlling health care costs in the USA, which mechanisms are the experts talking about that need to be changed or finetuned? Are they the capitation systems under HMOs, the reimbursements-based diagnosis-related grouping of diseases for hospitals under Medicare, the individual negotiations between drug plans and the pharmaceutical industry under the Part D prescription drug benefit program rather than the federal government negotiating with the pharmaceutical industry on behalf of all plans to control drug costs?

And what about the collision course Medicare finds itself on with the demographic future of America? Can the USA continue to expand the program with continuous new benefits such as preventive care services as millions of new Medicare beneficiaries, the baby boomers of the 1940s and beyond, soon begin to enter Medicare rolls, almost doubling the size of enrollees from about 37 million in 2006 (12% of the US population) to about 71.5 million in 2030 (20% of the US population)?[12]

The elderly are entering a market in which there is a severe shortage of specialists in geriatric medicine. The specialists who do practice are underpaid, and Medicare fails to provide for team care that many elderly patients need. Medicare may even prevent the elderly from obtaining the best care because of its low reimbursement rates for primary care relative to other medical specialties and its emphasis on treating short-term health problems rather than managing chronic conditions.

Meanwhile, the number of people in the work force supporting the social security and Medicare population through payroll taxes is shrinking, not getting larger, so fewer and fewer workers are supporting more and more of the elderly (Figure 13.1). So do the taxes of the workforce increase or does Medicare itself begin to shrink in terms of benefit coverage? Or is more and

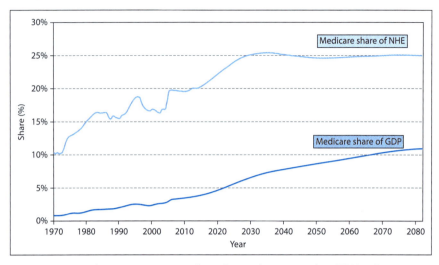

Figure 13.1   Medicare as a percentage share of gross domestic product (GDP) and as a percentage share of national health expenditures (NHE) 1970–2082. Note: For Medicare share of GDP, historical data are used before 2007 and projections from 2007 forward. For Medicare, share of NHE historical data are used before 2006 and projections from 2006 forward. Source: Centers for Medicare and Medicaid Services, Office of the Actuary, and as cited in Caldis T G (2008) *The Long-term Projection Assumptions for Medicare and Aggregate National Health Expenditures*. Baltimore, MD: Centers for Medicare and Medicaid Services: 15.

more of the cost sharing placed on the beneficiaries themselves according to their ability to pay? In 2005, the General Accountability Office reported the ratio of overall workers to retirees will change in ways that threaten the financial solvency and sustainability of these entitlement programs (Medicare and social security). In 2000, there were 4.8 working-age persons (20–64 years old) per elderly person, but by 2030 the ratio is projected to decline to. 2.9.[13]

And what about the oldest of the oldest, those 85 years and older who are one of the fastest-growing demographic groups in the USA as modern medicine increases our age span. Life expectancy for men was 74.1 years in 2000, up from 68.2 years in 1950. Among women, life expectancy was 79.5 years in 2000, up from 71.1 in 1950.[14] And those who reach the age of 65 are now expected to live an average of 19 more years, or 7 years longer than people who had reached age 65 in the year 1900.[12] With an increase in longevity come diseases that had not been treated before in great numbers because people didn't live as long, as well as the necessity and costs of developing more nursing homes, home care programs and other institutional and noninstitutional care that will increase America's health care bill with their attendant costs. Sicknesses such as Alzheimer's disease and other illnesses have added and will continue to add to the financial strain under which the US health system currently operates. In March 2008, a report by the Alzheimer's Association entitled *2008 Alzheimer's Disease: Facts and Figures* predicted that one out of eight baby boomers will be diagnosed with Alzheimer's and, if no cure is found, the nation will be faced with a half-million new cases in 2010 and almost a million new cases a year by the middle of the 21st century.[15] In 2005 Medicare spent $91 billion on Alzheimer's and other dementias, and spending could increase to $160 billion in 2010 and $189 billion by 2015.[15] Even some hospices are beginning to be accused of treating patients longer than their Medicare benefit duration allows, with the federal government asking some hospices to return the monies they billed the government for such treatment services because the government claims the patients did not die within the expected time.

All these are serious questions which programs such as Medicaid and Medicare must confront in future years because, just like state government, the federal government also has responsibilities to its citizenry in areas other than health care, such as defense, transportation, energy, agriculture, and education. Does the government continue to raise more and more taxes as health care begins to absorb more and more of America's annual gross domestic product (the value of all the output of its goods and services), not only to fund federal health programs but also these other programs, with the consequent impact of higher taxes on the economy?

The socioeconomic and political problems posed by Medicare and Medicaid, as described herein, are just one of many aspects of the crisis in health care today. A society that is not in good health cannot be as economically and politically viable as a society that is healthy. So, by cutting Medicare and Medicaid and perhaps rationing health care in this country, is this good or bad for American society as a whole? Yet, on the other hand, how much of an economic burden can America's health system place on society without it being or becoming an impediment to resolving the nation's other domestic and international problems posed by the other areas of societal interest, like energy, defense, and education, which are important pillars that hold up and make American society a viable entity relative to the other countries in the world? These are ramifications that one problem such as health care costs poses relative to the nonhealth problems that America must resolve in the ensuing years. These are extremely difficult choices America must face. The nation has no past experience to rely upon for guidance on how to deal with or make decisions in regard to its current socioeconomic dilemma because this is the first time in America's history that it is confronted with an increasing graying and aging population as modern medicine improves the quality and length of American lives. Yet, while everyone wants these scientific medical advances to continue, accompanying the benefits of this scientific progress come societal choices of a socioeconomic nature that America has never had to consider previously.

The description of the broadness and complexity of the Medicare program along with that of Medicaid illustrates the difficulties that are inherent in resolving America's health care cost crisis. Verbal platitudes as if America's health care system is monolithic in its character are far easier to enunciate in resolving America's health care crisis and problems than are the development of concrete proposals and actions to achieve the same goals because in actual fact American health care is a most complicated and diverse system of delivering health care services to its citizenry who are seeking care that is accessible, affordable, and of highest quality for all.

References

1. *A Commission Report: Intergovernmental Problems in Medicaid.* Washington, DC: Advisory Commission on Intergovernmental Relations, 1968: 3-4.
2. Clinton signs welfare reform amid turmoil. *Washington Post* 1996; August 23: A17.
3. What Medicare will (and won't) do for you. *Changing Times* 1979; 33: 40.
4. US Department of Health, Education, and Welfare. *Your Medicare Handbook.* Washington, DC: Social Security Administration, 1978: 13.
5. Crenshaw A R. Changes in 'Medigap' law revive duplicate coverage. *Washington Post* 1995; February 5: H1.
6. Braverman J. *Your Money and Your Health: How to Find Affordable, High-Quality Health Care.* Amherst, NY: Prometheus Books, 2006: 270.
7. Hoffman E D Jr, Klees B S, Curtis C A. Overview of the Medicare and Medicaid programs. In: *Health Care Financing Review/2005 Statistical Supplement.* Baltimore, MD: Centers for Medicare and Medicaid Services, 2006: 7.
8. Espo D. Drug companies, White House reach $80 billion prescription drug deal. *Huffington Post*, June 20, 2009; available online at: http://www.huffingtonpost.com/2009/06/20/deal-reached-on cutting-p_n_ 218431.html); accessed on June 20, 2009.
9. New study examines impact of 'doughnut hole' on people enrolled in Medicare drug plans in 2007. Menlo Park, CA: Henry J. Kaiser Family Foundation, August 21, 2008: 21, 26 (Table 2); available online at: http://www.kff.org/medicare/medicare082108nr.cfm; accessed on September 5, 2008.
10. Goldstein A. States cut Medicaid coverage further. *Washington Post* 2008; December 26: A1, A4.
11. Goodnough A. States turning to last resorts in budget crisis. *N Y Times* June 21, 2009; A1, A12.
12. Steenhuysen J. Older Americans wealthier, living longer. Reuters 2008; March 27.
13. *Long-Term Care Financing: Growing Demand and Cost of Services Are Straining Federal and State Budgets.* Washington, DC: US General Accountability Office, 2005: 8 (report number GAO-05-564T).
14. *65+ in the United States.* Washington, DC: US Department of Commerce, Bureau of the Census, 2006.
15. Fackelmann K. 18 percent of all boomers expected to develop Alzheimer's. *USA Today* 2008; March 18: 6D.

14

Health care fraud and abuse

Introduction

A very important issue that contributes to the rising costs of health care in the USA is the fraud and abuse of these services. In fact, the National Health Care Anti-Fraud Association has estimated conservatively that 3–5% of the nation's total spending on health care is lost to fraud – expenditures that had reached slightly more than $2.2 trillion in 2007 and may increase by as much as 20% in the next decade. That means more than $100 million a day is diverted from patient care to fraudulent activities or $66 billion in 2007, based on the Association's lower 3% figure.[1]

Where there are financial transactions, fraud and abuse of the health care system becomes an ever-present problem. The various estimated costs of fraud vary according to which groups are performing the calculations. In May 1992, citing health insurance industry sources, the US General Accounting Office (now renamed the General Accountability Office) reported to Congress that the loss amounted to as much as 10% of the nation's total annual health care expenditures.[2] Based on health care expenditures of slightly more than $2.2 trillion, 10% would amount to a loss of $220 billion in 2007 that was due to fraud. On the other hand, using the 3–5% figures of the National Health Care Anti-Fraud Association, fraudulent health care transactions in 2004 accounted for $94 billion of the $1.9 trillion spent on health care in that year, based on the 5% figure.[3] Then again, in regard to Medicare claims, in particular, the Office of Inspector General (OIG) of the US Department of Health and Human Services (DHHS) estimated in a report to Congress that 14% of Medicare claims dollars or $23 billion were paid inappropriately in fiscal year 1996, due to fraud and/or abuse and/or lack of medical documentation to support claims.[2] But, regardless of the time interval, 1996 or 2004 or 2007, or the various amounts that are involved, the trend in committing fraud and abuse in our health care system is on the rise and becoming larger each year. How large can health care fraud and abuse become?

On June 26, 2003, the US Department of Justice announced that HCA, a for-profit health care company that includes hospitals, agreed to pay the USA $631 million in civil penalties and damages arising from false claims the government alleged that HCA had submitted to Medicare and other federal health programs. In addition to some previous settlements such as on December 14, 2000 when HCA subsidiaries had pleaded guilty to substantial criminal conduct and paid more than $840 million in criminal fines, civil restitution, and penalties, the federal government by 2003 had recovered $1.7 billion from HCA.[4]

Definition

In order to understand the issue of fraud and abuse, it is important to define these terms. According to Empire Medicare Services, a Medicare contractor that was renamed National Government Services as of January 1, 2007, *fraud* is the intentional deception or misrepresentation that an individual knows is false or does not believe to be true and makes, realizing that the deception could lead to some unauthorized benefit either to himself/herself or some other person.[5] In regard to Medicare, in particular, the most frequent kind of fraud results from a false statement or misrepresentation made, or caused to be made, that is material to entitlement or payment under the Medicare program. The perpetrator may be a participating Medicare provider, a Medicare beneficiary, or some other person or entity, including the billing service or a Medicare contractor employee.[5]

On the other hand, the term *abuse* describes incidents or practices which are not usually fraudulent but also are not consistent with accepted sound, medical, business, or fiscal practices.[5] The practice may directly or indirectly result in unnecessary costs to the program, improper payment, and payment for services which fail to meet professionally recognized standards of care or services which are not medically necessary. For example, one major form of abuse to which Medicare is vulnerable involves the overutilization of services. Overutilization occurs when a patient receives services that are not medically necessary, or reasonable. Examples of abuse include not only services which are not medically necessary, as already noted; but also screening services; violation of Medicare assignment agreements; and/or waiver of copayments.

An abusive situation can become fraudulent if the abusive situation is brought to the attention of the provider or beneficiary, and the abusive situation continues even after the Medicare carrier has made an educational effort with the perpetrator of the abuse to correct the situation.[5] A carrier is a private organization, usually an insurance company that finances health care services. Carriers pay Part B Medicare bills (while fiscal intermediaries, also insurance companies, pay Part A Medicare bills).

Nature of fraud

Fraud in the Medicare program may assume many guises, though these forms are not confined to the Medicare program itself but are cited as examples that any third-party payer, public or private, may encounter. Fraud and abuse permeate many elements of the health care field, including hospitals, nursing homes, home care, prescription drugs, and physicians as well as other professional and institutional groups. However, one of the major programs where all these groups come together and receive payments for providing health care services is the Medicare program with its diverse benefits. Therefore, much of the discussion in this chapter will center on the Medicare program as an illustration or case study as to how fraud and abuse are perpetrated and combated in the health care field, even though these activities are not exclusive to the Medicare program alone but also embrace others such as Medicaid which is a state program of public assistance for persons whose income and resources are not sufficient to pay for health care, regardless of their age. These fraud and abuse activities include:

- incorrectly reporting diagnoses or procedures to maximize payments
- billing for services not furnished
- billing that appears to be a deliberate application for duplicate payment of services or supplies
- misrepresentation of dates and descriptions of the services furnished or the identity of the beneficiary or of the identity of the individual who furnished these services
- billing for noncovered or nonchargeable services as if they are covered items
- incorrectly apportioning costs in cost reports
- including costs of noncovered services, supplies, or equipment in costs that are allowed
- billing Medicare for costs not incurred or which were attributable to nonprogram items or other enterprises, or personal expenses
- repeatedly including unallowable cost items in a provider's cost report except for purposes of establishing a basis for appeal
- claiming bad debts without first genuinely attempting to collect payments.

Other fraudulent situations are less succinct. As two examples:

- Sometimes the coordinator-of-benefits provision of an insurance plan is circumvented by failure to disclose the existence of other insurance that also covers the claim at issue, leading to duplicate payments that may exceed the amount of medical expenses incurred.
- Coinsurance and deductible provisions in an insurance plan are designed to reduce costs by requiring the insured to have a financial stake in his or her own medical expenses by paying for part of these expenses out of his/her own pocket. When a doctor increases the charges by the amount of the deductible and coinsurance, and then

accepts the insurer's benefits as payment in full from the insured, the impact of such cost containment features no longer exists and the cost of everyone's insurance also rises.

By far the most challenging fraud is the professional schemes that often victimize the insured as well as the insurer. For example, let us look at the pharmaceutical industry.

Essentially, any services or benefits that are obtained by misrepresentation or suspicion can be classified as pharmaceutical fraud. Some of these common problems may include kickbacks, diverting drugs, and a drug company misrepresenting or falsifying clinical trial data; patients stealing prescription pads to forge prescriptions or drug shopping among several doctors in order to obtain multiple orders of a drug; and drug trafficking by physicians and pharmacists. Pharmacies may also fill prescriptions with generic drugs but charge the consumer-patient for brand-name drugs or may take prescriptions that are never picked up and place them back into their stock but bill the health plan for them and sell them to someone else. Cases of pharmacists diluting medications have also been observed in the legal system. Even pill shortages take place: charging $2.00 per pill might not seem like a lot of money, but shorting two pills out of a prescription can very quickly add to a profit when charging the patient for the full amount.[6]

However, scams perpetrated by professional groups and organizations, as already noted, affect public programs such as Medicare. How large a financial target are Medicare and Medicaid for the fraudulent and abusive schemes that are directed against them? Well, in 2007 both programs for older Americans and low-income groups cost $627 billion and accounted for 23% of all federal spending. With no change in existing law, the Congressional Budget Office has stated that the cost will double in 10 years and the programs will account for more than 30% of the federal budget. Some of the Medicare scams in the past, as reported in Florida, for example, included the following:

- Bribes for Medicare cards – beneficiaries have been offered money for their Medicare card number. Providers then used these numbers to bill Medicare for services they did not deliver.
- Bribes for medical services – beneficiaries have been offered cash or gifts to go to a mobile medical clinic for 'free exams' and tests. Medicare is then billed for the services as if the patient's physician had ordered them.
- Door-to door solicitation – beneficiaries were solicited in their homes and offered free groceries, medical equipment, and home cleaning services. Medicare was then billed for home nursing or home aide services.

Thus, by whatever standard used, health care fraud has constituted and continues to constitute a tremendous financial drain on both our private and public health care systems.[7,8]

US initiatives against fraud and abuse

To combat fraud and abuse, the federal government in the 1990s enacted and continues to propose new kinds of programs and legislation toward this effort, as well as relying on programs and laws created in the not so recent past and even a century ago.

Two good examples of the latter statement is the OIG of the US DHHS that seeks to identify and eliminate fraud, abuse, and waste in health and human service programs. The mission is performed through a nationwide program of audits, investigations, and inspection.

On the other hand, to fight overbilling, for example, the federal government has used a 19th-century law called the Federal False Claims Act. Prior to that Act, fraud was rather difficult to prove as it required 'knowledge of falsity.' The False Claims Act was originally enacted during the American Civil War to permit civil prosecution of widespread fraud among military contractors supplying the Union Army. Under the False Claims Act, a preponderance of evidence of actual knowledge, deliberate indifference of truth or falsity, or reckless disregard of truth or falsity is sufficient. There is also a Qui Tam (who also) provision, often called the 'whistleblower' provision, that permits persons who are knowledgeable about fraudulent claims to report the claims to the authorities and to share in their recoveries. Even if the government decides not to do anything, the private citizen may take responsibility for the case, sue on behalf of the government, and enjoy a greater part of the recoveries. The complaint is 'sealed' until such time as the government decides to prosecute the case, but the complaint and the name of the 'whistleblower' become public after the decision is rendered. The penalties of the False Claims Act include treble damages, a fine of $5000–10 000 per claim, interest, and possible exclusion from doing business with the government. It is becoming clear from these penalties as well as the risks inherent in the lower levels of required evidence that many organizations will settle, even if they believe they have not broken the law. The fear of paying $5000–10 000 per claim or perhaps even treble damages will motivate many to settle quickly.[9]

Despite the existence of various programs and laws, the federal government in the 1990s enacted new legislation and instituted new programs to buttress its efforts in fighting fraud and abuse. The federal government has also enlisted the efforts of the private sector to resolve these problems. This partnership has been forged between public and private entities to fight fraud and abuse. Members of this partnership include Medicare beneficiaries, Medicare contractors, state Medicaid fraud control units, quality improvement organizations (formerly named peer review organizations under Medicare), the Centers for Medicare and Medicaid Services (CMS), the OIG, the DHHS, the Federal Bureau of Investigation, and the Department of Justice.

During the 1990s, in terms of legislation, Congress enacted the Balance Budget Act of 1997 and the Health Insurance Portability and Accountability Act (HIPAA) of 1996. In terms of pilot programs, the federal government established Operation Restore Trust.

Health Insurance Portability and Accountability Act of 1996 (PL 104–191)

Often called the Kennedy–Kassebaum bill after its US Senate sponsors (Edward M. Kennedy (D-MA) and Nancy Kassebaum (R-KS)), HIPAA establishes a comprehensive program to combat fraud against public and private health plans. HIPAA required the Secretary of Health and Human Services, acting through the Inspector General, to establish a 'fraud and abuse control program' that would coordinate, among other activities, federal, state, and local enforcement programs and expand their activities on a nationwide basis. The goals of this program are as follows: coordinate federal, state, and local law enforcement efforts related to health care fraud; conduct investigations, audits, and evaluations relating to health care fraud; facilitate enforcement of civil, criminal, and administrative statutes applicable to health care; provide industry guidance relating to fraudulent health care practices; and establish a national databank to receive and report final adverse actions against health care providers.

Toward these goals the OIG and the Department of Justice have issued extensive guidelines for the operation of the fraud and abuse control program, have established a process for issuing 'advisory opinions' as required under law, and for expanding efforts to establish law enforcement task forces in each of the judicial districts in the USA in conjunction with other health-related Inspector Generals (Department of Labor, Department of Veterans Affairs, Office of Personnel Management, and Department of Defense).

In addition, the Kennedy–Kassebaum bill added Section 1843 to the social security law. The section's purpose is to promote the integrity of the Medicare program. The Medicare Integrity Program (MIP) was established to strengthen the DHHS Secretary's capability to prevent fraud and abuse in the Medicare program through various measures. First, it created a separate and stable long-term funding mechanism for program integrity activity which up to that point was subject to fluctuations in funding levels from year to year. The stable mechanism would permit the then-named Health Care Financing Administration (now renamed CMS) to shift its emphasis from postpayment recoveries on fraudulent claims to prepayment strategies that are designed to ensure that more claims are paid correctly for the first time. Second, by allowing the DHHS Secretary to use full and open competition rather than requiring that DHHS only contract with current intermediaries to perform MIP functions, the government is seeking to find the best value for contracted services. Also, MIP allowed the CMS to address potential conflict-of-interest situations.

Prior to the passage of the Kennedy–Kassebaum bill all contractors performed all aspects of the program integrity work. With highly specialized contractors focusing on fraud and abuse, prevention, and detection DHHS hopes to obtain a cost-effective and efficient pool of contractors. Contractors focus on program integrity activities for a given geographic area, rather than by provider type, as had existed until then. In this way DHHS hopes that contractors will have a more comprehensive picture of activity, and will be able to monitor, for example, whether doctors' bills match hospital bills, in terms of procedures performed and date of service.[10]

To achieve these various goals, CMS, the operator of the Medicare program, is to enter into contract with eligible entities to perform the following activities: medical review, utilization review, and fraud review; conduct audit cost reports; determine whether payments should or should not have been made under this Title and recover payments that should not have been made; educate providers, beneficiaries, and other persons in regard to payment integrity; and develop and update a list of durable medical equipment that is subject to authorization under this section and is frequently subject to unnecessary use in accordance with section 1834(a)15(A) of the Social Security Act.

As already noted, the law expanded CMS's authority by allowing the agency to contract with eligible entities to perform Medicare integrity activities and having new entities called safeguard contractors perform one or all of the activities then performed by Medicare intermediaries and carriers. While intermediaries and carriers could then qualify as safeguard contractors, they could not duplicate activities by performing them under both an intermediary contract and safeguard contract. It is either/or, but not both. To be eligible an entity must demonstrate its ability to perform such functions and agree to cooperate with DHHS and other law enforcement agencies investigating and deterring fraud and abuse. In addition, the entity must comply with conflict-of-interest standards applicable to accession and procurement and meet other requirements the Secretary of DHHS proposes.

Civil Monetary Penalties Law

Another important aspect of the Kennedy–Kassebaum bill should also be noted. Section 23 expands the prior Civil Monetary Penalties Law (CMPL) which was enacted in 1981 for fraud and abuse violations. This law allows the DHHS to bypass the criminal justice system in favor of a less restrictive administrative procedure, which can produce more extreme financial penalties than those established by federal courts in criminal cases. Imprisonment is not included in the range of sanctions for breaking the

CMPL rules. However, in addition to enormous fines and penalties, exclusion from participation in government health care programs is common. Moreover, because these are civil penalties, the government has an easier burden of proof. For the CMPL rules, the government merely has to demonstrate by a *preponderance of evidence* that a violation has occurred, which is a far easier standard to meet than the 'beyond reasonable doubt' standard under criminal fraud law. The following are the new CMPL rules.

First, the HIPAA of 1996 extended the CMPL jurisdiction to practically every federal health program. Thus, CMPL penalties now apply to programs such as TRICARE, veterans' benefits, and public health programs, in addition to Medicare and Medicaid. Formerly called the Civilian Health and Medical Program of the Uniformed Armed Services or CHAMPUS, the TRICARE program is a Department of Defense health program for active duty and retired uniform service members and their families. Along similar lines, the CMPL penalty amounts have been greatly increased from $2000 to $10 000 per violation. This change is important because the penalties apply for each claim form line item or prohibited practice. Thus, if during a patient visit a physician takes the patient's history, gives an injection, and diagnoses a specific pain, the 10- or 20-minute visit results in three or more line items on the total bill. If, for example, the services were found to be medically unnecessary and fraudulent or abusive, the medical practice would be looking at a minimum penalty of $30 000 from that brief visit.

In addition, the government may apply a damage assessment to increase this penalty, based upon aggravating or mitigating circumstances. Previously, the damage assessment was up to twice the amount of the claim. Now the law permits this damage assessment to be as much as three times the amount of the claim. Conceivably, the government could set a fine and penalty of $90 000 for that 10- or 20-minute visit. An effective internal compliance program will have a substantial impact on reducing the amount of the fine and penalty under these laws. To ensure adherence to the Act, experts advise every provider and managed care organization to establish an internal compliance program, including mechanisms for investigating and resolving reimbursement errors and other inappropriate activity. Laziness, sloppiness, and ignorance can all be construed as fraudulent activities under the new law.

To amplify upon the latter position, HIPAA's changes to the CMPL rules also include the imposition of penalties when the government can demonstrate that 'upcoding' or 'unnecessary care' in claims submitted for reimbursement was the result of extreme laziness or sloppiness. Upcoding is when a provider notes a code for procedure or treatment whereby the provider can receive a higher reimbursement because it is more complex than the actual procedure or treatment for which the provider is paid less. This lack of due care can be considered a false claim. A pattern of practice of upcoding and unnecessary care can also constitute a basis for civil money penalties and exclusion, even without the necessity of depending upon a false claim theory to justify the penalty. In other words, not only has the HIPAA of 1996 endorsed the government's previous position that repeated coding or other billing errors can make up a false claim, but a new civil penalty law imposes fines for excessive upcoding or unnecessary care even if the government cannot show that there was a 'false claim.'

The 'knowledge' requirement has been modified under the HIPAA. Whenever the law imposes a penalty in wrongful behavior that the provider 'should have known' that he or she violated the rules, this means that the provider must have actual knowledge of the wrongdoing or be so indifferent to whether wrongdoing happens that the provider 'recklessly disregards' the violations. This requires more outlandish behavior than mere negligent supervision. Thus, systemic indifference to billing errors, or continued tolerance of internal procedures that fail to monitor the accuracy of claims or that encourage upcoding or other violations may well be considered 'reckless' by the government and be subject to legal actions. The CMPL was originally intended to help enforcement agencies in situations where wrongful conduct escaped punishment because the 'knowing and willful' standard required under criminal law could not be met. Until the HIPAA's modifications, the knowledge standard was essentially one of negligence.

In February, 1998 the DHHS's OIG published a compliance program guidance for the health care industry. Its intent is to help hospitals and their agents and subproviders develop effective internal controls that promote adherence to applicable federal and state law, and the program requirements of federal, state, and private health plans. While the document presents basic procedural and structural guidance for designing a compliance program, it is not itself a compliance program. Rather, it is a set of guidelines for a hospital to consider if it is interested in implementing a compliance program. Fundamentally, compliance efforts are designed to establish a culture within a hospital that promotes prevention, detection, and resolution of instances of conduct that do not meet federal and state law, and federal, state, and private payer health care program requirements, as well as a hospital's ethical and business policies. In practice, the compliance program should effectively state and demonstrate the organization's commitment to the compliance process. Among the many topics the OIG document covers are standards of conduct, risk areas, claims development and submission process, medical necessity – reasonable and necessary services – anti-kickback and self-referral concerns, bad debts, credit balances, retention of records, and compliance as elements of a managerial performance plan. Overall, the OIG believes that an effective compliance program is a sound investment by a hospital.

Balanced Budget Act of 1997 (PL 105-34, Tax) (PL 105-33, Spending)

In addition to the HIPAA of 1996, the US Congress passed in the following year the Balanced Budget Act of 1997. Among its many provisions, including an expansion of Medicare program benefits and the addition of new kinds of program coverage for Medicare beneficiaries, the Act also provided new sanctions that the federal government can use to combat fraud and abuse. Among these sanctions, government could permanently exclude from Medicare or any state health program those convicted of three health-related crimes. The DHHS Secretary was also given the authority to refuse to enter into any Medicare agreements with individuals or entities convicted as felons. In addition, an entity controlled by a family member of a sanctioned individual could be excluded from the program. The Act also imposed various civil penalties. In more specific terms, the law includes:

- penalties for services offered by a provider who has been excluded by Medicare and Medicaid
- penalties for hospitals that contract with providers who have been excluded by Medicare and Medicaid
- civil monetary penalties levied on providers that violated the anti-kickback statute, under which the physician received some kind of incentive for referring patients. Medicare's anti-kickback statute 'penalizes anyone who knowingly and willfully solicits, receives, offers, or pays remuneration in cash or in kind to induce or in return for: referring an individual to a person or entity for the furnishing, or arranging for the furnishing, of any item or service payable under the Medicare or Medicaid programs or purchasing, leasing, or ordering of any good, facility, service or item payable under the Medicare or Medicaid program'
- requiring that health providers applying to participate in Medicare or Medicaid provide their social security numbers and their employer identification number so that CMS can check an applicant's history for past fraudulent activity
- barring felons from participating in Medicare and Medicaid
- establishing a prospective payment system for home health services, to be implemented by October 1, 1999. DHHS establishes in advance what it pays for a unit of service, how many visits will be included in that unit, and what mix of services will be provided. The prospective payment system is intended to be a very important tool to stem the flow of home health dollars
- paying home health services based upon location where the service is provided – the patient's home – as opposed to where the service is billed. This will stop agencies receiving higher urban reimbursement when, in fact, the services occurred in a lower-cost rural setting

- eliminating periodic interim payments to home health agencies. These payments were previously used to encourage Medicare participation and are no longer necessary
- developing guidelines for the use of home health visits such as how many home health visits should be required for various conditions. These standards will empower DHHS to crack down on providers who are offering excessive services for various conditions
- tightening eligibility for home health services so that providers can no longer game the system by certifying that patients are eligible for home health services simply because they need blood drawn on a regular basis. There is a specific benefit for drawing blood.[11]

Operation Restore Trust

From a historical perspective another major effort by the federal government to combat fraud and abuse began in May 1995 as a 2-year demonstration project and concluded on March 31, 1997. Inaugurated by President Clinton, its name was Operation Restore Trust. An initiative against waste, fraud, and abuse, the purpose of the project was to determine new partnerships and approaches to stop Medicare and Medicaid fraud and abuse and it represented the first comprehensive effort at collaboration between CMS and law enforcement agencies.

As a pilot program Operation Restore Trust proved successful. While the initial target states were New York, Florida, Illinois, Texas, and California, where more than one-third of all Medicare and Medicaid beneficiaries were located, other states were eventually involved. Some of the new approaches demonstrated under the Operation Restore Trust initiative included employing sophisticated statistical methods to identify providers for investigations and audits such as facilities with high reimbursement rates, the planning being coordinated among the CMS, Department of Justice, and other law enforcement agencies, as already noted. In addition state and local aging agencies/organizations and ombudsmen were trained and given authority to detect and report fraud in nursing homes, and other settings, with state survey officials who were experienced in monitoring home health agencies and nursing homes helping to identify inappropriate and fraudulent billings.[12]

As part of Operation Restore Trust, the Department of Justice involved the Federal Bureau of Investigation and US Attorney's offices across the country, while the US DHHS not only employed its CMS but also its OIG and its Administration on Aging. In addition, within the Public Health Service, the Health Resources and Services Administration designed, implemented, and operates a national data bank called the Healthcare Integrity and Protection Data Bank (HIPDB) that reports on final adverse actions that are taken against health care providers. The HIPDB was established under Section

1128E of the Social Security Act as added by Section 221(a) of the HIPAA of 1996. As already noted, the intent of the HIPDB is to combat fraud and abuse in health insurance and health care delivery. The HIPDB contains the following types of information: (1) civil judgments against health care providers, suppliers, or practitioners related to the delivery of a health care item or service; (2) federal or state criminal convictions against health care providers, suppliers, or practitioners related to the delivery of a health care service or item; (3) actions by federal or state agencies responsible for the licensing and certification of health care providers, suppliers, or practitioners from participating in federal or state health care programs; (4) exclusions of health care providers, suppliers, or practitioners from participation in federal or state health care programs; and (5) any other adjudicated actions against health care providers, suppliers, or practitioners.

HIPDB information is available to federal and state government agencies, health plans, health care practitioners/suppliers (self-query), and researchers (statistics only). The HIPDB is prohibited from disclosing specific information on practitioners, providers, or suppliers to the general public. (On May 1, 2007 the Data Bank's Proactive Disclosure Service went online. This service offers health care providers, such as hospitals, managed care organizations, and medical groups, the opportunity to monitor practitioners continuously. Health care entities who subscribe to the Proactive Disclosure Service will receive notification within 24 hours of the Data Bank's receipt of a report on any of its enrolled practitioners.)

These various agencies will be combating fraud and abuse on many fronts. In fact, the three fastest-growing areas in regard to Medicare and Medicaid fraud, for example, are:

1 *Home care industry*: billing for excessive services, billing for services not rendered, use of unlicensed or untrained staff, falsified plans of care, forged physician signatures, and kickbacks
2 *Nursing homes (including hospices)*: inappropriate payments and overuse of services
3 *Durable medical equipment*: similar abuses as above.

The federal government, in partnership with diverse elements of the private sector, has framed its attack upon the fraud and abuse of public programs such as Medicare and Medicaid. Some of the past investigations of the OIG involved such diverse issues as physician services at teaching hospitals, hospice eligibility and inappropriate payments for care, and laboratory fraud. As a 2-year pilot program, Operation Restore Trust proved very successful. Among its many accomplishments were the following:

• It identified $23 in recoveries for every $1 spent on Operation Restore Trust.

- It identified a total of more than $187.5 million in fines, recoveries, settlements, audit disallowances, and civil monetary penalties owed to the federal government.
- It achieved 74 criminal convictions, 58 civic actions, and, as of 1997, 69 indictments. In addition, 238 providers were excluded from the program.
- It established a special hotline (1-800-HHS-TIPS) in June 1995 which was still in operation in 2009 and receives thousands of complaints related to DHHS programs.[13]

In addition, the Administration on Aging's Ombudsman Program, as a partner in Operation Restore Trust, trained thousands of paid and volunteer longterm care ombudsmen and other aging services providers to recognize and report on fraud and abuse in nursing homes and other long-term care settings.

Also, CMS's contractors were educating the provider billing community, including hospitals, physicians, home care agencies, and laboratories about Medicare payment rules and fraudulent activity. This education covered current payment policy, documentation requirements, and coding changes through quarterly bulletins, fraud alert seminars, and, more importantly, policy through local medical review. The importance of education cannot be emphasized enough. For example, unintentional or not, hospitals may commit fraud in several ways. The first occurs when a patient is discharged and readmitted without leaving the hospital because the maximum insurance payment for the first stay expired. The potential for this occurring was revealed indirectly in an article published in the *New England Journal of Medicine* on April 2, 2009.[14] Though not about fraud, the article noted that during 2003–2004 almost one-fifth (19.6%) of the 11 855 702 Medicare patients who had been discharged from a hospital were rehospitalized within 30 days and 34.0% within 90 days. In the case of 50.2% of the patients who were rehospitalized within 30 days after a medical discharge to the community, there was no bill to the physician's office between the time of discharge and rehospitalization. The study estimated that the cost to Medicare of unplanned rehospitalizations (a sign of poor care) in 2004 was $17.4 billion. The second occurs when the hospital sends a bill for medication never given. The third happens when the hospital does not report a double payment from the insurer.

In still another effort to control waste and abuse in health care, CMS (then called the Health Care Financing Administration) initiated in 1996 the Correct Coding Initiative to develop a correct coding policy for all physician billing codes, which are referred to as current procedural terminology codes. Begun in 1996, this improved prepayment, control, and associated software update resulted in savings of about $217 million in its first year.[11,14]

As already noted, one area of the health care field that is subject to fraud and abuse is the area of prescription medicines. In 1996, for example, the

DHHS Inspector General found that Medicare payments for 22 commonly billed drugs exceeded actual wholesale prices by $447 million. For more than a third of the drugs, Medicare paid more than double the average wholesale price.[11] Apparently, this practice continues today as the following case demonstrates. In a class action lawsuit that claims that drug companies unfairly adjusted prices of medication, the plaintiffs received a major victory when the judge found that the defendants 'unfairly and deceptively caused false average wholesale prices to be published knowing that payers and the government did not understand the truth and severity of the markups.' In her opinion, dated June 21, 2007, the judge wrote that 'unscrupulously taking advantage of the flawed AWP [average wholesale price] system … by establishing secret mega-spreads far beyond the standard industry markup was unethical and oppressive.' The judge also wrote that such practices 'caused real injuries to the insurers and patients' who paid inflated prices for life-sustaining drugs.

Such drug-pricing fraud is part of a broad category of pharmaceutical fraud. In fact, the 2010 fiscal budget of the US DHHS is investing $311 million over a 5-year period by improving oversight and stopping fraud and abuse within Medicare and Medicaid programs, with particular emphasis on Medicare Advantage (Part C) and the Medicare Prescription Drug program (Part D), which could yield $2.7 billion in savings to the federal government.[15,16]

Two other areas open to prescription drug fraud are drugs bought over the internet and foreign-sourced pharmacies. Some websites are set up in states with few or no regulations. People can usually find a doctor somewhere to prescribe medication for a fee. Drug importation is another important issue, with many states advocating its activity because the price of a drug is lower in another country. There is also a representation issue in that, because a drug comes from country A, the purchaser may believe it is manufactured in that country, when, in fact, the drug may be manufactured in country B and the payment deposited in a bank account in country C. Also, there is the quality control issue as to whether patients really know the chemical composition of these drugs. Suggestions have even been proposed to reduce prescription drug fraud and abuse in the workplace, in addition to the use of hotlines, security staff, compliance, and internal audits. These include: education and preventive programs; the possible use of random drug screens, including prescription medications that are known to be abused, as a condition of employment; periodically comparing prescription, enrollment, and eligibility data with the pharmacy benefit manager (PBM) plan; advocating the use of picture identification, in addition to health plan membership cards, to hinder unauthorized use; encouraging the plan or PBM to analyze claim and utilization data to detect areas of potential fraud and abuse; and monitoring the use of expensive drugs or drugs prone to overuse or abuse, especially tracking prior authorization requirements.[6]

Thus, the federal government has instituted a number of programs to fight fraud and abuse in the financing of health care services not only within the public sector through such large entitlement programs as Medicare, but also in the private sector through the use of organizations especially established for these efforts.

Necessity of US fraud initiatives

As of 2008, the Medicare program was still considered prone to fraud and abuse since the program automatically paid bills it received from companies that possess federally issued supplier numbers. Rather than concentrating on fraud, the computer and audit systems in place at the time to detect problems generally concentrated on overbilling and unorthodox medical treatment. Employees reviewed fewer than 5% of the nearly 1 billion claims filed each year. The contractors, generally private insurance companies, review the claims and pay the bills for Medicare.

As another example, the necessity for the federal government to undertake programs and enact laws to combat fraud and abuse is underscored by a government report that was published in 1997. On July 16, 1997, federal investigators stated that the US government overpaid hospitals, doctors, and other health providers in 1996 by $33 billion, or 14% of the money spent in the standard Medicare program. According to the DHHS Inspector General, the books and records of the Medicare agency and its contractors were in such disarray that they could not be thoroughly audited. Hence, there was no way to determine how much of the overpayment was due to fraud. The report also stated that the government had no reliable method to stop or determine improper Medicare payments, and no reliable estimate of what it might owe on unpaid claims for service, as already provided.

Audits discovered a $4.5 billion 'computer error' in the agency's estimate of unpaid claims. They found that contractors sometimes mixed up Medicare's two trust funds for hospital and doctors' services. Other contractors confused amounts owed to the federal government with amounts owed by the federal government.

The 1997 report illustrated Medicare vulnerability to fraud and abuse as it made the following points:

- Controls over cash were not tight. Checks were signed by persons who had no authorization to do so.
- Medicare's huge computer systems have so little security that records can be easily altered or destroyed with few safeguards for the privacy of sensitive medical history, information, personal beneficiary data, and claim information.
- Payments were classified as improper because medical records did not show a need for the services provided, or the services were not covered by

Medicare. Routine billing errors and improper diagnostic codes accounted for only 9% of the improper payments.[17,18]

In the report, the Inspector General noted that Medicare was by its nature vulnerable because it had 18 million beneficiaries and paid million of dollars in claims through 59 contractors which are governed by a complex set of reimbursement rules. The Inspector General noted that CMS, then named the Health Care Financing Administration, had not sufficiently policed these contractors.

The Inspector General also provided several illustrations of erroneous payments. In one case, a nursing home was paid $15 362 for a 61-day stay by an elderly patient. Medical records did not reveal any condition that required skilled nursing home care. In another instance, a nursing home billed Medicare separately for routine services already included in the fixed amount paid by the federal government for each day of care. In other cases, auditors discovered that patients' medical problems were much less severe than indicated on the claims, so doctors should have received less money than they were paid.

Medicare fiscal intermediaries and carriers

One of the agents Medicare relies on to help fight fraud and abuse is the program's fiscal intermediaries and carriers. When Medicare became effective as a program in 1966, the US Department of Health, Education, and Welfare established a system in which fiscal intermediaries and carriers would administer a part of the Medicare program. CMS's current contracts with fiscal intermediaries and carriers were signed with the knowledge that the contractors were all involved in the commercial insurance business. As a condition of those contracts, fiscal intermediaries and carriers agreed to keep separate their commercial and Medicare business lines to avoid any potential conflicts of interest between the two lines of business. Essentially, the carriers perform a dual role. On the one hand, they are responsible for reimbursing Medicare providers for the services rendered; on the other hand, they evaluate physician practices and utilization patterns of Medicare recipients.

As already noted, the first part of the Medicare program is known as Part A, as the law is contained in Part A of Title XVIII of the Social Security Act. Coverage under Part A is for the costs of inpatient hospital care, other inpatient care, or home health or hospice care. Fiscal intermediaries under Part A perform the following responsibilities: claims processing, medical review, utilization review, auditing, and beneficiary relations.

The second part of the Medicare program is often referred to as 'supplemental Medicare' or Part B Medicare. This program, as already noted, is the voluntary supplementary program covering the costs of physician services and a number of other items and services not covered under Part A.

Enrollees in Part B are charged a monthly premium for the coverage. The carriers are responsible for claims processing, utilization review, audit activity related to fraud and abuse, and provider and beneficiary relations for the Part B portion. Medicare also has two additional parts. One is called Part C or Medicare Advantage, which is managed care. The other is Part D, the Medicare prescription drug benefit program. For purposes of discussion at the moment we shall concentrate on Part A and Part B.

In view of the dual nature of the Medicare program in respect to Parts A and B, the government decided that two different entities were required to administer each separate part. Claims under each separate part are paid differently in that there are different codes, payment systems, and contractors, as already noted. In addition, as another problematic example, the Medicare carriers' role is complicated by their position in the middle line of accountability in the Medicare Part B program. As already mentioned, the carriers evaluate and pay Medicare providers; however, the federal government, through the CMS, evaluates and pays the carriers. Just as Medicare providers are responsible for reporting their claims to the carriers to receive payment, the carriers are also responsible for reporting data from their utilization review program to CMS to receive their administrative payment.

In summary, then, the fiscal intermediary (Part A) and carriers (Part B) have many responsibilities in the Medicare program, including functions such as claim processing, audits, medical/utilization review, and finally, provider/beneficiary relations. For the purpose of understanding, a brief description of each activity follows.

Claims processing

Both fiscal intermediaries and carriers are responsible for reimbursing providers for Medicare-covered services. This includes a timely turnaround of payment from the receipt of invoice and the continuous following of beneficiary eligibility (i.e., payment of deductibles and coinsurance, use of lifetime reserve days). This responsibility also includes the development of electronic transmittal systems.

Audits

The fiscal intermediaries are responsible for performing Medicare audits on hospitals and other health care institutions. These audits verify expenditures and allowable costs.

Medical/utilization review

Fiscal intermediaries are responsible for conducting medical reviews of services such as home health, hospice, comprehensive outpatient rehabilitation facilities, and Part B outpatient physical therapy bills. Carriers also perform a limited medical review; however, these reviews are part of fraud and abuse investigations. Medical and utilization reviews by fiscal intermediaries and carriers do not include medical and utilization review activities that are conducted by the quality improvement organizations, formerly called peer review organizations.

Provider/beneficiary relations

Both fiscal intermediaries and carriers are responsible for provider and beneficiary relations. This includes the dissemination of information on new CMS initiatives to providers; verbally explaining policies and procedures to both providers and beneficiaries; and general public relations activities. In the past, hospitals and other health care institutions have complained that they have been placed in the position of explaining Medicare coverage, the diagnosis-related groups system, and eligibility requirements to an increasingly confused public. Many patients were obtaining their information about Medicare from the news media or information given by friends. Various providers have complained that the Medicare program, through its fiscal intermediaries and carrier system, has neglected the responsibility of informing beneficiaries of changes in the program.

Coding issues

Issues in regard to coding can assume many guises. Hospitals, for example, may unbundle tests that a patient receives. 'Unbundling' refers to the practice of submitting individual bills for separate tests that should be bundled together into a single bill for a group of related tests. The amount under Medicare for this 'bundled' amount is less than the sum of the amount for tests billed separately.

Another issue relates to billing service companies. Past OIG investigations have revealed that billing service companies which work on behalf of physicians have upcoded and/or unbundled procedure codes to maximize Medicare payments to physicians.

In addition, the OIG has found that physicians are not accurately or uniformly using visit codes in locations other than teaching hospitals and that it is not known whether carriers are adequately monitoring physician codes.

Another problem relates to whether physicians are using modifier 25 on their Medicare Part B claims to increase reimbursements. Modifier 25 is intended to be used to claim 'significant, separately identifiable evaluation and management of service on the day of surgery.'

Another issue relates to whether hospitals are incorrectly coding hospital charges for Medicare payment. Also, do the diagnosis codes on claims match the reasons for ordering and providing various services?

The aforementioned represent the kinds of coding problems that Medicare and the carriers as well as fiscal intermediaries encounter when processing claims and which can lead to incidents of fraud and abuse within the Medicare program.

Managed care

One aspect of the health care field which has developed dramatically within recent years and has had an impact upon fraud and abuse activities has been the organizational implementation of a concept called managed care. With the growth of managed care, federal fraud efforts are increasingly focusing on quality of care issues and watching for poor patient care resulting from fraud. By its very design, managed care has checks and balances. Its network care is provided with the gatekeeper's approval. Surgery usually requires a second opinion and authorization is required for expensive tests and procedures. Because of these restrictions, many employers and others view managed care as a foolproof defense against fraud, but they are wrong. According to the National Health Care Anti-Fraud Association, fraud in managed care can be more subtle and very hard to detect. The organization cites examples of automatic referral of sicker and more costly patients, perhaps in exchange for kickbacks, to providers outside the capitated network and the creation of inconvenient service location and/or appointment hours to decrease the patient's use of the managed care system. Others have cited failure to provide services, deficient treatment, falsifying credentials and deceptive enrollment practices such as selling insurance through bogus companies that had no licenses and no intention of paying for health care claims as other ways of committing fraud. While indemnity insurance may encourage overutilization of services, a capitated managed care system can increase the temptation of providers to maximize their income by withholding treatment.[19]

The aforementioned are some of the ways fraud can be committed under managed care. Fraud under managed care can become exceedingly important because, with the passage of the Balanced Budget Act of 1997, Medicare recipients, in addition to the traditional fee-for-service option, began having an opportunity to enroll in a variety of managed care programs from health maintenance organizations (HMOs) to preferred provider organizations (PPOs), also known today as Part C of Medicare or Medicare Advantage plans. These concerns were buttressed in May 1998 by a report (OEI-02-097-00070) released by the Office of Evaluation and Inspections, DHHS OIG, which reported that overall physicians' satisfaction with Medicare HMOs was low. While most physicians believe that their Medicare patients receive good care, their own misgivings with Medicare HMOs included a lengthy referral process, restricted clinical independence, limited access to care, an unsatisfactory complaint and appeals process, inappropriate utilization and quality assurance reviews, and questionable marketing. Many elements of these physicians' concerns can contribute to poor care and, perhaps, fraud and abuse activities, which can be documented, rather than good care that is based on medical subjectivity. Thus, safeguard contractors in regard to fraud and abuse activities will be witness to and have to increase their vigilance of a variety of settings and circumstances under which fraud and abuse in the Medicare program can transpire.

Impact of drug industry activities on public programs – view of DHHS

On February 9, 2007 the Chief Counsel of the OIG of the US DHHS testified before House Oversight and Government Reform Committee of the US House of Representatives about the federal government's view of fraud and abuse in the pharmaceutical industry. His testimony was titled 'Allegations of Waste, Fraud and Abuse in Pharmaceutical Pricing: Financial Impacts on Federal Health Programs and the Federal Taxpayer.' In his testimony the General Counsel identified three categories of fraudulent and abusive schemes that the OIG identified: fraud in prescription drug pricing, fraud in prescription drug marketing, and fraud in the dispensing and delivery of prescription drugs.

The Chief Counsel noted the important role prescription drugs assume in health care today. The expenditures for drugs by the federal health programs, including Medicare and Medicaid, are increasing rapidly. Medicaid expenditures for prescription drugs in 2005 were estimated as $41 billion, more than four times the amount of $8.9 billion spent in 1994. Prior to 1996, Medicare covered a limited number of prescription drugs. But despite this fact, Medicare expenditures for prescription drugs increased from $1.4 billion in 1994 to $10 billion in 2005. In 2006, the Medicare Part D program greatly increased Medicare's coverage of prescription drugs. In August 2008 researchers at the University of Minnesota stated that drug manufacturers are quietly raising drug prices by 100% – or even more than 1000% – for a very small but increasing number of prescription drugs which, in turn, drives up the cost for insurers, patients, and government programs.[20] Many of the pharmaceuticals are older medicines that treat fairly rare, but often serious or even life-threatening, conditions. One manufacturer in 2007 which manufactures a drug that treats spasms in babies increased the price of the medication from about $1650 a vial to more than $23 000. In 2007, the average wholesale price of 26 brand-name drugs increased 100% or more in a single cost adjustment compared to 15 drugs in 2004. In 2006, another drug manufacturer raised prices on four drugs by 3436%. Express Scripts, which manages drug benefits for large employers and insurers, noted that in 2007 prices rose an average of 7.4% for 1344 brand-name drugs. Stephen Schondeimeyer, director of the PRIME Institute of the University of Minnesota, which studies drug industry economics, stated, 'There's no simple explanation. Some companies seem to figure no one is watching so they can get away with it.'[20]

The Chief Counsel of the OIG of DHHS stated that Medicare and Medicaid have paid too much for prescription drugs because of fraudulent and abusive schemes that have targeted the federal health programs. He noted that some of the behavior contributes to the increases in the costs of health care programs and can distort medical decision-making by placing the financial interest of the prescribing physician ahead of the well-being of the patient. In other instances, unscrupulous providers take advantage of vulnerabilities in the reimbursement schemes, resulting in additional costs to taxpayers. He stated that the investigations by the OIG, working with its law enforcement partners, in regard to the pharmaceutical industry have resulted in more than $4 billion in recoveries. (This figure includes criminal and civil resolutions with pharmaceutical manufacturers, PBMs, retail pharmacy chains, and institutional pharmacies since 1999.)

Fraud in prescription drug pricing: manipulation of wholesale prices

According to the Chief Counsel, prior to 2005, Medicare Part B and Medicaid programs used as the basis for paying prescription drugs the manufacturer's 'average wholesale price' (AWP). Medicare has now changed the basis of its reimbursement methodology, but many states continue to use AWPs as the basis for Medicaid reimbursement for certain drugs. Generally, drug manufacturers send an AWP for each of their drugs to data collection agencies. In turn, each state obtains the AWP information from such agencies and uses it to establish Medicaid reimbursement for prescription drugs. However, the Chief Counsel noted that the AWP is prone to abuse. For example, if a manufacturer reports an inflated AWP, Medicaid reimbursement for the drug will, in turn, be inflated. By reporting an AWP that exceeds the price at which the drug is sold to providers, including physicians, the manufacturer creates a significant price difference between the provider's cost for the drug and the amount the provider will obtain in reimbursement for the drug from Medicaid. This price differential is known as 'the spread' and physicians who purchase drugs administered to their Medicaid patient can profit from it. In other words, if a drug X is sold to a provider and costs the provider $5 but Medicaid believes the AWP for that drug X is $10 and reimburses the provider $10 for dispensing the drug, the provider has made a profit of $5.

The Chief Counsel noted that some manufacturers have aggressively employed an inflated price spread as a marketing tool, to gain market share for their products. Purposeful manipulation of the spread to induce purchase of federally payable drugs implicates the criminal federal anti-kickback statute. For example, a manufacturer purposefully manipulated a drug's AWP to create an artificially high spread and then had its sale representative show to doctors the reimbursement comparison sheets that graphically showed the profits the doctor would obtain by purchasing one drug over another.

Fraud in the Medicaid drug rebate program

Another area of pricing fraud involves the Medicaid drug rebate program. The purpose of this program is to decrease the expenditures of the Medicaid program and the program mandates that drug manufacturers provide Medicaid with certain rebates on drugs provided to Medicaid patients. A statutorily defined rebate formula determines the amount of the rebate. Manufacturers must report to the CMS certain pricing information by drug, including the 'average manufacturer price,' and for some drugs, the 'best price.' OIG cases have concentrated primarily on abuses related to best price, which, subject to certain exceptions, should be the lower price (net of most discounts and rebates) at which a manufacturer sells the drug.

The following is how the rebate system works. Let us say, for example, the best price for a drug is $50.00 per 100 tablets or 50 cents a tablet. The pharmacist buys the drug at $70.00 per 100 tablets or 70 cents a tablet and bills Medicaid for reimbursement of 70 cents per tablet (the cost to the pharmacist) times the number of tablets dispensed to the patient in addition to a dispensing fee of $3.00. If the prescription was for 50 tablets Medicaid will ask for 50 (because 50 tablets were dispensed) times the 20 cents difference between what the pharmacist paid (70 cents for each tablet) and the best price for that tablet (or 50 cents) or a total of $10.00 (50 tablets × 20 cents) in rebate, but a claim may be sent monthly or quarterly for the aggregate number of pills dispensed during that period.

For many drugs, the lower a manufacturer's best price is, the higher that manufacturer's rebate liability to the state will be. Most discounts must be included in the calculation of the best price and manufacturers understand that giving a discount could increase the rebate owed to the Medicaid program. Because rebates are based on the total volume of the drug reimbursed by the state, even a small per-unit increase in the rebate can dramatically increase the amount of the total rebate owed to the state. To avoid this, the Chief Counsel noted that some manufacturers have knowingly mischaracterized discounts by structuring them as educational grants, sham data-processing fees, or similar arrangements in trying to disguise their status as discounts. The object is always the same – the preferred customer gets the drug at deep discounts and the manufacturer avoids additional rebate obligations to state Medicaid programs.

Impact of Medicaid drug rebate fraud on the 340B program

Errors or fraud in the Medicaid drug rebate information also have harmful effects on the 340B program, which is a disproportionate-share hospital

(DSH) program for pharmacies. In general, under a DSH program the US government provides special funding to hospitals which treat significant populations of indigent patients. There are two primary DSH programs, one for Medicare, and the other for Medicaid. The 340B program is managed by the Health Resources and Services Administration of the DHSS and provides for sales of outpatient drugs at or below a specified maximum price to certain health safety net providers (340B entities) such as DSHs, federally qualified health centers, and the Ryan White CARE Acts' AIDS Drug Assistance Programs. The Health Resources and Services Administration estimated that almost 12 000 340B entities would spend $4 billion on outpatient drugs in fiscal year 2007. The Chief Counsel noted that, although the 340B program differs basically from Medicare and Medicaid since it does not involve the submission or direct payment of claims, the prices at which 340B entities buy drugs are statutorily linked to the Medicaid drug rebate program. Under the 340B program, participating drug manufacturers sign an agreement stating that they will charge 340B entities at or below the maximum amount, known as the 340B 'ceiling price.' The ceiling prices are guaranteed whether the 340B entity buys drugs directly from the manufacturer or through a wholesaler. The ceiling price for each drug is calculated using a statutorily defined formula that is based on the drug's average manufacturer price and the Medicaid rebate amount per unit. Thus, if a drug manufacturer reports a best price that does not include all discounts for Medicaid rebate purposes, both the rebate amount and the 340B ceiling price may be adversely affected – the Medicaid program may receive smaller rebates and the 340B entities may pay too much for the drug.

Fraud in the marketing of drugs

The illegal kickback is one type of fraud in the marketing of drugs. The federal anti-kickback statute is a criminal prohibition against remuneration (in any form, whether it be cash or in kind, direct or indirect) that is made on purpose to induce or reward the referral or the generation of federal health business. Thus, there may be sales practices that are common or practiced for a long time in other sectors of business but they are not necessarily lawful or acceptable when federal health programs are involved. Illegal marketing activities, including the payment of kickbacks to prescribing physicians or the use of kickbacks to promote drugs for unapproved uses, present a risk to patients, as well as to the integrity of federal health care programs. Perpetrators of unlawful kickback schemes may be subject to criminal, civil, and administrative sanctions. There are a number of important reasons for the existence of the anti-kickback statutes, two of which are especially important in regard to the marketing and sale of prescriptions drugs. Kickbacks potentially increase the costs of federal programs because they encourage overutilization and may encourage the prescribing of more expensive drugs when clinically appropriate and cheaper options (such as generic drugs) may be equally effective. Equally disturbing, kickbacks can compromise the independence of medical decision-making by placing the financial interests of the physician ahead of the patient. In the OIG's experience, kickbacks offered to prescribing physicians by pharmaceutical manufacturers come in many forms, ranging from free samples for which the physician bills the programs to all-expense-paid trips and sham consulting agreements.

Fraud also involves 'off-label promotion,' which is the promotion of a product for a use that the Food and Drug Administration (FDA) has not approved. The FDA approves drugs for only those particular uses proven to be safe and effective and sometimes approves a product for only a single, narrow use. While physicians may lawfully prescribe a drug for an off-label use, manufacturers are prohibited from promoting a drug for uses other than FDA-approved uses. The General Counsel noted that the OIG had identified many situations in which promotional and marketing efforts have gone far beyond the approved use. By promoting their products for non-FDA-approved uses, manufacturers may cause the submission of false or fraudulent claims to Medicare, Medicaid, and other federal health care programs. Moreover, many of these off-label marketing schemes also involve illegal kickbacks to encourage sales for non-FDA-approved uses. OIG investigations suggest that some pharmaceutical manufacturers may be involved in a wide range of abusive practices that provide false and misleading information about the safety or efficacy of products for nonapproved uses. These practices include:

- using so-called 'medical science liaisons' that present themselves (often falsely) as scientific experts in particular disease to promote off-label uses
- sponsoring supposedly objective 'independent' medical education events designed to discuss off-label uses. In fact, the manufacturer provides extensive subjective input about the topics, speakers, contents, and participants of events
- proffering ghost-written articles about off-label uses. In these schemes, manufacturers pay physicians to write advocacy articles about off-label uses for products that are written, in fact, by the manufacturer. This practice is especially insidious, according to the General Counsel, because the publication of such articles in certain compendia may be enough to qualify off-label use for reimbursement under some state Medicaid programs.

Financial harm to Medicare and Medicaid is only one problem that off-label promotion causes. Off-label promotion may lead physicians to prescribe a product for nonapproved use based on false, misleading, or erroneous information, to the medical detriment of their patients. Also, off-label promotion gets around the FDA approval process, on which Americans rely to evaluate the safety and efficacy of pharmaceutical products.

Fraud in the delivery of prescription drugs

The OIG has not only investigated drug manufacturers but also investigated and resolved cases involving PBMs and pharmacies. These schemes typically involve fraud and abuse cases in the delivery of drugs or other operational aspects of the program. For example, the OIG has investigated a number of cases involving retail pharmacy chains that allegedly billed Medicaid for prescription drugs that were not provided beneficiaries. OIG and its law enforcement partners have also been involved in cases in which pharmacies switched the drug prescribed to the patient to exploit Medicaid reimbursement rules. For example, in one instance a national pharmacy switched generic Zantac tablets with capsules to avoid a federal payment upper limit established by CMS and the maximum allowable cost set by the state Medicaid programs for the tablets. By these and other switches, the pharmacy received additional federal and state dollars to which it otherwise was not entitled.

The OIG has also dealt with PBMs. Their function may include price negotiations with drug manufacturers, the development of formularies, and the provision of mail-order pharmacy services to members of health plans. In one instance, the government found that a PBM had solicited and received kickbacks from manufacturers to induce the PBM to promote their products, submitted false claims to health plans for services allegedly provided by the PBM's mail-order pharmacy business, and offered and paid kickbacks to health plans to induce them to enter contracts with the PBM. The government stated that their actions harmed Medicare and other federal health programs.

To counter these various fraud and abuse activities, the OIG is increasingly using its administrative authorities to sanction individuals engaged in such practices, in addition to criminal and civil enforcement. The OIG has the authority to exclude individuals and entities from the federal health care programs and to impose civil monetary penalties for a range of abusive practices, including kickbacks and false claims. For example, the OIG has pursued administrative cases involving kickbacks to physicians from pharmaceutical manufacturers, as already noted. According to the General Counsel, a physician who accepts a kickback from a pharmaceutical manufacturer in return for prescribing its drugs to Medicare patients is as culpable as the drug company that provided the kickback. In some cases, the physician has initiated the crime by demanding the kickback as a condition of prescribing a drug to patients. In the past, criminal prosecutors directed their limited resources toward companies paying kickbacks and generally did not focus on these physicians. The OIG has now taken steps and is using its authority to impose program exclusions and significant monetary penalties to target also physicians who thought they could demand kickbacks from drug companies without punishment.

To help safeguard the integrity of the federal health programs in regard to drugs, the OIG has issued a compliance program guidance for pharmaceutical manufacturers.[21] The compliance program guidance provides detailed information for drug manufacturers on establishing and operating an effective internal compliance program and identifying fraud and abuse risk areas, as it has developed similar compliance guidances for the various other health care sectors such as hospitals. The guidance describes the relevant fraud and abuse authorities and the major risk areas under these laws. It also offers concrete suggestions on how manufacturers can lessen their risk. For example, the risk areas include reporting data used to establish or determine government reimbursement, discounts, product support services, educational grants, research funding relationships with formulary committee payments to PBMs, formulary placement payments, average wholesale price 'switching' arrangements, consulting and advisory payments, business courtesies and other gratuities, relationship with sales agents, and drug samples.

Although the guidance is directed to manufacturers, much of its content relates to PBMs, customers, prescribers, and other parties involved in the provision of prescription drugs as well as serving as important guidance for participants in Medicare's new Part D prescription drug program. While the Medicare and Medicaid programs are subject to fraud and abuse schemes, the federal government continues to develop proactive enforcement strategies against those who are skillful in modifying their schemes to changes in reimbursement systems and government enforcement tactics.[21]

The future

Fraud and abuse activities within the health care field are likely to continue and increase as health expenditures become a higher and higher percentage of America's gross domestic product in future years. In addition, the demand for and the delivery of health services will continue to escalate as America's general population grows, especially the numbers of the elderly who have reached the ages of 65 or older, along with the various diseases that accompany old age and their attendant costs. Why are public programs such as Medicare and Medicaid such easy marks for fraud? The General Accountability Office has stated that the programs are fragmented, poorly supervised, and awash in public money. Much of the money is available to practitioners and entrepreneurs who have little accountability and can order goods and services as they wish; on the other hand, their clients have no incentive to care about costs, all of which are paid by a distant third party. A DHHS official once stated that more than 90% of Medicare spending, for example, is for payments to providers, yet claims processing and activities to prevent inappropriate payments account for only 1% of total program spending, with only 0.25% allocated for checking erroneous or necessary payments. In fact, physicians, supply companies, or diagnostic laboratories have about three chances in 1000 of having Medicare audit their billing practices in a given year. The DHHS official noted that, while 92% of Medicare providers do bill appropriately, the remainder could have received more than $3 billion in unwarranted payments between 1997 and 2002.[22] Concerned about this latter problem, DHHS began in 2004 a recovery audit program that Congress authorized as permanent in 2006. Beginning with only three states – California, Florida, and New York – contractors reviewed about 930 million claims submitted to Medicare, in 3 years returned to the federal government $300 million from these states, and identified errors in less than 0.2% of the claims reviewed. (Among the errors: in 3 years a hospital billed Medicare for conducting multiple colonoscopies on the same person on the same day. In another claim a provider billed for one type of diagnosis, respiratory failure, but an examination of the medical record indicated another principal diagnosis, sepsis, which is a potentially deadly infection.) DHHS expects to cover 24 states by the fall of 2008. When providers overcharge the government, they also have to refund any overcharged copayments or deductibles to the patient. If providers need more time to pay the government, they can apply for a repayment plan. If the provider refuses to pay, the Medicare contractor processing their claims will deduct future payments until the debt is paid.

In addition to overpayments, auditors also look for underpayments which they return to health care providers (which by 2008 amounted to about $20 million, mostly to hospitals). The tremendous size of the Medicare program with more than 1.2 billion claims each year not only makes it very susceptible to fraud but also to mistakes. The Office of Management and Budget estimates that payment errors total about $10.8 billion a year. To look at Medicare claims from another perspective, Medicare deals with 4.5 million claims each work day and 9579 claims per minute. In 2008 Medicare served about 44 million elderly and disabled people.[23] Perhaps, through the experiences CMS has received through the Medicare Integrity Program and working in coordinated fashion with law enforcement agencies and state agencies and employing tools such as review of provider activities, including medical, utilization, and fraud reviews; cost reports and audits; Medicare secondary payer determinations; provider and beneficiary education relating to payment integrity; and developing and updating a list of durable medical equipment that is frequently subject to unnecessary utilization in accordance with Section 1834(a)(15)(A) of the Social Security Act, the DHHS will be able to get fraud and abuse of various health programs under control and begin its diminishment in the ensuing years. Hopefully, DHHS will be able to transfer the experiences it has gained in combating fraud and abuse activities to other organizations, be they public or private, which are seeking to achieve the same goals in ridding the health system of wasteful expenditures, which could be used instead for improving the health care status of all Americans.

References

1. NHCAA releases fraud fighters handbook outlining strategies to protect the public against health care fraud. Washington, DC: National Health Care Anti-Fraud Association. (press release, undated).
2. *US Health Care Spending and the Impact of Health Care Fraud.* Washington, DC: National Health Care Anti-Fraud Association, 1997: 2–3.
3. *Blue Cross and Blue Shield Plan's Anti-Fraud Savings and Recoveries Increased 11 Percent in 2006.* Chicago, IL: Blue Cross and Blue Shield Association, 2006.
4. Largest health care fraud case in U.S. History settled. HCA investigation nets record total of $1.7 billion. Washington, DC: Department of Justice, 2003: 1 (press release).
5. Empire Medicare Service. Fraud and Abuse. New York: 1, 2 (press release).
6. Maas A. Pharmaceutical fraud: Rx for trouble. *Employee Benefit News* 2004; October: 1, 3.
7. Florida Department of Elder Affairs. *Shine the Light on Medicare Fraud and Abuse.* Florida: Florida Department of Elder Affairs, 1996.
8. Pear R. About those health plans by the Democrats. *N Y Times* 2008; March 3: A18.
9. Englander J R. Medicare fraud: a federal priority. What is it and how to avoid it. *NAHAM Manage J* 1996; fall: 8.
10. Prevalence of Health Care Fraud and Abuse. Statement of Bruce C. Vladeck, Administrator, Health Care Financing Administration before the Senate Committee on Government Affairs, Permanent Subcommittee on Investigation. Washington, DC: US Senate, 1997; June 26.
11. *The Clinton Administration's Comprehensive Strategy to Fight Health Care Fraud, Waste, and Abuse. HHS Fact Sheet.* Washington, DC: US Department of Health and Human Services, 1997: 2–5.
12. Secretary Shalala launches new 'Operation Restore Trust.' In: *HHS News.* Washington DC: US Department of Health and Human Services, 1997: 2–3.
13. *Operation Restore Trust Accomplishments.* Office of the Inspector General. Washington, DC: US Department of Health and Human Services, 1997.
14. Jencks SF, Williams MV, Colman EA. Rehospitalizations among patients in the Medicare fee-for-service program. *N Engl J Med* 2009; 360: 1418–1428.
15. Auerbach M. Federal judge rules drug companies engaged in drug price deception. *Pharma 101-Pharaceutical Fraud* 2007: 3–4.
16. HHS budget puts reform first. Washington, DC: US Department of Health and Human Services, 2009: 1–2 (press release).
17. Pear R. Audit of Medicare finds $23 billion in overpayment. *N Y Times* 1997; July 17: A21.
18. Johnson C. Medical fraud a growing problem. *Washington Post* 2008; 1: A20.
19. New ways to fight fraud. *Bus Hlth* 1995; August: 41–42, 44.
20. Appleby J. Drug prices up 100% – or higher. *USA Today* 2008; August 8: 1A.
21. Testimony of Lewis Morris before the House Oversight and Government Reform Committee, Allegations of Waste, Fraud and Abuse in Pharmaceutical Pricing: Financial Impacts on Federal Health Programs and the Federal Taxpayer. Washington DC: US House of Representative, 2007: 1–15.
22. Korcok M. Medicare, Medicaid fraud: a billion dollar art form in the US. *J Can Med Assoc* 1997; April 15: 1196–1197.
23. Freking K. Audits sting hospitals, physicians. Associated Press 2008; March 3: 1–2.

15

National health insurance

Introduction

The political party was quite clear when it called for 'the protection of home life against the hazards of sickness, irregular employment and old age through the adoption of social insurance adapted for American use.' These were not the words of Presidents William J. Clinton, Jimmy Carter, Richard M. Nixon, Lyndon B. Johnson, John F. Kennedy, or Franklin D. Roosevelt. No, these words were enunciated a century ago when Theodore Roosevelt ran for president on a political platform advocating national health insurance as the candidate of the Progressive 'Bull Moose' Party in 1912, Almost 100 years later Barack Obama, first as a candidate for nomination, then as the Democratic Party's nominee for president in 2008, and now the 44th president of the USA, took up the call for the establishment of a national health insurance program in the USA.

From ancient Greece

While every generation may think that the idea of national health insurance is a new and pressing issue to its time in history, the concept upon which national health insurance has evolved can be traced as far back as ancient Greece. Although issues related to national health insurance have been noted in various chapters, it might be useful at this juncture to recapitulate its history both in this country and abroad. As already noted, Theodore Roosevelt first proposed a national health insurance program for the USA in 1912. But, in fact, the very principle of compulsory participation can be traced as far back as 1798 when the US government created a marine hospital service (forerunner of the US Public Health Service) and required the owners of merchant vessels to contribute 20 cents a month into a sickness fund for each of their seamen.

The basic principle of individuals combining their resources in order to spread their economic risks can be followed as far back as the so-called funeral societies of ancient Greece, which ultimately became involved with a variety of social and relief functions, other than their original purpose of paying for members' funeral costs. Similarly, medieval craft guilds, heralds of the modern labor unions, often established welfare funds to help their sick or needy members. As the industrial revolution gained impetus in the 19th century, a number of labor unions and individual employers required that their workers join relief funds, many of which came under government control.

The concept that government should bear some of the responsibility for health care can also be traced as far back as the Greek city-states where tax-supported public physicians provided services to their citizens.

In 1854 the state of Prussia established the first broad-gauged compulsory health insurance law, 29 years before Otto von Bismarck unified Germany. The Chancellor was thus able to seize upon the precedent in 1883, when he convinced the German Reichstag to expand compulsory health insurance to workers throughout the German nation. When Bismarck's program proved very successful, the concept was soon adopted by other European countries, notably the UK, and eventually expanded into the comprehensive system of worker protection known today as 'social insurance.'[1]

At the beginning of the 20th century Great Britain was at the zenith of her power when it was said that 'the sun never sets on the British Empire,' thus admired and imitated in the USA. As a result, some groups began to push for a similar program of social insurance in the USA. This early promotion between 1910 and 1920 even originally had the support of the American Medical Association (AMA). However, professional opposition soon developed and, at its annual meeting in New Orleans in 1920, the AMA House of Delegates established a basic policy that the AMA followed for many decades to come. At that time the AMA stated that:

> The American Medical Association declares its opposition to the institution of any plan embodying the system of compulsory insurance against illness, or any other plan of compulsory insurance which provides for medical service to be rendered contributors or their dependants, provided or controlled by any state or federal government.[2]

Despite the AMA statement, interest in the subject did not disappear. By 1925 and 1926, a number of conferences were called to formulate plans for a study of the structure of medical services in the USA, culminating in the creation of the Committee on the Costs of Medical Care (CCMC). The Committee's final report was published in 1932. The majority of the Committee members held that medical service, both preventive and therapeutic, should be provided largely by organized groups of physicians, dentists, nurses, pharmacists, and other associated personnel and that the costs of medical care be placed on a group payment basis, through the use of insurance, taxation, or both. The minority report, which was supported by the AMA, objected to the proposal for group practice and the adoption of insurance plans unless sponsored and controlled by organized medicine.

After the CCMC report was issued, a movement began for the enactment of a national health insurance program. Originally, it was supposed to be included in the Social Security Act in 1935, but was omitted for various political reasons. In 1939 Senator Robert Wagner (D-NY) introduced the first national health insurance bill (S.1620) with the Roosevelt's administration's approval. Subsequently, additional efforts were made via the Wagner–Murray–Dingell bills of 1943, 1945, 1947, and 1949, during first the Roosevelt and then the Truman administrations, to enact this legislation. Despite a great amount of interest and support, these bills never passed either the House or the Senate. Recognizing that a universal national health insurance program could not become law in the foreseeable future, organized labor and other interest groups went back and reorganized their strategy. It was then that the long successful fight for Medicare which now provides care for many millions of elderly Americans began.

Burdens and stresses

Ironically enough, it was the very enactment of Medicare (Title XVIII) and Medicaid (Title XIX) amendments to the Social Security Act which served as the catalyst for precipitating the current crisis in the health care field and has led to renewed interest, impetus, and agitation for a more adequate and a more comprehensive system of financing and delivering health care to the American people. Hoping to alleviate, in part, the medical care ills and problems of the American people, Medicare and Medicaid only brought new burdens and stresses to an outmoded nonhealth system already under severe strain.

Except for its outdated statistics, one of the best descriptions of the ills and problems which plague the health care system in the USA at the beginning of the 21st century was enunciated in 1969 by Wilbur J. Cohen, former Secretary of Health, Education, and Welfare, when he stated:

> American health care is not really a 'system' but is essentially a mosaic of public and private health programs – one that has grown piecemeal to meet needs as they arose. A multitude of people, institutions, and arrangements are involved. There is a total of over 3 million health workers, including 300 000 physicians in a variety of practices and 700 000 nurses. There are 7000 hospitals varying greatly in size and in operation and some 20 000 long-term care facilities; there are local and national voluntary health agencies and professional groups, medical schools, hundreds of insurance companies, local, state and federal agencies, consumer groups and a variety of payment mechanisms, including fee for service, prepayment and charity, which further complicate the system.

This dynamic pluralistic arrangement has definite advantages. It provides opportunities for innovation and competition for quality development and incentives for organizational and quality improvements. And it has produced amazing medical miracles.

But out of it has evolved a number of serious problems that are likely to continue to face us in the decade ahead. Among the most serious, I would include the fact that the supply of certain services, such as those of physicians, dentists, and nurses, is inadequate. There is often an excess in supply-duplication of some services and facilities for high-income individuals, including some very expensive hospital services, and health facility planning is not now performed adequately. Also, children, the poor, the disadvantaged, the blacks and other minority groups often have inadequate access to medical care. There are shortages in less costly alternatives to hospital care such as outpatient care, home health services, extended care facilities, and nursing homes. Some costly services, especially hospital services, are sometime utilized unnecessarily. Many private health insurance plans produce undesirable incentives to use the most expensive methods of care; there are substantial gaps in coverage of health insurance. The cost of many drugs is too high. Many possible hospital management improvements have not been adopted. The growth of group practice has been retarded by legal bars and restrictive attitudes. Productivity in the provision of medical care has not been defined and measured. Insufficient attention has been given to preventive care and health education. There are insufficient financial incentives to restrain mounting hospital costs while maintaining high-quality medical care. Ignorance of quality comparisons or failure to undertake them has resulted in the purchase of high-priced drugs or unnecessary services. There has been unsatisfactory organization of activities at all levels – public and private – in the health care field. In summary, there are serious deficiencies in the organization, financing and delivery of health care in the United States.

These problems create obstacles to the provision of adequate health services for all Americans. Although the poor suffer from the inadequacies of the system, American families of all income levels are experiencing the consequences of our piecemeal system.[3]

When these words were spoken in 1969 the USA spent about $70 billion or about 7.2% of gross domestic product (GDP) on health care services. By 2008, the country's expenditures were slightly more than $2 trillion, or about 16% of GDP, and rising. Despite the $2 trillion in health care expenditures, the nation still has a shortage of health professionals like physicians and nurses. More nursing homes, extended care facilities, and home care programs are needed to meet the health demands of an increasingly aging population.

While in 1969 the internet and its websites were still at least two decades away from being invented and made available to the public, in the internet era at the beginning of the 21st century there is still a relative lack of quality comparative information available to the public regarding the provision of health services by and among health institutions and health professionals. Hospital costs continue to increase despite prospective payment and other systems now in place and these costs constituted almost 31% of total health expenditures in 2006 – the largest share of the total amount of national health care spending in that year. Forty-seven million Americans cannot afford health insurance at all and remain uncovered. Health insurance premiums have grown faster than inflation or workers' income since the turn of the 21st century, while industry spending on administrative and marketing costs, plus profits, consumes 12% of private insurance premiums. While legal barriers have fallen in regard to prepaid group practice, the development of managed care organizations and their provision of health services have received much criticism from the American public. Prescription medicine prices are still considered too high by the public and drug spending has increased as a share of overall expenditures since 2000, though drugs only represent 10% of national health care expenditures.

There is still a problem of health care access to the system for the poor, African Americans, and the disadvantaged. A funding increase in the state health insurance program for children was vetoed by President George W. Bush in 2008 to cover more children. Hospital services are still subject to duplication and their expensive equipment to idle use, while a national health planning law that was passed in 1974 to plan the expansion of health services on the community level, 5 years after Secretary's Cohen remarks, was repealed a decade later by the Reagan administration in efforts to reduce the federal budget. Only 36 out of 50 states as well as the District of Columbia have certificate-of-need laws in effect to control such hospital planning and expenditures.

Preventive health care such as warning the public against eating too much, exercising too little, or the hazards of smoking is more widespread today than in the past, but experts state that such activities which are modifiable still account for 25% of US health care costs. While more and more preventive care is paid for by third parties such as Medicare, its coverage is not as extensive as it should be. Even though the public may perceive that lawsuits against doctors are one of the major reasons for the increase in health care costs, this is not really the case. According to a 2004 study by the Congressional Budget Office, malpractice insurance premiums and liability awards account for less than 2% of overall health care spending.[4]

As in 1969, the government continues to play a predominant role in America's health care system. Although the government directly controls only 46% of national health spending, many of its policies still affect the bottom line of the health care industry, for example, by establishing Medicare reimbursement rates for physicians upon which private insurers base their own rates, or by requiring health insurance coverage for our citizenry, as the state of Massachusetts requires of its residents. So, while many circumstances within the health care field have changed since 1969, many others have remained the same.

Coalescing of forces for national health insurance

Given the ever-mounting socioeconomic and political burdens that the American public must bear in regard to receiving and paying for medical care, by 2007 a coalescence of forces within American society, including consumers, business, physicians, and others, began to become increasingly outspoken about their desires for health care reform, some through a national health insurance program. In a survey of 1200 adults in November 2007, *Consumer Reports* noted that a minimum of at least 50% to as high a figure as 88%, depending upon income levels (less than $50 000, $50 000–100 000 and more than $100 000) and the issues involved, were very concerned about not being able to pay for health care when they would require it. They were worried about being able to pay for health care in retirement, about being bankrupted by medical costs due to illness or accident, losing their health care coverage due to being laid off or leaving their job, and being unable to pay for the health care of aging parents. Consistent with these worries, more than 80% said the system should be reformed and should guarantee: coverage for all uninsured children; protection against financial ruin due to major illness or accident; the ability to obtain coverage regardless of pre-existing conditions; coverage that continues when people are laid off, changing jobs, or starting their own business; premiums, deductibles and out-of-pocket expenses that are affordable relative to income; and the ability to keep their current health insurance if they choose.[5]

In a survey of 2000 physicians in 2007, more than one-half (59%) now favored changing to a national health care plan and fewer than one-third (32%) opposed the idea.[6] This was a change from 2002 when 49% of physicians supported national health insurance and 40% were against it. One of the study's authors, Dr. Ronald Ackerman, said that 'as doctors, we find that our patients suffer because of the increasing deductibles, co-payments and restrictions on patient care ... More and more, physicians are turning to national health insurance as a solution to this problem.'[7] Ackerman added, 'across the board, more physicians feel that our fragmented and for-profit insurance system is obstructing good patient care, and a majority now support national health insurance as a remedy.'[7] The Indiana survey, which the researchers believe is representative of America's 800 000 physicians, found that 83% of psychiatrists, 69% of emergency room physicians, 65% of pediatricians, 64% of internists, 60% of family physicians, and 55% of general surgeons favor a national health insurance plans.[7]

Not only are consumers and physicians asking for health care reform, insurance companies, retailers, and other employers have joined forces with labor unions and other interest groups to propose their own plans. One group which has a vested interest in having the US health care system reformed is American business. Employers are steadily reducing medical coverage for employees and eliminating it for retirees. As American companies increasingly confront competition from foreign companies which don't directly cover their own workers, the trend will only increase. Yet, medical costs continue to rise at rates that far exceed any increases in incomes. When the costs borne by government, the private sector, and individuals are taken into account, the USA spends slightly more than $2 trillion annually on health care costs, more than any other industrialized country in the world. Researchers at the Johns Hopkins University School of Medicine estimate that the USA spends 44% more per capita than Switzerland, the country with the second highest expenditures, and 134% more than the median for member states of the Organization for Economic Cooperation and Development (OECD).[8] Some of the 30 members of the OECD in 2008 included Australia, Germany, Italy, Poland, the UK, Spain, Japan, France, Canada, Korea, Norway, and Turkey. These expenses have led to fears that an increasing number of American businesses will outsource jobs overseas or move their business operations totally offshore, leading to more job losses in the USA. According to 2005 data from the US Census Bureau, the most recent data available, in an American population of 290 million about 60% or 175 million were covered through employer-provided health benefits.[8] Those numbers have declined since 2001 when 65% of the population had some form of employer coverage. On the other hand, premiums have very rapidly increased, rising 87% since 2000. In 2004, health coverage became the most expensive benefit paid by American employers.[8]

These enormous health care expenses exert a heavy financial burden on businesses that are operating in the USA and can place these businesses at a very great competitive disadvantage when doing business abroad.

A good example is General Motors (GM), which provided coverage for 1.1 million workers and former employees. The company's health care expenses were enormous – about $5.6 billion in 2006. GM stated that health care costs alone added $1500 to the sticker price of every automobile it manufactured and estimated that by 2008 that figure could be more than $2000. Well, on June 1, 2009 GM finally paid the price of its high health care costs. On that day GM could no longer sustain its business operations as performed since 1908, when founded, and filed for Chapter 11 bankruptcy – the fourth largest in US history and the largest for an industrial company. While the costs of health care were not the only reason for the bankruptcy of GM, it certainly was an important one. GM followed a similar course taken by one of its US competitors, Chrysler LLC, which filed for Chapter 11 bankruptcy on April 30, 2009 and on June 10, 2009 found most of its assets owned by Italy's Fiat and under the new name of Chrysler Group LLC. In the end, even the $19.4 billion in federal government assistance was not sufficient to keep the nation's largest auto manufacturer out of bankruptcy and the federal government was expected to channel another $30 billion into GM to fund operations during its reorganization. Not only will many thousands lose their jobs, with GM plants closing as product lines like Pontiac were eliminated, but more than 650 000 retirees and family members who depended upon the company for health insurance will experience reductions in their coverage. Expecting to come out of bankruptcy within several months of its bankruptcy filings, even if GM builds 2 million vehicles per year in the USA, it will still spend $300 in retiree health care costs per vehicle it builds in the USA. The bankruptcy filing moves billions in retiree health care costs off GM's books.[9,10]

Health care does affect every level of US industry. Not only do large businesses cover their current workers but also, as already noted, they have large costs associated with insuring their retired workers. Health care expenses can devastate small businesses even more than larger companies. Many small businesses not only cannot afford the costs of health insurance coverage, but the expense of health care can impede their ability to hire the workers they wish to employ. Businesses contend that a wasteful public–private system is pushing health care costs higher than they should be. Jeffrey Rideout, a physician and the leader of the Internet Business Solutions Group at Cisco System's Healthcare Practice, says that the costs of businesses buying employee health insurance is just one factor of a company's total health care costs and that businesses pay a triple tax. First, they pay for insurance programs through health benefits. Second, companies indirectly subsidize Medicare and Medicaid by paying higher insurance premiums to make up for the fact that Medicare and Medicare reimbursements often do not equal the total costs hospitals incur in providing care to these patients. Third, businesses also subsidize the strain on the health care system that is brought about by the cost of providing care to America's uninsured, again through higher health insurance premiums. Given this situation, no one knows what kind of political storm it will take to reform the health care system, but increased pressure from the business community has made the possibility of change increasingly likely.

What's past is prologue

Back in 1969, America's health care system was deemed to be in crisis and the advisory committee to the Health Committee of the Senate Special Committee on Aging advocated a national health system, in part because, although acknowledging that millions of Americans had some form of health insurance, it stated that 'such coverage pays for only about one-third the cost of all consumer expenditures for health, while Medicare pays less than 50% of all medical costs of the elderly.'[11] At that time, the late Walter Reuther, president of the United Automobile Workers Union, stated the following in advocating that a national health insurance program be established in the USA – words that are as relevant today as they were when spoken in 1969.

> The insurance industry has worked hard. They have made a constructive contribution over the years. It has become increasingly obvious, however, that the health care crisis is beyond the insurance industry's capability of controlling costs while medical costs are spiraling. They lack the capability of assuring quality. They lack the capability of providing universal coverage ...
>
> We have therefore arrived at these conclusions after sober and careful reflection. We believe that this is a time of crisis and a time of decision and that we cannot afford to postpone facing up to the real challenges of this crisis. The people of America have a decision to make. We believe the choice is clear. We can continue to accept the status quo and spend increasingly billions each year to meet the skyrocketing costs of health care services; we can go on subsidizing the built in waste and inefficiency of a system that will continue to fail to meet our essential health care needs; or we can act in the knowledge that we must develop new ideas and new concepts and, through new social invention, create an appropriate system of national health insurance that will provide adequate and workable financial mechanisms to make high quality comprehensive health care available to every American.[12]

Thus, the proponents of a national health insurance plan are beginning to marshal their forces, develop their strategy, disseminate the arguments for such a proposal by citing the weaknesses of the current health system and, most importantly, are beginning to gain the necessary adherents and support for such a proposal among the business community, health professionals such as physicians, labor unions, the insurance industry, universities, national health associations, and others. As an example, in December 2007, the Centers for Disease Control and Prevention issued a report which stated that nearly one in five US adults – more than 40 million people – reported that they do not have adequate access to the health care that they need. In addition, nearly 20% of adults reported that they needed and did not receive one or more of these services in 2007 – medical care, prescription drugs, mental health care, dental care, or eyeglasses – because they could not afford them.[13]

Socialized medicine

When the issue of national health insurance is discussed in the USA, one of the first characteristics which is attributed to it is socialized medicine. Essentially, socialized medicine implies that physicians and others will all go on the public payroll and that government will take over the operation of the total health care system. So one of the first problems to overcome in educating the American public about the concept of national health insurance is a clarification of what any national health proposal seeks as its goals. A poll of American citizens was taken in January and February 2008 by the Harvard School of Public Health and Harris Interactive about their understanding of the meaning and consequences of socialized medicine in this country and the results were mixed. Socialized medicine was defined in the poll as single-payer government-run health care system. About 67% of those polled stated that they understood the concept very well or somewhat well, while 30% said they didn't understand the term at all or not very well. This seems to imply that public education about any future proposals concerning the establishment of some kind of a national health insurance plan in the USA in terms of its purpose and scope will be needed if those seeking to enact a particular plan are to gain public support for their own proposal. When those polled who stated that they understood socialized medicine 'very well,' 'somewhat well,' or 'not very well' were asked three questions, they noted those which they considered were applicable to socialized medicine. The poll showed that 79% thought that, in a socialized health system, the government makes sure that everyone has health insurance, 73% thought that the government would pay most of the cost of health insurance, and 32% said they thought that the government tells doctors what to do. When those who stated that they understood socialized medicine 'very well,' 'somewhat well,' or 'not very well' were asked whether socialized medicine would improve the US health system or worsen it, the results were as follows: 45% thought it would improve the health system, 39% thought it would worsen the health system, 4% did not think it would make any difference, and 12% did not know or did not answer.[14]

But, as defined in this poll, none of the candidates for the presidency has proposed socialized medicine as part of their campaign platform. Rather, various constituencies in the private sector have proposed different approaches or alternatives in regard to areas such as financing, benefit coverage, and administration or control. For example, if the national health insurance proposals of the past are any harbinger of what may come in the future, some may wish such a program to be completely voluntary, others may wish it to be wholly controlled by government, while still others may wish a mixture of the two, namely a voluntary program with minimum of government controls.

If concepts are needed of how other governments have established their own health system, there is no shortage of foreign approaches to examine. For example, the US health care system costs 83% more per capita than the Canadian system, where public funds collected through taxes pay as much as 70% of health care coverage. A number of East Asian health systems also deliver high-quality care for a much lower cost, such as in Hong Kong, Malaysia, and Singapore. The legacy of British colonialism, it is argued, has encouraged a strong state presence in the health care system. Taiwan's system is usually singled out as a model for cost-effectiveness. The system, implemented in 1995, provides comprehensive universal health coverage for Taiwan's population. Those who have studied the system conclude that savings from the national health insurance system largely offset the cost of covering those who were previously uninsured. In 2008 Taiwanese were assessed about $20 a month for full health coverage.[8]

Of course, when socialized medicine is discussed, one other nation, perhaps more than others, is usually mentioned – the UK. Long before Aneurin Bevan, health secretary, initiated the National Health Service (NHS) which began operating on July 5, 1948, the idea that medical care was a basic human right was institutionalized in England when the British Parliament passed the National Health Insurance Act in 1911. Under this 1911 Act, all manual workers whose income was below a certain level were protected by mandatory health insurance whose income level for health insurance was gradually raised until the NHS was enacted in 1946 and became effective as a program, as already noted, on July 5, 1948.

The central principles of the NHS were quite clear: the health service would be available to all and financed entirely from taxation, which meant that every tax payer contributed to it. Coverage is universal, covering all citizens and legal residents. Ninety-five percent of funding comes from taxes, and 5% from user charges, such as a copayment for prescription drugs. Half of England's population receives drugs for free, based on exceptions of age, disability, and pregnancy. The rest of England pays copayments. Wales and Scotland have abolished all copayments. Under the British system the government pays the doctor and hospital fees directly, although some doctors accept private insurance or fees directly from patients and some hospitals accept some funding from private insurers. Patients do not receive bills for NHS care.

The government's National Institute for Health and Clinical Excellence advises which high-cost treatments should be covered. The NHS administers the country's health care and dental services, with funding and support from the UK Department of Health. The system is divided into 10 regional strategic health authorities, and within those it is divided into trusts: primary care trusts, which administer public health and primary care; foundation (specialized hospital) trusts; and ambulance trusts. While general practitioners and dentists are paid per patient registered with them and hospitals and specialist services are provided in government hospitals and other facilities by salaried professionals, local health authority services provide maternity and child welfare, home nursing, and other preventive services. The NHS provides care through gatekeeper general practitioners who direct patients to specialists and more complex care as needed.

The NHS is the name commonly used to refer to the four publicly funded health care systems of the UK, collectively or individually, although only the health service in England uses the name NHS without further qualification. Each system operates independently and is politically accountable to relevant devolved governments of Scotland (Scottish government), Wales (Welsh Assembly government), Northern Ireland (Northern Ireland Executive), and to the UK government for England.

Since 1990 many changes have been brought about within the NHS. In 2007 the introduction of robotic arms led to groundbreaking operations to treat patients for fast or irregular heartbeats; in 2004 all patients waiting 6 months or longer for an operation were given a choice of an alternative place of treatment; in 2002 primary care trusts were established to improve administration and delivery of health care at the local level; in 2000 new health facilities opened offering convenient access, round the clock, 365 days a year; in 1998 a nurse-led advice service provides people with 24-hour advice over the telephone; and in 1990 the NHS and Community Care Act introduced an internal market, which means health authorities manage their own budgets. However, despite these changes, the NHS continues to confront the problem of maintaining a steady source of government funding in view of the costs of growing expensive treatments.

The necessity for the USA to reform its health care system was borne out by a survey of 12 000 adults published in 2007 by the Commonwealth Fund of New York City. The study compared the characteristics of US health care with that of Australia, Canada, Germany, the Netherlands, New Zealand, and the UK. Except for the USA, all the surveyed countries have universal health insurance systems. The survey results were as follows:

- US adults encountered the highest rates of overall errors, including laboratory and medication errors, among adults in the seven countries. One-third of US patients (32%) who had chronic conditions reported medical, medication, or laboratory test errors in the prior 2 years, compared with 28% of patients in Canada, 26% in Australia, and fewer patients in other countries.

- In the USA, 37% of all adults who were surveyed – and 42% with chronic conditions – did not take their medications, did not visit a doctor when ill, or did not obtain recommended care in the previous year because of the cost. These rates were well above those rates recorded in the other six countries. Few people in Canada, the Netherlands, and the UK reported that they had missed care because they could not afford it.
- A high proportion of US adults also have serious problems paying their medical bills – nearly one-fifth (19%), more than twice as high as the rate in the next highest nation. Nearly one-third (30%) of US survey respondents spent more than $1000 in the previous year in out-of-pocket medical costs. Nineteen percent of Australian and 12% of Canadians spent this much; rates were lower in other countries.
- Despite the arguments that countries with universal health systems have long waits to receive care, or even rationing of care, one-half or more of the adults in Germany, the Netherlands, and New Zealand reported having rapid access to physicians. Yet, in the USA, only 30% of adults stated that they could receive appointments on the same day with their doctors when they were ill. In addition, two-thirds of US adults – as well as two-thirds of adults in Canada and Australia – reported difficulty in obtaining care on nights, weekends, or holidays.
- US adults reported high rates of coordination and billing problems. For example, 23% of US adults stated that either test results were not available at the time of the appointment or the doctors ordered duplicate tests. In comparison, 19% of Germans and 18% of Australians reported these problems; rates were lower in other countries.[15]

For these and other reasons there is now a national call in the USA for reforming and rebuilding the American health care system.

American proposals

One of the leading issues which was debated in the 2008 American presidential election concerned national health insurance. During his campaign as presidential candidate of the Democratic Party, then Senator and now President Barack Obama outlined his proposal for a national health insurance plan to provide access to health care services for all Americans who wish it. His plan would add public plans or purchasing pools through which people could buy comprehensive, affordable health insurance, expand public programs like Medicaid and the State Children's Health Insurance Program (SCHIP) to cover more people, provide subsidies for families that do not qualify for Medicaid and SCHIP, and expand access to current private plans. In addition, his plan would add federal requirements that now only apply in individual states, such as requiring mental health coverage, mandates that could increase the costs of health insurance. He would also mandate coverage only for children.

President Obama has stated that consumers should not be required to purchase health insurance policies until costs can be reduced enough to make premiums affordable which, in his opinion, is the basic reason people do not buy health insurance today. His plan also includes subsidies to employers to reduce the employer's cost burden by partially reimbursing employer health plans for catastrophic expenses. Also as a presidential candidate President Obama stated that he would require employers to make a contribution toward health care or pay a percentage of their payrolls into a purchasing fund. His campaign estimated that the plan would save between $110 billion and $200 billion per year in health care spending, but outside health experts are not certain. As a presidential candidate President Obama stated that his administration would reduce premiums by up to $2500 for a typical family per year in his first term by investing in disease prevention, not just disease management; encourage 'team care' for treatment coordination of chronic conditions, recognizing the fact that about 80% of the health care dollars in the USA is spent on about 20% of people suffering from chronic illnesses and other serious medical problems; by investing in a paperless health care system (electronic medical records and other health information technology), reduce administrative costs; and by covering every single American and ensuring that they can take their health care with them if they lose their job.[8,16–18]

In keeping, in part, with this promise, President Obama announced on April 9, 2009 that the federal government is establishing a new system for updating medical records for servicemen and women during and after their military careers. The joint virtual lifetime electronic record will, among other things, help ensure a streamlined transition of health records between the Pentagon and Veterans Administration and give health care providers the opportunity to deliver high-quality care while reducing medical errors. When separating from the service, the veteran will no longer have to take his/her own paperwork from the Department of Defense duty station to a local Veterans Administration health center because it will now transition with the serviceperson and remain with the person forever.

In summary, then, President Obama campaigned on the idea of bringing down medical costs, improving quality, and eventually realizing universal insurance coverage. As already noted, he pledged to cover every child and reduce the average family's medical bill by $2500 a year. He fulfilled this former pledge as President Obama on Februay 5, 2009 when he signed into law an expansion of the SCHIP program, increasing its coverage from 6 million to 11 million children. (SCHIP is a program for parents who earn too much to qualify for Medicaid but still cannot afford private health insurance.) He also advocated initiating policies in promoting generic drugs and repealing the ban on direct price negotiation between Medicare and drug companies as well as placing a greater emphasis on prevention and expanding participation in the government-subsidized Medicare and Medicaid programs.

To back up President Obama's campaign promise to reform America's health care system, the administration in the winter of 2009 established a $634 billion health care reserve fund over 10 years in its fiscal 2010 budget. The purpose of the fund is the president's attempt to show how the country could expand health insurance to millions more Americans, improve quality, and at the same time begin to control escalating medical bills that threaten the solvency of families, business, and government.

But not all suggestions for health care reform are coming from politicians. They are also coming from the private sector as well, as in the case of Ezekiel J. Emanuel, chairman of Department of Clinical Bioethics at the National Institutes of Health Clinical Center, and Victor R. Fuchs, former president of the American Economic Association. They believe that five essential changes must be made within the American health care system to achieve comprehensive reform:

- Get business out of health care. Health care is not part of their core competencies but something they use as part of labor relations. It creates job lock and distorts employers' hiring and firing decisions.
- Guarantee every American an essential benefits package. This package – modeled on what members of Congress get – should be provided by qualified plans that would receive a risk-adjusted payment for each enrollee. Americans could choose their health plans with guaranteed enrollment and renewability; 'cherry-picking' and 'lemon-dropping' would be minimized. [In insurance by only insuring healthy people and refusing to insure those who were unhealthy or are likely to become unhealthy, a health insurance company can 'cherry-pick' the most profitable customers. Some say 'cherry-picking' or 'lemon-dropping' is when customers are charged higher premiums because of their medical history.]
- The universal package should be financed by a dedicated tax that everyone pays, such as a value-added tax. [A value-added tax is a fee that is assessed against businesses by a government on the increased value of goods and services at each discrete point in the chain of production and distribution, from the raw material stage to final consumption, thus ultimately passed on to the consumer. It is a common form of taxation imposed upon the member states of the European Union.]
- Administer the program through an independent National Health Board and regional boards modeled on the Federal Reserve System. They would oversee health plans, define the benefits package, and, through strong

incentives, facilitate adoption of patient safety measures and electronic management of medical records.

*   Establish an independent Institute of Technology and Outcomes Assessment to systematically evaluate new technologies and quantify their health benefits in relation to their costs. These evaluations would be used by the National Health Board and health plans.[19]

The authors believe that the aforementioned reforms would get rid of job lock, increase workers' earnings, and make labor more efficient. It would also provide Americans rather than their employers with their choice of health plans, physicians, and hospitals. They also believe the reforms would eliminate the $200 billion tax deduction for providing health coverage. But, most significantly, the authors believe that such reforms would improve efficiency and provide cost control for the health care system. The authors noted that the US health care system wastes money on administration, unnecessary tests, and marginal medicines that cost a great deal for small health benefits. It also provides strong financial incentives to preserve inefficiency. Getting rid of an employer's vetting of insurance companies and all the costs associated with it would save tens of billions of dollars. Since all Americans would be guaranteed coverage, according to the authors, means testing and determination of subsidies necessary for Medicaid and SCHIP would be eliminated. Finally, the expected consolidation of the health insurance industry would also increase efficiency.

The authors believe our health system is broken and that only a comprehensive change can provide universal portable coverage, lessen inefficiency, control costs, and guarantee health care for all Americans for very many years to come.[19] The aforementioned were but just a few of the ideas being put forward in 2008 and many more are to be expected as the debate of national health insurance reform in the USA is renewed once again.

Conclusion

For the past century national health insurance has appeared to be more of a dream than a coming reality, despite the number of presidents who advocated its passage. The social and economic conditions which exist in this country will, of course, determine whether this promise becomes law, and if so, the kind of program and the degree of involvement government and the private sector of society will have in such a plan. Health authorities state that certain conditions must continue to exist for government to have greater control over the health care system than it has at present (and to which many groups and organizations may not be willing to acquiesce). They state that as long as:

*   the costs of medical care continue to increase faster than the Consumer Price Index

- the amount of health care spending continues to be an increasing percentage of America's GDP, to the detriment of there not being enough monies to meet America's nonhealth care needs
- the number of people who are financially unable to buy health insurance continues to increase
- physicians, pharmaceutical companies, and others become more and more the object of public and Congressional criticism
- Medicaid problems worsen instead of improve, to the detriment of state government finances
- public objections against the high cost of medical care worsen
- Congress reacts with more and more investigations into the abuses of the system by those who provide health care services
- business believes that the health insurance which it purchases does not adequately cover health care services due to increasing costs and as long as the health insurance contributions it makes on behalf of its employees reduce its own profit margins

then the convergence of all these aforementioned forces may impel Congress to enact a program which, it believes, will ameliorate the conditions about which the public, big business, and labor are most vocal, namely, the high costs of paying for ill health. And the public may not be too discriminating as to the methods used to accomplish this task, as long as its own personal pocket book is aided by such a measure and the medical costs which it must bear are controlled. As far back as 1977, the warning signs were there, as when Robert D. Kilpatrick, then president of the Connecticut General Insurance Company, stated:

> If the private sector cannot show that it is able to control these rapidly rising costs, business managements, unions and everyone else concerned may well throw in the towel and seek a government takeover out of despair.[20]

Thus, social planners in the interest of national health insurance may have to reorder the approach of the health care field, assign new roles, and develop new kinds of organizations for the delivery of the highest quality of health care at reasonable costs. The politics of health care costs are based on false assumptions on a massive scale. Most Americans think that someone else is paying for their health care. Workers with employer-provided health insurance think that their employers are paying. Retirees and the poor think that state and federal governments through Medicaid (the poor) and Medicare (retirees) are paying. Because people believe that if spending is controlled someone else – not they – will be harmed or affected, the public has no interest in controlling expenditures. The various groups which compose the health industry have no interest because the more money that is spent on health care services and products, the higher is their income and profits.

If we examine the debate today on health care costs, there are a number of measures and programs that are not very successful in their intent to control health care costs or improve access to health care services. The physician reimbursement formula under Medicare has not brought about a redistribution of primary care physicians into rural or inner-city locales where they are in short supply and would receive higher reimbursements. Those states that still enforce the certificate-of-need laws after the repeal of national health planning in the 1980s have not stemmed the proliferation and duplication of expensive medical technology in their areas. Only a few states have even maintained health planning agencies on the local level to control costs in their own communities. Medicare's prospective payment systems have not stemmed the cost increases in hospitals, nursing homes, or home health agencies, though, perhaps at times, have slowed down their rate of increase. Abuse and fraud of the Medicare program are still rampant. Despite the enactment of Medicare's Part D drug program, many of the elderly are finding prescription drug prices prohibitive in their personal budget.

To be sure, there will be new kinds of delivery systems developed in the future, whether they are called health maintenance organizations, preferred provider organizations, convenient care centers in retail outlets, or other innovative mechanisms such as health savings accounts which make consumers more sensitive to the costs of care and what they are spending. But the underlying tenet of our health care system as it evolves in the future will be controls, whether they are instituted by state government or the federal government, or a combination of both. Thus far, voluntary controls over the costs of health care or even monitoring the quality of care of those who deliver such services have not been very successful in the view of those who advocate controls.

It must be remembered that the various elements making up our health care system are not isolated entities but rather interlocked and interrelated with all other activities. For example, the core of our system may begin with the doctor–patient relationship but their interaction eventually affects other segments of the health care field. Thus, when a patient visits a doctor the following interactions occur throughout the system:

- whether or not a health insurance company pays the benefit claims for the patient's visit
- whether or not a laboratory is used to assist in the patient's diagnosis
- whether or not other specialists – medical or paraprofessional personnel – are called in for consultation
- whether or not the doctor has to use expensive medical technology like magnetic resonance imaging to help in the diagnosis
- whether or not a short-term acute or a long-term institution is used in the patient's treatment

- whether or not a pharmaceutical firm's drug product is prescribed for the patient's ailment.

When a reform to improve the system is addressed to one group within the industry, its impact eventually has a ripple effect on other groups. Consequently, the problems that beset the health care system must be viewed and resolved as an organic whole rather than as isolated entities. For this and other reasons there is now a drive to reorganize and restructure the health care system by means of a national health insurance program by shaking up the old system of cottage industries and hopefully creating a system that is coherent, organized, and integrated such as, in part, through the greater use of information technology. Through such a national health insurance program, the system hopefully will become more accessible to those who are underserved while its quality will be controlled, and health care will be delivered at prices which are fair to both the consumers and providers of care.

However, not everyone believes our present health care system requires reorganization. If you believe that the health care system should remain as it is, then consider the organization where you work, especially if it operates on the profit motive. Look at your organization and ask yourself the following questions: Are the management functions of your establishment integrated and coordinated? Does your business have a department whose sole purpose is corporate planning? Does your department operate within a defined budget determined in advance of the business year? Is there a chart defining the lines of departmental authority and responsibility as well as interdepartmental relationships through the organization? Do you know the specific purpose of your department as well as that of others within your company? Does your establishment maintain some kind of training program for new employees and encourage taking educational courses outside employment hours to keep abreast of developments in the field? Does your Board of Directors oversee your business operations and give guidance and direction towards its future operational goals? Does your organization strive for management efficiency and economy in its operations? Does your organization maintain affiliation with other companies which are part of its overall corporate structure?

These same questions defining the structure of your organization's operations have great relevance to the health care field, but, in some instances, the concepts to which they refer have different names. They are called prospective reimbursement, rate review, cost commissions, prospective budgeting, health care planning, institutional affiliation, continuing education, and more. If your organization operated with duplicative departments and services, without an organizational chart as to functional responsibilities, without interdepartmental support, without organizational planning as to its future goals, without hierarchal oversight or direction as to its future operations, your organization and its stockholders would go out of business and become bankrupt quickly. Because of the latter characteristics, the health care system, as we know it, also appears to be going out of business. Its stockholders – the American consumer-patient whose finances support the system, both publicly and privately – are becoming bankrupt because of its present methods of operation. If it is not fair to ask your organization's stockholders to lose their money because of the way your company operates, is it any fairer to ask American consumer-patients to lose theirs? President Obama does not think so.

On September 8, 2009 President Obama appeared before a joint session of the US Congress and outlined in language more specific than his campaign rhetoric what he is seeking in a national health insurance plan that would meet three major goals: provide more security and stability to those who have health insurance; provide health insurance to those who do not have health insurance; and slow the growth of health care costs for American families, businesses and government.

- First, in regard to security and stability, for those covered by health insurance through their jobs, Medicare or Medicaid, nothing in the plan will require anyone to change the health insurance coverage of their employer or change the physician they have. Upon his signing of the law it will be immediately illegal under the president's plan for an insurance company to deny coverage because of pre-existing conditions. It will be illegal for an insurer to drop anyone's insurance coverage or water it down when they become sick or need it the most. Insurers will not be allowed to place an arbitrary limit on the amount of coverage a person receives in a given year or a lifetime. There will be a limit on how much a person can be charged for out-of-pocket expenses and insurance companies will be required to cover at no extra charge routine checkups and such preventive measures as mammograms and colonoscopies to save lives and money.
- Second, a new insurance exchange will be created for those without health insurance who may lose their job, or change jobs or go out on their own and start a small business so that they can obtain coverage. The exchange is a marketplace where individuals and small businesses can shop for health insurance at competitive prices. As one large group, the customers will have greater leverage to bargain with insurance companies for better prices and quality coverage. For those small businesses and individuals who still cannot afford the lower priced insurance available in the exchange, tax credits will be provided the size of which will be based on the individual's need. And all insurance companies that want access to the new marketplace will have to abide by the consumer protections outlined by President Obama. The exchange will take effect four years after the signing of the law. Meanwhile, for those Americans who cannot obtain health insurance at the present time because of pre-existing

medical conditions the plan will immediately offer low cost coverage that will protect them against financial ruin if they become seriously ill.

Also, the President sought a nonprofit public option within the insurance exchange that would only be an option for those who do not have insurance. No one would be forced to choose the public option and it would not impact upon those who have insurance. The US Congressional Budget Office estimates that less than 5 percent of Americans would sign up. Taxpayers would not subsidize this public option. The public option would have to be self sufficient and rely upon the premiums it would collect. By avoiding some of the overheads that get consumed in private companies by profits, excessive administrative costs, and executive salaries, the public option would keep pressure on insurers to keep their policies affordable.

- Third, individuals will be required to carry basic health insurance just as states require persons to carry auto insurance. Businesses will be required to either offer their workers health care or contribute to help cover the costs of their workers. There will be a hardship waiver for individuals who still cannot afford coverage and 95 percent of all small businesses would be exempt from these requirements because of their size or profit margin. His plan would not insure or apply to those who are illegally in the United States. Also, President Obama stated that no federal monies would be used to fund abortions and federal conscience laws will remain in place. These laws express the decided opinion of the US Congress and the American people that no individual – doctor, patient or other health professional – should be forced to violate his or her conscience in the provision of medical care. To save money in Medicare and Medicaid unwarranted subsidies to insurance companies will be eliminated because, according to the president, they pad profits and do nothing to improve a patient's care. Also, an independent commission of doctors and medical experts will be created to identify waste and inefficiency, and the commission can also encourage the adoption of best practices by doctors and medical professionals that offer high-quality care at costs below average, everything from reducing hospital infection rates to encouraging better coordination between teams of doctors. No money will be taken from the Medicare trust fund to help pay for the plan. Rather, most of the plan will be paid for, in part, by eliminating waste and inefficiency in Medicare and Medicaid as well as the Obama plan charging insurance companies a fee for their most expensive policies to encourage them to provide greater value for the money.

In addition, in his Congressional address the president noted that there were other issues related to his plan that had not been worked out as yet but the president neither specified nor discussed their nature.

So the question arises. Will President Obama's new health reforms make costs affordable for the American consumer-patient, while improving its quality and access to those who lack it now? Only time will render the ultimate verdict.

Perhaps, if the system could become organized and integrated then the cost of health care can truly be brought under control and its quality improved. No other measures seem to be working at the moment. Then, and only then, will the consumer-patient benefit from a system that realizes its full potential of providing quality health care at costs which are reasonable for the American public to afford.

References

1. Corning P. *The Evolution of Medicare . . . From Idea to Law*. Research report no. 29. Washington, DC: Social Security Administration, 1969: 3–4.
2. Seidman B. National health insurance: arguments for it. *Hosp Progr* 1969; 50: 60.
3. Cohen W J. Current problems in health care. *N Engl J Med* 1969; 281: 193.
4. High costs: who's to blame? *Consumer Rep* 2008; March: 16–17.
5. Six prescriptions for change. *Consumer Rep* 2008; March: 14–15.
6. Carroll A, Ackerman R. Support for national health insurance among U.S. physicians: 5 years later. *Ann Intern Med* 2008; 148: 566–567.
7. Doctors support universal health care survey. Reuters 2008; March 31.
8. Teslik L H, Johnson T. Healthcare costs and U.S. competitiveness. Council of Foreign Relations March 18 2008; available online at: http://www.cfr.org/publication/13325/healthcare_costs_and_us_competiveness.html; accessed on July 7, 2008.
9. Helliker K, King Jr N, Stoll J D. GM files for bankruptcy protection. *Wall Street J* June 1, 2009; available online at: http://online.wsj.com/article/SB124385428627671889.html; accessed on June 12, 2009.
10. Isodore C. GM bankruptcy: end of an era. CNNMoney.com June 2, 2009; available online at: http://money.cnn.com/2009/06/01/news/companies/gm_bankruptcy/); accessed on June 10, 2009.
11. United States Senate. *Health Aspects of the Economics of Aging*. Washington, DC: Special Committee on Aging, 1969: 41.
12. Reuther W. The health care crisis: where do we go from here? *Am J Publ Hlth* 1969; 59: 1.
13. US Centers for Disease Control and Prevention. *Health United States, 2007, With Chartbook on Trends in the Health of Americans*. Hyattsville, MD: National Center for Health Statistics, 2007.
14. Poll: U.S. split on socialized medicine. February 15, 2008; available online at: http://www.cbsnews.com/stories/2008/02/14/health/webmd/main3832537.shtml?source=R; accessed on July 11, 2008.
15. Schoen C, Osborn R, Doty R R, *et al*. Toward higher-performance health systems: adults' health care experiences in seven countries, 2007. *Health Aff* web exclusive 2007; 26: w717-w734; available online at: www.commonwealthfund.org/publications/publications_show.htm?doc_id=568237; accessed on July 14, 2008.
16. Andrews M. Candidates write their prescriptions. *US News World Rep* 2007; June 11: 32–33.
17. Sack K. Clinton details caps on premiums. *N Y Times* 2008; March 28.
18. Henig J, Robertson L. Obama's inflated health savings. *Newsweek* 2008; June 16.
19. Emanuel E J, Fuchs V R. Beyond health-care – Band-Aids. *Washington Post* 2007; February 7: A17.
20. Schwartz H. Health insurance: a fight for survival. *N Y Times* 1977; October 30: 3f.

Index